CRYPTIC CODE
OF THE TEMPLARS
in AMERICA

CRYPTIC CODE

OF THE TEMPLARS

IN AMERICA:

ORIGINS OF THE HOOKED X™ SYMBOL

BY SCOTT F. WOLTER

NORTH STAR PRESS OF ST. CLOUD INC.
WWW.NORTHSTARPRESS.COM

First Edition
ISBN: 978-1-68201-101-0

Printed in the U.S.A.

North Star Press of St. Cloud Inc.
www.NorthStarPress.com

Cover design done in collaboration by Dan Weimer and Elizabeth Dwyer.

Text set in Study, titles in Mason Serif OT, subtitles in Marion.

ALSO BY SCOTT F. WOLTER:

The Kensington Rune Stone:
Compelling New Evidence

The Hooked X:
Key to the Secret History of North America

Akhenaten to the Founding Fathers:
The Mysteries of the Hooked X

DEDICATION

This book is dedicated to Corinne Dwyer, who had faith in me and believed in this controversial subject matter enough to produce three wonderful books. I will be forever grateful.

Contents

Contents

Contents

Contents

Contents

A NOTE ABOUT THE COVER

The cover is a combination of the artwork of Dan Wiemer and the design work of Elizabeth Dwyer. The North American continent was the primary focus of pre-Columbian Knights Templar activity. This was featured on the covers of my two previous books and is continued here. Two Templar crosses symbolically represent the twin pillars of Freemasonry, Jachin and Boaz, and the twin obelisks at the entrance of the ancient Egyptian Temples that inspired them. In the lower left is the Flower of Life carved on Templar gravestones in Scotland, first-century ossuaries in Jerusalem, and the oldest known examples are found in Egypt including the Temple of Osiris at Abydos. In the lower right is the symbol for the Phoenician goddess of Carthage, Tanith, also known as the Queen of Heaven.

The equilateral triangle represents the three Grand Masters of Freemasonry, King Solomon, Hiram, King of Tyre (Lebanon), and Hiram Abiff, the Master Builder of the Temple in Jerusalem. The purple colored tiles were inspired by the incredible tile work inside the chapel in Lakewood Cemetery in Minneapolis, Minnesota. The chapel is a replica of the Little Hagia Sophia Chapel in Istanbul, Turkey. It was completed in AD 536 and served as a Knights Templar Commandery in the twelfth century.

The broken arm of the triangle represents the allegorical death of Hiram Abiff and is very important in the Third Degree of Blue Lodge Freemasonry. The trowel, symbolic of the building of the Temple, and the sword, symbolic of chivalry of a Templar knight, are crossed forming a Hooked X. The Ankh symbol tiled in gold represents the resurrection of Hiram Abiff. The ankh is a tau cross with an egg-shaped handle intentionally positioned over the symbolic Hooked X to complete the Hooked X/tau Cross symbol carved into a now world-famous first-century ossuary. The incredible discovery of that ossuary will be revealed in the pages that follow.

xvi

FOREWORD

BY William F. Mann

I first met Scott Wolter in Halifax, Nova Scotia, some ten years ago while attending the Atlantic Symposium, which was centered on the then-available evidence supporting a voyage by Prince Henry Sinclair in AD 1398 to North America. Initially, I was skeptical of the evidence contained within Scott's own presentation surrounding the Kensington Rune Stone and its relation to one of many pre-Columbian inland journeys of those medieval warrior-monks known as the Knights Templar. His scientific analysis of the stone was verifiable and sound but when compared to the broader research of others, including my own, Scott's thought process and inherent speculation at the time appeared somewhat forced and arbitrary.

Needless to say, I was somewhat suspicious of Scott's rationale in that he didn't share any of the ancestral bloodline nor Masonic/Native American spirituality deemed necessary to solve the larger puzzle. Many of the earliest clues of Prince Henry Sinclair's voyage came from the secret knowledge shared by the native Mi'kmaq, my brother Algonquins, who greeted Prince Henry and his fugitive Knights Templar as they landed on the shores of Estotiland (Nova Scotia). Scott would not have been privy at the time to the native whispers of strategic intermarriages, which occurred between Native North Americans and those of the Grail Bloodline between the 12th and 14th centuries.

One thing I was impressed with right from the start, though, was Scott's enthusiasm and self-assuredness. In a rather admiring way, as we have grown to become the best of friends, I have come to greatly appreciate Scott's determination and drive for what it truly is—unabashed enthusiasm for the truth. Where other people would have given up a long time ago, Scott's rugged doggedness for the truth has proved to be his greatest asset in this life-long journey we have come to share. In fact, in typical Scott

Wolter fashion, he jumped with both feet into hosting the immensely successful TV series, *America Unearthed,* for an initial run of five years and did a terrific job of exploring what many consider to be the hidden history of North America/Turtle Island.

As I have taken a slightly different pathway along the same journey, culminating to date with the publishing (www.InnerTraditions.com) of a trilogy of "hidden history" books centred on the Knights Templar in the New World, two of Scott's books (*The Hooked X* and *Akhenaten to the Founding Fathers*) have proved in a synchronistic way to compliment my own (*The Knights Templar in the New World*; *The Templar Meridians*; and, *Templar Sanctuaries in North America*).

Being a Canadian, I guess I'm not used to someone of Scott's uncompromising nature and pointed determination, as we tend to be more conservative and self-questioning than Americans. Scott's penchant to put his head down like a fullback charging through the defensive line, openly confronting both his critics and established academia, has certainly made him a target of academic criticism and troll dismissal, but what Scott has unveiled is both rational and, thus, undeniable in its scope and conclusions.

Scott has now brought forward a far-ranging and timely missive in the appropriately-titled *Cryptic Code of the Templars in America.* As I read the draft of *Cryptic Code* for the first time, I couldn't help but smile at the way Scott has linked his past research and historical interpretation into a fascinating summation of seemingly-unrelated historical facts and spiritual insight. His mind and spirit have definitely soared since that first time I met him.

Of course, I believe that his self-illumination is in no small part due to the personal path that he has chosen. What was always missing from Scott's research was an exposure to and understanding of Freemasonry's basic principles and beliefs. In no small part due to his recent initiation and rapid advancement in Freemasonry, specifically Scottish Rite Masonry and York Rite Templarism, Scott has now gained the spiritual insight and retrospective to put many of the pieces of his personal puzzle together. He certainly has gained tremendous insight into recognizing those signs, seals, and tokens, which, for a very long time, have been hidden in plain sight for only those with the eyes to see.

Where has all of this taken him? Well, I believe that he has once and for all proven beyond a doubt that the Kensington Rune Stone, including its many layers of cryptic code, is real and not a hoax; and, therefore, is of tremendous historical and cultural importance. In addition, his cumulative work on the Hooked X is fascinating in itself but, when applied to the spiritual mystery surrounding the Knights Templar, is nothing short of pure genius. His work with respect to the Cremona Document, in conjunction with his friend Don Ruhl, is also extremely significant, along with the exposure of errors in interpretation presented by an earlier author. I can't wait to see where all of this accumulated insight leads him next.

What Scott's work within *Cryptic Code of the Templars in America* has exposed, and in so doing confirmed, is that no one individual has all of the answers to the question of pre-Columbian exploration of North America by the descendants of the Jewish High Priests of the Temple of Solomon, and their co-habitation with the indigenous North American people. Many now see that beyond any doubt the original nine Knights Templar, who discovered something of immense historical and spiritual value under the Temple of Solomon ruins prior to their official recognition as an Order by the Pope in AD 1126, viewed North America as the New Jerusalem. It was here that the Knights Templar looked to establish a brave New World, one where the sacred feminine would take her rightful position and grow and flourish, all the while embracing the principles of freedom to worship and acceptance of all races.

The Founding Fathers of America embraced this concept of dualism all too well— one where the male and female aspects of life and death would come together. Unfortunately, the original tenets of the Knights Templar have been buried by the current evangelical penchant to overwhelm and dismiss any and all Mystical Christian philosophies, which do not conform to their own beliefs.

Fortunately for the world and its survival, the noble concepts of the original Knights Templar are still valid and lay in wait to be embraced by those who seek the truth and light defined through the much-misunderstood Christian Mysteries. Scott may very well be one of those initiates who unveil the truth once and for all.

R. Em. Kt. William F. Mann, KCT
Deputy Grand Master
Sovereign Great Priory—Knights Templar of Canada

FOREWORD

BY ALAN BUTLER

It was in 2000 that Scott Wolter began his work on one of America's most contro-versial and enigmatic artifacts—the Kensington Rune Stone. This large, flat, inscribed stone was found by immigrant farmer Olof Ohman while he was clearing land on his farm in western Minnesota in the autumn of 1898. Everything that springs forth in the pages that follow has its starting point amongst the tangled roots of a tree stump, where the Rune Stone was first discovered.

No matter how they are interpreted, the existence of the words carved onto the Kensington Rune Stone can have only one of two explanations. If they are genuine, the Kensington Rune Stone represented a message from the distant past—way before Christopher Columbus and the 'official' discovery by Europe of the New World. Alter-natively, the whole thing is an elaborate hoax.

Scott Wolter is, first and foremost, a forensic geologist with a proven track record when it comes to analysing and dating rocks, which is why he came to look at the Kens-ington Rune Stone with the most critical of eyes. Although a scientist, and therefore unfettered by prejudice or preconceptions, Scott was not expecting what he discovered, and he certainly had no idea just what sort of influence the weathered rock found by Olof Ohman would have on his life.

After exhaustive investigations there was no doubt about it—the inscription on the Rune Stone was genuinely medieval and amongst the characters carved onto the stone was one that would prove to be both curious and fascinating. It was an X, but one that carried an extra stroke. Scott Wolter christened this character the Hooked X, and it would come to be an extraordinarily important part of his life.

Where did the Hooked X come from, what did it mean and how far back in time did it go? These were questions that occupied Scott through a number of books and throughout his many appearances on television. Across thousands of miles and back into the mists of time, Scott Wolter chased the enigmatic Hooked X and he was eventually able to answer most of his own questions regarding a symbol that indicated the survival, across countless generations and a multitude of civilizations of a belief pattern and a way of seeing the world that seemed to be incredibly old. As testimony to its ancient pedigree, Scott and I were able to stand together on one misty day at the entrance to the Chambered Tomb of Newgrange in Ireland and view a row of Hooked Xs carved into the lintel above the entrance of a structure that was erected as long ago as 3,200 BC!

But even after the careful research and publications of three books there were still questions that deserved fuller answers, which is the reason for the writing of *The Cryptic Code*. Much of this most fascinating of stories is tied up with a medieval order of fighting monks, known as the Knights Templar, and with their companion order, the Cistercians. It is to these two enigmatic monastic orders that the evidence keeps returning. What true part did they play in the continued use of the Hooked X, why and how did they adopt it, and were they responsible not only for the Kensington Rune Stone, but for the other examples of such stones and inscriptions from across the United States?

The episode of the story of the Kensington Rune Stone and its companions laid out in this book represents the most compelling of all Scott Wolter's books. It will take you on an enthralling journey across thousands of miles and far back into the very origins of civilization. It will offer you an entirely different view of aspects of history that have been fudged and misrepresented and give you an insight into a way of thinking and being that a small but crucially important group of people have nurtured and perpetuated against incredible odds and in the face of tremendous challenges.

I would not dream of telling the reader any more about the incredible evidence that is presented in the following pages—that is a treasury for you to explore—but I will suggest that what you are about to read is more important to humanity than anything to be gleaned from generally accepted history books.

When criticism was everywhere, and orthodox experts refused to listen, Scott Wolter soldiered on and at last has discovered the secret of secrets. It has been my great pleasure and privilege to be associated with this most fascinating of adventures.

Introduction

It has taken eighteen years and three books, but I now believe I have finally reached the bottom of one of the most important mysteries in history: the origin of the Hooked X™ symbol. If you have followed my research journey to this point, you know the Hooked X is an enigmatic symbol carved into five different runic inscriptions found in North America that has stumped scholars for one hundred and twenty years. I have argued the symbol represents an ancient ideology called *Monotheistic Dualism* whose origins date back to the ancient Egyptians and beyond. I have also emphatically stated these five rune stones, four of which are self-dated to the late medieval period (1300-1500), were created by the most successful monastic order in history: the Cistercians and their military brethren, the Knights Templar. The evidence presented in my three previous books has proven the most enigmatic of them all, the Kensington Rune Stone, is a Knights Templar land claim placed along the north-south continental divide in the geographic center of the continent. In essence, the Kensington Rune Stone marks the beginning of the founding of the United States of America.

This research has also proven that every aspect of the Kensington inscription, including the language, runes, dialect, grammar, and dating features, has been found to be from medieval Scandinavia. Nearly all the questions pondered about the artifact have now been successfully answered. However, there were two lingering questions that now are answered here: where did the Templars acquire the symbol, and is the inscription really a tragic tale of medieval exploration or is there something else going on? The answers will startle and amaze, and perhaps most importantly, finally explain why scholars have struggled so mightily to solve this enigmatic inscription.

The mystery began in the fall of 1898 with a highly controversial discovery by an

1

immigrant farmer who was clearing trees on his land among the rolling glacial hills and lakes of western Minnesota. At first, the sturdy 44-year-old Olof Ohman thought the rectangular-shaped tombstone sized slab of stone he and his two sons, 12-year-old Olof Jr., and 9-year-old Edward, had unearthed wrapped within the roots of a 25-30-year-old Aspen tree was an "Indian almanac." Shortly thereafter it was realized the twelve-line inscription was carved in medieval Scandinavian runes and self-dated to 1362. Within months of the discovery it was realized this was no ordinary runic inscription and would incite a heated controversy among scholars in Europe and America for the next century.

The face side of the Kensington Rune Stone with the first nine lines of the inscription which reads, "8 Goths and 22 Northmen on this acquisition journey/taking up land from Vinland far to the west. We had a camp near 2 shelters one day's journey from stone. We were fishing one day, after we came home found 10 men red from blood and dead. *AVM.* Save from evils." The Hooked X symbol was used twenty-two times in the Kensington Rune Stone inscription. (2010/2002)

The message skillfully inscribed on the rectangular shaped stone chronicled a voyage, "…from Vinland far to the west," by a party of the thirty men comprised of "8 Götalanders…," from the southern Baltic region, "…and 22 Norrmen." The inscription then says, "…found ten men red from blood and death." The strange message was confusing and appeared to be a fanciful tale of Norsemen who penetrated the vast wilderness of the mid-continent region of North America in the fourteenth century, long after the Viking era had ended. Doubting runic scholars have argued, sometimes fanatically over the past one hundred-plus years, both for and against its authenticity, but neither side was ever able to gain consensus.

Looking back on the history of the debate about the inscription has been a real eye-opener for me. It has revealed the myriad of problems within academia in the largely opinion-driven disciplines of history, anthropology, linguistics, runology, and archaeology. At times, it has been painful to witness the repeated use of improper scientific methods which led to the wrong conclusion. It seems the more certain some academics were of their conclusions, the weaker their arguments. The fundamental mistake made was trying to tell the Kensington Rune Stone what it is supposed to be, instead of letting the artifact say what it is.

At the time of its discovery one of the main things scholars struggled with were several mysterious characters within the inscription. The meaning of most of the symbols was deduced by their position within words and similarity to already known and understood medieval runic characters throughout Scandinavia. By 2005, all the strange characters within the inscription had been found in accepted medieval documents except one; the Hooked X. The never-before-seen character was used for the *a* and *ä* sounds appearing twenty-two times within the Kensington Rune stone inscription. The problem was that it was not the expected runic symbol, and in fact, had never been seen before by runic scholars. It was truly a mystery and led many academics to mistakenly dismiss the inscription for this reason alone. The reason scholars have been unable to solve the Kensington Rune Stone is abundantly clear. They were more concerned with 'being right,' rather than getting the right answer.

When my time came to study the stone, beginning in July of 2000, I concluded it was a medieval artifact after comparing the weathering of key minerals to those in self-dated slate tombstones dating back to the American Revolutionary War era. At the time, I knew nothing about rune stones and was hired to examine the artifact purely for my knowledge of forensic geology. By relying solely on the geological aspects of the stone it told me all I needed to know about whether the artifact was genuine or a late nineteenth-century hoax as so many believed. Knowing that I could trust the rock, I knew it would tell me the truth. Just like it told the truth back in 1909 when the first State Geologist of Minnesota studied the weathering of the artifact and concluded it was genuine. For that brilliant work, Professor Newton H. Winchell deserves credit for being the first to solve the Kensington Rune Stone.

Eventually, I turned my attention to the mysterious character I named the "Hooked X." Because the geology told me it was a genuine medieval artifact, I knew everything within the inscription had to have a medieval explanation. As true as this was, it was no guarantee that an explanation would be found. However, knowing an answer had to exist somewhere was a powerful motivator for me, as was the endless criticism I received from those more interested in being right. What at first seemed like an impossible task became ever more doable with each discovery of yet another example of the X-shaped character with the small hook in the upper right arm. Having now worked thirty-three years as a forensic scientist, experience has taught me if you follow the facts, wherever they might lead, eventually they will take you to the truth. This has been the road map I have followed because regardless what the issue might be, there is always an explanation. Therefore, I knew this also had to be the case with the Hooked X. Discovering its symbolic meaning was one thing, but learning the truth about where the Knights Templar and their Cistercian brethren discovered the sacred symbol was almost unbelievable.

There are many other symbols the Templars, Cistercians, and traditions that came before, and after, that I will share in this book. The key to unlocking the truth behind these mysterious historical groups and the knowledge they carry lies in the symbolism they use routinely. Once you know the signs, symbols, tokens, and codes, those truths are revealed and enlightenment occurs. It is my hope the symbols and codes I reveal in this book with bring such enlightenment and, along with it, a richer understanding of the workings of the universe. While there is an undeniable spiritual aspect to enlightenment and revelations of historical truth, the scientist in me is omnipresent. That pragmatism led to the discovery of a previously unknown chapter in the history of America, added to the narrative that was first set forth by William F. Mann. His 2016 book, *Templar Sanctuaries in North America: Sacred Bloodlines and Secret Treasures,* revealed the approximate location of the Templars' secret vault in Montana and the "secret work" conducted by important historical figures to first confirm the location of the crown jewel hidden within the Louisiana Purchase, and to where the contents were most likely taken.

As has become my custom, I provide updates on what I have learned on my travels and about significant events related to important artifacts I have studied. These include the recovery and relocation of the Narragansett Rune Stone and new discoveries in the Newport Tower. In my previous book, *Akhenaten to the Founding Fathers: The Mysteries of the Hooked X*, Chapter 8 was titled "The C-Doc" because I agreed not to reveal the full name of the document in respect for my two colleagues, Donald Ruh and Zena Halpern, who were planning to publish their own book about the research based on documents left for Ruh by his lifelong friend, Dr. William Jackson. Sadly, disagreement between them led Halpern to hastily publish the book in 2017. Unbeknownst to her, it contained false information unrelated to the Cremona Document that made its way into her book. Important new information recently provided to Ruh will be presented in this book to put the incredible story into proper context with what we now believe to be the truth about one of the earliest voyages to North America by the Templars in the twelfth century.

This research journey that began with the Kensington Rune Stone has had many twists and turns with incredible highs and lows, and has always been interesting, enlightening, and rewarding. One thing is certain, throughout the entire history of the research and debate, the artifact has stood tall and is only now being seen by the world as the amazing historical document it is. In fact, this incredible artifact has triggered a major rewrite of world history that stretches back far beyond its existence, at least 3,500 years.

This incredible journey has allowed me to meet many interesting people I would not have met otherwise. Many have become close friends while others became adversaries for reasons that eventually revealed themselves. This journey opened my mind to new avenues of research, such as runology, medieval and ancient history, symbolism, esoteric thought, archaeoastronomy, and many other topics I never dreamed I would delve so deeply into. It has also led me to become initiated as a Freemason which was another watershed moment I will share details of later in the book, but first we must start at the beginning.

For those interested in learning more about the details of my past work on the Kensington Rune Stone, along with many other artifacts and sites connected to the discoveries presented here, there is a trilogy of books that chronicles my research, discoveries, the people, and the many travels it took to get here.[1] On the one hand, this is the culmination of an eighteen-year-long journey of investigation into the mysteries of the Kensington Rune Stone. On the other hand, it marks the beginning of a brand-new journey to flush out the veracity of new historical information that has yet to be revealed publicly. Many major new discoveries will be shared in this book including the historical origins of the Hooked X symbol and the final piece of the puzzle to the mysterious artifact that launched the founding of a new nation.

---

[1]   The three books written by Scott Wolter that will be referenced often in this manuscript are: *The Kensington Rune Stone: Compelling New Evidence*, herein referred to as *Compelling New Evidence*; *The Hooked X: Key to the Secret History of North America*, herein referred to as *The Hooked X*; *Akhenaten to the Founding Fathers: Mysteries of the Hooked X*, herein referred to as *Akhenaten*.

CHAPTER 1:

Tracking the Templars: America Unearthed

At the suggestion of a friend, I decided to start this book with a summary of the two most successful episodes of the television show I hosted for three seasons (2012-2015) and thirty-nine episodes on the cable network H2, called *America Unearthed*. The highest-rated episodes of all three seasons turned out to be the last two which morphed into a two-part story as we filmed it. The incredible historical romp of investigation began in southern Pennsylvania. Following up on a tip from a viewer, I examined what I hoped would be the new discovery of a medieval runic inscription that included the all-important Hooked X symbol. This enigmatic symbol is found on five other mysterious North American runic inscriptions and in other carvings and documents in Europe. Through years of research, I found that every example of the Hooked X was connected to either the medieval Knights Templar or modern Freemasonry.

My excitement to see this new inscription that was self-dated to 1208 using Roman numerals was off the charts, but I was also guarded as I arrived to examine the carvings with the discoverer and his friend who had originally contacted me with the news. With cameras rolling, I introduced myself and asked to hear the story from Bill Carney, who told me how he found the inscription several weeks earlier. My skepticism started as I listened to his somewhat odd story of "looking for carvings and inscriptions." I then turned my attention to the inscription at the base of a large sandstone boulder on the steep, wooded hillside.

It didn't take long for more red flags to appear, most notably tiny parallel ridges in mud that had been mixed with glue and pressed into the freshly carved grooves to make them appear old and weathered. The final test that exposed the fraud was performed by using my toothbrush and water to scrub the mud and water-soluble glue mixture from one of the grooves. I then splashed water onto the surface and as the mud and glue dripped off the recently carved characters, white lines were exposed. Needless to say, I was angry and let the two locals know it. A couple days after the episode aired, Carney admitted carving the hoax to his cousin who passed along the damning Facebook correspondence.[2]

On September 18, 2013, I examined a newly discovered runic inscription in Pennsylvania that included a Hooked X (left). While filming the discovery for *America Unearthed*, I revealed a hoax by using water and a toothbrush to remove mud that had been glued into the grooves to make them look old (right). (2013/2013)

The silver lining to this fiasco was this carving made a perfect example of what I have been saying for a long time, that fakes reveal themselves quickly under scientific examination and the real (genuine) artifacts keep hanging around no matter how hard people try to dismiss them. The Kensington Rune Stone is a perfect example of an artifact that has endured.

That first episode then took me from the woods of Pennsylvania in North America, to the city of Troyes, France, where I met up with longtime friends and co-researchers Steve St. Clair and Alan Butler. Together we visited a number of Cistercian-Knights Templar sites in the Lombard region, which included a restored Templar Commandery at Sir Aude, and St. Remi Basilica. We then traveled to Paris to St. Martin de Champs Chapel, and the site of the death by burning at the stake of Knights Templar Grand Master, Jacques de Molay, along the Seine River, on March 18, 1307. We were tracking the rise and eventual fall of the Knights Templar order, which along with their Cistercian brethren, I've proposed were founded and guided by direct bloodline descendants of the biblical Jesus and his wife, Mary Magdalene, along with the descendants of Jesus' brothers and sisters.

Part two of the "Tracking the Templars" episodes took place at multiple Templar

---

sites in Tomar, Portugal, and ended with a visit to Westford, Massachusetts. This culminated in the discovery of two new Hooked X symbols. Starting the episode in Tomar, we began inside Santa Maria do Olival Church, where twenty-two Grand Masters of the Portuguese Knights Templar are interred. Inside the twelfth-century church, the audience saw Steve St. Clair "discover" the Hooked X carved into one of the stone columns. For me, this was the most important and emotional scene in the entire three seasons of shows we made.

In reality, the discovery of the Hooked X on the column was actually made by my wife, Janet, who came with me to Tomar. While Steve and I were filming a scene outside the church, she had time to wander around and search inside. After finding the Hooked X, she took a picture on her cell phone and quietly shared it with Maria Awes, co-owner of Committee Films and the episode's producer. They decided not to tell me about it so they could capture my genuine reaction after seeing it for the first time. Word quietly spread among the film crew of Janet's discovery while I remained totally oblivious. After filming the scene, Steve immediately fessed up and said, "I didn't find it, Janet did." The smile on her face told me all I needed to know. Who else but her, someone who has been my primary colleague in this research for the past eighteen years, would make the most important discovery of the entire shoot?

After filming the discovery of the Hooked X scene at Santa Maria do Olival Church, it was late afternoon. Hoping to get inside the Templar castle, Janet, Steve, Maria and I raced in our rental car to the top of the bluff hoping to get inside the castle church before it closed for the day. Because we were flying home the next day, we knew this would be our only chance to see this amazing medieval Templar castle. We arrived with only a few minutes to spare. The stunning beauty of the fully illuminated, two-story tower comprising the altar (charola) at the eastern end of the church nearly brought us to our knees. As we wandered around with our mouths hanging open in awe, we noticed there was a very prominent round rose window on the west side of the sacred structure. After checking the compass on my cell phone, I quickly verified the church was aligned exactly east-west with the telescoping rose window on the west wall. As I pondered the possible significance of the east-west alignment of the nave, something dawned on me as I looked back to the east at the charola. Could there be an illumination event in this octagonal-shaped Templar tower as well?

I quickly ruled out a solstice alignment due to the east-west orientation of the church, which left the only realistic possibility of a solar alignment being on the vernal and autumnal equinoxes. The question was; what exactly was supposed to be illuminated within the charola to the east? It didn't take long to figure out it had to be the statue of Jesus hanging on the cross in the east archway of the charola. The problem was we were still three weeks away from the vernal (spring) equinox on March 21st, and there was no way I could test my theory on this trip. Fortunately, there was still hope.

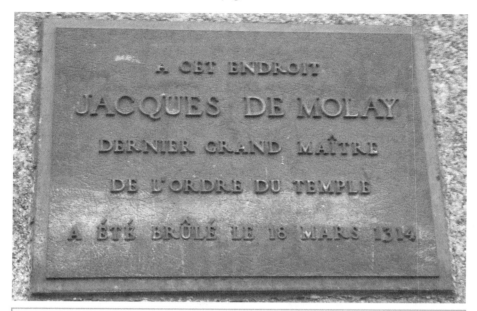

This plaque is on a wall next to the Seine River in Paris. Translated from French to English it reads: "At this place Jacques de Molay, last Grand Master of the Order of the Temple, was burned on March 18, 1314" (2014)

At the Templar Hotel where we stayed in Tomar, the bartender turned out to be a fan of *America Unearthed*. On the flight home it occurred to me to email our friend and ask if he would be willing to help. Francisco Vero Santos was thrilled to be of assistance. After cloudy weather on the 21st and 22nd, he was able to capture the illumination event two days later on March 23rd. Since the sun moves higher in the sky at a very rapid rate at the equinoxes, the head of the statue of Jesus was now in shadow whereas two days earlier it would have been fully illuminated by the sun piercing through the round oculus-shaped window in the west end

While filming in Tomar, I made another important discovery that is directly connected to a Knights Templar site in the United States. The Newport Tower in Rhode Island, which was first documented by the state's first governor, Benedict Arnold, in his will in 1677, is the oldest known stone and mortar structure in the United States. Research by myself and others has led to the conclusion the structure is a round, two-story chapel and astronomical observatory, constructed by the Knights Templar most likely around 1400.

On the morning of December 21st of 2007, I witnessed a life-changing event when the only true keystone found inside the structure, at the top of one of the eight rounded archways, became fully illuminated by a rectangular-shaped light box produced when the sun's rays passed through the structure's second-story south window. When the tan, egg-shaped granite keystone lit up at exactly 9:00 a.m. on the winter solstice, it was a moment of validation that the Templar research I had been following for the past seven years had been the right path all along.

Another discovery happened while filming in Tomar that is a direct parallel to the winter solstice illumination discovery in the Newport Tower. This time it was another illumination event at the Templar castle overlooking the city that would serve as corroborating evidence the Newport Tower winter solstice illumination research is connected to the medieval Knights Templar.

A tan colored, egg-shaped granite keystone is illuminated when a rectangular box of sunlight shines through the south window of the Newport Tower in Newport, Rhode Island. It was engineered to only happen annually at 9:00 a.m. on December 21st, the winter solstice. (2007)

The significance of the illumination in the charola of the Templar castle in Tomar and the Newport Tower in Rhode Island is self-evident. For our *American Unearthed* trip to Portugal, it was an "icing on the cake" discovery on a journey that also yielded a new Hooked X in a place that could not have been more appropriate; the city of Tomar that was founded by the Knights Templar in 1160, and inside a church where 22 Grand Masters of the Order are buried. We will later see the number of Grand Masters interred was no accident.

As previously mentioned, the final scene of the second episode was filmed at the Westford Knight site in Westford, Massachusetts, where I confirmed the authenticity of the discovery of yet another Hooked X! I had visited this site at least a half dozen times over the years and it never occurred to me to even look for a Hooked X character on this famous bedrock outcrop. In hindsight, it makes all the sense in the world for the Templar symbol to be here, but it took someone with an unbiased eye to see it. In later chapters, you will understand why finding a Hooked X with a carving of a

The charola inside the altar of the Templar church at the Templar castle in Tomar, Portugal, is a two-story tower built on eight columns and was inspired by the sacred octagonal architecture the Templars saw on the Temple Mount, in Jerusalem, during the time of the Second Crusade (left). The round rose window in the west end of the church as seen from the center of the charola (right). (2014/2014)

At 9:00 a.m. on March 21st and September 21st, the figure of Christ on the Cross inside the charola of the church at the Convent of Christ castle in Tomar, Portugal, becomes illuminated by the sun's rays that pass through the round window on the west side of the church on the equinoxes (left). This annual illumination event is analogous to the illumination of the egg-shaped keystone in the two-story octagonal tower in Newport, Rhode Island, at 9:00 a.m. on the winter solstice. This statue of Gualdim Pais, the First Grand Master of the Knights Templar in Portugal, stands in the square of the city of Tomar, which he founded upon returning from Jerusalem after the Second Crusade in 1160 (right). (2014/2014)

medieval sword and the Westford Boat Stone, near an ancient Native American site likely repurposed by the Knights Templar in Westford, Massachusetts, makes sense.

The two newly discovered examples of the Hooked X were added to the rapidly growing list of examples of the mysterious symbol that has only been found associated with two specific groups: the medieval monastic order of Cistercians and their warrior brethren the Knights Templar, and within Freemasonic secret societies that evolved directly from the earlier esoteric-leaning leadership of the order of "warrior monks."

The Hooked X at Tomar is not the only Templar secret that would be revealed during filming in Portugal. In April of 2015, just over a year after my first visit, I traveled to Tomar again with a different film crew for a different History Channel show about Templars, Freemasons, and pirates called, *Pirate Treasure of the Knights Templar*. This time I interviewed two experts on the Portuguese Templars, one of whom was a Freemason. The first Portuguese Templar expert, Manuel Gandra, told me the founder of the city of Tomar was Gualdim Pais, the first Grand Master of the Knights Templar of Portugal.[3] Upon his return to Portugal from Jerusalem after fighting in the Second Crusade, he laid out the new city of Tomar in 1160 as a replication of the sacred sites he had seen in the Holy City. The castle of the Convento de Cristo (Convent of Christ) built atop the *seven hills* overlooking the city represents the Temple Mount in Jerusalem. The Nabão River running through Tomar, with its multiple mills for grinding grain, represents the Gihon River running through the Kidron Valley, with the Santa Maria do Olival Church being symbolic of the Mount of Olives on the hillside east of the Temple Mount.

In the final episode in season three of *America Unearthed*, two new examples of the Hooked X were introduced. The first was found carved into a stone column within an inscription inside Santa Maria do Olival Church, in Tomar, Portugal, built by the Knights Templar in the twelfth century (left). The second is a highly-weathered example carved into bedrock a few inches from the sword carving known as the Westford Knight in Westford, Massachusetts (right). (2014/2014)

It made sense the Grand Master of the Portuguese Templars would want to build a New Jerusalem in his homeland. Perhaps it may have been a directive of the Order after they captured and controlled the original sacred city in the twelfth century. The Templars in Portugal were engaged in multiple wars with the Moors throughout this time and Tomar became an important line of defense for Christendom. The Templar castle at Tomar served as both a monastery and a church where I would learn from our second guest, a Freemason named João Fiandeiro Santos, about two of the most important rituals of the medieval Portuguese Templars.

The first was the initiation ritual for becoming a Templar knight that took place deep inside the bowels of the hilltop castle. Brother Santos explained how the candidate for knighthood was led into a rectangular-shaped room with four angels carved into the corner capitals at the base of the stone ribbed vaulted ceiling. At one end of the room, the candidate stood before wooden doors that would soon be opened to him. He was then told to look up to the central keystone with a strange carving. The initiate was told he stood before the "wise man with three faces" who passed judgment about his past, present and future. After a period of reflection, the initiate was then blindfolded, led through the wooden doors and down a spiral staircase to the lowest recesses of the castle. Both the blindfold and winding stairs were designed to disorient the initiate and test his resolve. Arriving at the bottom of the stairs, the initiate then stood at the top of a series of seven, unevenly spaced steps designed to distract his mind as he descended into another large rectangular-shaped room called the Initiation Chamber. The initiate was then prompted to slowly walk down the center of the long room as he unknowingly passed by Templar knights lining both sides watching the procession of their potential brother-in-arms.

Before descending a spiral staircase to the initiation chamber in the Templar castle in Tomar, Portugal, the initiate stood beneath the carving on a keystone of a wise man with three faces who passed judgement on his past, present, and future (left). Candidates for knighthood walked blindfolded down a long rectangular initiation chamber lined on both sides with Templar knights (right). (2015/2015)

Upon reaching the far end of the chamber and having passed under eight keystones overhead, the initiate stood beneath the ninth keystone. Unbeknownst to the Initiate there were two, large moveable blocks of stones in the floor under his feet. After instructions were given, the two stone blocks were removed revealing an underground chamber the initiate was then lowered into. The stones were put back into place and the initiate was left alone for three days with only bread and water. If he called out to be released before the end of the third day, he failed the initiation and could not become a member of the Order. If the initiate endured the full three days, the stones were pulled up and he was then raised. While in a depleted physical state, and likely fragile mental state, the initiate was asked to answer three questions. If answered correctly, the blindfold was removed and the initiate was told to look up. It was then he realized he was standing beneath the ninth keystone upon which was a carving representing the sun (male), with a rose (female) in the center symbolizing Dualism with its rays symbolically illuminating the newly initiated Templar knight.

Two large stone blocks in the floor were removed and the initiate was lowered into the chamber below for three days with only bread and water (left). Upon completion of three days in darkness inside the chamber, and correctly answering three questions, the blindfold was removed and the new Templar knight completed his initiation standing beneath the ninth keystone with a carving symbolic of a rose inside the sun (right). (2015/2015)

Having experienced multiple Freemasonic initiations, including being knighted, the description of the medieval initiation resonated deeply with me, even if the personal reflection aspect of the three days locked inside an initiation chamber was not nearly as lengthy or intense.

Santos later shared another Knights Templar ritual that took place inside the church in the area surrounding the charola before they headed into battle. He explained how knights, dressed in full armor with their horses behind them, surrounded the octagonal charola and then raised their swords in unison toward the top of the two-story altar. The top of the charola is beautifully illuminated in gold and represents the heavens with the sun, symbolic of Deity, at its center. The ritual was designed to call down the power of Deity into the knights and their steeds, giving them superior courage and strength in battle. This sacred ritual performed by Templar knights about to enter battle was somewhat reminiscent of what I have experienced myself before college football games in my playing days. Coaches and players, including me, gave inspired speeches designed to get players mentally prepared to do battle on the gridiron. We used to call it getting ready to "run through a brick wall."

Understanding what must have gone through the minds of these medieval warrior monks, and their Cistercian brethren, helped me better understand what likely happened during the post put-down period of the Templar order that did not simply end with a thud as many historians believe. As you will find out, the knights who escaped persecution in France did not simply grow old and die, eventually dissolving the order by attrition.

Unlike their brethren in France who escaped to Scotland, the Baltic Region, and other countries, the Templars in Portugal continued on as an official military monastic order until the mid-nineteenth century as the Knights of Christ. Most of the famous early Portuguese ship captains during the Age of Exploration were members of the Order of Christ who sailed their ships into the Atlantic Ocean from the port of Lisbon, and on to all the continents of the globe. The new evidence I have found of the medieval Templars in North America was discovered in medieval Templar documents originally purchased in Italy, and then brought to the United States in 1971. I will also present new evidence about the ideology of Monotheistic Dualism that began over two millennia ago as what some Biblical researchers now call *Jewish Christianity*.[4]

The top of the inside of the beautifully illuminated octagonal charola in the altar of the church inside the Templar castle in Tomar, Portugal, is symbolic of the heavens with Deity (the sun) at its center. In an important warrior ritual, Templar knights would surround the charola with their horses behind them and raise their swords to the center and symbolically draw the power of Deity to give them superior strength in battle. (2015)

During a rare moment of down time from filming, I visited another church in Tomar located in the middle of town directly below the Convento de Christ castle on the hillside to the west. The Church of São João Baptista (Church of John the Baptist) is similar in architectural design to Santa Maria do Olival Church that also has a tall

4   Bütz, 2010, page 3.

bell tower with the top half that is octagonal in design. While standing on the beautiful black and white pavement in the courtyard in front of the church, I noticed something interesting on the tower just below the bell.[5] On the west facing wall was a large clock. It was originally inside the Templar castle and moved to the tower centuries ago. What caught my eye were four carvings in the corners around the clock of a woman's head in the upper left corner, a badly deteriorated head of a man in the upper right corner, and the busts of two skeletons in the lower corners.

My first thought was the woman was Mary Magdalene and the man was Jesus. As I looked closer at the carvings, even though much of the man's face was missing, they both had distressed looks on their faces. This seemed to be consistent with many artistic depictions of Jesus and Mary Magdalene in distress at the time of the Crucifixion. If these were depictions of Jesus and Mary Magdalene, who were the people depicted as

The Church of São João Baptista (Church of John the Baptist) in Tomar, Portugal, has an octagonal shaped bell tower with a clock containing interesting carvings. The courtyard has black and white Masonic pavement with a bronze statue of the founder of the Templar city, Gualdim Pais. (2015)

---

5   The black and white pavement so common within modern Masonic lodges was inspired by the black and white pavement pilgrims must walk across to access the tomb believed to be that of the biblical Jesus inside the Church of the Holy Sepulcher in Jerusalem. I walked across this very pavement while in Jerusalem in 2015.

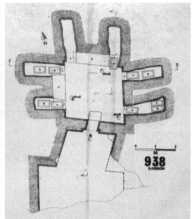

The antechamber, or front room, open to the south, of the Talpiot tomb in Jerusalem, was destroyed by blasting during construction of apartment buildings in 1980. Above the entrance to the burial chamber is a chevron-circle design (left). A schematic of the burial chamber shows three skulls that were placed on the floor and six tunnels, called Kokhim, containing ten ossuaries (right). (Internet/Internet)

The clock on the bell tower at the Church of John the Baptist in Tomar has four carvings in the corners that could be Mary Magdalene and Jesus, or maybe John the Baptist. Perhaps their bones below symbolize life and death. Could the skeletal remains be symbolic of the sacred remains collected by the Templars in Jerusalem during the Crusades? (2015)

skeletons below them? The carvings on the lower right below Jesus had crossed femurs beneath a skull—classic skull and crossbone symbolism. I let my mind entertain the idea this could be a veiled reference to the Templars having removed at least some of the bones of Jesus and Magdalene from the Talpiot tomb.[6]

---

6   https://en.wikipedia.org/wiki/Talpiot_Tomb

On the altar in the church dedicated to John the Baptist in Tomar are statues in great sorrow, the Virgin Mary on the left, and what appears to be Mary Magdalene on the right. (2015) See color section for detail.

The Talpiot Tomb is a first-century underground tomb in Jerusalem, discovered in 1980, where Israeli archaeologists found ten ossuaries, or bone boxes, that included inscriptions with the names believed to be the biblical Jesus and Mary Magdalene. During their excavations archaeologist discovered the tomb had been entered in the past. Whoever entered the tomb, some estimates put it at the time of the First Crusade, did not replace the stone that sealed the entrance. This allowed sediment from the rose gardens above to flow into the tomb, filling the burial chamber with up to two feet of mud. As the mud was carefully removed three skulls were discovered on the floor of the burial chamber. These skulls were in relatively good condition, as opposed to the bone fragments inside the ossuaries which were in relatively poor condition due to being roughly a thousand years older. Based on this evidence, it seems reasonable those who entered the tomb were not grave robbers, as ossuaries are commonly stolen and sold on the black market. They appeared to have entered with reverence, possibly leaving the three skulls as offerings.[7]

Perhaps it was Gualdim Pais, the first Grand Master of the Knights Templar in Portugal, who was involved in entering the Talpiot tomb during his time in Jerusalem in the Second Crusade. It was impossible to know with any certainty, but fun speculation nonetheless.

The question I asked myself is why was an apparently grieving Magdalene so prominently featured in a church dedicated to John the Baptist? As interesting as the carvings on the clock were, I was anxious to explore the attached church dedicated to

---

7   See pages 247-258 of *Akhenaten* for additional information regarding my discoveries about the Talpiot Tomb and the Jesus, son of Joseph ossuary.

John the Baptist. Once inside, I noticed people milling about preparing the church for a service, but they left me alone to explore. As I approached the altar in the east end, I noticed something peculiar. There were two figures on either side of the altar dressed in familiar colors: the Virgin Mary dressed in blue, gold, and white, the colors of Jerusalem on the left side, and what could only be Mary Magdalene on the right, dressed in green, red, and gold. Both statues on the altar were depicted in great sorrow, likely due to the tragedy of the beheading of John the Baptist. But if this was Mary Magdalene, what was she doing on the altar in a church dedicated to John the Baptist? I am certainly no biblical scholar, but this seemed odd and did not make any sense to me. For now, we will leave it a mystery, but as you read on the answer should come into focus.

Before moving on from Tomar to the next chapter, I want to share another potentially amazing discovery that happened while searching my files for pictures of John the Baptist I had taken inside the Templar church at the Convent of Christ castle. I discovered something very familiar that was literally hidden in plain sight. During my 2015 trip filming the *Pirate Treasure of the Knights Templar* show, I was allowed to enter the beautifully illuminated charola inside the altar. I took full advantage of the moment and snapped several photos from the interior, including directly overhead in the center. I didn't notice it at the time, but while looking at photos from that trip on July 12, 2017, I spotted it—another Hooked X! This time it was on the gold-painted, octagonal-shaped boss hanging in the center of the charola two stories above me. The letters XPS, a Latin sigma for Christ, were painted in gold and the letter *X* was clearly hooked.[8] Some might argue it is nothing more than flourishing of the script and this could be the case. However, based on the undeniable association of the structure with medieval Portuguese Templars, and its highly sacred location inside the church, my money says it is yet another example of this sacred Templar symbol. In chapter 9, the reader will finally learn the origin of this symbol and why it was so sacred to the medieval Cistercians and their Knights Templar brethren.

---

8   http://www.newworldencyclopedia.org/entry/Christogram

On July 12, 2017, while searching through my photo files from my trips to Tomar, I made an important discovery. On the boss hanging in the center inside the charola in the altar of the church at the Convent of Christ castle are the gold painted letters *XPS*, the Latin sigla for Christ. Sure enough, when I looked carefully at the *X* I found a familiar hook in the upper right arm. In this most sacred place to the Portuguese Templars I found one of their most sacred symbols. (2015)

CHAPTER 2:

UPDATE ON ARTIFACTS AND SITES

As has become my custom in the Hooked X series, I would like to share new information about important artifacts and sites I have previously written about that merit mention. These three Templar artifacts, all near each other, experienced historic events I was able to witness firsthand.

WESTFORD KNIGHT

In June of 2015, Janet and our friend and researcher, Jerry Lutgen, traveled to Westford to attended the dedication ceremony of a life-sized bronze statue of a fallen Templar knight believed by many to be Sir James Gunn. Less than a year earlier while filming what would be the final of thirty-nine episodes of *America Unearthed*, I examined what appeared to be a highly weathered Hooked X symbol, discovered by David Christiana only a couple of months earlier, carved into the glacially striated mica-schist bedrock near the sword. The event was well attended and included representatives from both the Sinclair and Gunn Clans. Our friend Steve St. Clair was appropriately dressed in a kilt, as were men from the Gunn Clan who remain close to the Sinclairs to this day. The artist who created the bronze statue, David Christiana, was at the ceremony and pointed out that he had cleverly hidden a Hooked X beneath the sword to honor his own discovery of the symbol I had verified several months earlier.

The addition of the bronze statue, along with a plexiglass cover over the sword and Hooked X carvings, add depth and credibility to the legend of Earl Henry Sinclair coming to North America in 1398. While it has not been definitively proven, if I were a betting man I would guess the sword was indeed carved to honor Sir Gunn.

Richard Gunn and Steve St. Clair, dressed in kilts with the colors of their Scottish clans, stand next to the bronze casting of a Templar Knight created by David Christiana, at right. (2015)

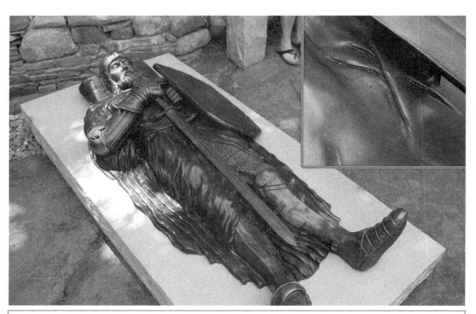

On June 13, 2015, a life-sized bronze statue was dedicated to a fallen Templar knight. The amazing bronze work done by David Christiana includes a Hooked X symbol under the bronze sword (inset). Christiana was also the person who discovered the Hooked X carved into the bedrock near the legendary sword. (2015)

Iᴨ Hᴏᴄ Sɪɢᴨᴏ Vɪᴨᴄᴇs Sᴛᴏᴨᴇ

June 14, 2018, was a big day in the history of the In Hoc Signo Vinces Stone carved into graywacke bedrock (Latin for "In this sign, thou shalt conquer"). It was barely protruding from the sand and gravel beach next to the seawall along the shore of Newport, Rhode Island. To the best of our knowledge, the Latin inscription was originally discovered sometime prior to the 1930s and exhibits extensive weathering whose age is difficult to pinpoint.

Our old friend Steve DiMarzo was the driving force behind getting permission and the permit to remove the inscription from the bedrock and transport it to the Newport Historical Society only a few blocks from the Newport Tower in Touro Park. Two years earlier when a group of us visited the stone we collectively agreed it was time for the inscription to be removed. Concern was raised about potential vandalism and the fact the inscription was now nearly buried in sand due to construction of a seawall only a few yards away that had caused changes to the shoreline. After the group that included Steve, David Brody, Richard Lynch and myself dug away the sand to expose the outcrop at low tide, I studied the structure in the rock and came up with a plan to carefully cut down to the fractures and then split out a large slab that included the inscription. Everyone agreed with the plan, though success depended on how well the rock split after the cuts were made.

Steve rounded up all of the equipment, including a concrete cut-off saw with a 16" diameter, diamond-studded blade. He also arranged to have plenty of people, mostly Freemasons, help place the slab onto a pallet and carry it out to a pick-up for delivery to the Society. Thursday, June 14, 2018, was the date selected when an extreme low tide occurred that would give maximum time to get the job done. To record this historic occasion I hired professional cameraman Brandon Bouley, whom I had worked with for three years making *America Unearthed*.

It was a bright, warm, sunny day as the water began to recede at noon, giving us over four hours to complete the task as low tide was to occur at roughly 2:00 p.m. A large group quickly assembled and had the sand dug away in short order. At 1:00 p.m. I fired up the saw and made the first approximately thirty-inch long cut across the back side down to the first fracture plane. I then took the largest steel chisel I had brought along and started splitting the rock to create space to cut down to the next fracture. After the first few swings of the hammer I knew it was going to be a much tougher job than we originally thought. The metagraywacke rock was much harder than I anticipated. After two more cuts, we were able to get a couple larger pieces to split out on the back side, but as the minutes dragged on it quickly became apparent to me the inscription wasn't coming out on this day. I knew the decision to stop was not going to be a popular one, but we had made significant progress and needed to come back with heavier equipment to make the extraction successful. To continue to cut and split away could have resulted in destroying the inscription and wasn't what anybody wanted. After a few initial complaints, everyone agreed it was best to wait and make sure the job was done right.

Steve DiMarzo watches as I make the first cut with a concrete cut-off saw during the initial attempt to remove the In Hoc Signo Vinces Stone on June 14, 2018. (Courtesy of David Brody)

The silver lining to an otherwise disappointing day was due to the unexpected toughness and competency of the bedrock. Given what we learned during the temporary setback in trying to extract the inscription from the bedrock, my opinion about the weathering and likely age of the inscription changed. I believed it was now possible the inscription could indeed be six-hundred years old and contemporaneous in origin as the Newport Tower. I was skeptical, but now there is a real possibility the two were created by the medieval Templar order at the same time.

Under specular light of Reflectance Transformation Imaging (RTI) the highly weathered In Hoc Signo Vinces inscription can be easily seen and measured. The length of the top line (18.58 inches) relative to the lower line (9.29 inches) is exactly 2 to 1. These exact lengths are consistent with the carver intentionally spacing the inscription to conform to this ratio, which was highly sacred to the medieval Knights Templar. (2019) This meant more scientific data was needed to try and draw a more definitive conclusion. That opportunity came on April 16, 2019.

As low tide receded, archaeologist Brad Lidge and I dug out the sand to expose the inscription, allowing Jerry Lutgen to set up his Reflectance Transformation Imaging (RTI) and photogrammetry equipment to capture digital images of the inscription for detailed examination. The process of data collection took about four hours and we finished just as the waves of the rising tide began to lap against the stone. A week and a half later, on April 28th, Janet and I met at Jerry's home in St. Paul to reexamine the data. The images of the inscription were excellent and after three hours of analyzing the three-dimensional images and taking detailed measurements I was ready to draw a definitive conclusion. With valuable insight and feedback from Janet and Jerry, I made the following interpretations:

1. The grooves of the inscription have a shallow *U*-shaped profile consistent with being made using a pecking technique, verses *V*-shaped grooves made with a straight chisel and hammer. Both the Westford Knight (sword) and the Westford Boat Stone were made using a similar pecking technique.

2. All sixteen letters are capitalized which is consistent with other medieval Latin inscriptions.

3. There is a possible man-made dot above the second *i* in *Signo* which is also consistent with other medieval Latin inscriptions.

4. The inscription exhibits advanced weathering in the otherwise very dense and hard metagraywacke.

5. The layout of the inscription and the raveling of the lines that cross the naturally formed cracks in the rock are consistent with the cracks already being present when the inscription was carved.

6. The length of the top line *In Hoc Signo*, and second line *Vinces*, are exactly a 2:1 ratio. 18.58 in. (47.2 cm) divided by 9.29 in. (23.6 cm) = 2. In fact, the disproportional spacing between the words *In* and *Hoc*, and *Hoc* and *Signo* in the top line, suggests the carver made every effort to ensure the inscription conformed to the sacred 2:1 Templar tradition.

The advanced state of weathering together with the inscription appearing to have been intentionally laid out to incorporate the sacred 2:1 dimension is powerful evidence the inscription is older than I previously thought. Based on this vital new information I am forced to change my previous opinion. The collective evidence listed above is consistent with the In Hoc Signo Vinces inscription being older than 200 years, possibly even 600 or more years old. The most likely candidate to have carved the inscription was a highly educated, and initiated, member of the medieval order of Knights Templar.

Return of the Narragansett Rune Stone

In *Akhenaten* I wrote about the theft and eventual recovery of the Narragansett Rune Stone. We also filmed an episode in season one of *America Unearthed* entitled, "America's Oldest Secret," that included the disappearance of the two-to-three-ton-sized glacial boulder from the shallow waters of Narragansett Bay, off Pojac Point, in the spring of 2012. The graywacke boulder has a mysterious two-line inscription comprised of nine runes carved into it that includes a Hooked X. Due in large part to the efforts of Detective Sheila Paquette, with the Rhode Island Department of Environmental Management, Division of Law Enforcement-Criminal Investigation Unit, the inscribed boulder was returned the following spring by Timothy Mellon, the owner of the property immediately adjacent to where the stone was previously located only dozens of feet from the shore.

After its recovery, plans were begun to find a home for the Narragansett Rune Stone when some unexpected and very troubling news came forward in June of 2014. In an interview that appeared in a local newspaper, a man named Everett Brown claimed to have carved the inscription when he was thirteen years-old in the summer of 1964. The news hit those of us who supported the authenticity of the inscription like a sledgehammer to the chest. We knew this person was not telling the truth and could only guess at his motivation for making up a story that threatened the efforts to protect the inscription. It was frustrating being in Minnesota realizing there was little I could do to help the situation. Thankfully, my good friend and then NEARA (New England Antiquities Research Association) coordinator for Rhode Island, Steve DiMarzo Jr., sprang into action. Being a man of great integrity with a passion for history, he took it upon himself to interview Brown to try and determine if he was being truthful and if the details of his story held together.

At about this same time, several residents read Brown's claims in the local papers. They were outraged and decided to come forward. These eyewitnesses said they had seen the inscription prior to 1964. One witness recalled seeing the inscription as far back as 1945. As welcoming and helpful as these statements were, Steve and I agreed it was vitally important a signed and notarized written affidavit was obtained from each witness. Steve again sprang into action, and over the next few weeks collected nine affidavits from these first-hand witnesses. Steve later confided he had personally interviewed Everett Brown who, he said, seemed to enjoy the attention he was getting in the newspapers.[9] However, as word reached Brown of the growing number of affidavits refuting his claim he suddenly went silent. Steve brought the affidavits to the attention of the local media and the heated controversy was quickly resolved.

---

9   http://m.independentri.com/mobile/independents/north_east/article_fe598e73-8b9f-548f-9130-9cce4460a356.html;   http://www.independentri.com/independents/north_east/article_9877ee-ab-8002-54f2-aa3b-d05867dbf4b9.html

Jerry Lutgen generated this image of the Narragansett Rune Stone inscription using Reflectance Transformation Imaging (RTI). The 2.38 in. tall by 2 in. wide area to the left of the *s* rune on line one appears to have been hammered on or chipped out indiscriminately. (Photograph courtesy of the Jerry Lutgen, 2014)

In fairness to Brown, he may indeed have recalled childhood memories of creating marks on the Narragansett Rune Stone. The difference between what he claimed in 2014, and what actually happened a half-century earlier, could be connected to what appears to be a damaged area immediately to the left of the first character on the top line of the inscription. This 2.38 in. tall by 2 in. wide area appears to have been hammered or chipped out indiscriminately in the past, and doesn't appear to be related to the inscription or natural weathering processes. If so, Brown may be right about his recollections of banging on the stone as a child. He apparently forgot the inscription was already there when he performed his youthful handiwork.

For eighteen months after the Rune Stone was recovered it was stored inside a warehouse owned by the University of Rhode Island. For the first time, being inside a secure, dry facility we were presented an excellent opportunity to examine the inscription without having to wait for an extreme low tide or fight waves that constantly lapped across the surface as we had experienced in past visits. On September 1, 2014, Detective Paquette helped make arrangements for my wife Janet, researcher Jerry Lutgen, and myself to examine the inscription inside the university warehouse near the bay. I was anxious to get a close-up view of the weathering aspects the inscription had endured, this time under ideal conditions. Jerry was also excited to test two advanced computational photography techniques, 3D imaging and Reflective Transformation Imaging (RTI). These techniques enable a more complete study of complex surfaces in stone than is possible with standard photography.

One of the first things we all noticed as we walked around the stone, resting on a large wooden pallet, were three deep gouges on the inscription end of the boulder. These marks were apparently made when Mellon's agents used heavy equipment to move the stone. Thankfully, the inscription wasn't harmed. As Jerry was setting up, Janet and I took close-up photos and carefully measured each carved character in the inscription. It measured 17 in. long by 6.25 in. tall. The edges and bottoms of all the carved characters were significantly rounded from weathering in this relatively hard

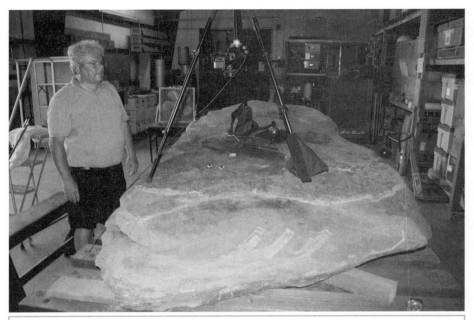

On September 1, 2014, Jerry Lutgen checks the set-up for photographing the Narragansett Rune Stone using Reflectance Transformation Imaging (RTI). Notice the three deep gouges on the end of the stone made when it was removed from the bay with heavy equipment. (2014)

and durable graywacke. In areas adjacent to the last three runes, on the first line, I noticed where some of the rock had spalled away. This made it difficult to determine which runic symbols they actually were. Overall, even though I cannot give an opinion on the exact age from a geological weathering perspective with reasonable certainty, I can say the inscription looked very old. At least well over a century, and possibly many centuries, based on the near-shore marine environment it was found in.

After finishing our work, we discussed the future of the inscription with Detective Paquette. She made it clear the university would not allow it to stay there permanently, but the town council of North Kingstown had stepped up and was willing to take possession of the artifact and proudly display it permanently in their town. The next day, on September 2, 2014, I gave a presentation on the Narragansett Rune Stone to the council. My goal was to try and help the council members understand the potential historical significance of the artifact and the need to protect and preserve it. My presentation was well received and it was gratifying to see the level of commitment to preservation of the artifact in the eyes of the members present.

The following summer, Janet and I were invited to the dedication ceremony in North Kingstown for the unveiling of the Narragansett Rune Stone in its new home. October 30, 2015, was a perfect, warm sunny day and a large crowd turned out for the ceremony. There were many familiar faces at the event and I was thrilled to be introduced to the nine individuals who signed the affidavits and shared their memories of the inscription. We thanked them for taking action for, had they not spoken up, the inscription might not have found a permanent home.

When it was my turn to address the large crowd, I did my best to explain the importance of preserving controversial artifacts until a consensus is reached based on sound and thorough scientific inquiry. Even though there were many people to thank for their support and efforts, I made sure to publicly acknowledge the hard work and commitment of two individuals. Detective Sheila Paquette deserved a ton of credit for tracking down the stolen historical artifact and ensuring its safe return, despite criticism by some for, "…spending her time trying to find a rock."

The other hero in this story is Steve DiMarzo Jr., who was relentless in making sure all the people signed the affidavits, and hounded them until they were legally notarized. Steve was also the heart and soul of the effort to ensure the preservation of the artifact. If not for Steve's unrelenting efforts, the artifact could have ended up in the proverbial dustbin of history.

Other very committed people like the North Kingstown historian, Tim Cranston, local representative and resident, Paul Roberti, and all the town council members also deserve credit for setting an example of what can be done when people work together. As wonderful as all of this was, their work is not yet finished. When the large boulder containing the inscription was finally unveiled I was very pleased with the location, the aesthetically-well-done design, and informative signage. However, I was still concerned to see it was uncovered. Hopefully, a secure shelter will be constructed around the artifact to protect it from the elements and potential vandalism. I know the town is committed to preserving this important piece of their cultural heritage and will get the job finished soon.

I'd be remiss if I didn't try to answer the question I've asked many times myself: what does the inscription say? The simple answer is we don't know. Scandinavian scholars are even more perplexed with the Narragansett Rune Stone inscription than either the Kensington or Spirit Pond Rune Stones. In 1971, the three Spirit Pond Rune Stones, self-dated to 1401–1402, were discovered shallowly buried together at Spirit Pond, near the mouth of the Kennebec River, in Maine.[10] At least they can decipher their messages to varying degrees, but the Narragansett inscription had defied all attempts to decode it by scholars. Runic scholars point out that even within the short, nine-symbol inscription there are significant inconsistencies with the runes used. Only the *s* rune and Hooked X symbol appear on either the Kensington or Spirit Pond inscriptions. The *h* and *r* runes on the Narragansett Rune Stone are different than those used on the other North American rune stones, and the rest are runic symbols seldom seen in Scandinavia.

An additional mystery includes the two runic symbols that date back to the Viking era, while others, like the Hooked X, date to the late medieval period. These facts make the inscription a nightmare for runic scholars to decode.

---

10   For more information about the Spirit Pond Rune Stones see Chapter 10 (pages 71-85) in *The Hooked X: Key to the Secret History of North America*.

What I suspect likely occurred, was the Templars carved a coded message meant only for those using a specific cipher to be able to decode the message. One example of what is believed to be a coded cipher is found in a copy of a twelfth-century document I will discuss in detail in Chapter 11. Because of the inability of runic scholars to be able to translate the Narragansett inscription, it has incited deep skepticism. However, like the Kensington and Spirit Pond Rune Stones, there is no factual evidence consistent with the inscriptions being modern, and the advanced weathering of the Kensington Stone suggests significant age. Until more data comes forward to shed new light on the Narragansett Rune Stone inscription it will remain a fascinating Templar enigma that must be preserved and protected.

On October 30, 2015, there was a very well attended ceremony for the unveiling of the new home for the Narragansett Rune Stone in North Kingstown, Rhode Island, not far from its original location. (Unknown)

CHAPTER 3:

†HE KEΠSIΠGTOΠ RUΠE STOΠE

For the reader to fully understand and appreciate the history revealed in this book, it is important to understand the journey I have taken in my research and the discoveries I have made investigating the artifact that started it all. These discoveries happened during my exhaustive investigation authenticating the artifact I now realize was the initial Knights Templar land claim, or "stake in the ground," that served as the beginning of the founding of the United States of America. These are strong words indeed, but words I am confident the reader will agree are true.

I had never heard of the Kensington Rune Stone before it was brought to my laboratory in July 2000, nor had I heard anything about the then century-old controversy surrounding its authenticity. When the representative of the Runestone Museum in Alexandria, Minnesota, started telling me the story, I could see the passion in his eyes and hear it in his voice. Barry Hansen was obviously an advocate of authenticity, and tried unsuccessfully to hide his bias, which triggered my caution radar to turn on. He explained how the Runestone Museum, located only a two-hour drive from my office in the Midway area in St. Paul, wanted a geological examination conducted on the artifact to try and determine if the weathering was consistent with the date on the stone: AD 1362. At that point, I recited the speech I give to all my customers who appear to have an agenda. I said, "I'll be happy to do this analysis for you, but you need to be prepared that I may come back and give you news you're not going to like, and you're still going to pay me regardless of the outcome." Barry and the museum agreed with the terms and we went to work.

The first time the Kensington Rune Stone was brought to the laboratory, I invited six geologists to the lab to perform a cursory examination of the artifact and offer comments about their observations and input into the analysis I was about to begin.

Three were my former professors from the University of Minnesota at Duluth: Professors Emeritus John Green, Richard Ojakangas, and the now-late Charles L. Matsch. July 10, 2000, was the first of many times we placed the artifact on a table-sized cart and wheeled it into the laboratory. The dozen or so geologists, which included several members of my staff, carefully examined the tombstone-sized 202-pound slab of graywacke while offering comments and suggestions. Little did I realize agreeing to this work would be the beginning of an incredible journey that would eventually lead to far corners of the world I never dreamed I would see.

Professor Ojakangas was the first to notice and comment on the root leaching on what we now call the back side of the artifact. As we closely examined the white, gently undulating, linear features that branched off twice, they began to fade and get thinner as they marched across the glacially striated surface. It was clear that if these features were caused by contact with roots, the widest end was closest to the trunk of the tree. All the geologists agreed the side of the stone had been intentionally split off before the last three lines of the inscription were carved on that surface. I later documented numerous crescent-shaped areas of impact along the edges of what I termed the split side that clearly indicated the carver started off with a larger slab of rock and skillfully split off a large piece to create the final rectangular shape. The split side would later become vitally important in the relative-age dating work I would perform because it was created at the same time the inscription was carved. This meant I did not have to take invasive samples from the carved runes to determine the weathering and eventually the age of the inscription.

This 1937 photo taken by Dr. Rodney Beecher Harvey shows two white and branching lineations on the glacial backside of the Kensington Rune Stone produced by contact with tree roots found wrapped around the stone at the time of discovery. (Photo courtesy of the Duerr/Harvey Family)

The distinguished group of geologists all agreed the rock looked like a metagraywacke. At one point, Dr. Charlie Matsch, my advisor in college who first sparked my interest in geology asked, "Are you going to take a sample from the stone to confirm the mineralogy?"

With little hesitation, I said, "Probably."

We both knew that to understand anything about the weathering aspects of the inscription meant I had to know exactly what the composition of the rock was. The only way to do that was to obtain a core sample from the artifact and examine thin sections under a polarized light microscope to identify the exact mineralogy.

The visiting professors also shared their knowledge about the controversial history of the artifact and that the consensus of experts believed it was a hoax. Knowing nothing about runes or Old Swedish at the time, I did not pay much attention to discussion about the message carved in medieval Scandinavian runes. My job was to focus on the physical aspects of the rock, most notably the weathering of the inscription. It came as a surprise to me the professors had all heard about the Kensington stone and its legend. It would be months before the gravity of the work I was about to embark on would become apparent to me.

Shortly after the professors' visit, I obtained permission from the museum's director, LuAnn Patton, to cut a one-inch diameter core sample roughly two inches deep into the back side of the stone. Examination of 25 micron thick slices of the rock revealed it was comprised of about a dozen different minerals and was indeed metamorphosed graywacke. Graywacke is a sedimentary rock that accumulates near the bedrock source where the particles of sand and clay that comprise it originated. The sediment is what is called mineralogically "immature," meaning it did not have a long history of transport to chemically break down the vulnerable minerals to quartz and clays. Because of this, there are many different minerals in greywacke that made it easier to pinpoint the bedrock source.

With the help of world renowned sedimentologist, Professor Emeritus, Dr. Richard Ojakangas, we concluded the Kensington Rune Stone was carved from a glacially transported slab of graywacke from the Thomson Formation that outcrops just south of Duluth in Thomson, Minnesota. I was very familiar with the Thomson Formation, having mapped sections of it as an undergrad. Exactly where the Kensington party in the fourteenth century found this particular slab of rock is unclear, but well-developed glacial striations on the back side suggest it could easily have been found on or near the property where Olof Ohman eventually discovered the artifact in 1898. The important point of this part of my analysis was my conclusion the rock is indigenous to Minnesota. This proved the Kensington party traveled to what is now Minnesota. Once there, they found a large slab of graywacke, split it down to its present shape, and then carved the inscription before shallowly burying it in the ground.

From 2000, when I performed my initial research, to 2003 it was an absolute whirlwind of mind-boggling events that came in rapid succession. It would certainly help those interested in additional details and context of these events and discoveries to read the chapter, "My Experience with the Kensington Rune Stone," in my 2006 book.[11]

The most important aspect of the geological work I performed on the Kensington Stone was the relative-age dating of the inscription that centered around two key minerals in the stone; pyrite and biotite mica. Before coming up with a method for using these two key minerals as weathering clocks, I first had to document several important geological facts about the rock and the inscription. The easiest way to explain these various aspects of the artifact is to list them chronologically starting with the initial

---

11   *Compelling New Evidence*, pages 249-386, 2006.

formation of the graywacke sediments that accumulated in a shallow ocean basin over 1.1 billion years ago.[12]

The second major event in the formation of the rock was the heat and pressure (metamorphism) it was exposed to after burial by more sediments that produced its overall very hard and dense physical makeup. Metamorphic processes also produced a two-directional foliation, or parallel alignment of elongate minerals, most notably the micas, that are unique to the coarser-grained sequences of the Thomson Formation the stone originally came from. Geological pressure produced stress and strain deep in the earth that produced both large and small-scale joint fractures.[13] The larger joint fractures influenced its eventual flat, slab-like shape. The small-scale jointing resulted in the tendency to fracture in predominantly one direction, called cleavage.[14] Cleavage within the rock influenced the relative smoothness of various surfaces when the rock would eventually be altered by man.

What formed next in the stone's geological journey was the white, triangular shaped area in the lower left of the face side with the first nine lines of the inscription. The white mineral is calcite that formed millions of years ago when groundwater solutions carrying the dissolved mineral crystallized within thin, sub-parallel joint fractures.[15]

Sometime in the last 20,000-50,000 years, during the last major advance of continental glaciers in North America, known as the Wisconsin Glacial period, deep parallel grooves and scratches running down the long axis of the back side of the stone were made. These glacial striations were made when sand and rock fragments imbedded at the base of the glacial ice deeply scratched and gouged the slab while it was still attached to the bedrock. Eventually, the original larger slab broke free within the ice along a large joint fracture and was carried by the glacier in a southwesterly direction, presumably into the area now known as Kensington, Minnesota.

Roughly 12,000-15,000 years ago, the continent-sized glacial ice sheet melted back and the large slab of graywacke was deposited, along with massive amounts of sand, gravel, and boulders that littered the landscape. After the glacier melted away, the tapering end of the larger slab was, at least partially, buried in glacial debris. Meteoric waters, made up of rain and melted snow, carried dissolved calcite solution that crystalized as intermittent secondary deposits on the surface of the lower back end.

For the next 10,000-12,000 years, natural weathering of the glacial surfaces produced a light gray color that is still present on all surfaces except the spilt side where the

---

12   https://books.google.com/books?id=hC_mtDrx8voC&pg=PA43&lpg=PA43&dq=Paleoproterozoic+Thomson+Formation&source=bl&ots=A_tPmvuC3K&sig=fEk79Ud4Kmk0183PAXUbozZcfw0&hl=en&sa=X&ei=OLBXVZ3YPMu2sAW8kYCwBg&ved=0CCYQ6AEwAQ#v=onepage&q=Paleoproterozoic%20Thomson%20Formation&f=false

13   A joint is a natural break (fracture) in the continuity of either a sedimentary layer or body of rock that lacks any visible movement parallel to the surface (plane) of the fracture. They can occur singly, but usually occur as joint sets and systems.

14   Cleavage is a type of planar rock feature that develops because of deformation and metamorphism. The degree of deformation and metamorphism, along with rock type, determines the kind of cleavage feature that develops. Generally, these structures are formed in fine grained rocks composed of minerals affected by pressure solution.

15   Calcite is what makes up hard water deposits that develop on leaky pipes.

Secondary calcite deposits developed on the glacial bottom end of the Kensington Rune Stone after it was deposited by glacial ice within the past 12,000-15,000 years. (2000)

last three lines of the inscription were carved. It has a much darker blue-gray color because it has been weathering for only six centuries as opposed to 10,000 years or longer.

The next chapter in the life of the Kensington Rune Stone began when a party of thirty Europeans reached what is the north-south continental divide of North America. If we rely on the inscription as it has been translated by Scandinavian scholars, it was a two-week journey west from the western tip of what we now call Lake Superior in the middle of the fourteenth century. For over a century it was assumed, "After we came home found ten men red from blood and death," meant they were killed in a battle with natives or even suffered from the plague. I never believed they were killed by Native Americans because, if they had not formed some kind of alliance with the indigenous people they would never have made it anywhere near the center of the continent. It was not until I was initiated into the York Rite degrees of Freemasonry that I realized this part of the inscription was simply an allegorical tale with hidden meaning, but I will save that story for later.

Before carving the runes, the carver started with a much larger original slab they found somewhere nearby and skillfully split it down by "bush-hammering," according to the former State Geologist of Minnesota, Newton H. Winchell, in his report to the Museum Committee of the Minnesota Historical Society in 1910.[16] Ninety years later I came to the same conclusion about the split side independent of Winchell, after documenting the rounded impact marks along the edges of that surface. It was not until after I had reached my conclusion regarding the age of the inscription, which proved it was a genuine medieval artifact, that I learned the first State Geologist of Minnesota,

---

16   Upon completion of his investigation, WInchell concluded in his report the Kensington Rune Stone was genuine. In a letter written to the committee that was separate from his 76-page final report he wrote, "The said stone is not a modern forgery, and must be accepted as a genuine record of exploration in Minnesota, at the date stated in the inscription."

and a giant in the field of geology during his time, had already studied the artifact. I was quite relieved when I read his conclusion that echoed my own. Upon reflection I realized I should not have been nervous as I had independently replicated the geological work Winchell had already done.

Three years after I documented the impact marks around the edges of the man-made split side surface, I was stunned to read that a team of scientists in Sweden had doubts, thinking the surface was more likely a glacial surface. I couldn't understand how they could possibly think this, and it was the first time I had serious doubts about the credibility and integrity of the Scandinavian scientists. It was especially disappointing considering the six-hour examination the lead scientist, a geologist named Runo Löfvendahl, and I performed on the artifact when it was on display at the museum in Hüdiksval, Sweden, in February of 2004. Afterward, in the lobby of the museum, Runo agreed with every geological aspect we discussed, including the man-made split side.[17] It would be the first of many disappointments I would witness from the Swedish scholars who would often offer bizarre and puzzling opinions on the artifact. The reason why would soon become apparent.

The importance of the man-made split side became especially relevant when I began the tombstone study phase of my work in 2002-2003. One of the unique features of the split side was its much rougher surface than the face side due to the irregular fracture caused by the inherent direction of the foliation and cleavage. The entire surface also had a different color, texture and weathering profile than all the other surfaces of the stone because the split side was thousands of years younger than the glacial backside. I do not believe for a second the Swedish scientists really believed this surface was of glacial age. I believe they intentionally tried to cast doubt on my

The split side of the Kensington Rune Stone contains the last three lines of the inscription and was created when the carver split the once larger slab of rock down to its roughly 2:1 dimensions. (2003)

---

17   I invite the reader to read about my experience with Runo Löfvendahl and our examination of the artifact in *Akhenaten* (page 137).

relative-age weathering conclusions, knowing the chip sample I obtained from the split side was critical to reaching a final conclusion. Keep in mind, they did not say it was of glacial age, they left the door open by saying, "it could be." Regardless, by making this statement they knew it would slow the ever-increasing momentum toward acceptance of the authenticity of the artifact. Authenticity would overturn a century and more of negative opinions by Scandinavian scholars who erroneously concluded it was a hoax. After interacting with Swedish academics for the past fifteen years, sad as it is, this is exactly what happens. These scholars have always maintained, and likely always will, the historical paradigm that the Kensington Rune Stone is a hoax, and all the facts in the world to the contrary isn't going to change it. So, we press forward without them.

After the carver split the slab down to its present shape, creating roughly a 2:1 ratio, he began to carve the inscription. As an experiment, having carved my own four-foot-tall rune stone into a large slab of granite gneiss of similar hardness and composition as the Kensington Rune Stone in 2005, I have a very good understanding of the difficulties the carver had as he crafted the inscription. I agreed with professional rune stone carvers in Sweden who examined the inscription and said the person who carved the Kensington Rune Stone had some experience, but was not an expert stone carver. Estimates on how long it took to carve the inscription range from several hours to several days. Assuming he kept his chisels sharp, which appears to have been the case, and from my own experience, I believe it took between six and ten hours.

There were at least two areas of the stone where the carver of the Kensington Rune Stone had difficulty. The first was at the beginning of line two, on the face side, as he was carving the fourth and final character in the first word, an *o* rune which is still partially present. Roughly a quarter-inch-thick, loose chip spalled off along an open natural cleavage fracture causing most of the first word on the second line to be lost. Likely sensing more trouble, he began the third line of the inscription on the right side of the edge of the quarter-inch-high step where the cleavage fracture had broken free from the bedrock at the base of the glacier thousands of years ago. On line four, the carver moved back to the left edge where he began the final six of nine lines in total on the face side.

The other area where the carver had difficulty was in the use of a punch chisel to make dots within the grooves of several runes *after* he had carved the character, and most likely after the entire inscription. We know this because of chipping of the top edges immediately adjacent to the already-present grooves of the original character. Ironically, the rune where the carver had trouble arguably turned out to be the most important runic character that by itself proves the Kensington Rune Stone is a medieval document: the Dotted R.

In the second *r* in the third word, *Norrmen*, on line one, the carver tried to make a dot in the upper loop of the character, but used too much force with his hammer, causing most of the plateau of rock to spall away. When working with the Scandinavian runologists, I learned the Dotted R rune is an extremely rare medieval character, used to indicate a different *r* sound, that was only discovered by modern scholars in 1935.

In May of 2005, I carved my own four-foot-tall rune stone to commemorate the publishing of my book, co-authored with Richard Nielsen, *The Kensington Rune Stone: Compelling New Evidence*. Using a hammer and chisels it took 40 hours to carve and paint the inscription. (2005)

This begs the question of how a forger could have known about the Dotted R in 1898? I will have more to say on that later.

It has long been a point of debate as to what the Kensington party did with the stone after the inscription was completed. It could be argued the stone is both a memorial, presumably for the "10 men red from blood and death," and a land claim. The memorial aspect of the inscription will be discussed in greater detail in Chapter 6. Many have argued the blank area below the nine lines on the face side suggests it was placed upright in the ground. This does not make sense to me for two simple reasons. The first is who would have been able to read it at the center of North America in the fourteenth century? Many have argued Native Americans would not appreciate the memorial to ten men many have claimed over the past century they were supposedly responsible for killing. The inscription says nothing about Native Americans, and the evidence of their compatible ideology suggests the opposite was true and they in fact were close allies, as will be discussed further on.

The second reason is because of the curved lower end on the back side, the 202-pound stone would have slumped onto its back with the inscription side facing up. In 1910, Newton Winchell argued that if the stone had been set upright in the ground, the sharp tapering end of the bottom edge wouldn't lend itself to being placed upright without the aid of other stones to keep it in place. Trouble is, there was no mention of Olof Ohman and his two sons finding other stones large enough to prop the Rune Stone up, so that scenario seems highly unlikely. Further, if the stone had been propped up by rocks or set up in the ground like a tombstone as some have tried to claim, there would be a weathering ground-line evidence when there is none.[18] In fact, the stone was found with the inscription side facing down as evidenced by the root leaching present on the back side. The evidence suggests the Kensington party buried the stone, face down, a foot or so below the surface which is exactly where Ohman said he discovered it in the fall of 1898.[19]

Roughly thirty years prior to Olof and his sons' discovery, the stone obtained one more important tattoo on its surface while still just below the surface of the ground. The 25–30-year-old aspen tree Olof pulled over with a winch had roots firmly wrapped around the stone enough to pull it from the ground as the tree fell. These roots left markings on the back side. Both Olof and his sons, Olof Jr. and Edward, wrote in their affidavits the roots over the back side were 3.5 inches wide and flattened from prolonged contact. During my cursory examination with six senior geologists we all agreed the two sets of half-inch wide, white, undulating and branching lineations running across the surface looked like scars from tree roots. At the time, I was troubled by the apparent discrepancy of the Ohmans' description of the tree roots being 3.5 inches wide, and the white lineations that were at most, half an inch wide. If these were the same roots from the tree the stone was discovered entangled in, shouldn't the white lineations be 3.5 inches wide also? This apparent inconsistency would eventually be cleared up by a plant physiologist named Paul Syltie, PhD.

During a personal visit to my home in June of 2004, I asked Paul about this root leaching discrepancy. He explained the active part of a root system was the leading tips that extract nutrients and minerals from soil and rocks. After looking at photos of the white lineations, he said, "They were definitely made by contact with roots from a young tree."

He then explained that as trees grow the root system expands, bark develops, and the active leading tips move on and the extraction of nutrients stop. Paul's explanation removed the inconsistency and the root leaching could now be logically explained.

The final event to impact the geological aspects of the artifact came while in the hands of the discoverer. In December of 1898, after being displayed in a jewelry store in Kensington, the stone was brought back to the Ohman farm where Olof Ohman began to study the inscription as winter set in. Keep in mind, being a Swedish immigrant, Ohman once said, "Every kid raised in Sweden knows what runes are." This included himself, but he said, "...but I don't know how to use them." In fact, his fellow Swedish immigrant neighbor, Andrew Anderson, gave him a book that contained a Viking era runic alphabet Ohman used in his studies.[20] With no electricity and long dark winter nights in 1898/99, Ohman studied the artifact by lantern or candle light. In 1909, Olof told Newton Winchell during his investigation he used a nail to clean the characters

---

18   For those interested in reading more about the weathering ground-line and other fraudulent claims please see the following article: http://www.kensingtonrunestone.us/html/_current_issues.html

19   *Compelling New Evidence*, pages 1-5.

20   Years later, when scholars learned of the book containing the Viking Age runic alphabet in Ohman's home, they claimed, even though it would have been impossible, that Ohman used the book to carve the Kensington inscription.

that were still packed with mud.[21] The fresh-appearing scratched-out bottom of the runes would cause confusion on the part of early skeptical researchers and scholars, as it also did with me initially. However, under microscopic examination, I could see the walls of the grooves were much darker in color and weathered, whereas the bottom of the grooves looked whitish and freshly scratched. Upon learning that Ohman had used the nail to clean out mud, this fact cleared up my initial confusion. It is amazing how so much of the geological history of the artifact could be deciphered so long after its discovery, and is an example of the ability to obtain important information through proper laboratory analysis. This investigation allowed for every physical aspect of the stone to be explained and led to a comprehensive understanding of both its geological and historical origins.

The last major and permanent physical imprint on the artifact, besides the *H* carved on the lower end of the split side by Hjalmar Holand in 1908, came when I made the decision to take a one-inch diameter core sample from the back side of the stone. It was not a decision I made lightly, but it was important to fully understand the mineralogical composition to make a proper interpretation of the weathering aspects of both the stone and the inscription. At the time, some criticized me for damaging the artifact. However, I would absolutely do it again, as it provided the critical mineralogical evidence for determining the authenticity of the artifact.

Along with taking the core sample from the back side, I also chiseled a tiny chip off the split side for the relative-age weathering study. Like Winchell in 1910, I determined there were three different weathering profiles representing three ages for surfaces of the slab of graywacke:

1. The glacial aged surfaces were 10,000-12,000 years old.
2. The freshly scratched surfaces at the bottom of the grooves made by Olof dated to 1898/99.
3. The age of the unscratched walls of the grooves of the inscription and the entire split side were unknown.

Because the artifact was too big to fit inside the vacuum chamber of a scanning electron microscope, I needed to take the core sample to make smaller test samples that would fit. This way I could closely examine the glacially weathered surfaces on the top of the core, and the fractured surface where the core snapped off which represented the non-weathered surfaces of the scratched-out bottom of the grooves. Since the split side was created at the same time the inscription was carved, the chip sample taken from that side would provide the control for the weathering profile of the original inscription.

---

21   In Winchell's report, he wrote the following about Ohman scratching out the runes, "The edge (split side) of the stone differs in this from the face, since most of the rune letters show the white powder from crushing the stone. This difference was said to be due to the fact that the runes on the edge had been filled with mud and had been cleaned out by scraping them with an iron nail. Indeed, in the runes in some places on the edge can be seen with a pocket magnifier small quantities of fresh metallic iron evidently derived from that process."

Armed with the core and chip samples, I made the three-hour drive down Interstate 35 to the Materials Laboratory at Iowa State University in Ames, Iowa, to examine the samples with a low vacuum scanning electron microscope (SEM) using energy dispersive analysis and elemental mapping to identify the surface minerals. As the images appeared under magnification up to 500X, things became clearer with regard to the weathering. As expected, the relatively soft mica minerals (Mohs hardness of 2 out of 10) covered most of the surface of the freshly fractured bottom of the core sample. This was due to the fracture following along the surface of the weakest minerals. Therefore, mica minerals would have heavily covered *all* surfaces of the original slab after the ice melted away because the rock was freshly scoured.

The top surface of the core sample was examined next and as expected, *all* micas that had once covered the glacial-aged surfaces had weathered away. This was due to thousands of years of exposure to repeated cycles of freezing and thawing and wetting and drying. What I did not expect was what I saw when the magnified surface of the

The three surfaces of the Kensington Rune Stone exhibit very different color, texture and weathering profiles. Left to right; freshly fractured bottom of the core sample and the bottom of the grooves of the inscription; the glacial aged surface of the artifact after 10,000-12,000 years of weathering; the spilt side surface that is the same as the original inscription made in 1362. Magnification is 50X (2000)

The same three surfaces under a scanning electron microscope. The freshly fractured surface of the bottom of the core is covered with flat, sheet-like mica minerals and represents the glacial aged surfaces of the stone, roughly 10,000-12,000 years old (far left). The micas are completely weathered away on both glacial aged surface (middle) and on the original inscription and the split side (far right). Magnification is 500X (2000)

chip sample from the split side came into focus: all the micas on that surface were also gone! In fact, the surface looked identical to the glacially weathered top surface of the core inside the scanning electron microscope. However, under reflected light at 50X, the surfaces looked very different. The glacial aged surfaces were a mellow, light gray color whereas the split side had a darker blue-gray color. The split side looked less weathered than the glacial surfaces, yet darker-colored and more weathered than the freshly fractured bottom surface of the core sample and the scratched-out bottoms on the grooves of the inscription.

Clearly, the original inscription was older than the bottom of the grooves scratched out by Olof Ohman. The question was, how much older? That would be my next challenge. To find the answer would require traveling to the east coast of the United States.

Tombstone Study

Early on, it occurred to me that tombstones might be a good way to measure weathering rates of mica minerals. With the death dates of the people carved on the tombstones, all I needed was to collect very small chip samples from the carved or polished surfaces of increasingly older tombstones and observe what happened as they weathered. I focused my experiment on the mica mineral biotite. There are actually four different micas in the Kensington Rune Stone, but I selected biotite because it contains iron in its elemental composition and therefore chemically weathers fastest. I did not want anyone to accuse me of choosing a mineral that would make the stone appear older.[22]

In March of 2003, I collected twenty-three chip samples from slate tombstones after obtaining permission from the trustees of the Hallowell Cemetery in Hallowell, Maine. Samples were collected up to six inches above, at, and up to six inches below ground level. The death dates of the tombstones ranged from 1796 to 1865, giving a sample range of weathering from 138 to 203 years. One of the key reasons the cemetery in Hallowell, Maine, worked so well was not only did the slate contain similar sized biotite minerals, but the area has a very comparable climate to Kensington, Minnesota.[23]

Armed with the tombstone chip samples, I drove back to the materials lab at Iowa State University to examine them in the SEM. While examining each sample, starting with the youngest, I could see the individual biotite crystals were slowly degrading on the exposed edges and eventually started to peel off the surface relatively intact. Repeated freeze-thaw and wet-dry cycles caused the biotite minerals to exfoliate off the surface like dry, flaky skin. Once the biotite minerals began to come off the surface of the tombstones, I knew the experiment was over. The average age the tombstones exhibited the exfoliating biotite minerals was 197 years, plus or minus five. At this point, I could quantify the age of the weathering and wrote the following in my final report:

---

22   The four mica minerals are muscovite, sericite, chlorite, and biotite. The other minerals and their percentages in the Kensington Rune Stone are listed on page 34 of *Compelling New Evidence*.

23   *Compelling New Evidence*, page 39.

Based on comparison of weathering characteristics of the chip samples obtained from slate tombstones, the biotite mica that was exposed at the time of the original inscription on the KRS, took longer than about 200 years to completely weather away. This eliminates the possibility that anyone living in the late 19th century could have been involved in a hoax.

Because the artifact had not been in a weathering environment since it was pulled from the ground in 1898, that is when the "longer than 200 years" estimate of weathering started from. This evidence pushed the most recent possible date of creation of the inscription to the very late 1600s. However, simple logic made the conclusion much easier to reach since there were only two realistic possibilities. The Kensington Rune Stone is either a late nineteenth-century hoax as so many believed over the past one hundred and twenty years, or it is a genuine medieval artifact. The tombstone study eliminated the hoax possibility leaving only one clear and obvious conclusion.

Some academics still have problems with this conclusion, yet the facts present a permanent roadblock to anyone who wants to believe the artifact is a hoax. Despite the sometimes-passionate insistence of their opinions, they are unable to produce any tangible facts to support a hoax scenario. Along with the scientific testing results, and basic logic, I was also able to prove the following specific points, further authenticating the Kensington Rune Stone as a genuine medieval artifact self-dated to 1362:

- All the language, runes, dialect and grammar features within the inscription are consistent with fourteenth-century Swedish grammar. They exist somewhere in the historic record.
- The inscription was carved into a slab of metagraywacke rock, indigenous to Minnesota.

Between 2003 and 2005, I took five trips to Sweden in search of the runic and linguistic evidence I knew had to exist, and with the help of many people, both American and Swedish, I was able to find everything. Working with Dick Nielsen and Henrik Williams, collectively, we also made important new discoveries that were an outgrowth of what arguably was one of the most important discoveries ever made relative to the Kensington Rune Stone. Olof Ohman, who never wavered in his denial of being involved in a hoax till the day he died, was telling the truth. Science has proven the Kensington Rune Stone is genuine! So, a Scandinavian party successfully traveled to Minnesota in the fourteenth century, for a reason, which meant there was also evidence to be found of motivation for such a journey.

Photo Library of the Inscription

In 2002, after enduring repeated criticism for my opinion of the Rune Stone's authenticity based largely on certain Scandinavian scholars' objections to aspects of the inscription, I decided to create a digital photo-library of every rune, number, Latin letter, and word separator within the inscription. I took over seven hundred photographs under both high and low angle reflected light to pull out the three-dimensionality of each carved character to understand exactly what was carved on the stone. My thinking at the time was that before any scholar could try to make sense of the inscription, they had to know exactly what was there. It turns out this basic process of detailed documentation ended up being the most important work I did with the artifact.

After the Runestone Museum accepted my proposal for doing the photo work gratis, the artifact was delivered to my laboratory a second time in the fall of 2002. The microscope was mounted on an articulated arm so I could move the lens freely over the stone. I completed the twelve hours worth of work over a weekend. Right from the start strange things began to show up I had not noticed with the naked eye, starting with the first symbol carved into the face side in the upper left-hand corner. As the Pentadic number 8 came into focus, I noticed something unusual. It didn't seem like anything important at first, but at the end of the second horizontal bar the carver appeared to have added a punch mark after carving the character. I looked at it repeatedly, wondering if my eyes were deceiving me Why would the carver do that? The next two characters also had strange anomalies. The two-dot word separator after the 8 had a third punch mark directly above the other two vertically aligned punch marks. The mystery continued when the next character, a g in the word göter, had a deep punch mark on the upper left arm. Tiny chips, or spalls, of rock along the edges of the original groove immediately adjacent indicated the punch mark was clearly added after the character was carved. I was puzzled, wondering what was going on with these added man-made punch marks?

The frequency of anomalous punch marks and short lines added to characters lessened as I continued. However, because of the three strange additions at the beginning of the inscription my awareness was heightened and I watched out for them. Eventually, I found over a dozen of the mysterious marks. Why did the carver add them, and, what do they mean? The questions swirled in my brain. It turned out these strange additions led to four important discoveries. Two were extremely important linguistically and runologically, and the other two were encoded secret messages.

HÄR

The first major discovery that came directly from the photo library was pointed out by Dr. Richard Nielsen. With a noticeably excited but serious tone in his voice he asked, "Are you sure there are two dots above the a rune in the word har on line ten?"

I said, "Absolutely, there are definitely two dots there."

He then took a devil's advocate approach to our discussion, telling me later the implication of these previously undocumented dots was significant, and, in his opinion, almost too good to be true. I then explained the likely reason the dots were previously missed. The medieval carver intentionally bush-hammered, or cleaved, the previously larger slab creating the split side. The newly created rougher surface was produced by the dominant foliation (preferred orientation of elongate minerals) that upon weathering made the two dots difficult to see. Satisfied with my geological explanation, Dr. Nielsen then explained the implication of this discovery.

It turned out the word *har* without the two dots *is* a modern Swedish word. For over a century it was the chief piece of linguistic evidence scholars used to claim the stone was a late nineteenth-century hoax. Dr. Nielsen then said, "These two dots change it from a modern Swedish word to an Old Swedish word."

The importance of these two simple dots suddenly came into focus and served as the perfect example of the value of the collaboration of our two disciplines. I had no idea how important those dots were, yet apparently, it took someone with no preconceived bias, and the proper geological knowledge, to properly document them.

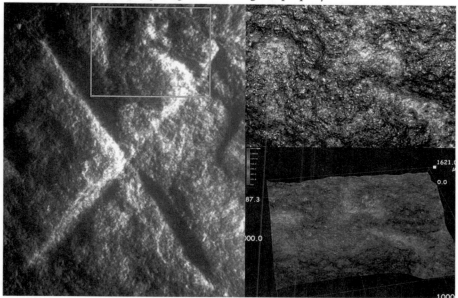

On line 10 in the second letter/rune of the first word on the Kensington Rune Stone is a Hooked X with two dots. Some scholars believed the carved line making the hook was connected to one of the two dots on the right side. Both reflected light imaging (upper right) and three-dimensional mapping of the surface (lower right), as well as a digital microscopic view of this area in the yellow box (left), clearly show the hook does not connect with the dot on the right, thereby confirming the carver made two separate dots above the Hooked X symbol. (2002/2011/2011) See color section for detail.

In 2003, Dr. Richard Nielsen and Swedish linguist and runologist, Professor Henrik Williams, co-authored a paper published in *Compelling New Evidence* (page 564) that included the discovery of the double-dotted *a* rune in *här*. Unfortunately for Henrik, his statement in the paper on the discovery of *här* demanded the Kensington Rune Stone be re-studied, and prompted a three-year punishment of additional administrative duties from the president of Uppsala University in Uppsala, Sweden. What should have been a watershed moment in the academic world was squashed without even the least bit of intellectual curiosity. They should have jumped on this exciting opportunity to open a new door to Scandinavian history. This was a glaring example of the sad and bizarre behavior of academia I would witness on this strange, yet fascinating journey with the Kensington Rune Stone.

Dotted R

Arguably, the most important discovery from the photo-library was a very small dot I had photographed, but didn't see at the time. Dr. Nielsen had been studying the runes and asked if I had noticed a dot in the upper loop of the first *R* rune on line six. I said, "No Dick, I didn't see a dot there."

After studying the Kensington Rune Stone for the previous twenty-five years he knew the inscription like the back of his hand. He then said, "The *R* in the word *w/var* or *were* in English, is a palatal *R* and there should be a dot in the upper loop."

This prompted me to pull up the two images on my computer and look closely in the area of the upper loop. Sure enough, there was a small, symmetrical, diamond-shaped hole right where Dick said it should be. I didn't understand the importance, but Dick was quick to explain.

The Dotted R was an extremely rare medieval Scandinavian rune. In fact, it was not discovered by modern runologists until 1935, when a rib bone was excavated from an archaeological dig in Southern Sweden. The bone had an inscription that included two Dotted *R*s. Ironically, during the excavation of a medieval church undergoing renovations that same year, a roughly five-feet long by two-feet wide medieval grave slab was unearthed with a long inscription carved around the perimeter.

In May of 2005 I visited this small church nestled in the rocky countryside of Ukna Parish, in southern Sweden. To photograph the grave slab was a top priority on that trip and my heart sank when I found the door to Ukna Church locked. After knocking on doors of nearby houses, I found someone to let me in and photographed the grave slab that had two additional, very clear examples of the Dotted *R*. These four examples were eventually published into the literature in 1938.

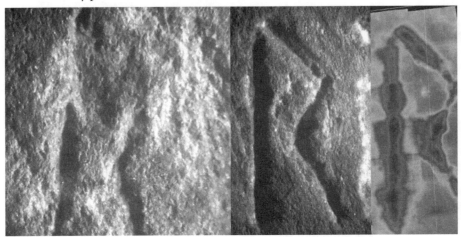

On line one, while trying to make a dot in the upper loop of the *R* the carver used too much force and caused the top half of the plateau of rock to break off (left). To avoid a similar problem, the carver used less force in the *R* on line six and made a shallower dot in the upper loop that was missed for over a century until it was documented in 2002 (middle). Three-dimensional image mapping clearly shows the shallow man-made dot (right). (2002, 2002, 2011) See color section for detail.

Dick then asked me, "If the Dotted *R* wasn't known to anyone in modern times until 1935, how did it get on the Kensington Rune Stone in 1898?"

It was a question that had only one answer. Upon reflection, it now made sense why this dot was so shallow and hard to see, and why the small plateau of rock in the *r* on line one had spalled away. The carver used too much force on the dot in line one and used less force on line six to avoid the spalling problem. This was why the Dotted R on line six was missed until Dick and I found it working together. The implications of this tiny manmade dot that was carefully cut into the small plateau of graywacke were enormous. This dot proved, all by itself, the Kensington Rune Stone was a medieval artifact!

Years later, in what can only be described as academic self-immolation, Dick would try to claim the dot on line six was not man-made and simply a pit in the rock. It did not seem to matter that he was not a geologist and therefore it was inappropriate for him to comment on this physical aspect of the rock. At one point, he even tried to argue the dot was the result of a dropped chisel. Sadly, the reason for this stunning turnaround was apparently due to his perception that someone else might receive credit for proving the authenticity of the artifact. He apparently decided if not him, then no one else was going to get credit for proving its authenticity, so he tried to kill it.

Looking back on this sad and mystifying experience brought to mind another strange event that happened after Dick and I were involved in a particularly testy debate with two Swedish scholars in Hüdiksval, Sweden, in February of 2004. The coastal city on the Baltic Sea was close to Forsa Parish, where the discoverer of the Kensington Rune Stone, Olof Ohman, was born and raised before immigrating to the United States. The Rune Stone was on display at the museum in Hüdiksval, and would be sent back to the Runestone Museum in Alexandria, Minnesota, in a few days. After the debate, several in the crowd of roughly 200 people came up and introduced themselves as descendants of Olof's brothers and sisters. One relative, Britta Blank, was still visibly upset at the rude behavior the Swedish scholars had exhibited and at one point said, "We do not treat our guests in Sweden this way." Moments later after calming down she quietly muttered, "This stone makes people do strange things." Truer words were never spoken.

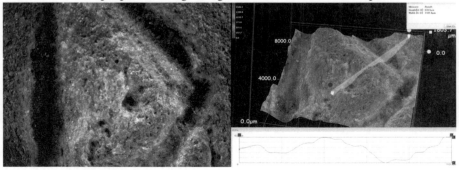

The dot in the *R* on line six of the Kensington Rune Stone inscription proves the artifact is medieval, since the Dotted *R* was unknown to modern scholars until it was discovered in 1935. (2011/2011) See color section for detail.

During that same trip, on the last day before I returned home, a visitor from Stockholm arrived at the museum. Geologist Runo Löfvendahl had been assigned to head up the scientific investigation team to study the artifact. The Runestone Museum had agreed it could stay four months in Sweden. On this last full day of the stone's visit, Runo decided to leave the intimidatingly skeptical environment of his Swedish colleagues in Stockholm, and sneak away to quietly examine the geological aspects of the artifact with me. After six hours of examining every carved character, the glacial striations, the two different kinds of calcite, the split side, and the scratches at the bottom of the grooves made by Olof Ohman, we concluded our study and then moved to the lobby to discuss our findings. Together, we wrote down all the specific findings we had just observed and agreed upon. After listing the dozen factual items, I made an *X* at the bottom of the paper, drew a line, signed my name on it and wrote the date. I then made another line and slid the paper across the table to Runo and said, "Sign it."

He looked back and with tears welling in his eyes he said, "I can't."

He then stood up, shook my hand, and caught his train back to Stockholm.

This experience told me all I needed to know about scholarship and anything that threatens the academic paradigm in Sweden in regards to the Kensington Rune Stone. Looking back with fifteen years of hindsight, I pity people like Runo who I know wanted to be honest and objective in his investigation of the artifact. The toxic environment within Swedish academia made it impossible for him and Henrik. What I've concluded about the continuing struggle of scholars trying to solve the Kensington inscription boils down to a lack of proper method of investigation.

The truth about the Kensington Rune Stone, and the history it represents, is more important than trying to protect the sorry state of scholarship, not just in Sweden, but in the United States as well. To be fair, the problem with our convoluted narrative of world history is more complicated than just the problems of certain aspects of academia. I will address some of these other points as we go along.

Acquisition Business or "Taking Up Land"

One of the issues that has long dogged the artifact was the second line of the inscription. When translated into English it reads, "…on this voyage of discovery, from Vinland far to the west." I remember thinking early on this seemed rather trite and unimportant as far as the purpose of why this intrepid medieval party traveled so far from their home in the Baltic region of northern Europe. It turned out the phrase was indeed trite, and everything changed regarding the context of the message after another discovery Dick and I made working together. It involved a little known linguistic detail found on medieval runic inscriptions on grave slabs. I examined these inscriptions when I visited the island of Gotland in 2004/2005. What we discovered was the *d* rune (called a thorn rune) used in the beginning part of a word, called the *initial position* as opposed to the last letter in a word called the *final position*, stood for the sound. This changed "voyage of discovery" to "acquisition journey, or taking up land."

Suddenly the rune stone had an important purpose: it was a medieval land claim. In the fourteenth century, both the French and the Dutch had a land claim practice whereby if explorers could prove they navigated to the headwaters of a river system and placed a land claim stone and/or plaque in the ground, they could lay claim to the entire river system and all the land associated with it. To my knowledge, I'm the first person to notice the Kensington Rune Stone was discovered on the north-south continental divide of North America at the headwaters of the Mississippi River and Red River watersheds.

This meant these medieval explorers could, theoretically, have laid claim to the entire Mississippi/Missouri River system to the Gulf of Mexico, and the Red River/ Nelson River system to Hudson Bay. When you include all the land in both watersheds it encompasses nearly half the North American continent. This was a key missing piece to the mystery of the Rune Stone. For decades, "…voyage of discovery" never made sense to many scholars and researchers, and they were right. These discoveries show that even the smallest linguistic or runological detail can have massive implications. I suspect there will be new discoveries in the future that will add even more context and understanding of this important artifact.

It later occurred to me the land included within the Kensington land claim was essentially the same land acquired by the United States and President Thomas Jefferson[24] in 1803 from Napoleon and the French with the Louisiana Purchase. In another episode of *America Unearthed* (Season 3, Episode 8: "The Plot to Steal America"), we explained that early eighteenth-century French explorer, Pierre La Vérendrye, placed lead land claim plaques at the headwaters and convergences of major rivers in North America while traveling with his four sons throughout the Great Lakes region, and west along the eastern front of the Canadian Rockies . These lead plaques served as the basis of the French claim of land that would later become the Louisiana Purchase. In the episode, I speculated La Vérendrye knew about earlier Templar land claims like the Kensington Rune Stone, and was searching to clear them out and replace them with the lead plaques that made specific reference to the land being claimed in the name of the French king. The Kensington party appears to have used the Hooked X as a unique symbol that was their specific mark. This identified them as the land claimants, as there is no mention of a monarch or country anywhere in the inscription.

This brings up another mystery that may have involved La Vérendrye. Before carving the Kensington inscription, the carver started with a much larger glacial slab of rock and split off what could be an even larger piece of the original slab that is now missing. This begs the question, where is the other half? It's quite possible it is still out there waiting to be discovered. The second possibility is Pierre La Vérendrye found it using the same sacred geometry triangulation of stone holes found at the Ohman farm at a different location.[25] Perhaps La Vérendrye removed the other half and replaced it with a newer French land claim lead plaque.

---

24   http://www.monticello.org/site/jefferson/louisiana-purchase
25   *The Hooked X*, pages 39-44.

This begs another question: If La Vérendrye knew of the earlier Kensington Rune Stone land claim, why did he not clear that one away too? Perhaps La Vérendrye either could not find it, or maybe didn't bother looking, knowing the 1362 land claim was obsolete by his time in the 1730s. It's likely he also knew the "Hooked X" Templars had morphed over four centuries into a modern Masonic group based in France, and that La Vérendrye may have been connected with them. I am speculating on the likelihood that knowledge of the Kensington Rune Stone land claim in North America was passed down through time within a specific European secret society whose roots date back to a medieval Templar order in the Scandinavian/British Isles region. However, what once seemed like a long shot speculation is actually quite plausible. In my *Akhenaten* book, I showed evidence that both Ben Franklin and Thomas Jefferson's names appear on the roles of the French Masonic lodge in Paris called The Lodge of the Nine Sisters. Could Franklin and Jefferson have learned about the extent of La Vérendrye's lead plaque land claims? Could they have known about the earlier Templar land claims, including the Kensington Rune Stone? The answer could be yes, and if so, it opens all kinds of possible historical secrets the world has yet to learn.

Dating and Gral/Grail Codes

Arguably, two of the most important breakthroughs made with the Kensington Rune Stone was our cracking of what Dick Nielsen and I coined the "Dating" and "Grail" codes embedded within the inscription. "Här" and the Dotted R were relatively easy. Having a person like Dr. Dick Nielsen, with over twenty years of knowledge of the runological and linguistic aspects of the inscription, was a huge help. Decoding the numerous other mysterious dots and short strokes added by the carver took a more concerted effort. Dick and I started by simply pulling out the singled-out characters as they appeared in sequence on the stone and things began to get interesting. When placed in sequence we got the following: *8, g, r, a, l, d, a, l, 10, M, u, 10,* and *w.* Curiously, this equaled thirteen modified symbols. As I wrote in *Akhenaten*, the number was very significant to the medieval Templars, and to related secret societies that continued on after the put down in 1307 and eventually morphed into modern Freemasonry. I will have a lot more to say about the number thirteen as you read on.

During this phase of the research, we concluded there were three examples of the Dotted R that made sense runologically, so they were not considered as part of the thirteen-symbol sequence. We also concluded the *R* on line four with two punch marks on the main vertical stave at the elevation of a double dotted word separator was a mistake. The carver made the word separator too soon and appears to have simply carved the *R* over it. After removing the four *R*s something very interesting jumped out. Skipping the number 8, the next four characters in sequence were letters that curiously spelled "gral." Dick pointed out that in medieval Old Swedish that word was "Grail." I remember very well the first time he focused his gaze at me and said, "That Grail!"

Dick then reminded me it was the Cistercian monks who wrote the Grail legends in medieval times. I remember thinking some people were going to think we were trying to create a real-life *Da Vinci Code* story around the Kensington Rune Stone which at the time was a worldwide media sensation. In reality, that was exactly what was happening except our unfolding story was not our intention and it most certainly was not fiction.

We had already concluded the carver of the inscription could only have been a Cistercian monk likely educated on the island of Gotland or from one of the Cistercian abbeys in southeastern Sweden that was feeding monks to the ninety-nine Cistercian churches on the island. I remember being impressed at how all the data was coming together so perfectly. The forensic scientist in me kicked in and realized everything in the inscription was consistent and if we continued to follow the factual evidence it would eventually tell us the whole story. The evidence was doing exactly what it was supposed to do and what an incredible tale it was telling. The big question now was; what was "Grail" doing on the Kensington Rune Stone?

To find the answer demanded a deep plunge into researching the legend of the Holy Grail and very quickly things took another unexpected turn introducing me to a branch of the Cistercians I had heard a lot about, yet did not understand. The Knights Templar were the military arm of the Cistercians. They were also monks who wore white tunics with black mantles and took strict vows of poverty and dedicated their lives to fighting for Christ.

Early in the Templar phase of my research, I stumbled upon an interesting book entitled *The Goddess, the Grail, and the Lodge*, written by a British author named Alan Butler. I quickly devoured the book and its fascinating subject matter. I especially enjoyed the captivating writing style of the author and his compelling argument that the standard academic view of the Cistercians and their Templar brethren were incomplete at best. He postulated their true ideology of what became the most successful monastic order in history by 1300, was much different than prevailing scholarly opinion. He wrote the long-held belief that the Cistercians were ideologically aligned with the Roman Catholic Church with the Templars being the Church's warriors for Christ was incorrect. Butler argued the early twelfth-century charismatic leader of the Cistercians, Saint Bernard de Clairvaux, was a mystic with a deep understanding of Gnosticism that influenced his teachings to the rapidly expanding order.

Alan, who subsequently has become a close friend to my wife Janet and me, wrote several books that shed invaluable light on these medieval orders who were responsible for inspiring some of the most significant events in world history. In 1090, Robert Molesme founded the Cistercians as a reformed order of the early Benedictine monks who had become "fat and lazy" by the beginning of the first millennia. Molesme envisioned this new monastic order would return to strict monasticism inspired by the motto that was carved in stone over the entrance of every Cistercian abbey, "Prayer and Work." The first Cistercian abbey was founded in Cîteaux, France, and was funded by donations and filled with the sons of the local counts of the Champagne region.[26]

The expansion of the Cistercian order began when Bernard of Clairvaux joined, along with thirty family members, in 1113. Some of these family members included uncles, like Hugh de Payens, who were members of the original nine knights who

26   Könemann, page 25, 1998.

fought in the First Crusade. Legend says they dug under the Temple Mount in Jerusalem between 1109-1118 and found incredible treasures. The impact of Bernard and the Cistercians on the Knights Templar, and modern Freemasonry, can be found if one knows where to look. One example was brought to my attention by a thirty-third-degree Scottish Rite Freemason named Richard W. Van Doren. In an article published in the Quarterly Bulletin of the Scottish Rite Research Society called, *The Plumbline,* Van Doren argued that modern Masonic Knights Templar meet in what is called *chapter* because its origins lie in the second most important building within a Cistercian monastery after the church.[27] The *chapter house* was built directly next to the south transept of the church in the eastern section of the monastery and served as the administrative headquarters where meetings were conducted by the abbot. Here complaints were heard, punishment was meted out, and initiations of new brothers were conducted.

The typical chapter house was rectangular with the long axis aligned east to west. I couldn't help but notice the rectangle was usually a two-to-one ratio or double square. We essentially see the same shape the carver of the Kensington Rune Stone intentionally split the once larger slab of rock down to before carving the inscription. It seems clear this sacred double square shape harkens back to the chapter house the medieval Cistercian monk who carved the inscription would have been very familiar with.

In the coming pages, you'll learn more about the Cistercians, their charismatic leader Bernard de Clairvaux, and about new evidence that sheds additional light on the veracity of this enduring Templar legend in Jerusalem.

---

27   Richard W. Van Doren, 33 degree, *Meeting in Chapter,* "The Plumeline," Summer 2006 issue, Volume 14, No. 2.

Chapter 4:

Invisible Runes in Icelandic Manuscripts

Exciting new discoveries were made in understanding the use of coded alphabets, as they relate to the North American rune stones, when Icelandic manuscripts were publihsed online in October of 2015. Two friends who had been researching various aspects of pre-Columbian European exploration in North America contacted me with news they were excited about. Steve DiMarzo, then Rhode Island coordinator for the New England Antiquities Research Association (NEARA), and Valdimar Samuelsson, a researcher who lives in Iceland, emailed images of drawings with many strange symbols that appeared in recently published Icelandic manuscripts dating back to the tenth century. One interesting aspect of the manuscripts was they were hand copied lists of hundreds of secret alphabets, many using Scandinavian runes with symbols familiar to me. One of those familiar symbols was the Hooked X!

Over the next several weeks the three of us began digging into the manuscripts, examining thousands of online pages of Icelandic text. We found a seemingly endless number of coded alphabets and secret numbering systems that in a few cases, Valdimar explained, were called *invisible* runes. To get a better understanding about the use of these strange runic codices I consulted a friend in Arizona named Ed Martinez, a Freemason and an Eastern mystic, who looked at some of the manuscripts using ligatures. Ed offered the following insights: "They are complicated symbolic instructions for magic, incantations, and rituals that were very Christianized, yet retained Pagan traits. These are sigil drawings using ancient Germanic and Nordic runes for witchcraft and ritual magic." He also said, "There are obviously Hebrew influences along with both Pagan and neo-Pagan ritual influences, and very clear Masonic connections." Ed also pointed out there are both Nordic/Swedish and Germanic influences in the manuscripts which we also have within the Kensington Rune Stone inscription.

According to Valdimar, "These coded invisible alphabets and complex ritual magic symbols were used for centuries by certain groups of people in Iceland, but were hidden away when Bishop Odd Einarson made it illegal to use runes. In 1625, the Roman Catholic Church began burning people who used witchcraft runes."

Considered heretical by the Church, these documents were hidden from Church authorities, only to surface again for the world to see. There is a lot of research to be done on these documents, but even with this initial study some incredible new knowledge is coming to light.

As I began combing through the mostly well-preserved pages that had recently been scanned and uploaded to the internet, my mind raced back to 2002. This was when I began my intense research at the Minnesota Historical Society into the history of the investigations into the Kensington Rune Stone. I spent the better part of three years digging through primary source documents, photographs, newspaper articles and books. I found a treasure trove of previously unknown facts that told a convincing story consistent with the authenticity of the artifact. What unfolded in that search was what amounted to puzzled scholars and people primarily looking for recognition and fame while fumbling in the dark.

Looking back now, it is easy to see how researchers in both Europe and the United States over the past century, using only the inscription to try and solve the mystery, were dealing with only some of the information needed. A vast amount of previously unknown but necessary information is only now being revealed. In hindsight, the one person involved in the early investigations who relied solely on following the facts, and using proper scientific method was Newton H. Winchell, the first State Geologist of Minnesota from 1875-1900. As I wrote in *Compelling New Evidence*,[28] even though I already knew Winchell was a giant in the world of geology, I had no idea he performed an in-depth study of the Kensington Rune Stone from 1909 to 1910. It came as a surprise to learn about his work. A part of me was a little worried what would happen if he had reached a different conclusion than the one I had already pronounced.

I spent roughly six months at the Society researching Winchell's personal and professional history and was even more amazed and impressed by this scientist who was relatively unknown outside of Minnesota. There were two items in Winchell's documents that were most important to me. The first was his geological field notebook that contained fifty pages of notes and drawings from his three trips to Kensington, the first in November/December of 1909 and twice again in the spring of 1910. They contain a wealth of information about his geological observations of the terrain at the Ohman farm and surrounding area, as well as detailed notes from his conversations with Olof Ohman, his family, friends and others, including some who doubted the authenticity of the artifact.

The second document was a handwritten letter that was most important of all. It was Winchell's final conclusion after completing his geological examination and testing

---

28   Pages 280-282.

of the stone and the inscription. I first read his words in the letter with some trepidation, but in the end I realized he was just as convinced by the hard science as I was ninety years later. There have been many people who have tried to claim they had solved the mystery over the years. There is only one who deserves credit as the first to reach the correct conclusion based on employing proper scientific method, logic, and common sense. That person is Professor Newton H. Winchell.

Winchell was not the only person who came to mind as I examined the flood of discoveries Steve and Valdimar were making in the Icelandic manuscripts. Theybrought back memories of another important discovery of a document that came shortly after my first trip to Sweden with the artifact in October of 2003. After attending a conference where I and others discussed the latest findings, retired Swedish researcher, Tryg-

On December 15, 1909, geologist Newton H. Winchell wrote this letter to the museum committee, stating his opinion that the Kensington Rune Stone was genuine. "I have personally made a topographical examination of the place where the Kensington rune stone was found, and of the region northward to Pelican Lake where the skerries are located, to which the inscription refers, and I am convinced from the geological conditions, and the physical changes that the region has experienced probably within the last five hundred years that the said stone is not a modern forgery, and must be accepted as a genuine record of an exploration in Minnesota, at the date stated in the inscription." (2002)

gve Skold, recalled seeing mysterious characters similar to those on the Kensington Rune Stone in papers recently donated to DAUM (Institute for Dialectology, Onomastics and Folklore Research in Umeå) that became known as the Larsson Papers. These papers contained obvious references to Freemasonry such as a long row of a Masonic box code, along with two runic alphabets. The second included several of the mysterious symbols never seen in a medieval runic inscription, including the smoking gun still billowing smoke from its barrel, the Hooked X symbol being used for *a* just like the North American rune stones. Surprisingly, Scandinavian scholars saw the smoking gun pointed at a different target. Professor of Runology at Uppsala University, Henrik Williams, who had previously stated he did not believe the Hooked X was legitimate because it had never been seen before in Sweden by modern scholars, thought the symbol somehow proved the Kensington inscription was the modern invention of a forger. His view was the Larsson Papers were proof that a late nineteenth-century immigrant in Minnesota could have had access to the secret papers in Sweden and used them to carve the Kensington Rune Stone inscription.

I found it very disappointing and, frankly, dishonest. Professor Williams did not bother to point out the fact the Larsson Papers proved the Hooked X symbol, along with other previously unknown runic symbols and Pentadic numbers, had existed all along. The papers also proved the strange runic alphabet had been secretly used, just like the "invisible" runes in Iceland, through the centuries by a secret society like Freemasonry, in Scandinavia. His instant rejection showed defensiveness and a desire to craft the discovery as evidence to maintain the status quo in Swedish academia which was hard to fathom. For Scandinavian scholars like Williams, the Kensington Rune Stone is a fake and all the facts to the contrary in the world will not change that position.[29] However, the discovery of the Icelandic papers led to a flood of examples of the Hooked X and many of the other strange symbols found on the Kensington Stone. These stretch back many centuries and make the opinion of scholars like Williams, no longer tenable. Beyond the fact, they had been proven wrong. The closed minds of Professor Williams and his colleagues had wasted a decade of potential progress. Better late than never as they say.

As each email arrived from Steve and Valdimar, they included more images of secret alphabets with examples of various types of *X* symbols for *a*. Several included the Hooked X symbol, and it became obvious this was a huge new discovery of previously unknown historical documents.

---

29   In fairness to Professor Williams, in a lecture at the Minnesota History Center in November of 2016, when asked about the authenticity of the Kensington Rune Stone, he reportedly replied, "I am 70/30 the inscription is a hoax." This is a significant change in his previous opinion, and I find it interesting that apparent shift came only a few months after the death of his research colleague and friend Richard Nielsen. Prior to that time, Williams had expressed his staunch belief the inscription was a late nineteenth-century artifact. Professor Williams reportedly also said in response to a question that, "Till the end of his life Dick Nielsen believed the Kensington Rune Stone was authentic."

The discovery of the Larsson Papers in Sweden in 2004, proved that many of the strange symbols found on the Kensington Rune Stone scholars said never existed, in fact did exist. The presence of a Masonic box code suggests the papers were kept within a Scandinavian Masonic secret society. (Internet)

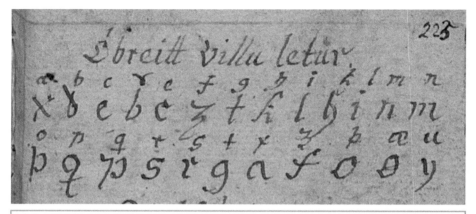

The Hooked X symbol being used for *a* exactly as found on the Spirit Pond, Narragansett and Kensington Rune Stones in North America is also found in this secret alphabet, recorded between 1750-1850, in recently published Icelandic manuscripts. (Internet)

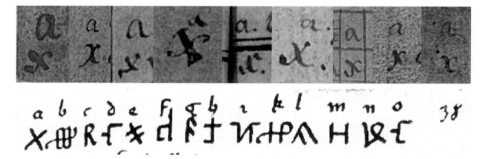

Above are only nine examples from the over 100 alphabets from the Icelandic manuscripts that begin with the *X* symbol for *a*. Eight years ago, I was ecstatic at finding and publishing one example in a coded alphabet from a fifteenth-century Cistercian manuscript in Germany. (Internet/Internet)

One manuscript I found while scouring the online database was of particular importance. It contained another Hooked X used not just for *a*, but for *aleph*, the first letter in the Hebrew alphabet. This immediately brought to mind the Hooked X (with the tau cross) carved on the lid of the Ossuary of Jesus son of Joseph (Jesus Ossuary) I discuss in detail in Chapter 9. I had long suspected the Hooked X might be a straight-line version of the Hebrew *aleph* stonemasons carved.

At this point, I must pause and give credit to a researcher who first brought up the possibility the Hooked X could be historically related to the Hebrew *aleph*. During a lecture I gave at the University Club in St. Paul in 2009, then host of the radio show *Coast to Coast*, Ian Punnett, asked a question if the two symbols could somehow be related. Ian was sitting in the back and I pondered the question I had previously not considered. I answered that I was not sure, but it could be. It turned out his speculation was right on the money as these Icelandic manuscript examples definitively show.

The past 15 years of research created a trail of evidence that started with the Kensington Stone in Minnesota, to the Cistercians on the island of Gotland in Sweden, to their ideological monastic brethren the Knights Templar, to the First Crusade and their control of the Temple Mount for nearly a century in Jerusalem in the twelfth century. It was the discovery of the Hooked X on the Jesus ossuary that pushed the symbol all the way back to the first century, and smack dab in the middle of Jerusalem as you will soon see.

Based on a cursory review of the Icelandic manuscripts we can already draw a few conclusions. The first is the X symbol for *a* was used extensively in alphabets within secret societies in Iceland dating at least back to the tenth century. Second, the Hooked X symbol was also used for *a* in secret alphabets within secret societies in Iceland dating back to at least the mid-eighteenth century. Third, at least one manuscript contains the Hooked X symbol being used for *aleph/a* in the Hebrew alphabet that dates to circa 1700, predating the Larsson papers by roughly two centuries and roughly three centuries after the Spirit Pond (1401-1402) and Kensington Rune Stones (1362) were carved.

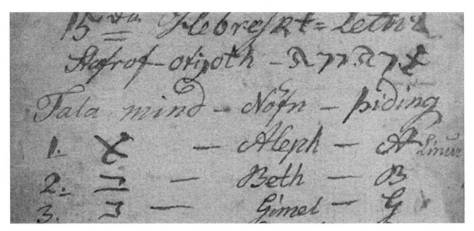

The Hooked X symbol is used for *aleph* in what is clearly a Hebrew alphabet, suggesting a connection to Israel and Jerusalem where we found another example of the Hooked X on the Jesus ossuary in the Talpiot Tomb. (Internet)

There is another very interesting thing that occurs in the manuscripts. Some are filled with highly complex interconnecting sigil drawings that incorporate Scandinavian runes and Masonic box code symbols. Other examples clearly indicate a Christian influence with repeated references to "Jesus" and "Yeshua." Scholars suggest these complicated coded drawings were used for witchcraft and ritual magic, which is likely true. This might explain why Roman Catholic Church authorities tried to round-up and destroy these manuscripts in Iceland circa 1600, as they were considered heretical and undermined Church authority and their intellectual control over the population.

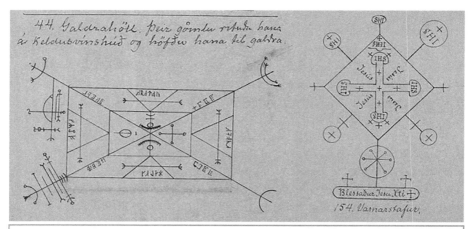

This document in the Icelandic manuscripts shows two examples of complicated sigil drawings that incorporate runes and Masonic box code symbols (left), and a heavily Christian-influenced drawing (right) the Roman Catholic Church claimed were used for witchcraft and ritual magic. (Internet)

The almost two-decade long trail of evidence I have followed that now runs through these Icelandic manuscripts has been consistent and convincing, but is it conclusive? From a truly scientific standpoint the answer is yes. However, until the Kensington, Spirit Pond, and Narragansett Rune Stones are accepted as the history changing artifacts they are, I and other dedicated researchers will continue to search for more factual evidence. The driving force of the geological aspects of these artifacts told me years ago the answers to the questions about their origins must be out there somewhere. The Icelandic manuscripts are simply the latest trove of evidence, with their invisible, secret alphabets, they were like finding a sunken ship filled with treasure. Researchers need to continue to comb through these pages to find more intellectual gold.

CHAPTER 5:

Raised as a Master Mason

The Icelandic manuscripts are a vitally important new resource to my research. Freemasonry is a new resource that has also become immensely beneficial in my quest for answers. I resisted becoming a Freemason for years, especially while hosting *America Unearthed* from 2012 to 2014. I did not want people to think I was biased toward the Craft. I knew the people who supported my research did not care if I was a Freemason and most of them would probably have been pleased. Eventually, I asked myself, "Do I care what my critics think about becoming a Freemason?" The answer was a resounding "No!" After years of waiting, I decided to take the plunge and asked if my friend and Masonic mentor, John Freeburg, would sign my petition to join. He did so, along with another friend and Freemason, Curt Quast, in front of a crowd at John's home Lodge in Anoka, Minnesota, in the spring of 2015.

I took my Entered Apprentice degree at my home lodge, Wayzata 205, on August 19, 2015, my Fellow Craft degree on October 21, 2015, and was raised as a Master Mason on November 21, 2015. All three degrees were memorable and impactful, especially the third degree when I was raised by another mentor and friend, Judge David Sinclair Bouschor, a Past Grand Master of Masons in Minnesota. I practiced the lengthy oral obligations with one of my best friends who had also decided to join, Richard Olson, who I have known since our college days at the University of Minnesota in Duluth. We had to memorize and then recite the obligations in front of the brethren prior to taking the Fellow Craft and Master Mason degrees. Going through the degrees with Rick was a truly enjoyable and memorable experience.

One thing I struggled with at the beginning of my Masonic journey was how to deal with answering the question all candidates are required to answer at the beginning of the first degree, "In whom do you put your trust?" As a young adult, I confidently called myself an atheist. I thought I had all the answers to life's big questions and was in complete control of my own destiny. Being a geologist had grounded my views that everything in the world could be explained scientifically using logic. The idea of a higher power watching over all people on the planet seemed ridiculous. I would laugh and shake my head at professional athletes who thanked God for helping them score touchdowns, score goals or hit home runs. I firmly believed that everything in life could be explained scientifically and I was one of the first to offer answers.

As I have grown older, I have come to realize that not everything in life can be so easily explained. It was not until my father passed away in a scuba diving accident in 1983 that the answers I thought I had figured out did not come. To this day, I still do not know exactly what happened and how he could have died in the Great Barrier Reef in Australia on that very hot and perfectly clear day. It was the next day that I found out my father was a Freemason when the coroner cut off and gave to me the old heavily worn ring my father always wore. I had no idea the curved sword on the ring meant he was a member of the Shrine. My mother eventually told me my father, grandfather and great grandfather had all been Freemasons yet they never talked about it. Freemasons today are more open to talking about being members which I think is a good thing.

Thirty-five years later the details of what happened that day no longer matter, but the mystery of what happened forced me to look inward and realize I did not have all the answers. Age has a way of humbling us all and forces us to rethink long held ideals and beliefs. As I pondered the question in the Entered Apprentice degree, I realized I could no longer call myself an atheist; far from it. I learned there is a force in life that cannot be fully explained . Something that makes plants, animals, and humans grow in a certain way. While science can account for most things on Earth and in the universe, it cannot explain everything. There are some things that happen in life we will never know the answers to and we have to learn to accept it.

So, whatever that "thing" might be that I am talking about, I do not believe it is necessarily gender specific. If so, I do not feel any sense of a masculine, or male aspect to it as most of the world's religions seem to favor. If Deity has any preference to gender as we understand it, there is no doubt in my mind it is associated with the life-giving attributes of the sacred feminine, the Goddess. I have no idea if that is what is going on or not, but it works for me as it does for many others going back thousands of years.

In the Entered Apprentice degree, each candidate must take an obligation with their hand on a Holy book of their choice. Depending on what religion a new Mason claims as the basis of his faith they can take the oath on either the Torah, Koran, Bible or the Book of Mormon. In fact, I've heard of Native American brothers who took their oaths on an eagle feather symbolic of the Great Spirit. None of these options made sense for me although the eagle feather was most appropriate. After much thought, I decided on something slightly controversial: the Thomas Jefferson Bible.

I had been researching Thomas Jefferson and just finished reading the bible he had literally retooled for himself. Beginning in 1820 at age seventy-seven, he assembled the document using passages from the four gospels, rearranging them into a logical chronology of the life of Jesus. Jefferson cut out the passages in four different languages, English, French, Latin and Greek. Gone were the gospel passages that did not make sense to him, such as the miracles that were in his words, "contrary to reason" which included the Resurrection of Jesus.[30] The "Jefferson Bible" as it has come to be called resonated with me as not something divinely inspired, but more in line with my own philosophy of sticking to the factual history and simply "doing the right thing."

I was raised as a Master Mason by Judge David Sinclair Bouschor, Past Grand Master of Masons, in Minnesota on November 21, 2015. In my left hand is a Golden Trowel the Judge gave me as a gift that memorable day. (Photo Courtesy of Richard Page Olson)

Although the Master of our lodge needed to get approval, the Grand Lodge said using the Jefferson Bible was fine. Just before the Entered Apprentice degree started, I handed the book to the Master of the lodge, another candidate saw it and said, "I want to use that bible too." Not knowing if I would have to make a statement to justify my decision, I was prepared to read the words of Jefferson that summarized his beliefs that so resonated with my own, "They are the result of a life of enquiry and reflection, and very different from that anti-Christian system, imputed to me by those who know nothing of my opinions. To the corruptions of Christianity, I am indeed opposed; but not to the genuine precepts of Jesus himself. I am a Christian, in the only sense in which he wished any one to be; sincerely attached to his doctrines, in preference to all others; he never claimed any other."[31]

---

30   Emerys, page 136, 2007.
31   Jefferson, page 25, 1820/2011.

Scottish Rite

As memorable and meaningful as the first three degrees were, it was only the beginning of my journey. My Masonic mentor, John Freeburg, had a lot more in store for me as a new Mason and signed me up to start the twenty-nine degrees of the Scottish Rite only a few weeks after I had been raised. What John had signed me up for was the two-day Centennial Weekend celebrating the one-hundredth anniversary of the Ancient and Accepted Scottish Rite of the Freemasonry Temple in Minneapolis, Minnesota. The Minneapolis Valley of the Orient of Minnesota performed the five terminal degrees that represent the concluding chapter of degrees that include the 4th degree called the Secret Master, the 14th degree or Perfect Elu, the 18th degree or Knight of the Rose Croix, the 30th degree or Knight Kadosh, and the 32nd degree called the Master of the Royal Secret. The Minneapolis Valley of the Scottish Rite is one of only a few jurisdictions in the United States that offers all twenty-nine degrees, each fall and spring. These build off the first three degrees of what is called the Blue Lodge of Freemasonry.

After completing the two days of incredible degree work I was officially a fully vested 32nd degree Scottish Rite Freemason. However, I did not feel complete without witnessing all twenty-nine degrees. In 2016, over the next two degree cycles, I completed the degrees I had missed which was well worth the time and effort. Thursday night is Rite Night in Minneapolis and one of the things I really enjoy is how welcoming the brothers are, not only to me, but my wife Janet also. Most nights when I was there as a candidate participating in the degrees, Janet was in the library conducting research or visiting with various brothers who had already completed the degrees. Although being a woman makes Janet ineligible to be a Freemason, she could still enjoy much of the experience at the Temple and further her own research at the same time.

York Rite

As if the Scottish Rite was not challenging enough, Brother Freeburg had more in store for me. John also signed me up for the three one-day sessions of York Rite degrees held at the Scottish Rite Temple in Minneapolis. On January 30, 2016, I participated in the four degrees that comprise the Royal Arch group of degrees. On February 13, 2016, I went through the three Cryptic Council degrees, and on February 27, 2016, I went through the three Chivalric degrees consisting of the Order of the Red Cross, the Order of Malta, and the Order of the Temple.

At this point, I am sure the reader will find it interesting the total number of York Rite degrees, that again build off the first three degrees of the Blue Lodge, is the number associated with the sacred feminine; thirteen. Since I took vows of secrecy I cannot share too many details about either the Scottish or York Rite degrees other than to say it was truly an enlightening and enriching experience.

The three Cryptic Council degrees were my favorite with the second, the Select Master degree, being the most interesting. The reason was due to an incredible realization I had as the degree unfolded, which I will share in the next chapter. It was a defining moment that was completely unexpected, although I had been hopeful something would happen during my Masonic experience that would lead to new discoveries related to my ongoing research on the Kensington Rune Stone. I could never have imaged how profound this discovery would be that serves as the final missing piece to the mysterious inscription that has eluded both seasoned scholars and capable amateur researchers. If it had not been for my deep understanding of the Kensington inscription I might never have caught what has turned out to be two vitally important and defining numbers—8 and 22.

The symbols for the York Rite bodies of degrees begin with the first three degrees called the Blue Lodge (bottom), the Royal Arch (left), Cryptic Council (right) and Chivalric degrees (top). The missing top side of the inner triangle in the Cryptic Council symbol represents the fallen Grand Master Hiram Abiff. (Internet/Internet) See color section for detail.

CHAPTER 6:

CRYPTIC CODE ON THE KENSINGTON RUNE STONE

As if my initiation into Freemasonry was not enlightening enough, something truly unexpected and amazing happened during the Select Master degree of the Cryptic Council that triggered a watershed of discoveries about the Kensington Rune Stone that, in my view, represents the missing key to solving the mysteries of the inscription. It appears certain the numbers chronicled within the Kensington Rune Stone inscription are connected to the Masonic legend of Hiram Abiff, the Grand Architect who, we are taught as Masons, oversaw the construction of King Solomon's Temple. Prior to my becoming a Freemason this information would never have come to me, and even if it did I would not have understood it. However, since I have been initiated as a Master Mason in the Blue Lodge which consists of the first three degrees of Freemasonry, and as both a Scottish Rite and York Rite Mason, my Masonic education gave me a whole new perspective.

To help the reader better understand how these two higher branches work, I will try to explain them. The first three degrees of Blue Lodge also serve as the first three degrees of both Scottish Rite, which has a total of thirty-two degrees, and the York Rite which has a total of thirteen degrees (see diagram). The basic story told in the first three degrees of the Blue Lodge is about the building of King Solomon's Temple overseen by Hiram Abiff.

In the higher degrees of the Scottish and York Rites, stories of legendary events from Old Testament times are told through a combination of theatrical performances and lectures. Essentially, the same Biblical stories are told in both branches, but neither presents the stories in chronological order which creates confusion at times. I am still not sure if this was by design or coincidence.

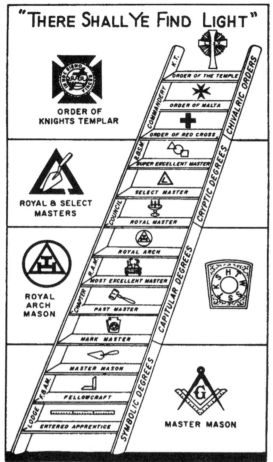

"THERE SHALL YE FIND LIGHT"

This graphic shows the thirteen degrees of York Rite Freemasonry. The first three degrees are called the Blue Lodge, the next four are called the Royal Arch degrees, the next three are called the Cryptic Council degrees and the final three are the Order of the Knights Templar degrees. The degree that tipped me off to the Cryptic Code numbers on the Kensington Rune Stone was the Select Master degree, the second in the Cryptic Council degrees. (Internet)

`Something caught my attention during a lecture portion of the Select Master degree, the ninth of thirteen total degrees in the York Rite branch. The story in this degree takes place shortly before the First Temple in Jerusalem was completed around 1000 BC. The key players are members of the Supreme Council of Grand Masters—King Solomon, Hiram-King of Tyre, and Hiram Abiff. Keep in mind it is not clear whether this story is historically accurate or simply allegorical. That debate has raged within academic and Masonic circles for centuries, but for the purposes of this research it is inconsequential. To aid the reader, the most current translation of the Kensington inscription, with the eight numbers (in bold) that I believe to be part of a Cryptic Code, is provided for reference:

Face Side
1. **8** Götalanders and **22** Northmen on
2. (this) acquisition journey/taking up land from
3. Vinland far to the west. We
4. had a camp by **2** shelter? **one**
5. day's journey north from this stone.
6. We were fishing **one** day. After
7. we came home we found **10** men red
8. from blood and death. AVM
9. Save from evil.

Split Side

10. There are **10** men by the inland sea to look
11. after our ships **14** days' journey
12. from this island/peninsula/hill. Year 1362

8 Arches and 22 Men

During the theatrical part of the degree we learned the three Grand Masters were entrusted with the writings of Moses, holy vessels, and sacred treasures which included the Ark of Covenant. To protect these treasures from being forever lost or taken by enemies, or if the children of Israel ever deviated from the sacred laws, a secret vault was constructed that was divided into nine arches or apartments. The three grand masters constructed the ninth arch where the sacred objects were hidden and secret rituals would take place.

After the theatrical performance of the degree, when a high-ranking Mason playing the character of Hiram Abiff said the following during his lecture, "There were employed on the other **eight** arches, **twenty-two** men from Gebal, a city of Phoenicia…" My ears instantly perked up as the two familiar numbers resonated in my head. I recognized them as the first two numbers carved on the Kensington Rune Stone, "**8** Götalanders and **22** Norwegians…" I did not hear much of the remaining lecture as my mind was elsewhere. After the degree was finished I immediately asked John Freeburg if there was a ritual book that contained the text of the lecture. He said, "Yes," and handed me his personal copy. As I excitedly read the degree, more important numbers connected to the Kensington inscription became apparent. The next number showed up in the following sentence, "…together with Ahishar and Adoniram, all of whom were well skilled in the arts and sciences generally, but particularly in sculpture." It quickly occurred to me that Ahishar and Adoniram are **two** individuals.

The next number to appear in the Kensington inscription after 8 and 22, is the number two, "We had a camp by **2** shelters…" The ritual book lecture continued, "One of King Solomon's particular friends, whose name was Zerubbabel, discovered that there was secret work going on…" This is **one** more person added to the story and if you have not already guessed, the next number in the Kensington inscription is one, "…by **2** shelters, **one** day's journey from this stone." Incredibly, we had the first four numbers in the Kensington inscription appear in the same sequence as the arches (8) and individuals (22, 2, and 1) in the York Rite Select Master ritual. However, this was not all.

In the theatrical part of the ritual one of the two guards, Ahishar, falls asleep at his post. Upon seeing the entrance unguarded, an overly inquisitive Zerubbabel ventures down into the secret vault. King Solomon discovers Zerubbabel inside the secret vault and is extremely angered. He then orders Ahishar to be executed, leaving Adoniram as the lone surviving guard of the original two. It then occurred to me that Adoniram was the second number <u>one</u> in the sequence on the Kensington Rune Stone. "We were fishing **one** day…"

At this point in the story, within the secret vault Zerubbabel discovers copies of the treasures in the Sanctum Sanctorum of the Temple above. We learn in the ritual the most important treasure is the Ark of the Covenant which contains the <u>Ten</u> Commandments. Could this be what the next number is referring to that appears within the inscription sequence ? "…after we came home we found **10** men…"

At this point in the ritual the story turns violent. As punishment for falling asleep at his post, Ahishar is killed by the other guards who slice him to death with their swords. Further, as punishment for entering the secret vault without permission, King Solomon orders Zerubbabel's eyes poked out. He is then paraded in front of the people with a bloody bandage over his empty eye sockets wearing a blood-spattered apron. It cannot be another coincidence the severe violence in the story occurs at the same point in the Kensington inscription that violence also occurs, "…we found **10** men **red from blood and death**."

The carver then offered two prayers. The first prayer appears to invoke Mother Mary with the only three Latin letters in the entire inscription, "AVM." The second prayer comprises the ninth line of the face side and almost appears to have been added as if to complete a symbolic aspect of the inscription, "Save from Evil."

Nine plus Three Equals Twelve

Indeed, it appears the ninth line of the Kensington Rune Stone was added by the carver to ensure the proper number of lines of text appeared on the face side of the inscription. In the Select Master degree ritual book there is a short paragraph that describes when the secret work was performed on the nine arches, "Their hours of labor were from nine at night until twelve, the time when all prying eyes are closed in sleep." If the labor was from nine p.m. to midnight, it means the laborers worked for a total of three hours. Suddenly, it appears we now understand why the carver added the ninth line of text to the face side of the inscription.

When the three additional lines of text on the split side are added to the nine on the face side, we end up with a total of twelve lines of carved text that coincide exactly with the number of hours of labor in the select Master degree: 9 + 3 = 12. Is this yet another coincidence? Not if one considers the importance of signs, symbols, codes, and allegorical messages so ingrained into the mind of the medieval monastic monk who has been initiated into the ancient mysteries. But the numbers do not stop with the first nine lines on the face side. There are two additional numbers on the split side that also figure into this Old Testament allegorical story; "There are 10 men by the sea with our ships, 14 days' journey from this island/hill."

Ten and Fourteen

Shortly after the three Grand Masters had completed the secret vault in the ninth arch below the Sanctum Sanctorum, three greedy fellow craft workers from the quarries

The typical *o* rune used in medieval Scandinavian runic inscriptions has two parallel lines angling down at roughly a forty-five degree angle and left from the main vertical stave. On the Kensington Rune Stone seventeen of the twenty *o* runes have the two parallel lines at ninety degrees left of the main vertical stave. The initiated medieval carver employed the Masonic moral allegory of, "Squaring our actions by the square of virtue." (2004, 2002)

confront and murder the Master architect of the temple, Hiram Abiff, for failing to reveal the secrets that would allow the men to receive more wages. The three ruffians bury the body and plant a sprig of acacia to mark the grave. Acacia is a famously hardy plant known for growing its own roots after being cut. In Egypt, acacia became a symbol of resurrection and restored life, and that same symbolism is very prominent in modern Freemasonry.[32]

As the story continues, King Solomon grows worried about his missing Master Architect and sends a party of twelve men to search for Hiram Abiff. The recently established Acacia plant tips off the search party and they discover Hiram's body after 14 days. Keep in mind, Hiram's murder and the subsequent discovery of his body happens after the story of the construction of the nine arches below the Temple. Based on this fact, and with the chronology of the Hiram Abiff legend in its proper sequence, we can now put the numbers in place that result in the exact same sequence as they appear on the Kensington Rune Stone inscription, 8, 22, 2, 1, 1, 10, 10 and 14! It would be easier to pick the correct lottery numbers, in sequence, than for these eight numbers to be coincidence. When we add in the lines of text on the face and split sides (9 + 3 = 12 lines of text in the Kensington inscription) we have incredible consistency of numbers. In my view, this goes beyond any possible random coincidence or chance.

†HREE GRAND MASTERS

When considering the Kensington inscription in context with Masonic symbolism, something else jumped out upon closer inspection of the three strange and ornately carved *o* runes within the inscription. Freemasonry puts utmost importance on the concept of the Rule of Three. First and foremost, the equilateral triangle is a symbol of Deity. In the Select Master degree the three sides of the equilateral triangle on the

32   https://www.buildingbeautifulsouls.com/symbols-meanings/flower-meanings-symbolism/acacia-meaning-symbolism/

lid of the Ark of the Covenant represent the three Grand Masters. The Kensington inscription has a total of twenty *o* runes within the inscription, seventeen of them are an unusual type that still puzzle runic scholars.

The standard medieval *o* rune is a vertical line, or stave, with two parallel lines angling down and left from the middle of the vertical stave at a 45-degree angle. On the Kensington Rune Stone, the *o* rune has the same two horizontal lines extending to the left, but they are at ninety degrees to the vertical stave instead of forty-five degrees. When viewed in a Masonic context it appears the carver "squared" the two lines, possibly invoking the axiom taught in Freemasonry, "squaring our actions by the square of virtue."

This leaves us with the three strange, but ornately carved *ö* symbols that continue to confound scholars. Runic symbols lend themselves for use on stone because they are dominantly comprised of straight lines that are relatively easy to carve. These three symbols require greater skill to carve being, comprised of a vertically aligned oval or ellipse. Inside the oval is an *n* rune with two dots above the oval. Linguists interpret the twin dots as umlauts indicating a different way of pronouncing the *o* sound. From a

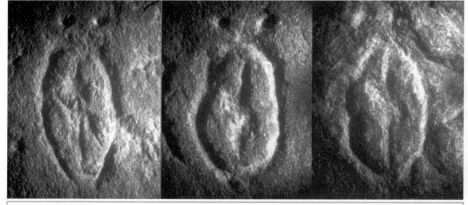

Three of the twenty *O* runes are ornately carved *n* runes inside vertically aligned ovals. Two dots above the three symbols represent umlauts indicating the *ö* sound. The Masonic concept of the Rule of Three appears to have been employed and could represent the three horizontals and/or three columns in the Tree of Life in the Kabbalah. (2002/2002/2002)

symbolic perspective, the three most ornately carved symbols in the entire inscription, together with the two dots, could also represent the three Grand Masters wearing their crowns.

Confirmation Code

One day while researching the angles of the hooks on the Hooked Xs in the Kensington inscription, I decided to count to see how many there were. I was surprised to find the number was **twenty-two**. This prompted me to look at the other odd runes and

Masonic News

NEW YEAR AND AUTO SHOW NUMBER
JANUARY - 1929

On the cover of this 1929 Masonic publication from Detroit, the auto manufacturing center of the world at that time, the sacred number 22 is hidden in plain sight in the number of leaves adorning the two vertical faces of the throne the Goddess is sitting in while holding a crystal ball with her hand, which is closest to her heart, and making the M-sign. (Courtesy of John Freeburg)

to my surprise three more of the numbers within the inscription were apparently confirmed. There are seven of the strange *g* runes, and if we include the never-before seen *u* in the word *Illu*, or *evil*, on line nine, there are a total of **eight** never-before seen *g/u* runes.

There are **ten** mysterious *v/w* runes, and **fourteen** individual numbers; 8, 2, 2, 2, 1, 1, 10, 10, 1, 4, 1, 3, 6, and 2. Keep in mind, the carver was likely a Cistercian monk and the Order did not believe in the concept of zero. Thus, it is no surprise that we do not see a symbol for zero. The carver used Pentadic numbers that include a single symbol for ten and not the two numbers 1 and 0. Confirmation of four of the important numbers within the inscription (8, 10, 14 and 22) are additional pieces of evidence consistent with a carver who was deeply initiated. The three mysterious symbols confirming three numbers are the backwards *g* (8), the *v/w* rune (10) and the Hooked X (22). The Pentadic numbers, which have never been seen used in a medieval inscription before, and the two number ones spelled out by the carver total the fourth confirmation code number of 14 (8, 2, 2, 2, 1, 1, 10, 10, 1, 4, 1, 3, 6, and 2).

So, what does all this mean? It tells us a lot; beginning with the fact the carver/author understood the ancient allegorical resurrection story found in every culture throughout time. One example that incorporates one of the important numbers is found in the Isis/Osiris legend of ancient Egypt. One version has Osiris being captured and killed by his enemies who then cut his body up into 14 pieces. [33] His distraught lover, Isis, goes searching and finds all but one of the pieces of his body—his phallus. Eventually, she impregnates herself with a reproduced phallus made of gold or beeswax, gives birth to her son Horus who grows into adulthood becoming Osiris, and the whole story begins again.[34] This story is an allegorical representation of the annual cycle of life on earth: new life in the spring, death in the fall, and resurrection of the sun on the Winter Solstice when the Goddess Isis becomes pregnant. The cycle then begins anew.

33   http://www.egyptianmyths.net/mythisis.htm
34   Hall, page 43, 1937.

As discussed in chapter one, this allegorical fertilization on the winter solstice is what the builders of the Newport Tower intended with the Illumination event. The rays of the sun (representing the male God) penetrate the womb/nave of the Tower symbolizing a Goddess temple, with the rectangular light box illuminating the egg-shaped keystone designed by the builders to be an allegorical fertilization reminiscent of the Isis/Osiris legend.

The second Resurrection legend that is relevant to our story is the Roman Christian version with the biblical Jesus taking on the role of Hiram Abiff. In this case, we have a real historical figure from the first century who was mythologized by the early Church fathers to create a Son of God with essentially the same allegorical death and resurrection story. In nearly every Catholic church around the world the Crucifixion and Resurrection story of Jesus is told in pictures by the Stations of the Cross. It is not a coincidence the number of Stations is 14 since the Resurrection story of Jesus in the Christian faith is an allegorical reboot of the resurrection of Osiris (the sun) on the winter solstice in the Egyptian mysteries.

Before anyone starts patting me on the back, these sacred numbers have been around Freemasonry for a long time. In fact, there is a direct connection between the sacred numbers 8, 14 and 22, and the oblong square in the construction of the Washington Monument. In a Monument fundraising effort begun in 1851 by the fraternity, donations of memorial stones specified dimensions of 4 feet by 2 feet (an oblong square) by 12-18" in thickness. Was it coincidence they received donations of 22 Masonic memorial stones contributed by 14 Grand Lodges and 8 individual Lodges?[35] These sacred numbers have an ancient history that has carried through into modern Freemasonry. The trail of this tradition weaves through the medieval Templars. This will be clearly demonstrated in Tomar, Portugal. The question remains where did these numbers originate?

KABBALAH

When studying the Cryptic Code of the Kensington Rune Stone inscription, an important question needs to be asked. What is the significance of the numbers? Knowing the medieval Cistercians and Knights Templar were well versed in Hebrew mysticism, they would certainly have understood and practiced the spiritual concepts and teachings associated with the Kabbalah Tree of Life. For a general understanding of the connection of what I have discovered, I should start with a basic explanation of what the Tree of Life is using the words of noted author and Templar historian Timothy W. Hogan, "In general, this Tree is composed of 10 spheres called sephiroth, along with 22 paths that connect these spheres, each of which is represented by one of the 22 Hebrew letters, and they rest on three pillars. Thus, there are a total of 32 emanations of Deity, with a possible 33rd hidden emanation."[36]

35   http://srjarchives.tripod.com/1997-06/Scott.htm
36   Hogan, page 14, 2009.

In Memoriam...

Igreja de S. Maria dos Olivais	✠	Panteão dos Mestres Templários

Gualdim Pais	1157 - 1195
Lopo Fernandes	1195 - 1199
Fernando Dias	1199 - 1206
Gomes Ramires	1206 - 1212
Pedro Alvito	1212 - 1221
Pedro Anes	1222 - 1224
Martin Sanches	1224 - 1229
Estevan Belmonte	1229 - 1237
Pedro Nunes	1238 - 1239
Guilherme Fulcon	1240 - 1242
Martin Martins	1242 - 1248
Pedro Gomes	1248 - 1250
Paio Gomes	1250 - 1253
Martim Nunes	1253 - 1265
Gonçalo Martins	1265 - 1271
Beltrão Valverde	1272 - 1280
João Escriptor	1280 - 1282
João Fernandes	1282 - 1288
Afonso Gomes	1288 - 1290
Lourenço Martins	1291 - 1295

Honra a *Vasco Fernandes*!... último mestre

Homenagem da Associação Cultural Templ'Anima, Câmara Municipal de Tomar, E. R. Turismo de Lisboa e Vale do Tejo, em 13/X/2011

Inside Santa Maria do Olival Church in Tomar, Portugal, are listed the names of the first twenty of a total of twenty-two Grand Masters of the Knights Templar who were buried inside the church. (2015)

Already, we have an uncanny connection with the Kensington Rune Stone numbers beyond what we have discovered in their sequence in relation to the Masonic/Christian/Isis-Osiris Resurrection story. It appears what we now have is: 8 Goter (Deity) and 22 Northmen (paths that connect the ten spheres); 2 shelters (Ahishar and Adoniram); and one day's journey (Zerubbabel). When we add these numbers up in sequence as they appear on the stone we have 8 + 22 + 2 = 32 + 1 =33. The fact this number sequence follows the Select Master ritual and the same numbers add up perfectly with the Kabbalah simply cannot be a coincidence. It appears certain the fourteenth-century carver of the Kensington inscription understood Hebrew mysticism and specifically the Kabbalah Tree of Life.

Shortly after sharing this discovery with a fellow Freemason, he reminded me about another connection to the numbers 8 and 22 that I had forgotten about. At the incredible Santa Maria do Olival Church there are twenty-two Grand Masters of the Portuguese Templars buried inside the Church, beginning with the first Grand Master, Gualdim Pais, who founded the city upon his return from Jerusalem after fighting in the Second Crusade in 1161. One of the major points we made in the *America Unearthed* episode was how the number eight was symbolically represented throughout the church. It begins by simply walking down the eight steps at the west entrance. Inside the church there are eight stone columns and eight windows, each one directly above a column. The origin of the sacred number eight is the five-pointed star in the small window high above the altar in the east end. The pentagram is symbolic of the planet Venus and the symbol it creates when viewed astronomically from Earth during its eight-year cycle.

As already pointed out, in esoteric circles the number eight and its association with the planet Venus has always been symbolic of the Goddess in the heavens. The Templars and their Cistercian brethren venerated the planet Venus, the sun, the planets, the stars and constellations. This is clearly on display in the church. Venus and the sun are symbolically represented in the east and west windows of the church. However,

At Santa Maria do Olival Church, Templar symbolism consistent with their true ideology of reverence of the Goddess is everywhere. The number eight is found in the number of columns running east-west down the nave (top left), windows above the columns and steps leading down into the church (top right). Eight is the number of earth years it takes to create the five-pointed star symbol when the movements of Venus are tracked from Earth. The five-pointed star is high up in the east window above the altar (bottom left). In the west end, there is a large rose window symbolic of the sun (bottom right), who in mystical circles is the eternal consort of Venus ,with the two being the ultimate symbol of Dualism in the sky. The five-pointed star is also seen in the rose window in Troyes, France. (2014)

the number eight is dominantly represented in the architecture which is consistent with the Templars veneration of the Goddess via the planet Venus, literally above the male sun God window in the west.

The important takeaway from this medieval Templar church is it gives us a peek in the minds of the Templars and what aspects of their faith were important to them. Many researchers, most notably Alan Butler, have written extensively about the Templars and Cistercians and their veneration of the planet Venus and other symbolic representations of the Goddess. By understanding Hebrew Mysticism and the religious ideology connected to the Templars/Cistercians, and the symbolism associated with it, one can also make sense of the sacred numbers and why those numbers appear on the Kensington Rune Stone.

The number twenty-two has significance not just in ancient Egyptian mysticism, but many scholars believe these principles were passed on to Hebrew mysticism where we find the same numbers being symbolically important in the Kabbalah. From there, the sacred twenty-two symbolic thread appears to have also been passed on to the Cistercians and Knights Templar. This is evidenced by the number of Grand Masters in-

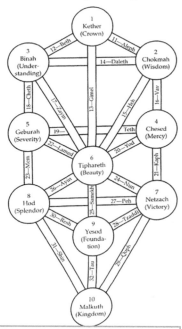

terred at Santa Maria do Olival Church. Keep in mind that scant documentation exists that can be referred to, as this esoteric knowledge was passed from master to initiate mouth to ear, most notably prior to medieval times.[37] In spite of this, the numbers that appear on the Kensington Rune Stone imply the carver was deeply versed in symbolism, allegory, codes, and specific sacred numbers that appear to have been passed on through mystical sects from Egypt to the Hebrews, to the Cistercians/Knight Templar, and finally into Modern Freemasonry.

Tim Hogan also brings up the concept of the same type of confirmation codes we see on the Kensington Rune Stone, specifically 10, 22 and 32, with some of the same numbers being confirmed by various references to God in the Torah and the Bible. Quoting Hogan, "Qabbalistic scholars have alluded to the fact that the 32 paths are suggested in the Torah by the 32 times that God's name 'Elohim' appears in the account of creation in the first chapter of Genesis. In this account, the expression, 'God Said' appears ten times, and these are the ten sayings with which the world was created.

This diagram shows the ten Sefirot (spheres) and the 32 paths of the Tree of Life in the Kabbalah as defined by the Ari (Rabbi Yitzchak Luria), considered one of the greatest Kabbalists of all time. (Internet)

The ten sayings seem to have a correlation with the ten sephiroth on the kabbalistic tree diagram, and alluded to by the Sephir Yetzirah, the Sephir Bahir, and the *Zohar*. The other 22 times that God's name appears in this account seems to match the 22 letters of the Hebrew aleph-beth (alphabet) and by extension the 22 paths."[38]

It appears we also have the ancient Kabbalistic tradition of using the same numbers and the same numeric confirmation codes known to have been used by the Cistercians/Knights Templar, also appearing within the Kensington Rune Stone inscription.

It would be several months later before I came to realize what was at the core of

---

37   Personal communication with Edward Martinez on November 24, 2014.
38   Hogan, pages 20-21, 2009.

these sacred numbers within the Tree of Life and the Kabbalah. One can think about the Tree of Life as a representation of the human body with the Crown sphere at the top being analogous to the head. It turns out there are an average of thirty-two vertebrae in the human body, which explains why there are the same number of emanations and, by extension, thirty-two degrees in Scottish Rite Freemasonry. This gives rise to the final emanation of the Tree of Life and the honorary thirty-third degree of the Scottish Rite. When thinking about the human body analogy the thirty-third bone would be the skull. Interestingly, the skull isn't comprised of just one bone. It is comprised of twenty-two bones, as if the reader needed any more proof the human body was the genesis of the philosophy and teachings of the Kabbalistic Tree of Life. The number of bones in the skull are comprised of two groups. There are fourteen bones that comprise the face and eight that make up the cranium in which sits the brain, considered by many to be the life force of humans.

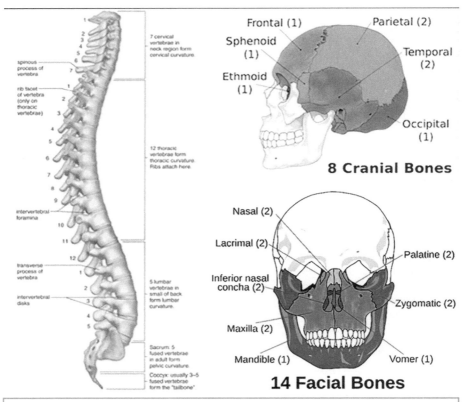

The Kabbalistic Tree of Life is largely patterned after the human body which contains important numbers of bones in the spinal column (32) and the skull (8 + 14 = 22). These same numbers are found in Scottish Rite Freemasonry (32 + 1 = 33 degrees) and the Kensington Rune Stone (8 Goths and 22 Northmen, 2 shelters? = 32 plus one days' Journey = 33) and (14 days' journey...).

(Internet)

FROM VINLAND, FAR TO THE WEST

The land claim thesis I proposed over a decade ago as the primary purpose of the Kensington Rune Stone is still firmly in place. However, my assumption of the meaning of what I perceived were the three practical elements has now changed. Originally, I believed, "…from Vinland far to the west," "…14 days' journey from this island/hill," and "…one day's journey from this stone," were part of what was essentially a land deed pinpointing the location of what is now the Ohman farm in Kensington, Minnesota. In light of the Cryptic Code discovery, it now makes more sense "…. from Vinland, far to the west" was the full extent of the carver's description of the land being claimed. One could argue this means the Templars were claiming the entire continent. So, if the first three lines of the inscription took care of the land claim and were the primary purpose of carving the inscription, what about the other two seemingly practical parts?

ONE DAY'S JOURNEY & 14 DAYS' JOURNEY

The other parts of the inscription that have changed in light of the new discoveries is my interpretation of these two lines in the text, "…one day's Journey from this Stone," and "…14 Days' Journey from this island/hill." I long thought they were describing the land associated with the actual discovery site at what is now the Ohman farm similar to a land deed description. In light of the new evidence, and the realization of the Masonic Royal Arch legend cleverly imbedded within the inscription, it struck me these could be directions to an actual secret vault "far to the west" of the Kensington Rune Stone discovery site. This idea took on increased credibility in light of the research of my friend and fellow Freemason, William Mann, who believes the Templars' secret vault is in the foothills of the Rocky Mountains.

If we follow the allegorical clues within the Cryptic Code taken from the Select Master degree, the words "days" could actually be a coded reference to degrees. If so, they could be interpreted as directions of one-day north, and fourteen days west, possibly directions to the location of a secret vault presumably filled with Templar treasures. While these directions would not take anyone directly to the exact secret location, they could lead to the territory of the Native American tribe guarding it. At that point, upon receiving the proper passwords, handshakes, and signs of recognition, the worthy party might then be lead to the secret vault.

Another possibility is after carving the 'business' part of the inscription on lines one through three, the Kensington Party left directions as to where they were headed. Knowing they were traveling and living with their Native American allies, they almost certainly assimilated with a local tribe and lived out their days as Native Americans. It is interesting that traveling roughly one day north and fourteen days west, depending on whether walking, in canoes, or on horseback, puts one in the territory of the Mandan/Hidatsa/Arikara Indians. The reader might recall the legends of the Mandan who were described by early missionaries and fur traders as the "blond haired, blue-eyed Indians." Is it possible the Kensington party assimilated with the Mandan? This might explain their sad extermination when the U.S. Army gave the tribe smallpox virus-infected blankets that all but wiped them out in 1837.[39]

At this point, we need to leave the interpretation of the directions in the Kensington inscription as unresolved. Regardless, this does not diminish the relevance or importance of the discoveries in the Cryptic Code which I will continue to present. Now that we have addressed what I consider are the practical aspects of the inscription meant to be taken literally, let us continue with other parts that were meant to be allegorical and symbolic in nature.

Jesus and Mary Magdalene

One would think that if the Kensington Rune Stone was carved by an initiated Cistercian monk traveling with Templar knights, he would have understood the historical truth about Jesus and his wife Mary Magdalene, and somewhere in the inscription there might be a clue to this knowledge. If a reference is there, to find it requires an understanding of certain esoteric principles, or what is sometimes called herbal knowledge of those who have the *eyes to see*. To the initiated, the biblical Jesus was known as the Fisher King, as he was initiated by John the Baptist as the first Grand Master of Freemasonry at the beginning of the Great Age of Pisces the Fish. In the Bible, if you were a follower of Jesus, you were a follower of the fish.

"We were fishing one day…" on line six of the inscription never made sense to me. It is obvious the Kensington party was fishing, likely on a daily basis to sustain themselves. However, when viewed through an esoteric lens by one who knew the secret about the humanity of Jesus and his marriage to Mary Magdalene, possibly one who may have been a direct bloodline descendent themselves, fishing seems more likely to be a coded reference to the biblical Jesus. The reference could also be a more general allusion by the carver that the Kensington party of Templars were followers of the same pre-Christian tradition of the Essene sect they were ideological, and likely bloodline, descendants of.[40]

Not to be excluded, the initiated will quickly see that his wife also appears to be acknowledged on line eight with the Latin letters *AVM* (Ave Virgo Maria). In *Akhenaten* I made this same point and whatever reservations I might have had as to which Mary the Latin letters were referring to, those doubts are gone. As if to emphasize the point, the carver made a punch on the lower right leg of the *M* as a coded acknowledgement to the sacred feminine representative of the Great Goddess they revered, in this case Jesus' wife, Mary Magdalene.

39   https://en.wikipedia.org/wiki/1837_Great_Plains_smallpox_epidemic
40   Knight and Lomas, page 73, 1996.

OBLOПC SQUARE

When John Freeburg reviewed an early draft of this manuscript he reminded me of the ten men in Alexandria, Minnesota, who began an effort to raise $300,000 to build a 204-foot tall obelisk-shaped monument at the discovery site on the Ohman

Farm in 1926. A local researcher in Alexandria, Minnesota, named Julie Snider, discovered these men were all Freemasons. In *Akhenaten* I speculated the ten men from Alexandria, who were all Freemasons, likely recognized the symbolism on the Kensington Rune Stone. Things such as the intentionally created sacred 2:1 dimensions of the artifact, the Latin letters *AVM/AUM*, and the 9 + 3 = 12 lines of text would have resonated with this group of men. The sacred space of a Masonic Lodge is specified to be the ratio of two squares in size called the double square or an oblong square. These are the same sacred dimensions found in the Temples of ancient Egypt, the Temple of Solomon, the Gothic Cathedrals of medieval Europe, most Native American lodges, modern Masonic lodges, and the Ark of the Covenant. Now that I have been initiated into the Craft I am even more convinced the ten Brethren in Alexandria absolutely understood the Masonic symbolism the Cistercian carver incorporated into what he considered to be a sacred object in the mid-fourteenth century.

I would be remiss if I failed to point out one more important symbolic aspect of the Kensington Rune Stone that needs to be addressed. The dimensions on the face side of the slab of stone was intentionally split down by the carver very close to 15.5 inches by 31 inches. Freemasons will instantly recognize these dimensions to be the double square. In the Entered Apprentice or first of three degrees in the Blue Lodge, the initiate is taught to place his right foot in the hollow of his left at a ninety-degree angle forming a symbolic oblong square. That oblong square is emblematical of the shape of a lodge whose floor is typically comprised of black and white Masonic pavement. The double square rectangular shape of a Masonic lodge, "...finds its prototype in many of the structures of our ancient brethren. The ark of Noah, the camp of the Israelites, the Ark of the Covenant, the Tabernacle, and, lastly, the Temple of Solomon, were all oblong squares."[41]

The Cistercian monk who carved the Kensington Rune Stone was initiated with a deep understanding of the ancient mysteries of the Craft. Based off this evidence, it is clear the carver intentionally split the previously larger slab of graywacke down to these sacred dimensions. The carefully crafted land claim inscription would have been considered extremely sacred and incorporating ritual in the process of creating it would have been standard procedure. According to Albert Mackey, "Altars, among the ancients, were generally made of turf or stone."[42] Therefore, it is likely the Kensington Rune Stone itself was used as an altar as part of a consecration ritual prior to being placed into the ground as a land claim. Keep in mind the artifact was discovered in what is the geographic center of the continent, symbolizing the center of the Temple,

---

41   Mackey, page 526, 1921.

42   Mackey, page 50, 1921.

or symbolic altar, of what they considered to be the New Jerusalem.

Everything involved in the creation of the Kensington Rune Stone land claim was considered sacred as evidenced by the following facts:

- The Dating code that incorporates the Pentadic number eight (Goddess).
- The word Grail was likely encoded within the inscription as a plea of protection for the land claim stone.
- The 8 (Gotalanders) + 22 (Northmen) + 2 (Shelters) = 32 + 1 (Day's journey) = 33 is the Scottish Rite degree system derived from the Kabbalah and Hebrew Mysticism.
- The total of eight numbers (8, 22, 2, 1, 1, 10, 10 14) within the Cryptic Code are a coded reference to the Goddess.
- 9 (3 x 3) lines of text on the face side plus 3 lines on the split side for a total of 12.
- The three Latin letters AVM are a veiled reference to Mary Magdalene/Goddess.
- The 31 inches by 15.5 inches or 2:1 dimensions of the slab form an oblong or double square.
- The Confirmation codes of the numbers 8 "g/u" runes, 10 "w/v" runes, 14 individual numbers (8, 2, 2, 2, 1, 1, 10, 10, 1, 4, 1, 3, 6, 2), 22 Hooked X's.

HALLiWELL MANUSCRiPT

One of the important takeaways of the Cryptic Code on the Kensington Rune Stone is it moves the discussion from the artifact being classified only as a Scandinavian style rune stone, which it certainly is in part, but it must now also be labeled as

The five-pointed star is symbolic of the planet Venus and a female Deity. It is featured here at the center and six more times around the black and white pavement in the shape of an oblong, or double square as part of a portable altar in Capitol City Commandery #2 in Albany, New York. (2017)

a Masonic document. In fact, the argument can now be made the Kensington Rune Stone takes the title of the oldest Masonic manuscript known to exist. The previous holder of that title is a document called the Halliwell or Regius Manuscript.[43] Some experts place the date of the manuscript to the mid-fifteenth-century, but Mr. James Orchard Halliwell, who was not a Freemason, first published the document in 1840 under the title of "A Poem on the Constitutions of Masonry," and places the date of the document to 1390. The 794-lined manuscript of rhymed verses is believed to be a Roman Catholic production which was the predominant religion in England and provides a clue to its age. Later Masonic documents lean more Protestant in character.

As I have already pointed out, the primary problem runic scholars had for over a century is trying to make the Kensington inscription follow the norms of Scandinavian runic practice. This consistently fundamental flaw in the process of investigation has led to confusion and erroneous conclusions. Instead of these scholars admitting they did not have a clue, they conveniently declared the Rune Stone a hoax. All that has changed with the discovery of the Cryptic Code and realization of the Masonic aspects embedded within this incredible document. Therefore, with the 1362 date the title of the oldest known Masonic document must now be handed to the Kensington Rune Stone. This document, created by the fugitive medieval Templars, was the first "Declaration of Independence" in North America, over four centuries before the more famous one.

The Kensington Rune Stone was intentionally split down by the medieval carver to an oblong or double square. These sacred dimensions allow for numerous geometrical teachings that incorporate, to name a few, the Vesica Pisces, equilateral triangle, and the Pythagorean Tetractys.[44] (2018)

---

43   http://www.freemasons-freemasonry.com/regius.html
44   Hutchens, page 66, 2017.

Jamestown Reliquary

I would like to veer off for a moment to discuss another recent discovery that may be connected to the Dotted M in *AVM* on the Kensington Rune Stone. In November of 2013, during excavations in the chancel of the original church in the settlement in Jamestown, Virginia, four bodies were found that had been buried between the years 1608-1610. On September 29, 2015, Janet and I visited the historic site and walked the grounds taking in the history. We became especially interested in the recent discovery of the original church and the four prominent individuals whose bodies had been discovered less than two years earlier. Outside the coffin of Captain Gabriel Archer, a small, hexagonal-shaped silver reliquary was discovered by archaeologists. The interpretive signs at the partially reconstructed church showed a picture of the reliquary and we noticed what looked like an *M* that had been scratched on the lid. Curious, we decided to investigate at the interpretive center.

At the entrance to the building we struck up a conversation with Senior Conservator Michael Lavin, who was particularly knowledgeable about the reliquary. After a few minutes, he asked if we wanted to see the artifact and invited us back into the lab. Janet and I jumped at the kind offer. We were introduced to other staff members and I explained some of my own experiences working on historical artifacts in a laboratory environment. After several minutes of conversation, the tiny silver reliquary was brought out from the storage vault in a small box. The box also contained replicas of the two lead ampulla and seven bone fragments the reliquary was thought to contain. They explained how the artifacts were replicated after a CT scan identified the contents.

We were thrilled to have this rare opportunity and asked what their thoughts were about the small cross scratched at the top of the far-left leg, and the additional scratches added to the bottom of the far-right leg of the *M*. The consensus was the bones were human and the lead ampulla probably contained Holy water, oil or blood. The obvious question was whose bones were they and how did they end up on the outside of the coffin of Captain Archer? One theory offered was Archer was believed to be Catholic and the reliquary was placed on top of his coffin by a family member or friend as part of a private ritual service.

On the drive back to our hotel, Janet and I talked about possible connections between the scratches added to the lower right leg of the *M* on the reliquary and the dotted lower right leg of the *M* on the Kensington Rune Stone. Could this have been the work of someone associated with a different cause, possibly Captain Archer himself? He may have been secretly involved in the establishment of a Free Templar State in the New Jerusalem during the earliest days of European settlement. Since the settlers at Jamestown had embarked on the perilous journey to the colonies, in large part to seek religious freedom, it seems highly likely there is a lot more to the story about the people at the Jamestown colony and that tiny silver reliquary.

Yet another example of the tradition of acknowledging the Virgin/Mary Magdalene/Goddess using subtle coded references was pointed out in June of 2018, by Patrick Shekleton. He examined a 1538 portolan nautical chart by the Italian cartographer,

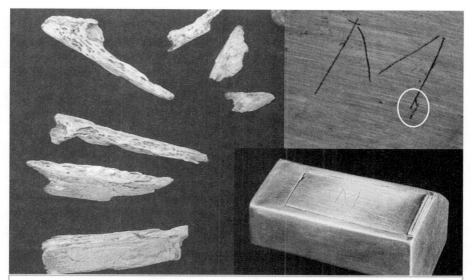

Although the small hexagonal-shaped silver reliquary found in the coffin of Captain Gabriel Archer (1575-1609/10) has not yet been opened, CT scans show it contains two nodules of lead ampulla and seven bone fragments which are assumed to be human. Whose bone fragments they might be, one can only guess. In addition, an *M* is scratched on the lid that includes a small horizontal bar added to the upper left vertical line, apparently making a cross, and two short lines on the lower right leg (circled) reminiscent of the Latin *M* with a punch mark on the Kensington Rune Stone. (2015, 2015, 2015)

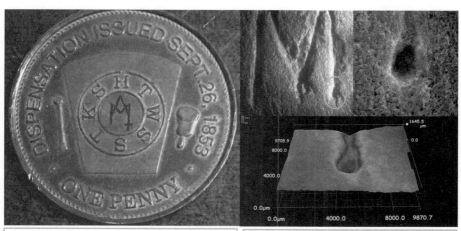

While having a beer with friend and 33rd Degree Scottish Rite Freemason, Monte Miller, he shared his personal mark he created after his initiation into the Royal Arch Degrees of York Rite Freemasonry. When I pointed out the cleverly crafted *AVM* and asked if the cross at the bottom of the right leg of the *M* was a coded reference to the Magdalene/Goddess like the M-sign, he smiled, winked, and took a long sip of his beer. (2018)

The carver of the Kensington Rune Stone added a deep punch mark on the lower end of the right leg of the *M* in an apparent acknowledgement to the Goddess, in this case, most likely Mary Magdalene. (2002/2011/2011) See color section for detail

Conte di Ottomano Freducci (1497-1539), that had a very interesting legend line at the top of the map. In bright red ink beginning at the top left was the *IHS* Christogram followed by an *a* above an *m* as an abbreviation for *AVM*. I saw similar examples in the religious houses in Goa, India.[45] However, in the Freducci map, Shekleton argues the *am* is followed by three curious letters that stand for Virgo. Most interesting to me was Shekleton also pointed out the *V* was made using an undeniably very clear Hooked X symbol! His final verdict on the legend phrase was based largely on the dots used to separate the words. This is the same as runic tradition in Scandinavia, it stands for In Hoc Signo Ave Virgo Maria, which is a reasonable enough conclusion.[46]

What is most relevant for me is the hidden meaning behind what portends to be a common symbolic Catholic reference to Jesus (*IHS*) and the Virgin Mary (Ave Virgo Maria). The first of two clues that reveal the true ideology of Freducci is revealed with the thin angled line added onto the lower right leg of the *m*. This angled line is analogous to the dot added to the lower right leg of the Latin *M* on the Kensington Rune Stone and the additional line to the *M* on the Jamestown reliquary. The second clue is the obvious hook added to the upper right arm of the *x* in Virgo. Later in chapter 11, additional evidence will be presented that appears to be confirmed here; the Hooked X symbol was believed to have been used as a "Cartographer's mark [by a] member of Poor Knights of Malta [as a] navigator or cartographer."

In the legend line of a portolan map made by Italian cartographer, Conte di Ottomano Freducci, in 1538, is an *IHS* Christogram, an *am* with an added line to the lower right leg of the *m* (circled), and a coded version for the word "Virgo" all separated by single dots similar to the runic tradition of Scandinavia. Patrick Shekleton believes it represents "In Hoc Signo Ave Virgo Maria." Carved on the wooden doors to a side chapel inside the Basilica of Bom Jesus, in Goa, India, is the Christogram (*IHS*) and a stylized *AVM*. (Internet/2015)

---

45   http://www.newworldencyclopedia.org/entry/Christogram

46   https://www.facebook.com/groups/1317343038292661/permalink/2235134319846857/

CHAPTER 7:

ΠEW DISCOVERιES

While standing firmly behind my thesis, the Kensington Rune Stone is, first and foremost, a land claim. Many people have wondered in whose name the claim was made. My argument has always been the Kensington party were the ideological descendants of the Knights Templar who were put down by the King of France and the Pope in 1307. Therefore, the land claim would not be made in the name of a monarch, and certainly not the Pope. However, in light of new evidence to come forward in my last three books and this one, I am forced to admit that I was wrong. It appears the land claim was indeed made in the name of a king. In this case, it was the Templars and Venus Families' ancestral and ideological Grand Master, the Fisher King allegorically referred to on line six with the words, "We were fishing one day..." As if to emphasize the point, there are twenty-two Hooked X's carved throughout the Kensington inscription; the same symbol found carved on the lid of the Jesus ossuary from the Talpiot Tomb. This incredible discovery is one of many made in the past five years that is worthy of presenting.

ΠEWPORt TowER

Upon reconsidering the implications of the Cryptic Code discovery within the Kensington Rune Stone inscription, the Newport Tower quickly came to mind. I went back and looked at my 2007 discovery of the long-range alignment that extends from the center of the tower through the only two true keystones in the structure, that are clearly symbolic, and intentionally constructed back-to-back in the north-northwest archway. I wanted to see if the new discoveries might somehow be connected. What instantly dawned on me was how much the notched keystone on the exterior side of the archway, together with the capstone ledges on the two stone columns on either side, looked strikingly like the artistic depictions of the Royal Arch symbol in York Rite Freemasonry. In fact, it is a spot-on match!

The notched keystone I discovered in the Newport Tower in 2007 sits in the rounded stone arch-way that rests on capstone ledges atop two heavy stone and mortar columns, and is an exact architectural match for the iconic symbolism of Royal Arch Freemasonry. (2016/2007/2007)

As we definitively proved on December 21, 2007, the illumination of the egg-shaped keystone on the inside of the archway symbolizes the allegorical resurrection of the sun on the winter solstice and was important enough to the builders, for both practical and spiritual reasons, to engineer the sacred solar alignment into the structure. This begs the question why bother to include the Templar/Masonic symbolism, and complex astronomical alignments, during construction of what many skeptics claim is simply a seventeenth-century windmill? This is pure nonsense for several reasons and is especially frivolous when knowing colonists at this time were struggling simply to survive. The obvious answer is they would not.

Due to the direct connection through the long-range alignment from the Newport Tower to the Kensington Rune Stone, the only logical conclusion that can be drawn is the same group of people created both.[47] And based on the collective evidence, the only candidates who could be responsible for both are the medieval Cistercians and Knights Templar. As if this miraculous connection were not enough, there is more that connects the two medieval artifacts. Like the 283.8-degree azimuth of the keystone's alignment to Kensington, there is another mathematical connection that is not subject to debate.

Since the publication of the Nova Scotia map in the Cremona Document, research-ers Patrick Shekleton, Jim Egan, along with Zachary Montello and Jesse Hauptmann, have made some interesting discoveries that relate to yet another connection between

---

47   The exact azimuth that produces a *rhumb* line through the center of the egg-shaped keystone to Kensington, Minnesota, was calculated by Patrick Shekleton, to be 283.8 degrees. http://www.mov-able-type.co.uk/scripts/latlong.html_

the Newport Tower, the Kensington Rune Stone and the Nova Scotia map dated 1179 (Pictured on page 282). For the first time, these researchers placed GoPro™ cameras inside the tower to record time-lapse videos of the movements of light boxes, created by five of the seven windows built into the structure, that move throughout the day.[48] The videos have documented several interesting and previously unknown alignments that have been published on the Phippsburg History Center Facebook page. However, there was one discovery that intrigued me above the rest. On May 1, 2018, the camera documented another incredible illumination of the egg-shaped keystone inside the west, northwest archway. This alignment corresponds with the cross-quarter day known as Beltane, the Pagan holiday of fertility that happens the first week of May.[49]

If the builders were Scottish Templars led by Earl Henry Sinclair, as oral tradition shared by Chief Black Eagle of the Wampanoag suggests, then documentation of Beltane is perfectly consistent. One of the most important Celtic traditions associated with Beltane is the Green Man, the personification of the young oak who legend says mates with Flora, the Goddess of spring when She is in her fullness, symbolic of fertility. In light of these facts the association with the medieval Sinclair Clan should come as no surprise as Rosslyn Chapel is, in part, a Temple honoring Beltane with literally dozens of examples of the Green Man among its incredible assemblage of carvings.[50]

This newly discovered cross-quarter day alignment provides yet one more nail in the coffin of the colonial windmill theory. It also adds to the mounting evidence that this structure could only have been built by medieval Templars. There will no doubt be more discoveries to come as this dedicated group of researchers continue to document the sun's movement throughout the year.

Shekleton also focused his research on two numerical parts of the Nova Scotia map that refer to latitude. The first are the Roman numbers *XLV 00* (45.00 degrees) with the word Nord (North) underneath, in the center of the map below the circle with two horizontal lines. In discussions with Patrick, he relayed at 45 degrees latitude north on the summer solstice there is exactly 8 hours and 22 minutes of darkness at night. This summer solstice 8/22 darkness band at 45 degrees latitude north appears to have had significance to the Templars who reportedly created this map in the late twelfth century. The significance, or more likely sacredness, of this latitude is underscored by the *X* in the number being a Hooked X.

Coincidentally, the 45th degree latitude line just happens to run through my hometown cities of Minneapolis and St. Paul. On a hot, sunny day on May 26, 2018, Janet and I took a drive to locate the brass plaque that is mounted into a large granite gneiss boulder located a half-block off the east-west running street of Roselawn (Rose line) Avenue. It seems early land surveyors and city planners who laid out the street system in Minneapolis and St. Paul, and cities throughout the United States, cleverly named the streets to preserve important information not readily apparent to the uninitiated. Montreal, Canada, is another place with Templar connections that is directly related to

48 The North and Dubhe windows built into the north side of the tower never receive light from the sun to create interior lightboxes.
49 http://www.goddessandgreenman.co.uk/beltane
50 Butler and Ritchie, page 151, 2013.

This photo of a newly discovered second illumination event of the egg-shaped keystone in the west-northwest archway of the Newport Tower, was captured on May 1, 2018. The medieval builders of the structure intentionally incorporated this solar event to coincide with Beltane, the Pagan holiday of fertility. (Courtesy of Zachary Montello and Jesse Hauptmann)

our research and falls within a half degree of the 45th parallel. One last tantalizing location on this sacred latitude is the city that is the namesake of the Templar document being investigated which has a latitude of 45.133862 degrees—Cremona, Italy.[51]

As if this new 8/22 revelation were not enough, Shekleton made another discovery that, once again, ties the Newport Tower to the Kensington Rune Stone and the Cremona Document. This discovery involves the two Venus windows in the southeast and southwest quadrants at the top of the Tower. In *The Hooked X*, I theorized the windows were important for making astronomical observations of the planet Venus because of its highly accurate and predictable movements.

Shekleton's discovery appears to provide additional support for my Venus windows theory in the form of mathematical details I had been unable to find. The circumference of the cylindrical tower is 360 degrees and corresponds to the twenty-four hours it takes for the earth to rotate on its axis in one day. When converted to minutes (24 x 60), one rotation of the earth's axis equals 1440 minutes. If we then divide 1440 minutes by 360 degrees, this equals four minutes for the earth to rotate one degree.

Shekleton measured the azimuth distance between the middle of the two Venus windows to be 125.5 degrees. When this value is multiplied by four minutes per degree (125.5 x 4) it equals 502 minutes. Now comes the amazing part. When 502 minutes is divided by 60 minutes to convert the time it takes for the earth to rotate the distance between the two windows to hours, the answer is 8.366667 hours. The final conversion comes when 0.366667 hours is converted to minutes (0.36667 x 60 = 22), the result is

51   https://www.latlong.net/place/cremona-lombardy-italy-22688.html

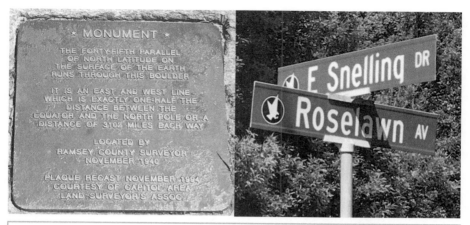

The plaque set into a large glacial boulder of granite gneiss marks the 45th parallel. This location is also marked by Roselawn (Rose Line) Avenue. The intersection at Roselawn is Snelling Drive, which is the north-south meridian and is exactly 90 degrees, or one quarter turn around the earth, west of the meridian that runs through Rosslyn Chapel. Curiously, these two streets marking important latitude and longitude positions are located in the city of Roseville, Minnesota. (2018/2018)

an astonishing 8 hours and 22 minutes. But that wasn't all. Patrick then relayed there was another 125.5 azimuth between the Venus window in the southwest quadrant (W-7) and the small Dubhe window in the north side near the top of the tower (W-5).

Dubhe is the star that makes up the upper front end of the Big Dipper which com-

The upper window on the north side of the Newport Tower marked the Dubhe star which is the top front star in the cup of the Big Dipper. This is part of the Ursa Major constellation also called the Great Bear. (2008)

prises the body and tail of the constellation of Ursa Major, which in Latin means *the greater she-bear*.[52] Dubhe and Merak, the star on the lower front end of the Big Dipper, form what are called *pointer stars* that line up and point to the North Star (Polaris) in the constellation of Ursa Minor. What likely made Dubhe so important to the Templars when the Newport Tower was built circa 1400, was that it never sets below the horizon in the northern hemisphere throughout the year. Because of the constant visibility of Ursa Major relative to Polaris, it has been used as a star clock by navigators and astronomers, including the Templars, throughout history.[53]

52   http://www.astronomytrek.com/star-facts-dubhe/
53   http://www.astronomytrek.com/step-6-interesting-facts-about-ursa-major-1/

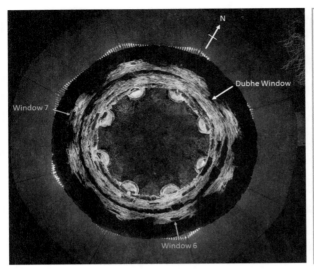

This overhead view of the Newport Tower has the location of the two Venus windows at the top of the cylinder labeled as Windows 6 and 7, and the Dubhe window on the north side. Patrick Shekleton measured the azimuth distance between the center of the two Venus windows on the south side, and the distance between the center of Window 7 and the Dubhe window, to both be 125.5 degrees. When converted to minutes of movement on the earth's axis (125.5 x 4), the result is 502 minutes, which converts to 8 hours and 22 minutes. (Courtesy of Matt Adams, 2018)

Yet again, the 8/22 numerical association with medieval Templars in North America appears consistently and is related to astronomical observations for navigation across both the oceans and the continents. A complete understanding of how the Templars used these numbers has yet to be known. However, recurrence of the numbers 8/22 in association with the activities of the Knights Templar in North America is beyond any question and provides yet another consistent and cohesive piece of factual evidence tying the Templars to all three of these artifacts, and to the founding of the United States of America.

As if this mathematical magic wasn't enough, Shekleton pointed out another discovery that might be the most amazing of all. Early on a Saturday morning in late May of 2018, I received a text message from Shekleton that simply said, "You up?" I responded, "I am," and a few minutes later the phone rang. He asked me to grab a pencil and write down a few numbers related to the dimensions of the egg-shaped keystone in the Newport Tower. Shekleton said, "The first number that is interesting is the length of the egg which is 20.625 inches. That is the same length of the Egyptian Royal Cubit." Shekleton then recited the length and maximum width of the granitic stone, in inches, and told me to add them up (20.625 + 12 = 32.625). He then said, "Now divide 32.625 inches by 12 and see what you get." Astonishingly, the answer was 2.719 inches, or a direct derivative of the megalithic yard! But that wasn't all. He then said, "Now divide the length of the keystone by the width," (20.625 ÷ 12 = 1.719). As I tapped away on my calculator and the number came up, something suddenly struck me. The megalithic yard derivative length of the egg-shaped keystone, and the result of the length to width number I had just calculated, was a ratio that is the Fibonacci sequence or the Golden Ratio. No wonder that egg is such a pleasing shape to the human eye.

Without a doubt, some skeptics will try to argue both the Kensington Stone and the Newport Tower were somehow products of York Rite Freemasons. This argument fails even under the slightest examination. If the Newport Tower was constructed shortly before its first historical mention in Governor Benedict Arnold's will in 1677, modern Freemasonry was still forty years away from officially coming into existence in England in 1717. However, any knowledgeable Freemason knows the Craft has existed for millennia and 1717 was simply the Craft's public coming out party.

Even if for argument's sake we accept that York Rite Freemasons built the Newport Tower, how were they able to create the incredible long-range connection to the Kensington Rune Stone that had already been buried in the ground for over three centuries? Applying logic to this argument creates huge problems on both ends. To accept this reasoning implies a connection between modern Freemasonry and the medieval Templars which is what I have been arguing for all along!

Conversely, if the Kensington Rune Stone is a late nineteenth-century hoax, as many have claimed, how could the builders of the Newport Tower be able to create the long-range alignment that passes right through the discovery site at the Ohman farm over two centuries before the inscription was supposedly created? Even more, how would the forger be able to carve and place the Kensington Rune Stone in the exact spot to align perfectly with another controversial stone and mortar structure on the East Coast that legitimate researchers have dated to roughly the same period? None of these scenarios make any sense and are physically impossible. This leaves us with the only scenario that fits all the facts to connect the two sites: the Kensington Rune Stone and the Newport Tower were created by two separate parties of fugitive medieval Cistercians/Knights Templar, staking their claim to their final sanctuary in North America.

The egg-shaped keystone in the Newport Tower that illuminates on the Winter Solstice (December 21st), and on the cross-quarter day of Beltane (May 1st), has dimensions of 12 inches wide by 20.625 inches in length. 20.625 inches is the length of the Egyptian Royal Cubit and when 12 inches is added it results in a total of 32.625 inches. When this total is then divided by 12 it equals 2.719 inches, a derivative of the megalithic yard. Further, when 20.625 inches is divided by 12 it equals 1.719 inches which when paired with 2.719 inches equals the ratio of two points of the Fibonacci sequence. (2015)

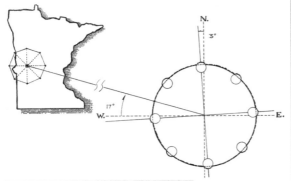

In 2007, I discovered if a line was made starting at the center of the Newport Tower and extended through the egg-shaped keystone on the inside of the northwest archway and the notched keystone on the outside of the same archway, and that line was extended westward, it would go right through the location of the discovery of the Kensington Rune Stone. (Illustration by Dan Wiemer, 2005)

This wood carving found at an archaeological site on Baffin Island dates to between AD 1250-1300 and depicts a person wearing a tunic with an equilateral cross on the chest reminiscent of the clothing worn by medieval Templar knights.[54] (Internet)

Perhaps the simplest way to answer the question of who built the Newport Tower is to ask the people who were here when it was originally constructed—the Wampanoag Tribe. On June 12, 2015, Janet and I were with a group of researchers and Freemasons visiting the Tower. Joining us was Daryl Black Eagle Jamieson, who is the current chief of the Wampanoag. While listening to Chief Black Eagle talk about what would have happened when early European explorers encountered his people, I pointed to the Newport Tower in front of us and asked the following questions, "So, flat out, who built this? Who do you think are the most logical candidates?"

While recorded, Black Eagle answered, "The most logical to me is the Sinclair(s) and the Templars that came through here, because they had some sort of an alliance, and they still do. They meet with the Mi'kmaqs every year. The flags are the same, only reversed. So, it doesn't make sense that the Mi'kmaqs would put a flag backwards, the same flag that the Celtic people had."

This testimonial confirms what the factual evidence has been telling us all along.

54   https://ottawarewind.com/2016/11/28/700-year-old-carving-found-on-baffin-island-depicts-figure-in-a-tunic-with-a-cross/

We can now add the Cryptic Code evidence that tells us the carver of the Kensington Rune Stone land claim was an initiated Cistercian monk who traveled with a party of brother Templar Knights to the geographic center of North America in 1362. The evidence for the Newport Tower suggests it was also the creation of a party of medieval Templar knights sometime around 1400. If true, the long-range keystone alignment to Kensington was engineered afterward and implies the builders of the Tower already knew about the land claim and exactly where it had been placed. The facts, incredible as they may seem, are consistent with these conclusions.

From a Templar/Masonic symbolic perspective, the Kensington Rune Stone to the Newport Tower alignment connection makes perfect sense. The land claim stone was placed at the geographic center of the continent with its sacred symbolic aspects within the inscription and physical dimensions that incorporate sacred geometry. For the Templars, it represented the allegorical keystone at the center of the new Temple they began to "build" in the fourteenth century. The responsibility of the completion of the Temple, where freedom from the tyranny of the monarchs of Europe and persecution from the Church could flourish, was passed on to the Founding Fathers, nearly all of whom were Freemasons who risked their lives to create the new sanctuary now called the United States.

13TH and 14TH Scottish Rite Degrees

I would be remiss if I didn't point out the symbolism in two of the twenty-nine degrees in the Scottish Rite. They are suspiciously connected to both the numbers on the Kensington Rune Stone and the famous legend of treasures found by the Templars under the Temple in Jerusalem around AD 1110 In the 13th degree, the ritual deals with the legend of a secret discovery inside a hidden crypt nine levels below the ruins of the Temple in Jerusalem. Enoch's crypt was built after he received a vision, and was later discovered by three brethren, called Master Architects, who removed a tabular stone, with a ring on top, hidden beneath moss. Upon removing the stone, they took turns lowering each other three levels until they reached the ninth arch. Inside the ninth arch, called the secret vault, they found an alabaster pedestal with a cube of agate resting on top. Set into the cube is a triangle of gold inscribed with the Hebrew, or Phoenician, letters for Deity: Yod, Heh, Vav, Heh.[55]

This legendary story was born from the ancient Enochian legend, but could the 13th degree of the Scottish Rite also be a record of real historical events? If the South Wall narrative in the Cremona Document is authentic, it could mean the 13th degree chronicles the discoveries made by Hugh de Payens and the other five knights veiled within an allegorical story.

The 14th degree of the Scottish Rite continues the story of the secret vault and appears to include specific reference to the Newport Tower and the Kensington Rune Stone. The association of nine arches, each with a sacred keystone, has already been

---

55   Hutchens, page 85, 2010.

shown to exist in the Newport Tower. The Masonic apron for the Scottish Rite 14th degree has a flat slab of stone with a ring on the flap. Could it be symbolic of the the the Kensington Rune Stone? Suddenly, we now have three apparent direct connections between the two Scottish Rite degrees and important documented facts:

1. The flat tabular slab of stone that is the key to the treasures in Enoch's secret vault in the 14th degree, and the flat tabular stone that is the Kensington Rune Stone that holds the directions to the Templar's secret vault in Montana.

2. The nine rounded arches with notched keystones of the Royal Arch in modern Freemasonry and the notched keystone in the rounded archway in the Newport Tower.

3. Both fourteenth-century artifacts are connected by archaeoastronomy and are in the 14th degree.

This suggests the Rune Stone is a representation of the now-missing stone that once covered the entrance to the Talpiot tomb. In *Akhenaten* I argued a mysterious late nineteenth-century glass slide with the image of a Templar knight holding a skull and kneeling in front of an open tomb was used in the York Rite degrees.[56] The rectangular slab of stone at the entrance is strikingly close in shape to the Kensington Rune Stone, right down to the dark shading in the lower-left side of the stone. I argued the scene could be a veiled depiction of the Templars paying respect before entering the Talpiot tomb of the royal family during the time of their legendary excavations in the First Crusade. Let us not forget about the three skulls found symbolically placed in

The Masonic apron for the Scottish Rite 14th degree has a flat slab of stone with a ring on the flap (left). Could it be symbolic of the Kensington Rune Stone? (left) This late nineteenth-century glass slide used in the York Rite degrees could be a clue to knowledge of Templar excavation activities in Jerusalem in the early twelfth-century that was passed down to modern Scottish and York Rite Freemasonry (right). (Bridge to Light, page 90; Courtesy of the Minnesota Masonic Historical Society)

56   Wolter, page 255, 2013.

the south, west and east quadrants of the tomb, most likely Templar knights who died during the siege of Jerusalem who would have been honored to have their skulls placed as symbolic guardians of their bloodline ancestors. The glass slide could be direct evidence and knowledge of those activities that have been passed down from the Templars into modern Scottish Rite and York Rite Freemasonry.

Since we have already demonstrated the carver of the Kensington Rune Stone must have been a Cistercian monk initiated in the Enochian mysteries and Kabbalah, there could be additional symbolism connected to activities in Jerusalem. The land claim stone could have been symbolic of both the South Wall stones that covered the entrance to the hidden chamber the Templars discovered beneath the Temple Mount, and the actual stone that once covered the entrance to the Talpiot tomb. In my view, to think all this evidence doesn't prove a connection between these two Scottish Rite degrees (and the Select Master degree in the York Rite) and the medieval historical truths unfolding before our eyes stretches skepticism to the breaking point.

GRASSY POND CHAPEL

During a visit to Westford, Massachusetts, to see our friends Kim and David Brody, they took us to a newly discovered site recently pointed out to them less than a mile from their home. On March 26, 2017, David and Kim directed us to a small park with hiking trails called Grassy Pond. The pond is located only a quarter of a mile from Stony Brook reservoir which is the start of the climb up to Prospect Hill and the Westford Knight/Hooked X carvings. This location is also less than a mile from the Westford Boat Stone and would have been right in the middle of the late fourteenth-century activity of Earl Henry's Templar knights.

Our friends led us through the woods and the week-old melting remnants of a blizzard. The trail led us to the center of a snow-covered open field. They explained the field had always been a water-filled pond that completely dried out the previous summer. This was the first time in many decades. There was still a fair amount of early spring snow on the ground, but the stones were protruding through and clearly visible. Exposed in the center were hundreds of mostly white-colored granitic glacial stones and large boulders. As we walked into the middle of what at first seemed to be an area of randomly strewn glacial boulders we noticed an order to their arrangement.

David then pointed to a circular cluster of small stones with a series of larger stones aligned due west on the west side of the roughly twenty foot diameter circle. A larger single boulder was at the center of the circle and struck me as either intentionally placed or was already there and the circle of stones were placed around it. As I stared at the larger boulder I noticed a small flat area on the top that could be a crude altar within a round symbolic chapel or outdoor lodge.

Knowing the Templars had been in this area most likely around 1400, the circumstantial evidence suggests this party ended up in what is now Newport, Rhode Island, and built the Newport Tower as the central structure within their permanent settlement. The circle of stones in this dried pond could have been a symbolic religious

Janet Wolter stands in front of the larger white altar(?) stone in the center of the white stone circle on the high point of Grassy Pond in Westford, Massachusetts, on March 26, 2017. (2017)

This picture of the white stone circle was taken in late fall and shows the eight stones running roughly east-west. (Courtesy of Cori Ryan)

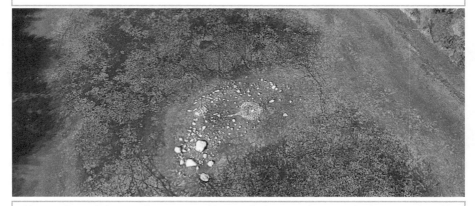

This Google Earth image of Grassy Pond in Westford, Massachusetts, clearly shows the white stone circle with the eight stones that looks like a stingray when viewed from above. (Google Earth)

structure the Templars used for rituals to honor Deity, or something much older that was already in place. Perhaps it was built by Native Americans or earlier European visitors?

Just as I was reigning in my imagination, Janet, who was standing by the line of stones on the west side of the circle said, "Hey, guess how many stones are in the line here?" We all looked over and started to count. There were eight roughly one-foot-wide stones. We all knew eight was a sacred number to the Templars, and to Native Americans, and it struck us what this could be. Janet then asked, "When a Templar approached the altar from the west following this line of stones, who would he then be facing?"

I smiled and replied, "The Master of the lodge in the east." Shen then pointed to a large boulder just outside the ring where a Master may have sat.

The other possibility to explain this circle of white stones with an apparent larger white stone altar was a Native American medicine wheel to track the movement of the stars, planets and the sun. Few realize the indigenous people were master astronomers who kept track of the annual movement of heavenly bodies essential to survival. It is also possible the stone circle was originally a native site that was later repurposed by the Templars in the fourteenth century.

If this pond was dry before urbanization it was the perfect location for an observatory, being lined with trees creating a consistent horizon for making accurate celestial observations. David confirmed this was the only location in the area for miles that was open to the sky except for deeper ponds or lakes. The proximity of the medicine wheel/chapel was too convenient to not at least be considered connected to the Templar party that likely wintered here circa 1400.

FISH SYMBOL

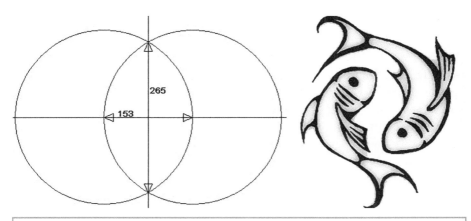

When two circles are joined that create three equal parts in the middle the vertical almond shape in the center has a height to width ratio of 265/153 (left). The symbol of the constellation Pisces is two opposing fish. (Internet/Internet)

This symbol of the fish is essentially the same modern Christian style fish symbol commonly seen on the back of automobiles, except with a rounded head instead of a pointed end. We see this rounded version of the fish symbol, often occurring in opposing pairs, in the handwriting of historical figures and artists suspected of being enlightened Venus Family members or initiated members of Masonic orders used when conveying secret messages to other members. The seemingly random position of individual fish or opposing pairs could also be a unique watermark used to authenticate writings to the initiated who understood the meaning of the symbols.

After pondering these symbols a short while, I eventually reached out to a friend with a deep understanding of esoteric knowledge. Brother Tim Hogan recognized the symbol as the Christian fish, created by the intersection of two equal sized circles spaced such that the central horizontal line divides into three parts of equals lengths. Quoting Tim Hogan:

> The ratio of the long axis to the short axis is 265/153. In the early writings of the Pythagoreans and the other Greeks, they abbreviated this measurement by calling it "the measurement of the fish" or sometimes just by the number 153. This is why, I believe, Jesus and Pythagoras were said to have caught 153 fishes, as it was a geometric metaphor. This "measurement of the fish" is what is used to make a perfect equilateral triangle. Interestingly, "the Magdalene" in Greek (Gematria) adds up to 153, and "Mary" adds up to 152.[57]

Much like the opposing fishes in the Pisces symbol, which also symbolize the concept of Dualism, an argument could be made the lone fish symbol itself represents the dualism of Jesus and Mary Magdalene.

My deep plunge into researching the esoteric aspects of the vertically aligned fish symbol reminded me of another artifact I examined a decade ago, the Westford Boat Stone, that contains what could be the same symbol, and along with other evidence, could be a direct connection to the Templar knights who stayed in North America in 1362. The Westford Boat Stone contains the signs, symbols, numbers and most importantly, advanced weathering of the carved lines that appear to indicate it could be connected to the party associated with Earl Henry Sinclair, whom legend says came to North America in 1398. Curiously, the Boat Stone also falls upon a very important longitudinal line of 71 degrees, 28 minutes. Many people do not believe the Templars were capable of determining longitude in the 1300s. Supposedly, the ability to determine longitude was not discovered until the seventeenth century. In his 2006 book, William Mann lists one of the important pre-Columbian Templar Meridians as 71 degrees west.[58] The following list of mysterious artifacts and sites fall very close to this meridian, and all but the Cumberland Monastery, America's Stonehenge and Old Quebec City are possibly connected to the Knights Templar and Earl Henry Sinclair in 1398. One

---

57   Hogan, pages 72-73, 2009.

58   Mann, page 69, 2006.

thing that seems indisputable is these locations indicate a keen understanding of how to calculate longitude:

1. Newport Tower...,..... (41.29 N, 71.19 W)
2. In Hoc Signo Vinces Stone...........................,...... (41.31 N, 71.19 W)
3. Narragansett Rune Stone................................... (41.38 N, 71.24 W)
4. Cistercian Monastery in Cumberland............. (41.56 N, 71.24 W)
5. Westford Sword and Hooked X........................ (42.35 N, 71.26 W)
6. Westford Boat Stone.. (42.36 N, 71.28 W)
7. Tyngsboro Map Stone.. (42.40 N, 71.25 W)
8. America's Stonehenge.. (42.50 N, 71.12 W)
9. Mystery Stone at Lake Winnipesaukee............ (43.34 N, 71.19 W)
10. Old Quebec City.. (46.48 N, 71.12 W)

The three symbols carved on the Westford Boat Stone are a single vertical line, a vertical fish symbol, and the number four, or the astrological symbol for the planet Jupiter. (2007)

There is no way in my mind this many artifacts and sites located in such close proximity to the 71st degree Templar meridian can in any way be dismissed as a coincidence.

As she was researching fish symbols, my wife Janet found something interesting in letters written by Founding Father and Freemason, Benjamin Franklin.[59] One letter in particular caught her attention, and Janet pointed out what looked like fish symbols in the flourishing of Franklin's penmanship. Sure enough, one could argue the letter *g* in the word "gentlemen" has two fish symbols. Adding more mystery to the Franklin letter written to The Committee of Secret Correspondence of the Continental Congress, on the back side of the letter in the upper left corner of the page Franklin wrote another stand-alone letter *G* that is an exact duplicate of the *G* at the beginning of the letter.

I could not help but notice the letter *G* is the first thing Franklin wrote in the upper left hand corner on both sides of this letter. Coincidentally, it is also the first rune/letter carved in the upper left hand corner of the Kensington Rune Stone and has a dot added

---

The first four runes singled out by the carver using punch marks made on the carved lines, or short lines on one side next to them, are put in sequence as the inscription spells *Gral* or Grail in Old Swedish. (2018)

Benjamin Franklin included mysterious elements in a letter written to The Committee of Secret Correspondence on January 4, 1777. The *g* in gentlemen and a standalone *G* on the back of the page contain opposing fish symbols that could be more than just flourishing in his penmanship. He also added a dot and the number 13 after the date that also contains the twin fish symbols. The number 13 is very important symbolically to both medieval Templars and modern Freemasonry as the number of the Goddess. (Internet) to the upper right arm, as if being singled out by the carver. In Freemasonry, the letter G appears in the middle of the compass and square which is said to represent God, Geometry, and some have suggested it could also mean Gnosticism or Gia. Perhaps the medieval carver of the Kensington Stone is telling us what the G really means as the next three runes he singled out, in sequence, are r, a and l. In medieval Old Swedish, the language used in the inscription, those four letters spell *Gral* or Grail. Could that be the secret message the Gs in Franklin's letter are referring to? He played an important role in the hidden history behind the founding of the United States and may have been communicating important messages to members of the secret committee.

An early example of George Washington's signature at the age of 12 in 1744/45, shows a young, educated man with beautiful penmanship. However, notable changes in his signature occur after he was raised as a Freemason at the age of 21, most noticeably a vertically aligned fish symbol over the *g* in his last name and within the *W*.[60] (Internet/Internet)

Another curious element in Franklin's letter is he added a dot, and then the number 13, after the date January 4, 1777. Other Franklin letters do not include these additions and begs the question, why add *that* number after the date? We have seen throughout this book the number 13 is of great symbolic importance to both medieval Templars and modern Freemasons. During my conversation with Tim Hogan about these additions to the date he said, "In certain Templar traditions people tended to hide things within written dates. Secret information could be passed on since most people do not pay close attention to dates." It's possible the number 13 was a clue used by Franklin to inform the initiated there was secretly coded information within the letter.

Another Founding Father, who was undoubtedly initiated with the same esoteric fish knowledge, was George Washington. When looking at his signature as a young man it is clear he was highly educated with beautiful penmanship.[61] However, there are notable changes to Washington's signature after he was raised as a Freemason in 1752.[62] The most notable change is the addition of a vertically aligned fish symbol above the *g* in his last name. Washington also appears to change the style of the capitol G in his first name that is reminiscent of the same Franklin made. Here again the letter G appears to be con-

60   https://www.pinterest.com/pin/40884309087430803/
61   http://www.ubooks.pub/Books/ON/B1/E1583R2959/16MB1583.html
62   http://americanbuilt.us/patriots/george-washington.shtml

nected to the fish symbol just like in Franklin's 1777 letter, and in the Kensington Rune Stone inscription. Prior to my own initiation into Freemasonry, I likely would not have taken any of this very seriously and written it off as speculation. However, after having gained a much deeper understanding of Masonic symbolism and the esoteric aspects of the Craft, I now understand when to pay attention to certain signs and symbols. Keep in mind symbols like these are designed to be subtle and innocuous, always leaving the door open for plausible deniability by the symbol maker.

One thing I have discovered is once you know what to look for, the signs, symbols and tokens seemingly jump out at you everywhere. The fish symbol is now one of them. Recently, while paging through an early twentieth-century book about the history of George Washington, my wife Janet found a portrait of General Lafayette. The artist, Charles Wilson Peele, painted the picture of Lafayette, a well-known Freemason, sitting inside a tent and incorporated interesting symbolism. Besides the obvious *M*s formed outside Lafayette's tent by the tents on the right side, the general's right arm is bent at a ninety-degree angle symbolizing his being, Masonically, on the square. His right hand is holding a book with his index finger separated from his other three fingers. This symbolizes a reference to pi (3 + 1 = 4 or 3.14) as an ode to science.[63]

What caught Janet's eye was something even more obscure, but patently obvious once she pointed it out. On the left edge of the painting was the corner of a rolled-up scroll. The word General in cursive writing can be seen on the small portion of the scroll. However, what immediately jumped out was a clear and obvious vertically aligned fish symbol the artist appears to have intentionally placed within the painting. Like the *M* sign, this is yet another esoteric symbol indicating knowledge about the truth of the first-century royal families.

This portrait of General Marquis de Lafayette by Charles Wilson Peele contains important symbolism. The general's right arm is at a ninety-degree bend or, "On the square," and his fingers are positioned to symbolize 3.14, or *pi*, as an ode to science. The tents alignment to the right depicts multiple *M*s, and on the far left is cursive writing on a scroll with the vertically aligned fish symbol (see inset).[64] (Internet)

63   Callahan, page 134, 1913.

64   This painting of General Lafayette was included in a Masonic publication in 1917 that was intended to raise money exclusively for the George Washington Masonic Memorial in Alexandria, Virginia.

In 2016, while attending the "Martin Luther: Art and the Reformation" exhibition at the Minneapolis Institute of Art, Janet and I noticed another very interesting letter. In addition to the two triple-barred Cross of Lorraine symbolism in his will we found an interesting letter with a familiar symbol dotting the page written by Luther to Georg Spalatin, a key figure in the early years of the English Reformation, in 1523.[65]

Of the numerous Luther letters on display, this was the only one that had twelve "fish" symbols randomly sprinkled throughout the handwritten lines of text. Later, I did an online search of letters written by Luther and found another with the same horizontal fish symbols. This letter, written in Latin, was addressed to Thomas Cromwell in 1536.[66] Cromwell was the first Earl of Essex and the chief minister to King Henry VIII of England. At the time, he was also one of the strongest advocates for the English Reformation. If indeed the numerous fish symbols in Luther's letter are part of a code to individuals initiated in the same tradition, Thomas Cromwell and George Spalatin would be strong candidates.[67]

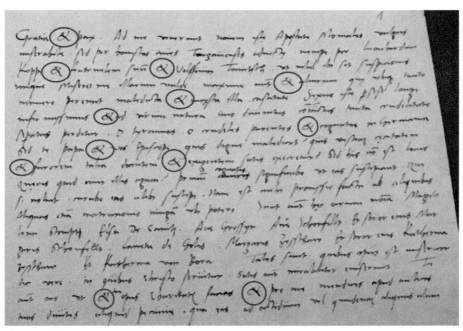

There are twelve fish symbols, swimming to the left, on this page of a letter written by Reverend Martin Luther to Georg Spalatin on April 10, 1523. Could these be some type of coded symbolism intended only for those initiated into certain esoteric traditions to understand? (2016)

65   https://en.wikipedia.org/wiki/George_Spalatin

66   http://www.gettyimages.co.uk/detail/news-photo/martin-luther-letter-in-latin-to-thomas-crom-well-secretary-news-photo/173279062?#autograph-martin-luther-letter-in-latin-to-thomas-cromwell-secre-tary-picture-id173279062

67   https://en.wikipedia.org/wiki/Thomas_Cromwell

While working on the subject of mysterious symbols, another example of a possible direct connection to the fish came to mind. I would like to direct the reader's attention back to the Hooked X/tau cross symbol on the Jesus ossuary that I believe ties the medieval Knights Templar/Cistercian leadership, and their Monotheistic Dualism ideology, back to the first-century Essene. For those who followed the years of controversy and drama surrounding the ossuaries from the Talpiot Tomb, believed to contain the mortal remains of the biblical family of Jesus and Mary Magdalene, they may know there is more to the story located only a couple hundred feet away. A second first-century tomb exists beneath a condominium complex that still contains seven ossuaries. Construction of the condominium was such that this second tomb, referred to as the Patio Tomb, is inaccessible primarily due to the objections of Orthodox Jews who aggressively protest if anyone tries to enter either of these ancient tombs.

In 2010, a hole was drilled through the basement floor of the apartment building and a robotic arm was used to film the contents of the tomb. Seven ossuaries were found tucked into four of nine tunnels, or niches, cut into the bedrock which made it difficult for the camera on the articulated arm to see the carvings and inscriptions on the sides of the bone boxes. On the so-called Jonah ossuary, besides what has been interpreted to be a large vertically aligned fish carved on one of the long sides of the ossuary, there are also six small fish symbols aligned horizontally along the top of the

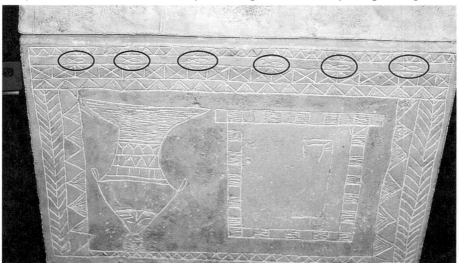

This replica of the Jonah ossuary from the Talpiot Patio Tomb in Jerusalem, has six fish symbols (circled) all swimming to the right at the top of the ornately carved box. The square to the right with alternating light and dark squares lining the perimeter are reminiscent of black and white Masonic pavement symbolic of dualism, representing balance. These carvings could be a clue to the ideological beliefs of the individual interred within the ossuary. These symbols could also represent evidence the ideology of monotheistic dualism, begun in Egypt by Pharaoh Akhenaten, continued into Jerusalem in the first century and carried forward. (Internet)

---

68   Jacobovici and Tabor, pages 59-63, 2012.

for, the bloodline families that descend back to the biblical Jesus, Mary Magdalene, and other family members? The answer is almost certainly yes, and begs yet another question: could there be more hard evidence to support the esoteric ideological symbolism of the fish that weaves throughout the Scottish Sinclair Clan and other Venus families who were "in the know?" The answer to that question also appears to be yes.

In early April of 2018, what appears to be new hard evidence of linking the fish symbol with the Sinclair Clan came unexpectedly, and unknowingly, from none other than a Sinclair. While scrolling through my Facebook feed on April 5, 2018, a couple photos appeared posted by my friend Steve St. Clair. Steve had called a few days earlier while conducting research into his family lineage around Edinburgh, Scotland. Steve posted photos of the family coat of arms carved beneath stone effigies within recessed niches built into Corstorphine Parish Church in the western part of Edinburgh. Steve pointed out one of his ancestors had married into the Forrester Clan with an image showing the coat of arms for both families carved into shields below the effigies. What immediately caught my eye were five examples of the Forrester coat of arms with a very familiar symbol. Each example had three curved powder horns with the hanging strings very prominent in the unmistakable shape of the vertically aligned fish.

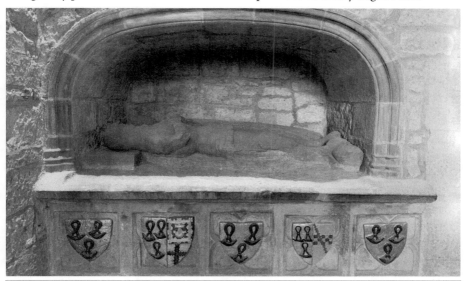

Carved inside this recessed niche in Corstorphine Parish Church in Western Edinburgh, Scotland, are the effigies of Sir John Forrester and his wife, Jean Sinclair, daughter of Henry Sinclair, First Earl of Orkney.[69] Carved on shields below the niche are the hunting horns and string in the symbol of the fish of the Forrester Clan along with the engrailed cross of the Sinclair Clan in the lower right quarter of the shield second from left. (2019)

This prompted an online search for examples of the Forrester coat of arms, and I quickly found several examples that matched the carvings Steve had found at Corstor-

---

69   http://www.clanmacfarlanegenealogy.info/genealogy/TNGWebsite/getperson.php?person-ID=I5606&tree=CC

phine Parish Church. The key fact that struck me was the obvious Sinclair coat of arms in the lower right quarter of one of the shields. This connection of the Sinclair clan to the Forrester clan prompted me to search genealogical sites where I made an interesting discovery: Sir Adam Forrester (circa 1361-1405), First of Corstorphine.[70] It was his son, Sir John Forrester (circa 1380-1448), Second of Corstorphine, who was buried at Corstorphine and whose effigy is carved next to one of his three wives, possibly his second wife, Jean Sinclair, the daughter of Henry Sinclair, First Earl of Orkney.[71]

The discovery of the veiled fish symbol as the string of the hunting horn in the Forrester Coat of Arms was exciting. However, even more fascinating was to find out the father of the knight effigy carved at Corstorphine Parish Church, whose wife was a daughter of Earl Henry Sinclair, means that Sir Adam Forrester not only knew Earl Henry Sinclair, but may have traveled with him to North America in 1398. The interconnecting thread of these late fourteenth/early fifteenth-century Templar families with the fish symbol cannot be a serendipitous set of coincidences. If Sir Adam Forrester did travel to North America, he did not stay behind in 1398. This means he returned to Scotland and, according to genealogical records, he was present at the Battle of Homildon Hill and taken prisoner in 1402. The bottom line is the known historical record provides a direct connection of the Forrester Clan to the Sinclair Clan by marriage in the early 1400s. This, along with the esoteric fish symbolism found on the Forrester Coat of Arms, leads one to believe both clans were deeply involved in the mission to establish the New Jerusalem in North America.

As compelling as these new discoveries were, it didn't end there. The Forrester hunting horn also appears unexpectedly within a mysterious mid-eighteenth-century encoded document that was finally decoded in 2011.

Copiale Cipher

In 2013, I wrote about the recently decoded 105-page handwritten manuscript in *Akhenaten* that dates back to about 1760 called "The Copiale Cipher." What interested me most at the time was the use of a familiar symbol, the Hooked X, one of a total of eight (that sacred number again) larger sized symbols, called *logograms*, used in the manuscript. The manuscript was a Masonic ritual of a high degree in France and/or Germany emphasizing scientific enlightenment by a secret society known as the Oculist Order.[72] The decipherment revealed the Hooked X symbol, called Big X by scholars who cracked the code, represented a rival Masonic order some believe are Freemasons that have not progressed beyond the Master Mason or third degree. These facts drive home the point that the Hooked X has been a sacred and secret symbol used by the Knights Templar. If you know where to look, you see the symbolism around us today.

70   http://www.clanmacfarlanegenealogy.info/genealogy/TNGWebsite/getperson.php?person-ID=I30482&tree=CC

71   http://www.clanmacfarlanegenealogy.info/genealogy/TNGWebsite/getperson.php?person-ID=I3813&tree=CC;   http://www.clanmacfarlanegenealogy.info/genealogy/TNGWebsite/getperson.php?personID=I3813&tree=CC;   http://www.clanmacfarlanegenealogy.info/genealogy/TNGWebsite/getperson.php?personID=I3813&tree=CC

72   https://stp.lingfil.uu.se/~bea/copiale/

FOSTER

The coat of arms of the Foster Clan includes a string with a tight loop attached to a hunting horn. The string of the hunting horn of the Forrester Clan is larger and shaped like vertically aligned fish. (Internet/Internet)

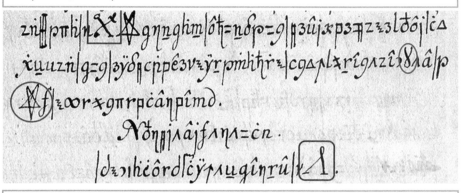

At the bottom of page 21 in the Copiale Cipher are three of the eight different larger symbols used in the manuscript, called logograms, and include a unique version of the Hooked X (line one), a downward pointing pentagram (line three), and small looped fish symbol (line five). A vertically aligned fish symbol with the head down (line two) is also used in the manuscript suggesting it has deeper meaning. (Internet)

While the Hooked X in the Copiale Cipher was an important new discovery, it isn't the only symbol used in the manuscript that is important to our story. It turns out the esoteric fish symbolism found woven through the works of important historical figures and the Cremona Document is prominently displayed in the Copiale manuscript. Specifically, another of the eight logograms was the fish symbol with a smaller loop at the top. The significance of this unique version of the fish symbol was realized after researching the hunting horn symbols on the Forrester Coat of Arms Steve St. Clair had brought to my attention. I quickly found numerous examples on the internet of the Forrester Coat of Arms as well as another closely related family name that has used essentially the same

At the end of the Copiale Cipher manuscript was a watermark in the paper that includes a hunting horn with a vertically aligned fish symbol consistent with the Forrester Clan Coat of Arms in Corstorphine, in western Edinburgh, Scotland. (Internet)

triple hunting horn symbol: Foster. However, there are two noticeable differences. The first difference is the larger end of the horn is facing to the right in the Forrester Coat of Arms, and to the left in the Foster Coat of Arms. The other difference is the fish symbol of the string attached to the horn in the Foster Coat of Arms is much smaller and looks exactly like the logogram used in the Copiale manuscript.

As we have seen in this research time and again, the connections between specific symbolism and the people using them, most notably the Venus Families connected to the medieval Knights Templar, and modern Freemasonic orders, are not by coincidence. In fact, they represent tangible connections between these orders throughout time, and with specific individuals from families comprising these orders throughout the centuries. The Copiale manuscript includes many esoteric symbols that are familiar to modern Freemasons, such as the downward pointing Pentagram, which is the physical manifestation of the Goddess in the heavens (the planet Venus), and used by the modern related Masonic order for women called Eastern Star.

These symbols were used from at least the fourteenth-century by the Knights Templar through the Enlightenment period (circa 1800), by modern Freemasonry and related secret societies. What is becoming clearer are the emerging connections of their use by specific clans and families.[73] Symbols like the various forms of the fish and the Hooked X provide compelling evidence of the centuries-long mission by the Venus Families they called The Covenant, that ultimately resulted in the founding of what was often referred to as the New Jerusalem, or what we now call the United States of America.

Rosslyn Chapel Forrester Fish

As if the Forrester fish didn't already have an interesting enough connection to the Copiale Cipher, it also has a connection to Rosslyn Chapel in Scotland. In January of 2019, during a trip to Rosslyn to film an episode for the reboot of *America Unearthed* on Travel Channel, I discovered something carved into a flower-adorned beam in the northeast corner on the interior of the chapel. Lying on its side was a beautifully carved fish symbol with a curved line attached to the tail. It was a spot-on match to the hunting horn

---

73   https://www.britannica.com/event/Enlightenment-European-history

symbol on the medieval Forrester Coat of Arms. At first, I assumed it was a mason's mark seen on hundreds of stones throughout the building. Upon reflection, it seemed like it might be something more. It wasn't shallowly carved and somewhat crude in appearance like all the other marks. This was larger in size, carved deeper in the stone and skillfully made. Perhaps there was something more to this carving that represented a nod to another prominent Scottish family that had a direct connection to the Sinclairs, evidenced by the effigies of Jean Sinclair, daughter of Earl Henry Sinclair, and her husband Sir John Forrester, carved in stone inside Corstorphine Parish Church.

William "The Builder" Sinclair's aunt would have been Jean Sinclair who married John Forrester, William's uncle by marriage, in the early fifteenth century. Sometime after the cornerstone was placed in 1446, William may have ordered one of the stonemasons to carve the Forrester fish symbol to honor the Forrester family who had become relatives during his lifetime. Details of those relationships are mostly unknown, but they are interesting stories lost to history behind the Forrester/Sinclair clans' relationship that included at least one bloodline marriage. If only that fish symbol could share its secrets.

Carved into a north-south trending, foliage-adorned, east facing beam in the northeast corner of Rosslyn Chapel is an apparent mason's mark identical to the Forrester Clan symbol of a hunting horn found in their family coat of arms. (2019)

Rosslyn Chapel Cryptic Code

During the same trip to Rosslyn Chapel, it occurred to me it was possible the Cryptic Code I found on the Kensington Rune Stone could also be here as well. While examining the detailed carvings both inside and outside the chapel, I kept noticing angels holding scrolls. Upon returning home, I kicked myself for not keeping track of how many there were at the time. During a Skype call with Alan Butler I shared my thesis and he suggested I start with the spires on the exterior which was easy. The total number came to thirty-two.

You might recall from chapter 6, the first four numbers in sequence on the Kensington Rune Stone are 8, 22, 2 = 32 + 1 = 33. If indeed the esoteric teachings of Hebrew

One of at least a dozen Scroll Angels scattered throughout the interior and exterior of Rosslyn Chapel. This carving sits above what many believe is the death mask of Robert the Bruce. What I believe is the 33rd spire is the only statue (spire?) on the inside of the chapel: the Virgin/Goddess holding her child. (2019)

mysticism were present in 1362 in the middle of North America, then it stands to reason the same teachings were present roughly a century later when the chapel was built. With the spires count showing promise right out of the gate it seemed a safe bet Sir William "The Builder" Sinclair was initiated with the same teachings. If so, then the Cryptic Code numbers must be present in the chapel, the challenge now was to find them, and to find the hidden thirty-third spire.

A day later, in a second Skype call with Alan, I explained how the exterior spires conformed to the Cryptic Code. I also shared where I thought the thirty-third spire was hiding. As usual, it was in plain sight inside the chapel in the most appropriate of all places. The core of esoteric teachings is how to achieve inner peace by finding a balance between one's self and the Godhead. Therefore, it stands to reason the symbolic representation of these teachings were of utmost importance to Sir William Sinclair and the Templar tradition. The beautiful symbolic carvings serve as evidence he revered the Great Goddess. One only needs to stand in the center of the chapel and She cannot be missed. I concluded the thirty-third spire of Rosslyn Chapel was the only lone statue in the entire building. It sits directly below the rose window where the Great Goddess is veiled as the Virgin and child.

The exterior spires and Goddess statue appear to be telling us the Cryptic Code of sacred numbers was intentionally incorporated into the building. If so, then the numbers 22, 14, 10, and arguably the most sacred number of all, eight, will be cryptically hidden within the amazing stone work, but where? On the plane back to Minnesota I scanned the hundreds of photos I took in the chapel. Could these angels holding scrolls be where one of the sacred numbers was hidden? After an exhaustive search of my photos, I lamented over why I had not noticed the code while still visiting the chapel. I found eleven scroll angels, but I knew I had not found them all. The odds are there will likely be twenty-two since the number fourteen came as quickly in the number of beautifully carved columns on the interior. This led to the windows in the building which resulted in the following: ten second story windows on the north and south sides, ten tall first story windows on the north and south, and two smaller windows above the north and south doors for a total of twenty-two. Of course, this leaves out the five additional windows in the east end and one in the west wall. As exciting as this discovery is, there is still more work to do.

Rosslyn Matrix

In *Hooked X* I introduced the research of Ashley Cowie where he explained how initiates learned how to calculate latitude using nothing more than a stick or rod. The exercise involves drawing a circle on a high point of land and then marking the four cardinal points. At sunrise, the stick is placed on the east point which casts a shadow across the circle that is drawn in. The exercise is repeated until either the summer or winter solstice is reached, and the shadow line drawn reaches its steepest angle from the east-west line across the center of the circle. At this point geometry comes into play, allowing the other three lines to be drawn (the shadows cast from the west point at the end of the day on the solstices and the shadows cast from the east point on the solstices) creating a lozenge with angles that correspond to a specific latitude.

Cowie proposed at the latitude of Jerusalem (31.7683° N) the shape of the lozenge has sixty-degree angles at the east and west sides that corresponds to the Seal of Solomon, the symbol on the flag of Israel. At the latitude of Rosslyn Chapel (55.8554° N), the east-west lozenge angles are ninety-degrees which forms a perfect square lozenge inside the circle. In *Hooked X*, I pointed out that Jerusalem and Rosslyn Chapel were both important places to fifteenth-century Templars and modern Freemasons. I also mentioned the 60 and 90-degree angles of the lozenges at these sacred locations also correspond to the angles of the two working tools that make up the most iconic symbol of Freemasonry, the Compass and Square.

I brought this knowledge to Rosslyn Chapel in January of 2019 while I examined the mysterious carving on the south wall of the sacristy just east of the doorway. Shallowly carved with precise straight lines is what looks like a power line tower with opposing curved lines at the top framing four lozenges of different shapes stacked vertically in the center. My mission was to measure the angles of the lozenges and check if they corresponded to the latitudes proposed by Cowie to be Jerusalem, Rosslyn, Orkney Islands (~59 degrees) and the Faroe Islands (~62 degrees). Indeed, the angles did correspond to these locations, suggesting the lozenges were a coded reference to Earl Henry Sinclair's

Carved into the south wall of the sacristy in Rosslyn Chapel is a grid system likely representing a map of the North Atlantic Ocean with two curved arms at the top with a series of four varying shaped lozenges in the middle (left). The lozenges are an ancient symbol representing the latitudes of approximately 32, 56, 59 and 62-degrees north. The five-pointed star of Venus on the left arm could represent the latitude of Newport, Rhode Island. (2019)

Tucked into the alcove in the exterior northwest corner of the chapel is a large, deeply carved "Awen" symbol. This Celtic symbol represents the rays of the sun on the equinox (middle) summer (left) and winter (right) solstices emanating from the horizontal line representing the horizon. (2019)

legendary voyage to North America in 1398, the grandfather of William Sinclair. The corn and aloe carvings inside the chapel have always defied conventional explanation and provide powerful supporting evidence. How could the stonemasons at Rosslyn have known about these North American plants decades before Columbus made his famous voyage in 1492? The implications are obvious, but the most compelling evidence of Earl Henry's voyage lies in the amazing carving on the south wall of the sacristy.

I already knew the lozenges corresponded to the latitudes mentioned, but what I was more interested in was the five-pointed star on the curved left arm meant to represent when Venus is an evening star in the western sky, the left arm of the Horns of Venus.`[74] On this trip, my third to Rosslyn, I had time to carefully study the walls throughout the chapel and the sacristy and noticed there were more than a dozen five-pointed star symbols etched into the stone blocks. Clearly, they were mason's marks and were the same size and shallowly carved as the five-pointed star in the Rosslyn Matrix carving. I quickly concluded the five-pointed star on the left arm was also a mason's mark that had been there before the tower and lozenges were carved into the wall. I also concluded the subsequent carvings were intentionally positioned to incorporate the preexisting five-pointed star into the exact position where it needed to be. The question was, did the five-pointed star also correspond to a specific latitude associated with a particular place? Granted, the star is rather large, but the center of the star is between the lowest two lozenges and the approximate latitudes of 32 and 56 degrees north. Since it was located on the left arm it seemed reasonable to assume the location represented by the star was to the west in North America.

The approximate latitude of the star relative to the lozenges was somewhere in the low 40s. As I stared at the carvings it suddenly dawned on me. Within that range of latitude, the most logical place in the New World that Earl Henry would visit and establish a settlement of fugitive Templars in the fourteenth-century is well known. That place is Newport, Rhode Island, in Narragansett Bay where we find the Narragansett Rune Stone, the "In Hoc Signo Vinces" Stone, and the Newport Tower.

Before leaving the chapel, I took one more walk around the building and discovered something I had never noticed before. On the wall inside an alcove created by the west wall and the westernmost buttress wall on the north side was a carving of the largest mason's mark I have ever seen at roughly 6" by 6". I recognized the Awen symbol, the Celtic symbol of the solstices on the two sides and the equinox in the middle radiating from a central point on the horizontal line representing the horizon.[75] I smiled realizing the mason who carved this must have known the ancient secret of calculating latitude, for the solstice lines were correctly drawn for the Rosslyn latitude.

---

74   Cowie, pages 87-88, 2006.

75   http://www.cassandraeason.com/divination/druidry/awen.htm

Rosslyn Chapel X

My visit in January 2019 was the third time I had been to Rosslyn. In preparation for the trip, I paged through a book I bought during my first visit to Rosslyn Chapel in 2006. As I studied the paintings and sketches, I found something that immediately caught my eye.[76] The book featured historic artworks of the chapel and castle, dating back to 1693. A familiar symbol appeared in an interesting series of sketches by William Delacour dated to 1761. In multiple perspectives of the exterior of the chapel I could see a very prominent X symbol in the stone tracery of the upper east facing window.

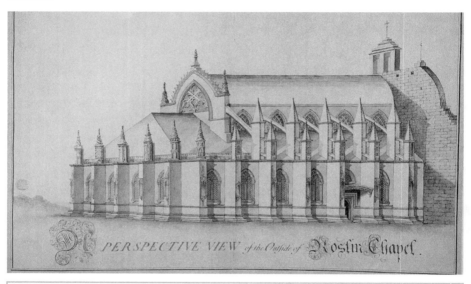

In this sketch from a northeast view of Rosslyn (spelled "Roslin" here) Chapel by William Delacour in 1761, a prominent X can be seen in the stone tracing of the upper east-facing window. (National Galleries of Scotland)

I previously did not notice the large X symbol and decided to dig into it. During both of my visits in 2006 and 2007, I had photographed the four X's at the top of the stone traceries of the lower corner windows on the east end of the chapel. Currently, the upper east window has an engrailed stone square inside of a circle design meant to invoke the geometric Masonic concept known as "squaring the circle." This mysterious X in the upper east window prompted me to look at the two books about Rosslyn Chapel written by my friend, Alan Butler, and his co-author, the late John Ritchie. Their book, *Rosslyn Chapel Decoded,* included photos of the east window from circa 1860, with what appeared to be newly installed stone tracery of a stylized cross resting on a heavy central column. Reportedly the tracery was redesigned at that time as a memorial to the sister of the Earl of Rosslyn.[77] The stone tracery of the upper east window must

---

76   Rosslyn and Maggi, pages 29 & 52, 2002.
77   Butler/Ritchie, page 115, 2013.

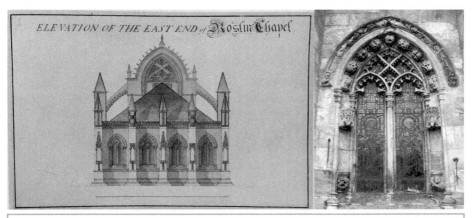

In William Delacour's east facing sketch of Roslin Chapel in 1761, a prominent *X* symbol can be seen in the stone tracing of the upper east window, and at the top of the north and south sides of the east facing lower windows. Two additional windows on the extreme east end of the north and south (pictured here) sides of the chapel also have *X*s at the top of the windows making a total of five original windows with *X*s. (National Galleries of Scotland; 2006)

have been redesigned and installed to its present design only a few decades later as the square inside the circle design is pictured in 1892.[78] Regardless, it appears all memory of the original *X* design was lost.

To try and confirm my suspicions I placed a Skype call to Alan Butler on January 11, 2017, and we discussed the history of the east window. To our surprise, neither he or John Ritchie were aware of the earlier *X* design. Alan noted that William Delacour's sketches looked like very accurate architectural rather than artistic drawings, and agreed the *X* design had to be Sir William Sinclair's original design. Another detail in Delacour's sketches was the presence of a peaked roof on the lower east end, directly in front of the upper east window that makes up the east end of the two-story nave of the chapel extending west. The apex of the peak was just below the level of the *X* tracing. The 1860 era photo shows the peaked roof over the Lady Chapel on the east end had been removed during renovations at that time.

At this point, some might ask why is this such a big deal? The original stone tracery design of the upper east window is important because it would certainly have been approved by Sir William Sinclair, 3rd Earl of Orkney.[79] If so, why did he choose the *X* symbol in his design that appeared five times in the Lady Chapel on the east end? It is a safe bet Sir William was also initiated into the medieval Freemasonry and Templarism mysteries and understood at its core is the veneration of the sacred feminine.

The stone window traceries at Rosslyn Chapel tell us that William The Builder understood the *X* was a symbol of those initiated into the traditions of the ancient mysteries of monotheism that trace back to Pharaoh Akhenaten in Egypt. He may also have been aware of the *X* carved in front of Jesus' name on his ossuary in the Talpiot tomb, signifying that he was likely also initiated into the same tradition. There were

---

78   Thompson, page 36, 1892/2006.

79   Sinclair/Me, page 392, 2018.

The stone tracing design in the upper east window of Rosslyn Chapel (upper left) has changed at least twice from the original *X* design of William Sinclair (left). In the 1850's the first renovation was made into a vertically aligned, stylized cross that was soon replaced with the current 'square inside the circle' design (right). (Internet/2006)

originally five *X*s in the stone window traceries at William Sinclair's Rosslyn Chapel. They were both surrounding and directly above the Lady Chapel, and likely were symbolic of the five-pointed star of Venus. Curiously, there are seventy-four carved into the peaked ceiling of the west bay symbolic of the Goddess omnipresent in the enigmatic fifteenth-century chapel. Based on everything we have learned in researching the history of the Templars/Cistercians and Monotheistic Dualism, it seems we now have a better understanding of the history and motivation behind the construction and design of this incredible building.

Looking up at the west bay of the peaked ceiling of Rosslyn Chapel are seventy-four, five-pointed stars symbolic of the planet Venus, the Goddess in the heavens. (2006)

Sklar/Sinklar/Sinclair?

Just when it seemed there couldn't be another potentially blockbuster discovery related to the Kensington Rune Stone, in February of 2018, the improbable may have happened. On Valentine's Day my friend, Patrick Shekleton, sent an email with a startling claim. He pointed out how the enigmatic word on line four of the inscription, *Sklar*, has been translated by modern scholars from Old Swedish into English as *shelters*? The question mark suggests the word might be something else entirely.[80] However, a little history about this word will be helpful.

The sequence of numbers and words at the end of line four of the Kensington Rune Stone are, "...2 sklar, one..." and show both a short horizontal bar in the *l* rune, and a longer horizontal bar in the *o* rune. These subtle differences in the length of the horizontal bar have big implications to the meaning of the inscription. (2011)

Early on in the investigation into the Kensington inscription the crossed *l* rune in *Sklar* was thought by scholars, like Eric Moltke, to be a *j* in the 1940s.[81] This was ultimately rejected, for no reasonable Old Swedish word worked with the *j* in that position. Scholars later thought it might be a *bind rune*, meaning two runes combined into one symbol built upon a common vertical stave. In this case, either an *el* or *le* bind rune, but in both cases the Old Swedish words did not make sense. The use of a bind rune also didn't make sense since the traditional use of bind runes was either many were used in lengthy inscriptions or none at all. The Kensington inscription has no other bind runes, despite the opportunity for several that were commonly used at that time. My co-author, Richard Nielsen, and I came up with another idea for the short horizontal stroke in the *l* rune that appears to explain the strange anomaly we named, the Dating Code.

Since the Dating Code appears to explain the short horizontal bar in the *l*, and the similarly strange horizontal bar in the *u* rune in the last word *Illu* (evils), on line nine, the rune in *sklar* stands as simply an *l* rune. This leaves us with the English translation to the problematic word *shelters*? The question mark added by runic scholars Richard Nielsen and Professor Henrik Williams in 2014, shows the lack of confidence in their translation. This begs the question: if not *shelters* then what does this word spell? This brings us back to Shekleton who in his email posed the word actually might be a name!

---

80   The question mark was added by runologists, Richard Nielsen and Professor Henrik Williams, in their most recent translation of the inscription in 2014, indicating they were not certain the English translation is correct.

81   Nielsen/Wolter, page 146, 2006.

That name was immediately known to all who have read this book, but not by the spelling carved on the stone. To try and determine if Sinclair could have been spelled this way in the past, I reached out to the best genealogist I knew, Diana Muir. It didn't take long for Diana to find a suitable reference. In fact, she found 241 examples ranging in dates from 1511-1807.

In all, Muir found ten different ways the familiar name was spelled that included Sklar, Sinklar, Sinklr, and Sinclair. The realization hit me like a sledgehammer. Could the name Sinclair, spelled *Sklar*, really be on the Kensington Rune Stone? If so, it could not be referring to Earl Henry Sinclair, who was only a teenager in 1362, but his father and grandfather, who were both Templar knights and respected leaders and navigators in their own right. For the Kensington Rune Stone to be directly linked to the Sinclair Clan would actually make sense, and be another conclusive connection of the artifact to the medieval Scottish Templar order, after the put-down.

OVERTON STONE

Roughly four years ago I was contacted by a fan who sent me pictures via email of one of the most interesting carvings relating to the history of Knights Templar in North America ever discovered. Upon opening the images, I could not believe my eyes. I stared in near disbelief at the incredible carvings that seemed tailored to the research I had recently published in *Akhenaten* about the strategic ideological alliance between the medieval Templars who secretly came to North America and their Native American brethren. I resolved to visit the site to try and understand the geology of the huge boulder hosting the carvings and if there was any possibility of dating them. Unfortunately, we were too busy to get there until July of 2016.

On August 31, 2017, Janet and I finally had a chance to visit the site. It was a perfectly sunny midday when we approached the two car-sized boulders that stood out on a slight rise, surrounded by vegetation, roughly 200 feet from the shoreline at low tide. The carvings were on the south-facing side of the larger boulder, roughly four feet off the ground. What stood out most prominently was the roughly six-inch tall, Templar-style cross encircled with an egg-shaped line that had four dots at the flared ends of the cross, marking the four cardinal points. The lower arm of the cross was longer than the other three, resembling a Christian-style cross some have interpreted to be connected to the Portuguese Templars.[82] Immediately to the right of the cross is what some say is a leaf, but looks more like a feather carved in detail. Underneath the feather are what appear to be crossed tobacco leaves in the form of an X. Immediately to the right is a carving of a crescent moon or possibly the crescent shape of Venus.

The first impression I had was the carvings represented the consummation of a alliance between a group of Templar Knights and the local indigenous people known as the Mi'Kmaq. If the carvings date back to the time of Earl Henry Sinclair, his descendants, or

82   New England Antiquities Research Association (NEARA) Past-President, Terry Deveau, published an article on the Overton Stone making the claim the cross was of Portuguese Knights Templar origin in 2015. His paper can be read at the following link: http://www.neara.org/images/OvertonStone.pdf

Janet Wolter points to the Overton Stone carvings of a Templar Cross, crossed tobacco leaves, a large feather, and a crescent moon. (Courtesy of Patrick Shekleton)

perhaps a group of Portuguese Templars who had contact at a later date is unclear. The key to answering that question could lay in whatever I might be able to do in the laboratory to somehow put a date on the carvings.

The boulder and surrounding area was made of a strongly foliated schist. Before leaving, I took a sample of the rock from the opposite side of the boulder for laboratory analysis. That sample had the same light-colored, deeply weathered surface as that which contained the carvings and helped answer several questions I had about the rock type, the weathering of the carvings and its possible age. Regardless, whether the carvings were made by Portuguese Templars believed to have traveled to Nova Scotia, or Scottish Templars we know were here, they represent potentially vital and important evidence of the pre-Columbian history of North America.

The rock flakes and cuttings from the carving process would have collected on the ground in the organic-rich soil directly below. A small-scale archaeological excavation could result in a carbon-14 date of the organic material of the soil layer the cuttings are in.

Roughly four feet to the left of the carvings near the ground are four additional carvings including a double fish-like symbol, a sideways *S* and below these are the numbers *06* and *07*. (2017)

CHAPTER 8:

Knights of Christ in Goa, India

Many researchers, myself included, believe the leadership of the medieval Templar/Cistercian order directly descended from the first-century royal families, or Venus Families, who embraced the ancient ideology that venerated feminine aspects of the Godhead. It was that heretical ideology, along with other political factors, the Roman Catholic Church found unacceptable. This prompted the suppression of the heart of the Templar order in France in 1307. No doubt it was a devastating and pivotal moment to the long-range plans of the Venus Families that forced the surviving leadership to continue "under the rose," or *sub-rosa*. In Gnostic circles, the rose is symbolic of a secret, specifically, the secret of Jesus and Mary Magdalene's marriage and the existence their descendants, and was one of the most important secrets the Templars, and other traditions, were in charge of protecting. As I have discussed in the *Hooked X* and *Akhenaten*, one of the ways they preserved the secrets was through symbolism embedded in artistic works.

In May of 2015 I took a trip to Goa, India, to film scenes for *Pirate Treasure of the Knights Templar*.[83] Goa is the city ruled by the Portuguese Order of the Knights of Christ, the name the Portuguese Knights Templar took on after the put-down. They from 1510 until the mid-nineteenth century. The Portuguese Templars built over a dozen beautiful churches in Goa. In addition to a chapel dedicated to St. Mary (Magdalene?), they also built the stunningly beautiful and gold-illuminated Basilica of Bom

---

83 *America Unearthed* was put on hold after season three aired in February of 2014. The reason was our host channel, H2, was sold to Viceland. Eventually, my agent said History decided not to continue our series because the content was "too smart" for the audience demographic.

Jesus, built between 1594 and 1604;[84] the massive Church of St. Francis of Assisi, built in 1661;[85] and the equally massive Se Cathedral, constructed between 1562 and 1619.[86]

Goa also had a massive church and monastery dedicated to St. Augustine that now sits in ruins.[87] The remains of the church include dozens of seventeenth-century grave slabs mortared into the floor near the main altar. I spent over an hour examining these on a blistering hot day. Many of the grave slabs were those of Portuguese Templars whose family crests revealed interesting symbolism. I will share an important discovery I made on those grave slabs in the next chapter.

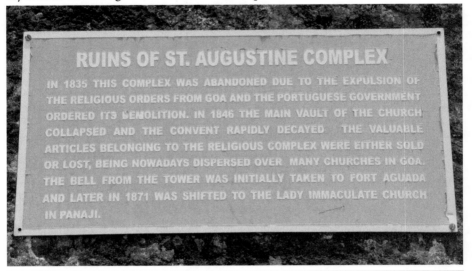

RUINS OF ST. AUGUSTINE COMPLEX

IN 1835 THIS COMPLEX WAS ABANDONED DUE TO THE EXPULSION OF THE RELIGIOUS ORDERS FROM GOA AND THE PORTUGUESE GOVERNMENT ORDERED ITS DEMOLITION. IN 1846 THE MAIN VAULT OF THE CHURCH COLLAPSED AND THE CONVENT RAPIDLY DECAYED. THE VALUABLE ARTICLES BELONGING TO THE RELIGIOUS COMPLEX WERE EITHER SOLD OR LOST, BEING NOWADAYS DISPERSED OVER MANY CHURCHES IN GOA. THE BELL FROM THE TOWER WAS INITIALLY TAKEN TO FORT AGUADA AND LATER IN 1871 WAS SHIFTED TO THE LADY IMMACULATE CHURCH IN PANAJI.

This plaque on the ruins of St. Augustine Monastery in Goa, India, explains the downfall of the Portuguese Templars, and the monastery, in India that coincided with the final suppression of the Templars in Portugal. (2015)

Even though these religious houses were built in the name of Roman Catholicism, certain members of the Portuguese Templars ensured that not-so-veiled symbolism was incorporated into the religious houses (monasteries, churches, and Se Cathedral) that reflected their true origins and Monotheistic Dualism ideology. During my whirlwind, three-day, on-camera investigation in Goa, I found numerous examples of the Venus Families' true ideology of Monotheistic Dualism. That ideology was alive and well for over five hundred years after the Templar order had supposedly been eliminated, and the heresy of their efforts to bring down the Catholic Church, from within, had been suppressed.

The first example of apparent heresy I noticed was in the Church of St. Francis of Assisi. Roughly three stories above the altar was a life-sized, three-dimensional wood carving of a monk (probably Bernard with the crown-of-thorns-style tonsure) taking

---

84   https://en.wikipedia.org/wiki/Basilica_of_Bom_Jesus

85   https://www.britannica.com/topic/Church-of-Saint-Francis-of-Assisi

86   https://en.wikipedia.org/wiki/Se_Cathedral

87   https://en.wikipedia.org/wiki/Church_of_St._Augustine,_Goa

Jesus down from the Cross. Later that night in my hotel room, while going through my photographs, I noticed Jesus had his arm around the monk's shoulder—that seemed to indicate Jesus was still alive. Then I realized his head was up, not drooped as if dead, and his eyes were open!

At the St. Francis of Assisi Church in Goa, India, the high altar has a monk with a Cistercian tonsure helping Jesus from a tau-style cross with his arm around the monk and his eyes open as if still alive. (2015/2015)

The shocking part was this life-sized, three-dimensional imagery was at the top of the high altar. It made me wonder how many people would even notice the still-living Jesus being taken down from the Cross? The other interesting thing about this strange Crucifixion scene was the cross was not the standard Christian style; it had a very short vertical beam extending barely above Jesus' head. This cross was the preferred style of Christian Cross we saw throughout Goa and while reminiscent of the *T*-shaped tau cross, it looked more to me like a unique form of the double-barred Cross of Lorraine. In fact, I only saw one example of a typical Lorraine style cross with both horizontal bars being of equal length. It was in a painting of a local Bishop at St. Francis of Assisi Church, holding a red, equal length double-barred Cross of Lorraine. The Templars reportedly carried it into Jerusalem during the First Crusade. As I stared at the painting of the Bishop in Goa holding the patron symbol, it felt like a nod by the Portuguese Knights of Christ to their early twelfth-century brethren who fought in that campaign.

This subtle yet unmistakable imagery of Jesus surviving the Crucifixion is now the third such example I have seen that makes this suggestion. The other two examples were in France: one, at a very small Templar Church in Champagne Sur Aude, a small wooden carving of the same image of a monk taking Jesus down from the Cross with

Outside a cemetery in Goa, India, is a monument with nine ascending steps that is topped with, what I coined, a Goa-style Cross of Lorraine. (2015/2015)

his eyes wide open; the second was an ornate, life-size sculpture of the entombment of Christ that came from a Knights Templar Commandery in Reims. That sculpture was ordered by Francois Jarradin, Commander of the Hospitallers, in 1531, and shows a still bleeding Jesus after he was taken down off the Cross. All three examples have a direct connection to the Knights Templar. This begs the question, did the Knights Templar have secret knowledge about Jesus that the Roman Catholic Church did not? If Jesus really did survive the Crucifixion, it opens all kinds of new historical possibilities for what really happened in Jerusalem in the first century.

One thing that has always intrigued me is the post-Crucifixion story of a deceased Jesus having been placed inside a stone tomb for three days only to be resurrected with his body and soul rising to heaven. Could it be the story is allegorical and is not really about the Resurrection of the Son of God, but in fact, is the story of the resurrection, or return, of the Sun God? Indeed, the Jesus Resurrection story in the Bible is more likely an allegorical tale about the age-old story of the return of the sun on the winter solstice. The *three days* refers to the time the sun appears to stand still before, during, and after it reaches its southernmost point in the eastern sky, at sunrise on December 21st. The shortest day of the year is called the winter solstice. If the biblical Resurrection story is really an allegory about the rebirth of the sun on the winter solstice, then what really happened to Jesus at the time of the Crucifixion? I'm sure there are many other examples of Jesus surviving the Crucifixion. My guess is the best place to look for them is sites connected to the Knights Templar and their Cistercian brethren.

Before moving on from the allegorical resurrection of Jesus and the sun, we must address another aspect of the story that is too often overlooked. According to the Bible, when Jesus emerged from the tomb on the third day, the only person to see this miracle was Mary Magdalene. Here again, the biblical version of the story can also be allegorical. In mystical circles, the sun and the planet Venus are known as the eternal travelers and the ultimate symbol of dualism in the heavens. We know when Venus is a morning star, She rises in the eastern sky followed shortly behind by the rising sun. As an evening star in the west, she gradually comes into view as the light of the setting sun fades, following her consort and eventually disappearing below the horizon. In light of these astronomical events, it makes sense that the symbolic female consort of Jesus, Mary Magdalene, was present at the time of the allegorical resurrection.

The discovery of the Talpiot Tomb led to a flood of evidence that supports not only the marriage of Jesus/Yeshua and Mary Magdalene/Mariamene, but that they had children, including a son named "Judah, son of Jesus." The presence of iron-rich sediments nearly two feet deep that flowed into the tomb encasing the entire burial chamber and all ten ossuaries suggests the tomb was entered by someone in the historical past. Because the stone sealing the entrance was not properly replaced, sediments from the rose gardens above flowed in over the course of what is believed to be the past nine centuries. I proposed it was the Templars who entered the tomb after capturing and maintaining control of Jerusalem at the time of the First Crusade.

I will reveal more details about the Talpiot Tomb in a later chapter, but it is now time to reveal what might be the most important discovery for me related to the Kensington Rune Stone. I have shared the stories about the discovery of every other aspect of the the Kensington Rune Stone that is consistent with its fourteenth-century creation. The one remaining mystery is the origin of the Hooked X symbol. While I firmly believe I have conclusively explained the meaning and significance of the symbol, what has eluded me are its origins. If given the opportunity to choose any place and period in history to explain its origin, I never would have chosen what turned out to be reality.

CHAPTER 9:

HOOKED X/TAU CROSS ON THE JESUS OSSUARY

Speculation of a connection between the Cistercians/Knights Templar and modern-day Freemasonry developed early on in my investigation into the Kensington Rune Stone. What started out as a logical assumption quickly became obvious, and then eventually, a certainty. Convincing others, including many Freemasons I have met along the way, was a more difficult task. Eventually, the evidence became too compelling and consistent to ignore. Not only did the trail run through Freemasonry and the Cistercian/Knights Templar traditions, but the rapid accumulation of facts were like standing dominoes that began to fall into place in 2012. The dominoes had many branches leading to unexpected, and for many, inconvenient and problematic places. The most important domino trail was the most unexpected, yet once they began falling they marched headlong back through time to an ancient tomb in one of the most sacred places in the world: Jerusalem.

First discovered in 1980 during blasting of the relatively soft limestone chalk in the East Talpiot neighborhood of southern Jerusalem, construction crews were preparing to build condominiums and accidentally unearthed a first-century underground tomb. Construction was halted and archaeologists were called in to document the tomb and its contents. Little did they realize the enormity of the situation they had literally walked into. Once inside the burial chamber, Amos Kloner, Jerusalem district Ph.D. archaeologist, and his assistants, archaeologist Joseph Gath and archaeology student, Shimon Gibson, documented ten ossuaries that were partially to completely buried in up to a two-feet deep accumulation of organic-rich Terra rossa soil.[88] Whoever entered the tomb roughly nine hundred years ago, did not put the seal stone at the entrance back into its proper position. This allowed soil to flow into the tomb roughly a millennium after it was initially sealed in the late first century.[89]

The tomb presented many questions, most notably, whose family tomb was this and who had entered it around the time of the First Crusade? The answers to these and other questions seemed to be inextricably connected to my search for the origin of the Hooked X and were found in the first book written about the Talpiot tomb by Simcha Jacobovici and Charlie Pellegrino titled, *The Jesus Family Tomb*. For anyone with even a passing interest in the biblical Jesus, whether in his story as interesting history, or in Him as your Divine Savior, this book should be considered required reading. It chronicles the tomb's amazing discovery and subsequent archaeological excavation and processing of the artifacts, remains, and ten ossuaries within it, seven inscribed with names, six in Aramaic and one ornately inscribed in Greek. The collection of names includes the following and their English equivalents:

Inscription on Ossuary	Description
1. Jesus, son of Joseph	Aka, Jesus of Nazareth
2. James, son of Joseph	Brother of Jesus
3. Yose	Like Joey in English, likely brother of Jesus
4. Judah, son of Jesus	Son of Jesus
5. Maria	Probably mother of Jesus, James and Jose
6. Mathew	Possible cousin of Jesus, James and Jose
7. Mariamene Mara (in Greek)	Likely Mary Magdalene and wife of Jesus[90]

Excitedly, I looked at the picture section to see the tomb and the ossuaries and what first caught my eye was a familiar symbol in front (on the right side, as like Hebrew, Aramaic is read right to left) of the "Jesus, son of Joseph" inscription. It was a large *X* with a ninety-degree bend to the left on the lower right leg, exactly like the first Roman numeral ten on the In Camera Stone found only a year before on Hunter Mountain.[91] Upon seeing the character and reading about other strange *X*s found on several additional first-century ossuaries in Jerusalem, I felt compelled to contact Simcha because in his book he wrote he didn't know what the *X* symbol meant. After finding his email address online I wrote offering my thoughts. I proposed the *X* was the symbol of someone who was initiated into the equivalent of the ancient priesthood of the Egyptians. I also suggested the Nazarene sect of Jesus and his followers could

---

88   Tabor and Jacobovici, page 23, 2012.

89   It should be noted that Israeli geologist, Aryeh Shimron, believes the sediment that entered the Talpiot tomb occurred in 363 BC when the blocking stone became dislodged and rolled away after a major earthquake. So far, he has offered no factual evidence to support his thesis that I am aware of.

90   There is much debate in the academic community as to who these people are. However, this collection of names in the tomb all match the names of known persons in the life of Jesus you would expect to see buried in his tomb and based on when it is thought that they died.

91   See *Akhenaten*, page 218.

be ideological descendants of the Pharaoh Akhenaten and the Monotheistic Dualism religion he tried to usher in when the celestial great age of Taurus the Bull gave way to Aries the Ram circa 1350 BC.

Simcha was intrigued by these ideas and asked if I had any other insights about the tomb. I explained that after reading about the three skulls the archaeologists found on the floor of the burial chamber that were in good condition as opposed to the badly decomposed bones in the ossuaries, it was clear they were intentionally placed by the Templars who controlled the city at that time. I then relayed the important symbolism I saw in the archaeologist's diagram of the burial chamber that showed the three skulls in an equilateral triangle—a tell-tale calling card of the Templars. Something else occurred to me that I could not pull out of my brain during our email exchange and told him I would forward it on when I figured it out.

What I finally remembered was a coin minted by the Crusaders in 1200, less than a century after they entered the tomb. I had seen the coin in a book on Crusader art in the Holy Land and it had the unmistakable chevron-circle symbolism of the carving into the bedrock directly above the entrance to the tomb. To me, minting a coin with secret Talpiot tomb symbolism was exactly the kind of thing the Templars would do. It was their way of quietly informing those in-the-know that they had successfully accomplished a very important part of their mission upon gaining control of the Holy Land. I'm also convinced the secret of the tomb has been kept tight within the medieval Templars, and their Cistercian brethren, who eventually passed it onto a secret society popularly known today as the Priory of Sion.

I give credit to the discovery I am about to share to my friend, and brilliant scientist, Charles "Charlie" Pellegrino. When I opened the first of five images of a symbol Charlie had emailed on May 24, 2014, I instantly recognized one of the two symbols before me. My eyes widened and my heart started pounding as I fixed my gaze on what I knew was of vital importance to my then 14 years of research on the Kensington Rune Stone that had never been made public before. In the email, Charlie explained the pictures he'd taken were of what he and other members of the Talpiot Tomb research team called a "star" symbol. He and the other researchers believed the symbol represented an important aspect of an ancient Jewish historical story. Almost everyone I later showed the pictures to agreed it didn't look like a star. The carved lines were asymmetric and didn't meet at the center as one would expect for a star-like symbol.

I immediately typed my response as fast as my fingers would go, "Charlie, the star carving on the Jesus Ossuary lid looks like a monogram to me of two separate symbols: a *T* and my Hooked X. Of course, I may be seeing what I want to see, but the top bar/ line of the *T* is slightly below the intersecting lines in the middle of the *X*. What do you think?"

He quickly responded, "Dear Scott: The top bar line of the *T* is certainly off line with the Hooked X—a seven pointed star with one of the points diverging into a *V*. I did not notice it in that way before."

I later explained, after a quick internet search of first-century alphabets, the symbols represented the first and last symbols of the Hebrew alphabet and postulated they represented the esoteric concept of *alpha-omega*, the beginning and end.

Excitedly, I started rattling off questions, "Did you take these pictures? When did you take them? Where did you find these symbols?"

A few minutes later my computer dinged and I read his reply, "Yes, I took the pictures a few years ago using a flashlight at a low angle to highlight the inscription, and yes, you're right. It's not a star symbol at all. The lines in the middle are not at the center and it does look like the symbols you suggest. I also agree with your interpretation, it represents one of the enduring legacies of Jesus, they no doubt represent the alpha and omega, beginning and end."

Carved into the lid of the Jesus ossuary from the Talpiot Tomb is a monogram of two important symbols. One is the Hooked X, and the second, just below the intersection of the *X* is the Egyptian-style tau cross. The Hebrew *aleph* (Hooked X) and Aramaic tau symbols likely represent alpha-omega—beginning and end. (Courtesy of Charles Pellegrino, 2014)

Amazingly, carved into the lid of the Jesus Ossuary from the Talpiot Tomb is a monogram of two important symbols. One is the Hooked X. The second symbol is carved just below the intersection of the *X* and is the Egyptian-style tau cross. After researching the symbols and various first-century alphabets there was no question this was the stone carver's version of the Hebrew *aleph* (Hooked X) and Aramaic tau symbols likely representing alpha-omega—beginning and end.

Charlie and I exchanged numerous emails and phone calls over the next several days and weeks as the enormity of the discovery sank in. The importance of these previously overlooked carved lines into the lid of the famous limestone box was crystal clear to both of us. For me, it was confirmation of the origin of the Hooked X symbol that first appeared on the highly controversial Kensington Rune Stone in 2000. What started off as a question of forensic geology quickly morphed into an investigation whose evidence trail traced back through the Cistercians to the Templars, and ultimately to Jerusalem. That journey culminated into the long forgotten first-century tomb in the east Talpiot neighborhood that was accidentally re-discovered in 1980.

Charlie's mention of the star-like symbol prompted me to go back to read the section in his and Simcha's 2007 book about the symbols on the "Jesus, son of Joseph" ossuary:

> In the case, the most glaring anomaly of all (if the cross was to be explained away as a mason's mark) was that instead of being matched by a large cross (or a cross of any kind) on the lid of the "Jesus" ossuary, there was, on the lid, a *V*, or chevron, and a deeply incised, six-spoked star (with one of its spokes diverging into a barely discernible *V*). What the cross, the star, and the *V* meant, they had no precedent in the realm of mason's marks.

When I first read this paragraph almost eleven years ago I had no idea what they were talking about, but after studying Charlie's photos things suddenly made sense. In one image, the tight *V*, or chevron symbol, is faintly visible below and slightly left of the Hooked X/Tau Cross symbol. It is still unclear to me what the chevron symbol may represent. However, I wholeheartedly agree with Simcha and Charlie's argument that neither the large *X* carved in front of "Jesus, son of Joseph" on the side of the box, the chevron, or Hooked X/Tau Cross symbols have anything to do with matching "makers marks" for lining up the lid on the box. Skeptics and doubters are sure to differ, but it is clear to me, Charlie, Simcha, and many other researchers these are stand-alone symbols with important meaning.

My joint discovery with Charlie Pellegrino of the Hooked X/Tau Cross was so important to my research I was determined to see the monogram with my own eyes, but knew that would be easier said than done. However, it occurred to me there might

One of Charlie Pellegrino's photos he sent of the lid of the "Jesus, son of Joseph" ossuary on May 24, 2014 has a tight chevron symbol (circled) carved approximately two inches below and left to the Hooked X/Tau Cross monogram. Other holes and marks on the surface are worm burrows and debris. (Courtesy of Charles Pellegrino, 2004)

be an opportunity. The Dead Sea Scrolls exhibition had recently concluded at the Minnesota Science Museum in St. Paul, and was currently on exhibition in Los Angeles, California. I did not attend the exhibition when it was here because I was unaware the Talpiot tomb ossuaries were part of it. It was not until after the Dead Sea Scrolls Exhibition had left town, that my friend and Talpiot tomb researcher, Jerry Lutgen, informed me that the Jesus and Mary Magdalene ossuaries were part of the display.

As luck would have it, the last stop for the exhibit was Los Angeles, California, and Janet and I had already made plans for a family vacation in San Diego during that time. Once we realized the fortuitous timing, we quickly agreed to take a day and drive to Los Angeles to see the exhibit.

On March 18, 2015, we jumped into the rental car in San Diego and made our way north to Los Angeles. Once at the California Science Center we bought tickets and made our way into the exhibit room. The ossuaries were inside a strangely designed display that had a tall glass viewing pane that was only about a foot wide. The stone boxes were placed on shelves and according to the interpretive sign the Jesus Ossuary was closest to the glass roughly a foot off the floor. Both Janet and I were surprised there was no mention of whose bones these boxes originally contained. One would think these names, that already had strong supporting evidence they were connected to the first-century royal family, would be included in the exhibit to boost attendance. There is no way it was a coincidence these ossuaries were randomly selected to simply show what first-century ossuaries looked like as was inferred by the display. It was truly bizarre and we still wonder if there was some alternate explanation?

The lighting was purposefully arranged to highlight the now familiar "Jesus, son of Joseph" inscription, with the large X in front of the name carved into the side of the 2000-year-old limestone box that was now only inches from my eyes. My heart raced as I knelt to scan the lid looking for the monogram. Unfortunately, the same overhead lighting that highlighted the vertically aligned inscriptions on the side of the box made it difficult to see the carvings horizontally oriented on the lid. Since I didn't know where on the lid the monogram was located, it took me a few seconds to find it. Suddenly, I saw it, and was surprised that it was larger than I imagined. I was also surprised to find the roughly one-inch tall symbol clearly carved on the inscription end of the lid. The symbol was carefully carved, centered perfectly, and placed in a prominent position on the lid due to its obvious importance.

Photographs were prohibited and, even if allowed, the direct overhead lighting would not have made for a good photo of the symbol. As soon as we exited the display area I immediately sat down at a table in the food court and sketched out what I had just seen on my exhibition ticket.

On the drive back to San Diego, my mind was spinning considering the historical implications of what we had just seen. If someone had told me the long and often tortuous evidence trail I had followed over the past fifteen years would eventually lead to the family burial tomb of Jesus and Mary Magdalene I would have laughed, but I am not laughing now. In fact, I am more involved than ever in this infinitely complicated

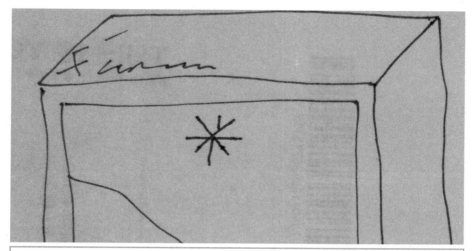

After seeing the Hooked X/Tau Cross symbol on the lid of the "Jesus, son of Joseph" in the Dead Sea Scroll Exhibition in Los Angeles, California, and not being allowed to take photographs, I drew a sketch of the symbol on my exhibition ticket. (2015)

and controversial investigation as we confidently stride into 2019. I am now armed with a boatload of scientific evidence that has blazed a trail to the truth about some of the most important moments in human history. What started out as a rather straight-forward scientific laboratory investigation plunged into the deepest recesses and dark caverns of symbolism, allegory, and the secrets of ancient mysticism. Long ago I realized it was necessary to expand the research beyond my everyday world of scientific method and logic. It was my only chance of solving the multiple mysteries behind the people responsible for the many artifacts and sites in North America that have puzzled scholars for over three hundred and fifty years beginning with the Newport Tower.

My search for answers has not been a solitary venture by any means. There have been many people who have contributed valuable research, insight, and inspiration. Most notably my wife Janet, for without her the journey would have ended years ago. Many times, when I was stymied or had run into a dead end, she came to the rescue with what should have been obvious yet eluded me. As trite as it might seem, this male-female team with its infinite intricacies and dynamics was crucial to the progress we have made.

Tau Cross

The amazing discovery of the Hooked X/tau Cross on the Jesus Ossuary in the Talpiot Tomb brings the search for the Hooked X full circle and solidifies the historical and ideological threads of the mission of the Venus Families quest to establish the New Jerusalem where they could pursue their spiritual journey unencumbered by dogmatic religious entities. The 3500-year long journey was completed with the establishment of the United States of America. While not a perfect utopia by any means, with the

The 110-pound bar of lead was discovered on a shipwreck in Pirate Cove in Isle St. Marie, Madagascar, in May of 2015. Discoverer Barry Clifford believes the ship is the Adventure Galley, scuttled in 1698 by the notorious pirate, Captain Kidd. The Triple Tau, seen here inside the equilateral triangle on the flap of a Masonic apron, is the most important symbol in Royal Arch Masonry and first appeared in Masonic writings around 1740. See color section for detail (Photograph courtesy of Rob Sixsmith, 2015)

recent ushering in of the new 26,000-year-long cycle known as the Precession of the Equinoxes, on December 21st of 2012, now is as good a time as any to pause and reflect. As I wrote in *Akhenaten*, the New Age of Aquarius was not only the beginning of a very long astronomical cycle, but should also be the beginning of a new age of truth and understanding about our past. As we learn new facts we need to use that knowledge to make better decisions globally to steer our species in a more positive and productive path going forward.

One of those exciting paths is researching the historical development of the tau cross from the time it was carved on the Jesus Ossuary in the first century. The discoveries made during my trip to Old Goa, India, were enlightening in many ways including my understanding of the Tau Cross. An important moment in this research occurred in May 2015 when Barry Clifford pulled out a 110-pound bar of what he thought was silver, but turned out to be lead. Clifford said it came from the captain's quarters of the Fiery Dragon ship that was reportedly scuttled in Pirate Cove on the island of Isle St. Marie, in Madagascar, by the notorious pirate Captain Kidd in 1698. [92] Once Clifford surfaced, he noticed two large symbols carved into the bar. What at first glance looked like a stylized capitol *T* and an *S*, didn't look quite right, especially when he looked at the number *95* stamped into the bar twice, presumably for the year 1695 when the bar was cast. When rotated one hundred and eighty degrees, the *T* looked very different and was a very important symbol in Freemasonry. I instantly recognized it as a triple tau.

The triple tau symbol is exactly what it sounds like, three tau crosses joined to-

---

92   A debate raged shortly after the metal bar was discovered on whether it was silver as Barry Clifford claimed, or if it was lead. Many people asked my opinion, but since I never saw the bar during the filming of the show I had no idea. A few weeks later I heard the bar was made of lead. If so, an argument could be made it was worth just as much, or perhaps more than silver. In the pirate culture at that time, silver was sometimes used as ballast whereas lead was valuable for use as ammunition. Despite this, for my purposes regarding the Triple Tau symbol on the metal bar, it did not matter if it was made of lead or silver.

gether at their bases. Upon realizing the connection of the triple tau with Freemasonry, and the tau cross within the monogram carved on the lid of the Jesus Ossuary, my first thought was to wonder if there could be a connection to the medieval Knights Templar. Like so many other symbols with connections to both Freemasonry and the Knights Templar, the triple tau was a natural to be included in that discussion. However, due to the presence of the tau cross on the Jesus Ossuary lid the importance of the triple tau suddenly increased in its significance and priority. The answers to the many questions that arose about the triple tau were found in a book recommended to me by a very knowledgeable friend who was of course, a Freemason. *Freemasons' Book of the Royal Arch*, by Bernard E. Jones, was a wealth of info that started with the realization the triple tau was the most important symbol of Royal Arch Masonry which dates back to the official start of Freemasonry when four English lodges joined together in 1717.

The triple tau symbol on Barry Clifford's metal bar was initially puzzling. This example predates the earliest recorded appearance of the symbol associated with Freemasonry by roughly a half-century. The *Encyclopedia of Freemasonry and Kindred Sciences*, by Albert G. Mackey, cites the origin of the Royal Arch Degree as beginning no earlier than the "…fourth decade of the eighteenth century." This meant that either the Royal Arch degree dates back much farther than was previously thought or it is associated with something else. The only other logical avenue of investigation to pursue was to determine if the triple tau was associated with the Portuguese Order of Christ, given their known presence of on Isle St. Marie, in Madagascar. Pursuing research in that direction paid immediate dividends.

The historical beginning of the Tau Cross, like so many other aspects of research into Freemasonry and Templarism, ultimately goes back to Egypt. According to Jones, the original Tau Cross was a simple *T*-shaped flood gauge used for measuring the water level of the Nile River. The lifeblood of the people in Egypt was directly dependent on the rise and fall of the Nile. If the river's water in the spring was too low, there would be drought and famine among the people. If too high, floodwaters would destroy their stores and homes leading to devastation of the people. Thus, the T-shaped flood gauge became an important symbol of life, and later, a talisman in Egyptian culture believed to avert evil and ward away sickness and disease. A loop was added to the Tau Cross making it the most common and important symbols in all ancient Egypt—the Ankh was symbolic of eternal life.

To have the tau cross so prominently featured on the lid of the Jesus Ossuary speaks volumes about his reported Egyptian heritage. Further, being intertwined with the Hooked X is also consistent with his ancestral connection to Egypt. In 2009, I argued the Hooked X symbol almost certainly evolved from the crossed crook and flail featured so prominently in the imagery of Pharaoh Akhenaten and his son, Tutankhamun.[93] The crook and flail represented the Egyptian gods Osiris and his wife, Isis. Crossed on the chest, the rods symbolize kingship and royalty. The hook at the end of the crook held the eggs of fertility.

---

93   Wolter, pages 86-98, 2009.

Coptic Christianity

In trying to understand the progression of the Hooked X/tau cross symbolism through time, it becomes rather murky after the first century. Specifically, how did the Hooked X symbol make its way over nearly a millennium to the medieval Templar tradition? It seems clear to me the Hooked X/tau cross appearing together as a monogram on the Jesus Ossuary in the Talpiot tomb is powerful evidence the Biblical Yeshua (Jesus) and his followers practiced an early form of Egyptian Christianity, and may have been early Coptic Christians.[94] The tau cross is a huge clue. Its Egyptian origin as the most iconic and important hieroglyphic of the symbol for life and resurrection, and it is perfectly appropriate carved into the ossuary lid. The connection to Egyptian iconography is further supported by the Hooked X symbol. I have long argued this is another iconic Egyptian symbol representing the new religion of Monotheistic Dualism Pharaoh Akhenaten ushered in over 1400 years before Jesus.

The Hooked X/tau cross provides compelling evidence of the form of Christianity, or Christ consciousness, defined as the highest state of intellectual development and emotional maturity, many believe Jesus and the people in his sect practiced.[95] This would suggest there was an Eastern mysticism influence in early Christianity which could very well have been possible. It has long been rumored Jesus spent years studying in India during the "missing years" of his life. If true, this could explain the Eastern Buddhist influence on the faith he would eventually teach. If Coptic Christ Consciousness Christianity (CCCC) was indeed practiced by the first-century royal family, it appears the ideology continued in secrecy as it had to for survival after the Roman Siege of Jerusalem circa AD 70. The two deeply meaningful symbols tell us a lot about the true ideology of the core members of medieval Templar/Cistercian leadership they appear to have inherited.

Like most symbols, the crook and flail have multiple symbolic meanings. One of which, related to Akhenaten, is directly connected to the precession of the equinoxes, a 26,000-year long cycle for the twelve primary constellations of the zodiacal belt that encircles the earth. Because of the slight wobble of the Earth, those constellations cycle through the eastern horizon. When the sun rose through the constellation at dawn on the spring equinox ancient astronomer priests deemed the event sacred. The length of time the constellation was present was labeled a "great year" by ancient astronomers. When the constellation eventually descended below the eastern horizon taking an average of 2167 years (26,000 ÷ 12 = 2167), the age changed and a new constellation replaced the previous one signaling the beginning of a new "great month."

When Akhenaten came to power in Egypt roughly 3,350 year ago, the age of Taurus the Bull was ending as the large constellation disappeared below the horizon and the age of Aries the Ram was ushered in.[96] That important change in the ages is

94   http://www.coptic.net/EncyclopediaCoptica/
95   https://www.gotquestions.org/Christ-consciousness.html
96   http://www.bbc.co.uk/history/ancient/egyptians/akhenaten_01.shtml

This stylized carving of the world is on the wall just below the clock on the tower next to the church dedicated to John the Baptist in Tomar, Portugal. The 45-degree angled band circling the globe represents the belt of the twelve primary constellations of the zodiac. The small sphere at the center represents the earth with the celestial sky surrounding it. On top of one of the two pillars in a Masonic lodge is a celestial sphere with a zodiacal band of the twelve primary constellations. (2015/Internet)

symbolized by the flail, which herds the bulls of Taurus symbolic of the followers of the old religion of Polytheistic Dualism. The crook herds the sheep of Aries symbolic of followers of the new religion of Monotheistic Dualism.[97] The two symbols crossed on his chest represented Akhenaten's attempt to unite the two religions which history shows failed. It is thought by many researchers that the followers of the new religion of Monotheistic Dualism were driven out of Egypt which is chronicled in the Bible and known as the Exodus.[98] That was how I believe Akhenaten's new religion made it into the Middle East, the Cistercians, Knights Templar and other traditions who embrace monotheism, and ultimately to Freemasonry.

Most historians and archaeologists do not understand why Akhenaten tried to change the religion in Egypt because they do not understand the importance of astronomy, precession of the equinoxes, and the ancient concept of "as above, so below." In other words, the ancient astronomer priests understood how the interactions between the sun, moon, planets, stars and constellations impacted life on earth for as long as humans have looked up into the night sky.

To the Cistercians and their Templar brethren, the Hooked X carried the same symbolism as the crossed crook and flail with Jesus (∧), Mary Magdalene (*V*) and their offspring with the little *v* symbolic of a daughter esoteric legends say was named Sarah, and served as a first-century allegorical analog to Osiris, Isis and their offspring. To have a monogram of two Egyptian symbols that includes one that is symbolic of what

97   https://www.merriam-webster.com/dictionary/dualism

98   https://www.sigmundfreud.net/moses-and-monotheism.jsp

This example (left) shows the Egyptian Ankh is a Tau Cross with an egg-shaped handle. Egyptian Pharaohs Tutankhamun (middle) and his father Akhenaten (right) both have the crossed Crook and Flail across their chests which was the earliest known representation of the Hooked X symbol and the ideology of Monotheistic Dualism it represents. (Internet/Internet/Internet)

Roman Christianity would later call the Holy Trinity (crossed crook and flail/Hooked X), and the other representing resurrection and eternal life (tau cross/ankh) carved into the limestone lid of the ossuary of what appears to be the biblical Jesus now seems perfectly appropriate.

One must always think of symbols in levels because they usually have multiple meanings. With this in mind it appears very likely the Hooked X/tau cross on the lid of the Jesus Ossuary has another possible meaning that is directly connected to the Biblical Jesus. Many have speculated the Hooked X symbol is a straight lined, carved-into-stone version of the Hebrew *aleph*, the first character in the Hebrew/Aramaic alphabet. The tau is the nineteenth character in the Greek alphabet, and *Tav* is the last letter in the Hebrew alphabet. This suggests the monogram could be the equivalent of *alpha-omega*. In the Bible Jesus reportedly said, "I am the alpha, omega, beginning and the end." Perhaps the Hooked X/Tau Cross symbol on his ossuary is evidence that the Biblical passage was indeed uttered by Jesus in his lifetime?

Five examples of the triple tau symbol I found on grave slabs within two churches in Goa, India. Four examples shown here were near the altar in the church at the ruined monastery dedicated to St. Augustine that date to between 1695 and 1706. The fifth example was on a grave slab near the high altar at the Church of Francis of Assisi built in 1661. (2015/2015/2015)

Getting back to the triple tau on Barry Clifford's metal bar, we eventually learned the original meaning of the symbol was a *T* over the *H* emblem which meant *Templum Hierosolymæ* or the Temple of Jerusalem.'The triple tau symbol can also be read as an *I* over *H* and a first-century Christogram of the Greek letters, *I* (*iota*) and *H* (*eta*), the first two letters for the Greek spelling of the name Yeshua/Jesus. Reportedly, an *S* was added in the second-century creating the well-known symbol of Christianity, *IHS*. Interestingly, a stylized *S* is also on the metal bar from Captain Kidd's scuttled ship in Madagascar. This begs the question, is it somehow related to the *IHS* and the Biblical Jesus? Considering the presence of the Portuguese Templars in the Indian Ocean for several centuries and specifically in Goa, India, a settlement they founded in 1510, the triple tau on the metal bar as a reference to Jesus begins to make sense.

Upon my arrival in Goa, my primary goal was to try and find a connection between the Triple Tau and the Portuguese Templars, who changed their name to the Order of Christ after the put-down in 1307. The King of Portugal was not about to disband the paid military force that protected the country from the invasion of the Moors from the south. King Afonse Henriques awarded the Templars roughly one-third of his territory for the knights' service.[99] The Portuguese Templars continued as the Knights of Christ for another 500-plus years until the Queen of Portugal ordered their dissolution in 1835.

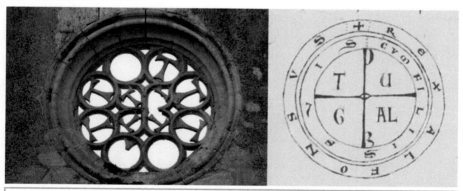

Twelve Tau Crosses, the outer eight within circles, are carved in stone in the now ruined rose window of the Church of the monastery and hospital of St. Anthony of Castrojeriz, in Spain. It was founded by King Alfonso VII, in 1146, with the aim of attending to pilgrims traveling along the Camino de Santiago and underscores the importance of the Tau Cross in Christianity. On the charter issued by King Afonse Henriques in 1159, he placed a seal that the initiated in esoterica could read as "Port tu Gral" (Port of the Grail).[100] (Internet/Internet)

The theory the Templars entered the Talpiot tomb at the time of the First Crusade, saw the Hooked X/Tau Cross monogram on the lid of the "Jesus, son of Joseph" ossuary, and thereafter used both as secret symbols of reverence to Jesus seems very plausible. It seems especially plausible if they removed at least some of the bones of Jesus (and

99   http://www.viewzone.com/templar/templar.html

100   https://esotericastrologer.org/newsletters/virgo-2016/#vir

Mary Magdalene) from their ossuaries as appears to have been the case.[101] Looking at the evidence so far, both symbols took on significance after the early twelfth century. At the same time, knowledge of the Templars having entered the tomb of the biblical Jesus appears to have been preserved within artwork by artists initiated into secret societies sworn to preserve it. Let us now take a look at examples of symbolism and the secret knowledge it preserves that have recently come to light.

---

101   Some believe the Templars brought the Mariamene Ossuary with her bones back from France to be reunited with her husband as part of their mission in Jerusalem during the First Crusade citing it being the only one with the inscription carved in Greek.

CHAPTER 10:

SUMMARY OF SYMBOLISM

The reader should find this chapter particularly interesting as it will help give a better understanding and appreciation for the language of symbolism related to this immensely complex historical investigation. The phrase "hidden in plain sight" is especially appropriate as so much symbolism related to this research has been encrypted into many famous works of art. We should start with one of the most interesting and common symbols in artwork that was introduced to the world on the last two shows of *America Unearthed*, titled "Tracking the Templars:" the so-called M-sign. The M-sign is a hand gesture where the subject's middle and ring fingers are held together, or with one finger overlapping the other, with the index and pinky fingers separated creating an *M* when the hand is pointing downward. In some works of art, it is obvious and overt while in other works it is subtler.

M-Sign

My research into this symbol shows that it began to appear in paintings and sculptures shortly after the put down of the Templars in 1307. Many have speculated that members of the fugitive Templar order disappeared into practical stonemasons' guilds who constructed the massive Gothic cathedrals, churches, and abbeys financed primarily by the Knights Templar and their supporters. While stone masons were important and highly revered for their craft skills, people often forget about the artisans who beautified those amazing buildings with paintings and sculptures. These artists had very special skills and knowledge passed on through progressive initiation rituals similar to the stonemason guilds. Painters, sculptures, metallurgists and experts in glassworks, especially stained glass, were highly skilled. Members of these unique orders held secrets of their craftwork very tightly. They also held onto secret information they preserved and passed on in their artwork. Arguably, during medieval times the most important secret was the truth about the marriage and family bloodline of Jesus and Mary Magdalene. It is speculated many members of the craft guilds were direct descendants and it was their own family lineage secrets they were helping to preserve. In most cases, this occurred right under the nose of the Roman Catholic Church, who in their minds were perpetuating lies about their ancient ancestors, their belief systems and traditions.

The letter *M* is the 13th letter of the alphabet since the time the letter *J* has existed and it should come as no surprise this number was branded as bad or evil by the Roman Church. The Church knew the secret and clearly understood the symbolic importance of the number. I will delve deeper into this shortly. While it is highly unlikely any Church documents will ever surface to prove their real motive, it was certainly no accident the date the arrest order was issued for the Templars was October 13 of 1307. Without a doubt the Roman Church selected that day as a way of sending a message to the Templars, and their Venus Families supporters, they weren't going to let anyone interfere with the Divinity of Jesus myth that made them so wealthy. It was after the put down in 1307 that the remaining Templars went underground and turned their attention in earnest to North America.

What many people do not realize is the arrest order only affected the members of the Templar order in France along with a couple of aging knights who were arrested in England. However, throughout the rest of Europe and Scandinavia they were essen-

At the Templar Commandery of Sur Aude in France, this statue of Jesus is making the M-sign with his left hand on his heart perhaps symbolizing his love for his wife, Mary Magdalene, and his right extended in the M-sign showing the stigmata. It is interesting he is depicted as very much alive and bleeding, as if human, and having survived the Crucifixion (left). This portrait of Mary Magdalene depicts her arms across her chest in the "Osiris" pose with her left hand making the M-sign (right). (2015/internet)

146

In a Time-Life book Janet Wolter found a picture taken inside a Dreamer Cult lodge of the Nez Percés tribe taken in 1860 (top). Sitting amongst dozens of fellow tribesmen and women in the front and center wearing white is the prophet Smohalla. His left hand is on his chest clearly making the M-sign with what appears to be a sacred Mi'gis shell between his ring and middle fingers (bottom left and right).

tially unaffected. It was a devastating blow to the order to be sure, but to say all Templars were rounded up and the order was permanently crushed is not true. As we just learned, in Portugal, the Templars simply changed their name to the Order of Christ and continued for another five centuries. As we will soon learn, the order also survived clandestinely in Scotland. The fact is, the Venus Families who founded and comprised the leadership of the Templars never went away. All they did was change the plan by setting their sights on a New Jerusalem in North America.

After the "Tracking the Templars" episodes of *America Unearthed* aired, and we had revealed the meaning of the hand gesture, my email became flooded with examples of the M-sign people were discovering for themselves. People wrote how surprised they were they had not noticed the hand gesture in art before and nearly everyone was positively excited about the revelation. Many were surprised the hand gesture had been out there in plain view for so many centuries and is still alive and thriving in modern artwork.

The most surprising and interesting examples came to light in the summer of 2015 when my wife, Janet, was in the dentist's office. While waiting to get her teeth cleaned, she found something shocking while paging through an old Time-Life book from the *Old West* series titled, *The Great Chiefs*. She excitedly texted me a photo from the book and I could hardly believe what I saw. It was a picture taken in 1860, inside a Dreamer lodge of the Nez Percé tribe, with the prophet Smohalla sitting amongst dozens of fellow tribesmen and women with his left hand on his chest clearly making the M-sign. While shocked at first, I realized that since the medieval Templars and certain Native American tribes had intermarried, forming strategic alliances and sharing sacred rituals, seeing this symbol being flashed by a Native American spiritual leader made perfect sense.

While looking more closely at his hand and the positioning of his fingers, there was no mistake it was the M-sign. However, it also looked like there was something very small between his middle and ring fingers. It looked like a small pebble and then it occurred to me it was likely a sacred mii'gis shell that resembles a cowrie shell.[102] It appears the M-sign is a sacred hand gesture alluding to the same secret knowledge the medieval Templars had within a secret society of the Nez Percé.

Now that the reader is aware of the M-sign, be on the lookout for the hand gesture and you will be surprised how often you see it. What it tells you is the artist, and often the subject of the artwork, was initiated into a tradition that understood and passed along the truth about the secret lineage of the biblical Jesus, his wife, Mary Magdalene, their children and other family members. Many of these artists are direct descendants of the first-century royal family, or their supporters, who preserved this secret knowledge of the humanity of Jesus and his marriage that was passed down to them. What is not a secret, was the Roman Catholic Church's brutal, and sometimes desperate efforts, to suppress this knowledge using persecution and often genocide. What happened to

---

102   https://www.sas.upenn.edu/dpic/traditionalmedicine/interviews/transcendingtime

the Cathars in the thirteenth century, and the indigenous people in North America after contact, was due in large part to wiping out those with knowledge that could potentially bring down the religious institution that perpetrated the biggest lie humanity has ever seen.

On the outside of St. Andrew's Church, at Foley Square in New York City, is a statue of St. Andrew holding the X-shaped cross he was supposedly crucified on. What struck one of my Twitter followers, @TruthSeeker2160, was how the sculptor placed the left arm of St. Andrew over the upper right arm of the cross making a Hooked X with his hand making the M-sign. (2018)

13

The Templars, the Venus Families, Native Americans and other traditions throughout history have always held the number 13 sacred, often sending out troops into battle, or knights on their ships in groups of 13, or groups of 26 (2 x 13) as symbolic acknowledgement of the Goddess/Deity to provide strength, courage and protection. This is why the Roman Catholic Church and the King of France, Philip the Fair, chose Friday, October 13, 1307, to arrest, torture, and burn at the stake over 100 Templar Knights in France. It was a not-so-subtle message to their ideological enemy they would no longer tolerate their covert veneration of the Goddess. The subsequent demonizing of the number 13 by the Roman Catholic Church as bad luck is still ingrained in society to this day, and almost no one understands why. However, the negative stigmatism toward the number 13 is changing with some embracing the number as good luck, especially when they understand its true history.

In fact, the number 13 is associated with the sacred feminine and the positive virtues of women. Most esoteric researchers trace the origin of the association of the number 13 with woman, in part, to the number of lunar months in a calendar year. A lunar month can be divided into two types. The first is called the "sidereal orbital period" which is how long it takes the moon to complete one 360-degree revolution around earth which is 27.3 days. The second is the "synodic month" or cycle, which is the time it takes for one new moon to the next new moon which is 29.5 days.[103] The average number of days for each cycle is approximately 28 days, the average length of a woman's menstrual cycle, which occurs 13 times in a calendar year, hence the logical link to women with the moon.

In esoteric circles, the number 13 is also associated with another physical manifestation of the Goddess in the heavens—the planet Venus. There are several important, highly accurate and reliable cycles associated with Venus that ancient astronomers have documented for thousands of years when its movements are carefully tracked. We will learn more about the cycles of Venus later in the book, but what is arguably the most important of all relates to eight earth years. If we multiply eight by the number of days in one earth year, (365 x 8 = 2,920 days), and then divide the number of days in one Venus year, which is 224.6 days (2,920 divided by 224.6), the result is 13. In other words, for every eight times earth revolves around the sun, Venus will revolve around the sun 13 times. As we find throughout Freemasonry and Templarism, it seems that every esoteric concept or idea traces back to legends in Egypt. The same is true with the number 13.

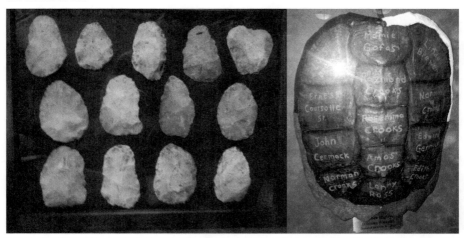

This cache of 13 scrapers buried in the past by a Native American was discovered by Marion Kincaid in a field in Kansas in 2016 (left). The turtle shell is considered sacred by Native Americans ,due in part to the 13 plates, called scutes, of the top of the shell, called the carapace (right). (Courtesy of Marion Kincaid/2018)

103 https://community.dur.ac.uk/john.lucey/users/lunar_sid_syn.html

There are 13 five-pointed stars in the seals of these branches of the United States government. (Internet)

Some might argue the number 13 represents the 12 constellations of the zodiac plus the sun, or Deity around which the constellations revolve. It's a good rule to know when studying the esoteric side of symbolism that regardless of which ancient culture's myths and legends you study there will ultimately be a connection to some aspect of astronomy.

Native Americans also hold certain numbers sacred and 13 is definitely one of them. Native cultures also kept close track of the movements of the heavenly bodies which included the moon and Venus, both considered to be associated with the sacred feminine or the Goddess (Great Mother). One example of the veneration of the Goddess by Native Americans was in the number of arrowheads or scrapers buried in the ground as an offering or cache to be recovered at some future time. The number of artifacts was an acknowledgement of the Goddess and/or a plea for protection for the important stash in hopes of still being there upon the owner's return.[104]

The number 13 is disproportionately featured on the back of the one-dollar bill —six times on the bald eagle side alone. In addition to the 13 rows of stones in the unfinished pyramid, there is the same number of letters in *E Pluribus Unum*, leaves and berries on the olive branch in the left claw, arrows in the right claw, stripes in the shield and stars above the eagle's head that are from the Seal of Solomon. (2017)

104   https://www.facebook.com/marion.kincaid/videos/g.285220768263598/1206201046124870/?-type=2&theater

The thesis that Washington D.C. is the City of the Goddess is convincingly argued by Alan Butler in his 2011 book, *City of the Goddess: Freemasons, the Sacred Feminine, and the Secret Behind the Seat of Power in Washington, DC,* and by Alan and Janet Wolter's book, *America, Nation of the Goddess: The Venus Families and the Founding of the United States.* Not only do we find undeniable symbolism in the numerous goddess statues in the capital city, and throughout all cities of the nation that reflect veneration of the sacred feminine, but we also see the number 13 quietly, yet undeniably woven into the symbolism of our country. It began with the 13 colonies that comprised the first union of territories that would become the United States. In virtually every great Seal of the major branches of American government, and of the individual fifty states and Puerto Rico, there is at least one five-pointed star, which is emblematic of the planet Venus. This is also the physical manifestation of the Goddess in the heavens, and quite often there will be 13 five-pointed stars.

Once armed with this knowledge it is a wonder anybody today would consider the number 13 to be anything other than sacred. Our own government quietly venerates this important number by prominently featuring it on the most common currency we carry in our wallets—the one-dollar bill. On the back side, we see the pyramid with the all-seeing eye on the left and the bald eagle on the right. Take a moment and count the number of horizontal beads on both ends in the middle of the bill, rows of stones in the pyramid, letters in the Latin phrases, *annuit coeptis* (Providence favors our cause) and *e pluribus unum* (out of many, one), fig leaves and berries in the left claw, arrows on the right, stripes in our flag, and stars over the eagle's head. All these symbolic references to the number 13 are claimed by some to represent the number of original colonies. That may be true, but does anyone ever wonder if the final number of colonies was simply a matter of chance or was it also intentional all along?

Pi Sign

Have you ever looked at a painting or sculpture where the subject is holding a book or had their hand on their hip with the index finger in an isolated position? If so, it is likely due to the artist conveying the symbolic message of the acknowledgement and support of science which was embraced and promulgated throughout history by the Venus Families, the Templars, and modern Freemasonry. In this case, the index finger is isolated within a book with the three fingers on the outer part of the hand representing the number three. The index finger represents the number one and the collective of the fingers used to make the gesture, excluding the thumb, is four. The symbolic meaning of the hand gesture is the number 3.14, or Pi, which is used to calculate the area of a circle and for calculating distances on a sphere, which is a vital mathematical tool for navigating the oceans.

In this beautiful monument to the Fridley family carved in granite in Lakewood Cemetery, in Minneapolis, Minnesota (left), a Goddess figure sits contemplatively holding a book in her right hand. Upon closer inspection in the inset photo, her index finger is inside the book with her three remaining fingers on the outside in the symbolic hand gesture of 3.14 or Pi. This wall painting (right) inside the altar of the Convent of Christ Church in the Templar Castle in Tomar, Portugal, shows a woman clearly giving the Pi sign. (2018)

OSIRIS POSE/X

The Osiris Pose is an ancient symbol made by crossing the arms across the chest forming an *X* that dates back time immemorial and is still used by many cultures around the world, including within Freemasonry as a form of prayer. Arguably, the pose is most well known in the ancient world of Egypt as every pharaoh was buried with their arms in this position. Templar tradition maintains the *X* is a symbol of one who has been initiated in the ancient mysteries which includes, but not limited to, the knowledge of the seven classic arts and sciences. Templar knights buried with their legs crossed into an *X* was a symbol they had served in the Holy Land during the time of the Crusades.[105]

We also see the *X* symbol carved in front of the words, "Jesus, son of Joseph" on the controversial ossuary. There is a lot of debate as to what this particular large *X* symbol means. Amos Kloner, a doctorate student in 1980, and one of the two Israeli archaeologists to investigate the tomb, wrote a report in 1996 and dismissed the large *X* as a mason's mark made either by a stonemason or the person who originally placed the bones in the box.[106] Carvings of matching *X* or *V* symbols have been documented

---

105   Hogan, page 44, 2015.

106   Jacobovici and Pellegrino, page 79, 2007.

on ossuaries that were made for proper alignment of the lid with the box. These maker's-mark symbols are much smaller in size and there is no matching *X* symbol to line up with on the lid.

It appears this large stand-alone *X* symbol in front of the inscribed name was made by a knowledgeable follower, or family member, to indicate "Jesus, son of Joseph" was initiated in the ancient mysteries, as has long been known within mystical circles for two millennia.

This effigy on the tomb of a fallen Templar knight has his legs crossed into an *X* is symbolic that he served in Jerusalem during the Crusades. On the "Jesus, son of Joseph" ossuary from the Talpiot tomb in Jerusalem, there is a large *X* carved to the right and in front of the name inscribed in Hebrew. (Internet/Courtesy of Charles Pellegrino)

AVM

I showed many examples of *AVM* and its hidden reference to Mary Magdalene in my *Akhenaten* book, but did not fully explain its meaning. In Catholicism, *AVM* represents *Ave Virgo Maria* which is a reference to the Virgin Mary. However, one of the cardinal rules of symbolism is every symbol can have multiple meanings depending on the point of view of the person considering them. We must also keep in mind that in medieval times the Latin *U* and *V* were interchangeable.[107] In esoteric circles, *AUM* was an important concept that was symbolic of a female Deity to the Venus Families and the Templars, it refers only to their much-maligned ancestral queen Mary Magdalene. *AVM/AUM* was one of those symbols at the heart of the battle between the two diametrically opposed ideologies of Monotheistic Dualism and Roman Catholicism. The Venus Families were trying to hold onto the historically accurate story of dynastic succession from the first-century royal family; the other wanted to hold onto power

---

107   http://medievalwriting.50megs.com/scripts/letters/historyuv.htm

and control over the people using the Myth of Christ that persists to this day.

The *AVM* on the Kensington Rune Stone is surely a coded reference to Mary Magdalene, and you can be confident the medieval carver knew full well she never experienced virgin birth. As if to secretly underscore who he was referring to, the carver added a punch to the bottom right leg of the *M* some skeptics still try to claim is not there. In 2011, the presence of the punch was definitively proven. While my interpretation of the meaning of the punch does not prove that was why the carver put it there, when considered in context with the collective evidence presented in this book, it is far and away the most plausible reason the punch mark is there.

On line eight of the face side of the Kensington Rune Stone the carver added a punch to the bottom of the right leg of the *M* of the only three Latin letters in the inscription. Microscopic three-dimensional image mapping clearly shows the dot in the *M* exists. Some have claimed there is no dot. (2011)

COLORS OF MARY MAGDALENE

One of the keys to understanding the true identity of individuals in historical paintings and drawings of biblical scenes involving Jesus and Mary Magdalene are the colors used in the artwork. This is especially true when determining if a figure is Mary Magdalene or the Virgin Mary.

In the summer of 2015, Janet and I visited Monticello, in Virginia, the home of Thomas Jefferson and toured the residence and grounds paying special attention to symbolism in the architecture and artwork of the third President's home. There were several paintings in the parlor with interesting symbolism that immediately jumped out at us.

Jefferson (1743-1826) had numerous paintings, drawings, and sculptures of people he admired. Some were contemporaries he knew personally along with other well-known historical figures from Europe. Contemporaries included philosopher and writer, Francois Marie Arouet de Voltaire (1694-1778); philosopher and revolutionary, Thomas Paine (1727-1809); astronomer, David Rittenhouse (1732-1796); lawyer, author and second President of the United States, John Adams (1735-1826); naval commander, John Paul Jones (1747-1792); respected political rival, James Madison (1751-1836); historian, banker and botanist, William Roscoe, (1753-1831); James Monroe

(1758-1831); Robert Fulton (1765-1815); General and President, Andrew Jackson (1767-1845); French General and Freemason, Marquis de Lafayette (1757-1834); artist and musician Maria Cosway (1759-1838); explorer Meriwether Lewis (1775-1809); monarch, Tsar Alexander I (1777-1825); and one of the most important of America's Founding Fathers, Benjamin Franklin (1706-1790).

Interestingly, Jefferson also had a marble bust of Napoleon Bonaparte (1769-1821), whom he considered, "…a cold-blooded, calculating, unprincipled usurper, with a virtue."[108] However, he reportedly said to General Lafayette, "Your emperor has done more splendid things, but he has never done one which will give happiness to so great a number of human beings as the ceding of Louisiana to the United States."[109] These somewhat contradictory opinions about the famous emperor begin to make sense as we continue to flesh out our thesis of pre-Columbian Templars bringing treasure to North America.

The question central to my theory and to the thesis presented by my friend and brother Freemason, William F. Mann, in his 2016 book, *Templar Sanctuaries in North America: Sacred Bloodlines and Secret Treasures,* is did Thomas Jefferson give specific instructions to Meriwether Lewis during his famous expedition with William Clark to find the secret vault? Jefferson must have learned of the vault's whereabouts while he was the American Ambassador to France from 1785-89. If so, these top-secret instructions would not have been written down and were likely passed on to Lewis from "mouth to ear." Jefferson also created a cipher exclusively for private communications with Lewis using the keyword "Artichokes." However, Lewis found no need to use it during the expedition, but it begs the question why there was a need to such secrecy between only those two?[110]

Since there is no known written record of such orders given to Lewis by Jefferson, could there be any circumstantial evidence that lends credence to the existence of a secret vault in western North America? If we take a close look at the evidence, the first clue appears with Jefferson's famous purchase of North American land from the French Emperor in 1803, in a transaction famously known as the Louisiana Purchase.

To get a better understanding of this mystery, we need to look at the people Jefferson associated with while in France where he likely learned about pre-Columbian Templar/Venus Family activities in North America. Jefferson met many well-known and powerful people in his lifetime, but the three men Jefferson wrote he admired most were John Locke (1632-1704), Isaac Newton (1643–1727), and Francis Bacon (1561–1626), whom he called, "My trinity of the three greatest men the world had ever produced."[111] Francis Bacon died over a century before Jefferson was born, but it is highly likely he played an important role in the early stages of the founding of the United States.

108   Stein, page 225, 1993.
109   Stein, page 225, 1993.
110   https://www.monticello.org/site/jefferson/jeffersons-cipher-meriwether-lewis
111   Stein, page 128, 1993.

Any knowledge about secret activities in North America by the Templars would have been passed down through secret societies in Europe like Freemasonry. However, specific knowledge this sensitive would only be known within a very exclusive and extremely secretive organization. The reason was their true ideology and activities were diametrically opposed and considered heretical to both the monarchs of Europe and the Roman Catholic Church. Anyone known to be associated with these secret organizations was at risk of disappearing and being put to death in a very painful way. The most likely organization whose activities directly undermined the Church and feudalistic system was a mystical sect that was believed to be a later revival of the medieval Templars—the Rosicrucians.

The Rosicrucian order first came into public view in Europe with the publication of pamphlets by anonymous authors in Germany starting in 1614. In addition to delving deep into alchemy the pamphlets included commentary about the abuses of the Catholic Church and blatant corruption of the monarchies against the people. Thomas Jefferson embraced similar views having been involved in the American Revolution that stood up against these forces of evil opposed to freedom and personal liberty. One of the most common symbols used by the modern day Masonic Knights Templar represents their success of achieving freedom from the oppressive forces of the medieval military order by the monarchies of Europe—the Crown, and the Roman Catholic Church—the Cross. This makes even more sense in context with the successful establishment of the Free Templar State of the United States of America that officially began in the 1362 with the Kensington Rune Stone land claim.

One of the most common symbols of the modern-day Masonic Knights Templar is the Christian style cross inside a crown many think represents, Jesus, King of the Jews. The symbol's hidden meaning refers to the Templar's successful establishment of the United States of America where they enjoy personal liberty and freedom from oppression and thus defeated the monarchs of Europe—the Crown, and the Roman Catholic Church—the Cross. (2017)

According to Timothy Hogan, all three of Jefferson's most admired men were members of the Rosicrucian order, with Francis Bacon being the leader during his time.[112] Whether Jefferson was an official member of the Rosicrucians is not definitivly known.[113] However, his known ideology was completely consistent with Rosicrucian ideals, so whether officially a member or not, for all intents and purposes he was a Rosicrucian.[114] Within esoteric circles, it is well known the Rosicrucians evolved directly from the fugitive Knights Templar Order. So, it should come as no surprise they knew who made the Kensington Rune Stone land claim and who deposited at least some of the Temple Mount treasures in the secret vault, which according to William Mann, is located along the "Great Western Meridian" in present day Montana. Thus, Jefferson could have learned about both from his colleagues who were members of the Rosicrucians, also known as the "Order of the Rosy Cross." The secrets about Templar activities in North America would have been held extremely tight. At this critical time in history, it would have made sense to share these secrets with Thomas Jefferson.

Among the many paintings in his home were those of the explorers Sir Walter Raleigh (1552-1618), Christopher Columbus (1451-1506) and Amerigo Vespucci (1454-1512) confirming Jefferson's interest in the early exploration of the Americas. He also had a strong interest in the first-century biblical stories including the life of Jesus.

I was sent the following information in an email from an initiate of the Cathar Tradition in March of 2017:

"Lineage of Christ and Mary Magdalene.

- John the Baptist married Mary Magdalene and had a boy, Jesus David.

- After John's death, Mary married Christ and he adopted Jesus David, then they had two children:

- Sarah Demarie (Sp?) who married a barbarian king in the south of France.

- Yeshuah Joseph who married a princess from the barbarian kings.

- Through the[se] marriages the Merovingian Kings line was established."

This was certainly news to me, but upon reflection the idea began to make sense and prompted me to go back and look at certain Renaissance-era paintings because art was frequently used to hide secrets. Many paintings of the Holy family were based on the official story the world had been told by the Roman Catholic Church. However, what appeared to be depicted in these paintings is in fact, something else completely.

---

112   Hogan, page 102, 2007.

113   As reported in my *Akhenaten* book in 2013, Thomas Jefferson's name appears on a roll of the Lodge of Nine Sister's Masonic Lodge in France. It was listed as indirect evidence, so it's possible he may have been a member and therefore a Freemason. See Weisberger, William R. (Editor), *Freemasonry on Both Sides of the Atlantic: Essays Concerning the Craft in the British Isles, Europe, the United States, and Mexico*, page 296, 2002.

114   On page 325 of *Revelation of the Holy Grail*, author Chevalier Emerys lists, among many others, Benjamin Franklin, Thomas Jefferson, Thomas Edison, Leonardo Da Vinci, John Dee, Albert Einstein, Nikola Tesla, Henry Ford, Walt Disney, Ludwig Van Beethoven, Thomas Paine, J.R.R. Tolken, Jules Verne, Carl Jung, Nicholas Roerich, Albert Pike and Francis Bacon, as members of various Rosicrucian orders over the centuries.

(Left) In Leonardo Da Vinci's "Virgin on the Rocks," the first version painted in 1486, was rejected by his client the Brotherhood of the Immaculate Conception. Perhaps it was due to the "angel" with auburn colored hair wearing the Magdalene's green and orange colors and her pointing, with her fingers making a compass and square symbol, to her other child fathered by deceased husband John the Baptist, as she watches over the infant fathered by Jesus. The Virgin watches over the children with her extended left hand nearly touching the "Mother of Two." (Right) In the second version, Da Vinci removed the tell-tale colors of the Magdalene's clothing, her pointing finger and added wings to ensure we know the woman is merely an angel. Haloes were added to the children to remind us of their divinity with a Christian staff carried by the son of John the Baptist. (Internet) See color section for detail.

It has long been rumored in esoteric circles that the people depicted in the biblical-era artwork of certain initiated artists were actually not who they were long thought to be. Artists like Michelangelo di Lodovico Buonarroti Simoni (1475-1564), Sandro Botticelli (1445-1510), Michelangelo Merisi da Caravaggio (1571-1610), and Leonardo Da Vinci (1452-1519) were initiated into orders that held knowledge of the secret truths behind the first-century royal family. When viewing their work, and other artists works, through the lens of a different narrative some interesting things begin to emerge. One of the paintings by Da Vinci that always puzzled me was *Virgin of the Rocks*. In his original version, painted in 1483, the woman on the right, believed to be an angel, is wearing the green and orange colors of the Magdalene. Cathar tradition says Mary Magdalene was the mother of the sons of both John the Baptist and Jesus. In light of this, what is actually depicted is Mary Magdalene and her two sons with her right hand pointing to her older son born of the seed of John the Baptist.[115]

115   While explaining the symbolism of these paintings to professional artist and long-time friend, Dan Wiemer, he noticed the fingers on the pointing hand of Mary Magdalene, in the first edition of "Virgin on the Rocks," form angles of sixty and ninety degrees resembling the Masonic Compass and Square.

It is no wonder the client, the Brotherhood of the Immaculate Conception, objected to this original version and had Da Vinci paint a second version with important symbolic aspects of the original changed.[116] Whether the client fully understood what was actually being depicted is unknown, but as was his practice, along with many other initiated artists of that time, they made sure there was plenty of room for plausible deniability in their artwork to escape suspicion and possibly persecution from paranoid Church authorities.

Many artists painted the same imagery of what was supposed to be the Virgin Mary with John the Baptist and Jesus as infants. However, in light of the ancient secret knowledge I can never again look at these paintings and not see the Magdalene with her two sons. One rendition of the Holy family painting resides in the home of Thomas Jefferson and is a copy of the work by Raffaello Sanzio da Urbino, known as Raphael, acquired by the third president while he was in France. Both children are easily identified and even though the Magdalene's clothes are more consistent with the diagnostic blue cape of the Virgin, her true identity is revealed with the yellowish-orange colored sleeve of her left forearm, along with the M-sign in her left hand as she picks up the child born of the seed of Jesus.

This painting (left) of what is purported to be the royal family by Bronzino, circa 1540, could actually be a pregnant Magdalene, and her second husband Jesus, looking adoringly at their son Judah(?), and her son with John the Baptist. Symbolism of her true identity includes both her and her son of John the Baptist making the M-sign and three round towers looming in the distance. The early Aramaic meaning of Magdalene/Magdala is Tower.[117] Jefferson purchased this copy of a painting (right) of the royal family by Raphael, while in France as the American Ambassador. See color section for detail. Right: a pregnant Mary Magdalene lifts her son Jesus using her left hand making the M-sign as her older son looks on cradling a cross symbolic of his father, and the Magdalene's first husband, John the Baptist (right). (Internet/Internet)

---

116   http://www.louvre.fr/en/oeuvre-notices/virgin-rocks
117   https://themeaningofthename.com/magdala/

This intriguing sixteenth-century painting (left) by Jacopo da Pontormo shows an elderly Mary Magdalene in a tender embrace with who has to be her daughter, Sarah, as an adult. Both members of the royal family have faint halos with Mary dressed in green and orange and Sarah in black symbolic of her having been veiled from history or in darkness. If there were any doubt who the Magdalene is, her daughter confirms her identity with her right hand making the M-sign on her mother's shoulder. In this watercolor and ink drawing (right) by Andy Warhol, circa 1955, the green (hand making the M-sign) and reddish-orange (hair) colors symbolically associated with Mary Magdalene are obvious. Subtler symbolism in the image includes the vine winding around her middle finger with a bud about to flower representing the continuation of the physical bloodline, and the gold arm holding a golden chalice containing "bread" (Manna) to the lips of the Magdalene. (Internet/2016) See color section for detail.

Colors of Jerusalem

The colors of Jerusalem are yellow (gold), blue (royalty) and white (purity) and are synonymous with the Templars and their Monotheistic Dualism ideology. As with nearly everything associated with this subject matter, the trail invariably begins in Egypt and then moves into the Holy Land. From Jerusalem during the Crusades, the Templars brought new knowledge, tangible treasure, and a multitude of esoteric symbolism to Western Europe and Scandinavia, eventually crossing the Atlantic to the New World in earnest in the fourteenth century. During my travels around the world tracking the Templars, I noticed these colors paralleled the movement of Goddess veneration that is at the core of Monotheism.

While symbolic colors can be somewhat subjective there are ancient traditions still in use today that use colors to convey messages to the initiated. During my filming for History Channel, I had the opportunity to see these symbolic colors in some of the

The symbolic colors of Jerusalem are yellow, blue, and white and likely originated in Egypt and were adopted by the Knights Templar for use in their abbeys and churches after returning from the Holy Land and the Crusades. King Tutankhamen's sarcophagus is primarily adorned with gold and blue stones; (top left) the Dome of the Rock Temple in Jerusalem is adorned with mostly blue and yellow tiles beneath the gold dome (top right). The yellow, blue and white colors of Jerusalem are featured in the tiles that adorn the Lady Chapel's in both Santa Maria do Olival Church in Tomar, Portugal (bottom left), and the ruined Abbey of St. Augustine in Goa, India (bottom right). They were built by the Portuguese Knights Templar in Tomar in 1161, and the Order of Christ, in Goa circa early 1500's. (Internet, 2015/2015/2015) See color section for detail.

most iconic places the Knights Templar were known to visit. It started in Jerusalem on the Temple Mount when I had the opportunity to enter the amazingly beautiful, octagonal structure adorned with dominantly white (bottom half) and blue (top half) mosaics topped with a gold dome known as Dome of the Rock.

In the Templar headquarters of the Iberian Peninsula in Tomar, Portugal, the entire Lady Chapel next to the altar at Santa Maria do Olival Church is adorned with the yellow, blue and white tiles of Jerusalem. In Goa, India, where the Portuguese Order of Christ built a massive monastery dedicated to Saint Augustine, the only surviving original tiles in the ruins are comprised of the same three colors. These colors also adorn the Nova Scotia flag where, as we will see in the Cremona Document chapter, the Scottish Templars made the first of many landfalls in the New World. Somehow, not only were these now familiar colors incorporated into the design, along with red of the Templars, but the enduring symbol of Jerusalem itself; the Lion Rampant, is curiously facing left to the west.

If you look carefully, you will also see these important symbolic colors when you least expect it within modern Freemasonry, both in the United States and elsewhere around the world. The Templar trail of Jerusalem colors left a clear path over the past millennia from the Temple Mount in Old Jerusalem, to the New Jerusalem in North America. I don't believe it is a coincidence both the Nova Scotia Lion Rampant and the Exxon Mobil logo with the Cross of Lorraine tilted to the left/west are both red in color.

The yellow, blue and white colors of Jerusalem were revered by the Templars, and along with the color red adorn the flag of Nova Scotia (left), a place pre-Columbian Templars frequented numerous times prior to 1600. The compass and square logo outside the Grand Lodge of Minnesota also has Jerusalem colors (right). (2012/2013) See color section for detail.

Number of Deity

When researching the symbolism and ideology of the Knights Templar it quickly becomes apparent the number 8 was very important. In fact, it is arguably the most important number to the Templars and their ideological ancestors dating back to time immemorial. Examples of this sacred number are found in the octagonal architecture of their sacred spaces and religious houses. Examples include the spectacular two-story tower that rests on eight columns inside the altar of the church at the Templar Castle in Tomar, Portugal, as well as the exact same architecture of the Newport Tower in Rhode Island, to the eight equally spaced points of the Templar Cross. Eight is the number that permeates all that was sacred to the Templars because it is directly related to the physical manifestation of the Goddess in the heavens—the Planet Venus.

Why is the number eight associated with Venus you might ask? Upon learning this association, I was prompted to find out how many people in our society understood the origin was of the five-pointed star also known as the pentagram. I have asked many people over the years and rarely will someone know the correct answer. It speaks to the lack of understanding by the vast majority of people living in America today. Our country's history and knowledge of symbols are right in front of our eyes daily, such as the American flag we pledge allegiance to every day. Like so many symbols found in our world today, the origins of the five-pointed star are found in the night sky. As ancient astronomers tracked the movement of the third brightest heavenly body in the sky behind the sun and moon, they documented the symbol of a five-pointed star it made over a period of eight earth years. It probably goes without saying the middle of the pentagram is a pentagon and it is here where the esoteric knowledge gets interesting. A quick Google search of "golden ratio of the pentagram" results in numerous hits that explain the mathematical and geometrical aspects found within the five-pointed star and how the Golden Ratio within it is intertwined with all aspects of nature.

 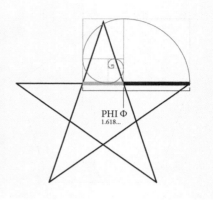

PHI Φ
1.618...

When astronomers track the movement of the planet Venus from earth during its eight-year cycle it creates a pentagram (left). The Golden Ratio is imbedded within the five-pointed star symbol as are other mathematical and geometrical aspects which in esoteric circles are called Sacred Geometry. (Internet/Internet)

Most people know the United States base of military operations is the Pentagon building in Washington, D.C., which was constructed with five sides, five rings and five floors. Is this a coincidence or yet another veiled reference by initiates who designed it to the Goddess planet in the night sky? Using basic gematria, three 5's = 555 and is the exact height in feet of the Washington Monument. Despite the obvious military purpose of the building as the brains behind the war machine for the United States, it could be argued the underlying significance of the pentagonal shape of the building and the association with Venus and the feminine aspects of the Goddess, is a symbolic reference to the underlying desire in our country for peace.

In esoteric circles, the number eight and its association with the planet Venus has always been symbolic of the Goddess in the heavens. The Templar's and their Cistercian brethren venerated the planet Venus, the sun, the planets and the constellations in the night sky. Veneration of these heavenly bodies is clearly on display in the Santa Maria do Olival church in Portugal.

When standing inside looking west, the large rose window is symbolic of the male consort of Venus, the sun. They are the ultimate symbols of Dualism that mystics called the eternal travelers. When Venus is a morning star, it rises before the sun leading her consort into the new day. Conversely, when Venus is an evening star, the sun sets in the west followed by the brightly shining planet slowly descending below the horizon in the darkness. Both heavenly bodies are symbolically represented in the church with the five-pointed star of Venus in the highest window in the east, and the large Rose window in the west representing the sun. However, because the number eight is so overwhelmingly represented in the architecture of the building, it suggests the medieval Templars venerated the sacred feminine of the Goddess above the male God. The beliefs that were important to the Portuguese Templars are incorporated into the architecture of Santa Maria do Olival. The symbolism of this medieval church provides a portal into the minds of the Templars who built it.

It has always puzzled me why the octagon and the number eight were, and still are, so prevalent in Templarism and Christianity. Most Christian churches incorporate octagonal architecture with the most obvious being the steeple. The Templar Cross has eight equally spaced points on its four arms, and let's not forget about the eight equally spaced columns in both the charola in the altar of the church at the Templar Castle in Tomar, and in the mysterious Newport Tower in Rhode Island. The answer as to why came from a friend named Ed Martinez, a Freemason, who has studied ancient esoteric aspects of the Eastern and Jewish mysteries.

Ed explained in the Jewish Kabbalah there are esoteric aspects to the science of numbers called gematria.[118] Each of the twenty-two Hebrew letters are assigned both an esoteric aspect, such as a constellation, planet, or the sun, and a numerical value starting with one and ending with 400. He relayed that every word in the Hebrew language can be assigned a single number using a mathematical concept called numerology reduction. "Let's take the name Jesus, or Yeshua as he was called in the first century, for example," Ed said. Each Hebrew letter in the name has a numerical value as follows: Yud = 10, Shin = 300, Vav = 6 and Ayin = 70. When those numbers are added together it equals 386. When numerology reduction is applied, the three numbers are added together, 3 + 8 + 6 = 17. To achieve the final single number, the 1 and 7 are added together to get 8.[119]

My eyebrows raised as Ed explained this ancient and ingenious mathematical process. "The number eight is associated with Deity or God," Ed said. Puzzled, I asked if this was because it was only due to the association with Jesus. I became even more confused knowing that Jesus was fully human after spending considerable time researching the Talpiot tomb, and being convinced the mortal remains of he and other

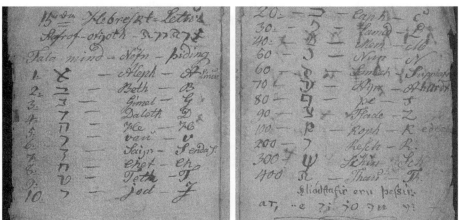

In Hebrew mysticism, gematria is the science of numbers where each letter in the Hebrew alphabet has a numerical value as seen in this hand-written eighteenth-century manuscript from Iceland. By adding the numeric values of the letters in a word or phrase, it results in a total that can be reduced to a single digit using a concept called numerology reduction. (Internet)

118   http://www.myjewishlearning.com/article/gematria/
119   https://astrologybay.com/hebrew-numerology

family members were interred there. Ed then said, "No, the reason is the number eight is associated with the ineffable Hebrew name of the Creator as found on the Tetragrammaton."

I was already familiar with the Tetragrammaton having explored its meaning in my *Hooked X* book. I had recited the Hebrew letter many times, Yod = 10, Heh = 5, Vav = 6, Heh =5. By applying numerology reduction, the numbers added together equal 26, and then when adding 2 + 6 = 8, we again arrived at the number of the Deity. This suddenly made sense and explained why the octagonal architecture associated with the Templars and their Cistercian brethren was so important and used in their most sacred structures.

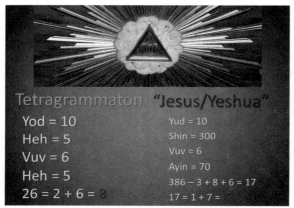

Using numerology reduction in the science of numbers called Gematria, the single number associated with Deity and represented on the name The Delta of Enoch, and of Jesus/Yeshua, is 8. (2016)

The realization the number eight was associated with Deity prompted a whirlwind of thoughts to rush through my head. For years, I had studied the rise of the Cistercians beginning with the first abbey at Cîteaux, France, that was founded in 1098, and eventually grew to about 700 monasteries by the year 1300. Eventually, they reached a total of 754 by the time of the French Revolution in 1789. The most sacred structures within the monasteries were a two-story, eight-sided fountain structure called a lavatorium. This fountain was where the monks would wash their heads, hands, and feet before and after every meal. In fact, one of the only surviving structures at the ruined monastery at Mellifont, in Ireland, is the lavatorium with rounded Romanesque arches between its eight columns that is eerily reminiscent of both the Newport Tower in Rhode Island, and the Templar charola in Tomar. It would be much later, after being raised as a Freemason, that I would understand the significance of the rounded arch Romanesque architecture between the eight columns of these structures.

All around us, especially in church architecture of all faiths and denominations, we see octagonal architecture designed to call down the power of Deity here on earth. The Cistercians, led by Bernard of Clairvaux who was deeply initiated into mysticism, certainly understood this sacred architecture and its Kabalistic roots. Clairvaux's own ancestry is rumored to trace back to Jesus and Mary Magdalene and the mystical Jewish Christianity they were teaching in their own time. Tracing this same line of research, I am convinced there is a bloodline connection between the first-century royal family, and their descendants and followers we have named the Venus Families. It was these wealthy families of like-minded ideology who founded the Cistercians and the Knights Templar. A strong argument can be made these bloodline families passed on the location of their ancestors tomb in Jerusalem to the Templars and therefore, are the only logical candidates to have entered the Talpiot Tomb at the time of the First Crusade. Who else would have had the knowledge of the location of the sacred tomb that was passed down through the family for generations? Who would have had the motivation to reportedly remove some of the bones of only the Yeshua and Mariamene ossuaries and leave three skulls on the floor of the burial chamber as symbolic guardians? And who else would have known where to correctly place those three skulls in the east, south, and west positions on the floor of the burial chamber where the three highest ranking officers sit in a Masonic Lodge or Templar Preceptory?

As I suggested in *Akhenaten* in 2013, there are clues permeating our modern society, from Disney princesses, to the utopian society story lines in the original Star Trek, to Oreo cookies' symbolism, and within certain Masonic rituals there are subtle clues about knowledge of the mortal remains of Jesus, Mary Magdalene, and other family members prior to the discovery of the Talpiot tomb in 1980.

I should remind the reader that my research over the past decade has revealed

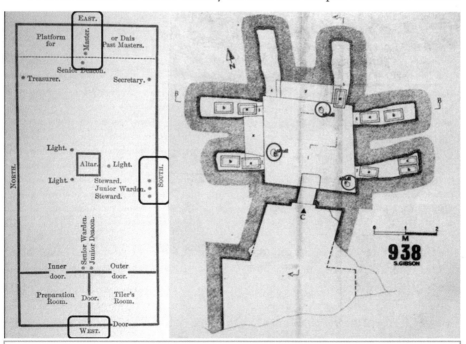

The three highest ranking officers in a Masonic Lodge or Templar Preceptory sit in the south (Junior Warden), west (Senior Warden), and the east (Worshipful Master). The three skulls (circled) placed on the floor of the burial chamber by someone who entered the Talpiot tomb at the time of the Crusades are placed in the south, west, and east quadrants. Could this be evidence consistent with the members of the Knights Templars who were bloodline descendants of the people interred in the tomb and who knew of its whereabouts? (Internet/Internet)

(Left) There appears to be incredible symbolism in this wall painting at the St. Mary's Cathedral Basilica of the Assumption in Covington, Kentucky, Janet and I visited in October of 2015. Inside we found a Crucifixion scene in Golgotha with an auburn-haired Mary Magdalene dressed in red and green, at the base of the cross were three skulls on the ground in the south, west, and east positions, just like the three skulls in the Talpiot tomb, relative to the walled city of Jerusalem in the distance. Right: a mosaic tile image shows Jesus after being taken down from what is suggested to be a Tau shaped cross as is depicted in both works of art. It is interesting there are four individuals in the mosaic with gold halos begging the question as to who they are. The female behind Jesus wears green and red colors of the Magdalene which would be heretical symbolism to Catholic Church authorities. (2015/2015) See color section for detail.

that the bloodline descendants of Jesus and Mary Magdalene, along with other family members, have survived persecution over the centuries to this day. Several prominent Merovingian (Vine of Mary) family lines existed in France into the latter part of the eleventh century and founded the Cistercians as a reformed order of the Benedictines, who in the eyes of the Venus Families, had become fat and lazy. The pivotal move came in 1113, when what I believe can only be described as the beginning of the greatest coup d'état in history, when a twenty-three-year-old named Bernard joined the Cistercian order with thirty other family members including his uncle André de Montbard.[120]

120 https://books.google.com/books?id=qbUk5OfLBNIC&pg=PT84&lpg=PT84&dq=bernard+de+clairvaux%27s+uncle+Andre+de+Montbard&source=bl&ots=NEw9MHXhwH&sig=88Bgvzgz6zJnakFEvib6qjEemVo&hl=en&sa=X&ved=0ahUKEwjt0Pd16bbAhUDmlkKHasXA7oQ6AEIQzAE#v=onepage&q=bernard%20de%20clairvaux's%20uncle%20Andre%20de%20Montbard&f=false

This bold move by the Venus Families of aligning with the Catholic Church by sending their sons to fill the monasteries launched the Cistercians, and their military brethren the Knights Templar, which quickly led to unprecedented growth and power.

I now propose conventional wisdom and academia missed this critical historical power play launched by a group of families with bloodline ties and, most importantly, knowledge that stretched back to the first-century royal family. Their ultimately successful, long-term plan to establish the New Jerusalem, the United States of America, came to fruition by direct descendants of the Venus Family members we collectively now call the Founding Fathers. Upon completion of the first phase of the mission, the second phase was to institute a spiritual platform for the people, characterized as freedom of religion, that above all else gave the ability to communicate with Deity to the individual, not kept by an institution (church) that mandated that communication be through a human conduit (clergy), and then relayed to the individual. This is the simple, yet powerful truth religious institutions of all faiths do not want the people to know.

Possibly the most controversial image with heretical symbolism I have ever seen was in one of the side altars in Se Cathedral, in Goa, India. It was a hot, muggy day and sweat was pouring off me as I quietly walked through the massive cathedral. I instantly recognized the image of Saint Bernard of Clairvaux, the charismatic leader of the Cistercian order and well-known mystic. He was wearing the usual white tunic with a black mantle symbolizing the concept of Dualism the Cistercians embraced. Dualism is what some might call the mystical concept of opposites that keep things in balance such as male-female, good-bad, light-dark, and heaven and earth. I would like to remind the reader the Hooked X symbol also represents Dualism. When an X is cut in half horizontally, it creates upward and downward pointing chevrons symbolic of male and female. The hook on the upper right arm represents a child or the continuation of that ideology and thought.

While filming in Goa, India, the director and cinematographer, Rob Sixsmith, our local fixer, Tony Cordeaux, and I wandered into a cemetery next to one of the older churches built by the Portuguese Templars. As we passed through the entrance gate we heard a loud banging noise and noticed a half dozen people standing next to the wall surrounding the cemetery. Upon closer inspection, we noticed the wall was made up of two rows of vertical monuments. After walking a short distance to the middle of the burial plots, we looked over and saw several human bones and a skull lying on top of a horizontal monument slab on the ground. Tony explained the people were opening the small space in the wall to reinter the bones of a deceased family member they had dug up earlier in the day. Traditionally in Goa when a person died they could only be buried in a cemetery for no longer than three years. The family must then dig up their loved ones remains and put them into a smaller space within the wall for their final resting place.

The heretical beliefs of at least some of the influential religious leaders of the Portuguese Order of Christ in Goa, India, were on full display in Se Cathedral. In this seventeenth-century painting, Saint Bernard of Clairvaux is symbolically depicted elevated above the Pope whose mitre and crosier are on the ground. The artist has painted Bernard with interesting hand gestures, his right making the 3 + 1 = 4 sign (3.14 or Pi), an ode to science, and his left making the M-sign an ode to Mary Magdalene, i.e. the Goddess. (2015)

While shooting B-roll in Goa, India, cameraman, Rob Sixsmith, and I visited a local cemetery and photographed the scene of a deceased person whose remains had been dug up earlier in the day by relatives. Local tradition requires family members to remove the bones of their deceased relatives within three years of burial and reinter them inside a monument space along the wall of the cemetery. (2015)

It quickly occurred to me this burial practice was eerily similar to the ossuary culture of the first-century royal family in Jerusalem. Could the Portuguese Templars have brought this unique burial practice with them and passed it onto the local population in Goa? Tony did not know where or when this burial practice originated and thought the reason for it was simply to save land space. After looking out past the cemetery walls and seeing nothing but jungle I concluded, at least at this location, the "saving space" reasoning did not seem to fit. India is soon to be the most populated country in the world and burial space likely will be a concern in the future. However, space does not appear to be the driving force behind the burial practice that dates beyond the memory of Goa residents I talked to. It is quite possible the burial tradition was brought to Goa by the Order of Christ who may have inherited the tradition from pre-putdown Knights Templar in Portugal, who had been to Jerusalem during the time of the Crusades.

DELTA OF ENOCH

Perhaps the most common symbol in Freemasonry, and also one of the most common symbols found around the world, is the triangle. Considered a symbol of Deity, it has many forms it can take that include an equilateral triangle or a right triangle. Within the triangle, or Delta, an eye (of Horus) is often found, as well as the four Hebrew letters known as the Tetragrammaton discussed earlier.

The triangle symbol is also associated with one of the most enduring historical legends in Freemasonry, the story of the biblical figure Enoch. According to the Book of Genesis, he was the seventh patriarch and great-great grandfather of Noah in the story of the creation of the Delta of Enoch.[121] The specific passage relevant to this discussion in the legend of Enoch concerns his building of a temple underground. Albert G. Mackey M.D. wrote the following on page 245 of his *Encyclopedia of Freemasonry*:

> *Enoch, being inspired by the Most High, and commemoration of a wonderful vision, built a temple underground, and dedicated it to God. His son Methuselah constructed the building; although he was not acquainted with his father's motives for the erection. This temple consisted of nine brick vaults, situated perpendicularly beneath each other, and communicating by apertures left in the arch of each vault. Enoch then caused a triangular plate of gold to be made, each side of which was a cubit long; he enriched it with the most precious stones, and encrusted the plate upon stone of agate of the same form. On the plate he engraved, in ineffable characters, the true name of Deity, and placing it on a cubical pedestal of white marble; he deposited the whole within the deepest arch.*

> *When this subterranean building was completed, he made a door of stone, and attaching to it a ring of iron, by which it might be occasionally raised, he placed it over the opening of the uppermost arch, and so covered it over that the aperture could not be discovered. Enoch*

121 Mackey, 1921, page 244-245.

himself was permitted to enter it but once a year; and on the death of Enoch, Methuselah and Lamech, that the destruction of the world by the deluge, all knowledge of this temple was lost until, in after times, it was accidentally discovered by another worthy of Freemasonry, who, like Enoch, was engaged in the erection of a temple on the same spot.

This intriguing story contains several important details that appear to be connected to the numerous aspects of the artifacts I have been researching. First, it mentions the sacred Delta of Enoch made of gold with the ineffable name of the Deity being buried nine levels down under the temple, which is what we now call the Dome of the Rock. The other important detail is the hidden vault was accidentally discovered by another, "…worthy of Freemasonry," who was also "…engaged in the erection of a Temple on the same spot." That spot must be the Temple Mount, or Dome of the Rock, in Jerusalem and the Enoch legend might be an allegorical tale of the building of the First and Second Jewish Temples. If so, then the existence of a treasure nine levels below the Temple Mount begins to make sense and may be supported by a mysterious Templar writing called the Cremona Document.

CHAPTER 11:

†HE CREMONA DOCUMENT

The mystery of my Hooked X/Templar research took an interesting and exciting turn in November of 2008, when friend and fellow Templar researcher, the now late Zena Halpern, asked if I would look at some artifacts while attending the NEARA (New England Antiquities Research Association) Conference. Janet and I went to Zena's room and together with Zena's tall and lanky friend, Donald Ruh, we were shown a curious, round, brass disk, shaped like a hockey puck. In her typically excited way, to the point of being almost breathless, Zena cryptically explained the discovery of the brass seal. It contained two small parchments with a rare ancient script called Theban, known to have been used by the medieval Knights Templar. Donald told us how, in 1968, he discovered the brass seal along the shore of Bannerman Island on the Hudson River. It was hidden inside a decorative lawn ornament.

Don shared an amazing story. Over the course of the next four years following the brass seal discovery, he and and his close lifelong friend, Dr. William Jackson, were led on an incredible journey of research and exploration. A few years after the seal was discovered Dr. Jackson purchased a document that chronicled an incredible three-year journey by the Knights Templar that began in England, in 1177. In a fleet of six ships, six Templar knights and their crew traveled across the Atlantic to what is now the Hunter Mountain area of the Catskill Mountains, in New York, eventually returning to Europe in 1180. The Cremona Document is actually a compilation of documents that includes the deposition of the Templar knight who led the voyage, Sir Ralph de Sudeley.[122] His deposition was coded into Theban and then signed by de Sudeley upon reaching his final destination at Castrum Sepulcher, in Seborga, Italy.[123]

The brass seal, its contents, and the story shared by Don was exciting to say the least. The photos I took of the artifacts that night prompted a flood of intense research by myself, Janet, David Brody, and another friend who lives in Corona, North Dakota, Judi Rudebusch, and others. It culminated into two trips to Hunter Mountain which I wrote about in *Akhenaten*. The research continued in earnest and has culminated in at least three books, two already published. In 2018, Donald Ruh published his own book about his experiences with Dr. William Jackson and the Cremona Document entitled, *The Scrolls of Onteora*. This book provides additional new facts and historical context that could lead to massive, history-changing discoveries.

In April of 2017, Zena published a book about her eleven years of research into the various aspects of the tangled web of information related to what she calls the Templar Document. This was edited by David Brody. To be blunt, the book has issues. There is a lack of citations for critical elements she builds her arguments upon, several errors of fact, the unintentional inclusion of fictional material, and the deliberate inclusion of unrelated material in an attempt to make a connection to Oak Island. She did this to garner interest from the then popular cable television series, *The Curse of Oak Island*. What Zena did well was to flesh out certain details related to the de Sudeley deposition about the voyage to North America, the recovery of first-century scrolls hidden on Hunter Mountain, and his successful return to Europe. The compelling narrative presents strong evidence that the Cremona Document could be an authentic record of twelfth-century Knights Templar activity in North America. Obviously, without the original source document, it makes the job of assessing authenticity of the story more difficult. However, even if the document is a first or second generation copy of the original, the historical accuracy of the story can still be vetted.

In *Akhenaten*, I wrote a short chapter called the "C-Document," with the C meaning *Cremona* (Italy), that was only known to exist within a tight circle of researchers. At the time, I promised to publish only certain aspects directly related to my own research, like the new examples of the Hooked X in the document and site visits I participated in personally. For four years, I waited for Zena to publish her book. Subsequently, I am now free to write about Sir Ralph de Sudeley's narrative and other previously unknown aspects Zena's book did not address. What I will also share is Dr. William Jackson's personal narrative about his experiences and feelings related to his twenty-six years of successful research that culminated in his selling the document in 1994. Dr. Jackson died in 2000 and in 2007, his son, Mark Jackson, turned over the Cremona Document's legal rights to Donald Ruh who graciously gave me permission to use it in this book.

---

122   https://www.geni.com/people/Sir-Ralph-de-Sudeley/4389989523420078700

123 https://en.wikipedia.org/wiki/Seborga

We six have now entered beneath the South Wall

The most important sections of the Cremona Document relating to the Templars in North America is comprised of two parts. The first part, entitled, "Aelia Capitolina," which was the Roman name for Jerusalem, reads as a first-hand narrative of six Templar knights who descended into the system of caves below the Temple Mount sometime between 1108 and 1118. The second part takes place roughly six decades later between 1178-1180, and is the deposition taken of Templar knight Ralph de Sudeley, who led an expedition to North America to recover scrolls hidden in a cave within a Temple complex in the Catskill Mountains of New York. These scrolls were brought over presumably by Hebrews in the first century. Knowledge of these ancient texts and their whereabouts was learned from the scrolls recovered under the Temple Mount in Jerusalem by the six knights who recorded their discoveries in the first part of the Cremona Document. The narrative of both parts was written in Theban, a known secret Templar script. The script was then translated into Latin, Italian, Old English, and finally into English, which took Dr. Jackson two years to complete (1971-1973). Based on the recorded names and events, the time period these events took place was most likely sometime between 1110 and 1120. The six knights named are Godfroi, believed to be Godfrey de St. Omer; a man referred to as Hugh, speculated to be Hugh de Payens, the first Grand Master of the Knights Templar Order; Beamont; Jacques; Buford; and Lionel.[124]

Before we begin with the narrative, I must share a previously unknown part of the story relating to the Templar discoveries under the stables in Jerusalem. This came to Donald Ruh's attention shortly after Zena Halpern's book was published. During my visit with Don in May of 2017, he handed me a large envelope that contained clear plastic sleeves with a document in each one. Two contained hand-drawn maps that looked familiar to me. One we named the Six Islands map and the other the Denmark map. Upon examination, it quickly became obvious what they were and more importantly, why they were not sold with the rest of the Cremona Document in 1994. Dr. Jackson kept these maps and passed them on to his daughter Melissa. Incredibly, they were detailed treasure maps marking the exact locations of stashes on six different islands and in Denmark.

The maps also provided what appear to be four new examples of the Hooked X symbol on the Six Islands Map, and on the Denmark map one Roman numeral ten is a Hooked X. For obvious reasons the entirety of the maps will not be published here, but it is my intention to follow up on these maps to see what can be learned. Stay tuned!

Besides containing a letter of explanation from Dr. Jackson to his daughter about the significance of the maps and why he left them to her, the third document was also vitally important. Don remembered the envelop after I asked him if there were any

---

124   Tim Hogan lists the nine original Templar knights who were the first to be in Jerusalem circa 1110 as: Geoffroy de Saint Omer, Hugh de Payens, Andre de Monthard, Andre di Gundomare, Payen (Nivard) de Montdidier (Montdesir), Archambaud de Saint Aignan, Deoffrey Bissor (Bisol), and Godefroy Roffal (Roral).

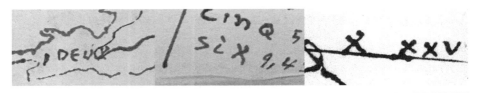

Three new examples of the Hooked X are seen here, two in the letter *x* on the "Six Islands" map (left and middle) and the Roman number ten on the "Denmark" map (right) from the Cremona Document. (2017)

photographs of the original Theban text pages in the Cremona Document narrative. When I pulled out the last plastic sleeve my question was immediately answered. As if on cue, inside was a page filled with Theban text and it was an original! For a moment, I couldn't believe my eyes. I looked up at Don and a knowing smile came to his face and he said, "Turn it over." When I flipped the page over there were six additional lines of text and below them was a compass with each cardinal point direction marked with a Theban symbol. Below the compass was a strange looking sketch that included two circles and a wavy line. Don said, "What do you make of that?"

We studied the drawing for several minutes when Don spoke up, "The Latin at the top of the page is the cipher code phrase needed to decipher the Theban text. Without it the narrative is useless." Don then relayed that Dr. Jackson had sold the document to Archbishop Paul Marcinkus at the Vatican in 1994.[125] Marcinkus was known as an enforcer and bodyguard to the Pope and was suspected to be involved, if not the perpetrator, of Pope John Paul I's death. The Pope died after thirty-three days as pontiff on

March 23, 1996

Dear Melissa

Keep these enclosed maps for me. They are from the thing I bought from Italy. Mike Kline had it tested to 1800's so the document is a copy or compilation of material from the 12th century. I think one is in Danish the other is definitely in French. The Danish one is probably the coat of Denmark around where Faro Island is now with what I called Esbjerg in my translation of the document but this map calls it "KINGS CAMP". The other is of Islands as you see but no names. I tried to match shapes to some in my atlas but got meager results. One could be Sandoy and another Rousay but am not sure. Number six might be Prince Edwards Island. I was there with Don. I do not want your mother to get to them or she will throw them out. You know how she is with this stuff. If anything happens to me see that they get to Don Ruh. Thanks.

With all my Love,
Your Father

R J Jackson

On May 19, 2017, Donald Ruh shared three previously unknown original documents, two maps and a page with Theban text and a map drawn on the back side, from the Cremona Document. This note, written by Dr. William Jackson to his daughter Melissa, in 1996, explains what he thought they depicted and what his wishes were for the precious items. (2017)

---

125 https://www.nytimes.com/2006/02/22/business/archbishop-marcinkus-84-banker-at-the-vatican-dies.html

September 28, 1978.[126] Suddenly, it dawned on me why Dr. Jackson pulled the Theban text page and the two maps from the Cremona Document prior to selling it. He obviously didn't want the Roman Catholic Church to have the treasure locations or the key phrase to deciphering the story encrypted within the Theban text. I laughed to myself realizing Dr. Jackson must have held contempt for the Roman Catholic Church and made sure they didn't have the "keys to the kingdom" of priceless historical information, and quite possibly, real treasures hidden in multiple locations by the Templars in the twelfth century.

What also struck me was the letter Dr. Jackson wrote to his daughter Melissa that made it abundantly clear where these documents were to end up, "If anything happens to me see that they get to Don Ruh. Thanks." Don then handed me another piece of paper and said, "This is my translation of the Theban. Tell me what you think." I read the translation Don had just completed of the first page of the twelfth-century narrative with great interest and anticipation having thought for the past ten years the page was missing:

> Achmed ben Yamani has been charged with possession. His wine is always cold no matter the heat of the day. He cries to Bernrd he is innocent the back wall of his stall is always cold. The wooden pegs which hang his wine skeins low on the wall touch it and remain cool. Bernrd puts his hand and ear thus and so does say he speaks true.

> We have broken through the ancient city wall the back of his stall that sells green cloth in the marketplace. There is a small pool of water from under the wall. A channel has been cut through the rock 10 hands high by wide 25 cubits.[127] We have opened it to the height of a man and found a tunnel cut for loculi and we are among the dead.[128] In the failing light, we see the odd green glow as the light passes through the green cloths spread out for sale from the awning of his stall. It is disquieting but disproved his possession. In search of relics we six enter beneath the south wall. Achmed's wine is made from honey. He uses it to set the green color of his hides and cloths.

What is apparent from Don's translation is this page describes exactly where the knights entered the underground cave system which was below the South Wall near the South Gate. It also makes clear the cave system entrance was cleverly attached to an existing tunnel, called a loculi (or Kokhim), where ossuaries are interred within underground first-century family tombs. I then looked again at the drawing of the back side of the Theban text page when it hit me. The curving line that started on the

---

126 https://www.crisismagazine.com/2009/a-quiet-death-in-rome-was-pope-john-paul-i-murdered

127 According to Donald Ruh, on page 133 of his manuscript, "Bill used what he thought would be a better set of terms for measuring distances than those mentioned in the original document. The document apparently used cubits, spans and hands as the measure of choice, but Bill translated these to chains, links, and hands."

128 http://www.dictionary.com/browse/loculi

outside of the South Wall, and then meandered as if a tracking device was attached to the explorers, terminated outside the perimeter of the walled city. This was where the knights discovered the secret chamber (secret vault?) and the legendary treasures speculated about for the past nine hundred years. Not only was the vitally important Latin cipher phrase needed to decipher the Theban text on this document, but also the exact location where the knights entered the underground tunnel system and the secret chamber. No wonder Dr. Jackson pulled this page along with the maps. It seems he wanted to protect the treasures from the clutches of the Roman Catholic Church.[129] Let us now turn to the rest of the story of the knights' exploration under the South Wall, in English, as translated and written by Dr. William Jackson:

> ...we six have now entered beneath the South Wall. The entrance is very narrow but opens soon into a large natural cavern of limestone. Godfroi says that we should remove our armor, you too Hugh he says to me and we all comply as it will be bulky in the confines of the crypts. Jacques leads the way with a lantern extended on a pole the ring fixed over the spike of the axe. The oil sputters in the dampness of the chamber. We retain our weapons and mail Godfroi and Beaumont have helmets to protect them from the falling debris from the roof. One end of the cavern glows with an odd green glow. We proceed towards it cautiously and see steps going down. Bernrd calls out de Payens you take the rear. Jaques keep the long ropes and Buford to go back for the scaling ladder. It will be slow going. I could smell the stench from the entrance. There were about a dozen steps down and we were among the dead. God save us.

Dr. Jackson offers the following comments: "The remainder of page one has been destroyed, page two and three are missing. The narration begins on page VI with Italian:"

> The Ivri [first-century Hebrews] have taken much care in the structure. We are now down to the fourth level. The smell from decayed and rotting flesh is almost gone here. Only bones are in the holes cut into the walls. Hugh's arm brushes a corpse and the head falls into the path. I cross myself and gently place it back.

Dr. Jackson comments:

> *I surmise that since Hugh is now mentioned not in the first person that the writer has changed. If the events described on page one are the same time frame as those mentioned on page four there is no indication but since the names are the same I believe it is. There is a space here due to the illegibility of the Theban writing and some deterioration of the page itself. The narration begins again from here in Italian.*

129 Photographs of these three documents, with redactions, will be published in Donald Ruh's forthcoming book.

The walls are mostly mud here but the path is set on stone and slopes steadily down. The entrance to this level was from the end of the last but not by steps as before but by a descending ramp turning on itself so we walk below the way above. The first level was about ten chains long the second nine chains the third and this about six chains and six rods. At the seventh rod we again descend by steps to another level below turning once again to now walk north as we did on the first level. This is poorly kept but there is(are) no bodies here. The way is narrow Godfroi's sword scrape the walls bringing down caked mud from above. Our feet are covered with water. There are rats and other vermin here. We have killed several. The air is close and it is hard to breathe. The candles flicker and the lamp has gone out twice.

We are several hands short of six rods when Bernrd suddenly cries out and disappears to his waist. He has fallen into a hole. Only his sword and scabbard turned on the trillion and frog have saved him from going down. To this he clings. The water suddenly drains into the hole. Beaumont and Jaques pull him up. Lionel has lit a torch and prepares to throw it into the hole but Bernrd cries "Ney." There may be oil below I smell something. Godfroi states it is the smell of the dead but Bernrd says "Ney." We lower the lantern by a rope into the hole. It is ten hands wide and very deep. From the sides around it are protruding old rusted metal points some sword lengths long. A man would be sliced up falling through that and the lamp reveals at the bottom spikes. Why such a trap almost to the end of a blank wall? What does it guard states Bernrd? Hugh probes the wall when the scaling ladder is brought forth and lain over the hole for us to walk onward to the far wall. It is mud but half his blades length he reaches something solid. Lionel uses the axe and we are through the timbers some two to three hands wide. We are into dirt and through it with half the length of a spear. We open the hole to reveal another huge chamber of natural rock.

The roof extends far above us but there is a small opening far above as we see light through it. It must be from the street above on the surface. We have entered this place two hours after Terce130 and by the candle mark it must be near Sext.131 There are metal sconces on the walls but they are very rusted and we do not use them to hold our lights. This is a curious place. It is almost a chain long and half a chain wide. There is a cross bar of metal at one end where a flat slab of rock rests. It has a groove at one end where and a hollow in its center. There is a dark stain all over it. Jaques states it is an Ivri sacrifice altar. The bones of sheep and birds beneath our feet tell that he speaks the truth.

---

130   https://en.wikipedia.org/wiki/Terce
131   https://en.wikipedia.org/wiki/Sext

Behind it the bronze bar forms a short rail from which seven small cups hang. The Ivri symbol states Bernrd.

The Ivri symbol is likely the six-pointed Seal of Solomon, also called the Star of David, which adorns the flag of Jerusalem to this day.[132]

The Ivri symbol mentioned in the Cremona Document is likely the six-pointed Star of David seen here on two flags of Israel flying over the city of Jerusalem. (2015)

There are no seats except around the walls there are flat stone pieces set upon other stones so as to provide a seating place but no evidence that was the use. There is a trough and water within, a ritual bath perhaps, it runs through a hole in the wall. This is where the water under foot came from. At the four corners of a squared floor defined by marble stones set in the floor forming an oblong square rests four limestone boxes.

As a Freemason, the mention of an oblong square resonates as the shape of Masonic lodges which is two adjacent squares or a double square. These dimensions are found in the layout of sacred spaces in churches and temples. Even the final dimensions of the Kensington Rune Stone was split down to an oblong square before the inscription was carved in 1362.

They are called bone boxes and the Ivri bury the bones of their dead in them. There is a loculi behind each one but no bodies are within. To the right of the Altar stone we open that one (ossuary) first it has a rosette of six petals interlaced with small dots and the flat lid is very pitted and worn as would be due to the damp. Writing on the long side indicates one dinar two obol and the writing may be a name but it is very worn and there is the bones of man within. We count the ribs. Hugh notes it is strange the head is separated not on the spine but cleanly severed. This man died when his head was cut off with a very sharp axe. The bones show little splintering where the axe slid over them. There is a name and I read a little Ivri it is to me that falls

132   https://en.wikipedia.org/wiki/Flag_of_Israel

the making out of what is written. It is Yon. Bernrd bags the bones.

In the box to the left are twelve long clay tubes with writings in one that we break the wax seal on. It is all in the Ivri text and I see that it is the book of God but in Scriptuo continua making it most difficult to read. There are others in a strange script too. We take them all of them. Bernrd we will bring all of them to Castrum Sepulchri [Castle of Burial Site] with us. There is a man called Jakobus there of the Germanic tribes who may be able to read them.

The box at the back now on my right is sealed with lead seals over a lip on the edge of the box and its cover. This is unusual. There is a design of pillars on long side. This could be a doorway to an Ivri Temple. We cut the seals off and Bernrd takes one to go with us. Within is some rotten sheep hides. Even after a long time the smell of the sheep remains in them. Below them and stacked in a pyramid shape are small elongated blocks of Gold each stamped with a seal that Beaumont recognizes as the of the Ivri King Solomon. This is a treasure beyond our wildest dreams. This will help the money moving plans.

The last box is now opened quickly expecting more Gold but below the sheep hides we find none. Instead there are five devices of metal and of curious type. Bernrd states we will bring them to Hildegard of Bingen who works on the Liber Subtilitatum Diversarum Naturarum Creaturarum in the ???? Mountains and may be able to discern their use. I will describe each as best I can.[133]

Now a shaft of light passes from the hole above and illuminates a spot on the marble floor. We stare as it reveals a big eye. When we place torches to it we see it is laid out with tiles once of many colors in the shape of a big fish. Beaumont thinks by the candle mark it is the noon mark we see. Since it is Midsummer's Eve Bernrd believes it sets a mark on the eye on purpose and this was an early Christian meeting place.

Upon reading this passage, I realized this must be the same round hole I saw cut into the limestone bedrock in the Dome of the Rock inside the gold-topped dome on the Temple Mount. The hole extends to the first level below which is now a sacred Muslim prayer site. This hole, called the Well of Souls, is designed to allow the souls of the dead to ascend to the surface. I had a rare opportunity to visit this sacred place while filming *Pirate Treasure of the Knights Templar* for History Channel in 2015. However, because the Cremona Document narrative mentions a "…shaft of light from the hole above…," this cannot be the Well of Souls because the hole is inside the Muslim temple

---

133   The detailed descriptions of these devices and replicas made by Dr. William Jackson and Donald Ruh are explained with commentary in Ruh's forthcoming book, *The Scrolls of Onteora*.

181

which existed in the twelfth century and therefore, sunlight could not pass down through it. This means the hole to the surface must be somewhere else within the walled city probably closer to the South Wall. Later in the narrative we find the answer to the mystery, "...from Adoniram's scrolls that were found below the stables of Solomon..."

The October Films crew and our guide stand below the round hole cut into the limestone bedrock called the Well of Souls. The vertical shaft extends to the surface of the Dome of the Rock inside the Muslim Temple. Because of the manmade floor there was no way to determine if the hole extended down a total of nine levels as legend says. (2015)

The first part of the Cremona Document struck me as vitally important. It could be the first tangible evidence supporting the long-standing Knights Templar legend. This document definitively proves treasure was discovered while exploring under the walled city after capturing Jerusalem during the First Crusade. It would also give support to the Masonic rituals of both the Royal Arch and Scottish Rite Degrees preservation of historical truth rather than just allegorical stories. Additionally, it supports the Templars did in fact return to Europe from Jerusalem and presented their discoveries to their leader, and bloodline relative, Bernard de Clairvaux around 1118. I have reached the conclusion that elements of the Templars' secret excavations found their way into Masonic ritual.

We see evidence of Royal Arch degrees in the pre-put down Portuguese Knights Templar initiation ritual I learned about in the castle at Tomar. In the basement of the castle, the candidate passed beneath eight keystones to eventually find their spiritual treasure under the ninth keystone. Carved into the limestone boss is the sun "shining its light" on the candidate with the omnipresent power of the Goddess symbolized by a rose in the center. The ritual illumination of the initiate appears to be connected to the vertical shaft of light the twelfth-century Templars in the caves under the walled city saw shining down onto the big eye in the marble floor. The fish symbol likely represents the Age of Pisces that was ushered in as the new constellation visible on the eastern horizon at sunrise on the spring equinox which occurred at the beginning of the first century. We will see more of this important fish symbol later in the book.

The presence of what appears to be at least two vertical shafts within the walled city in Jerusalem suggests an ancient tradition existed where sacred rituals were performed deep within the Earth. The Well of Souls shaft appears to extend much deeper as suggested in the sketches made by Brother Charles Warren during his teams' excavations under the Temple Mount from 1867 to 1880. These sketches clearly show the shaft extending beyond the first level below. How deep it goes and what lies at the bottom is still a mystery.

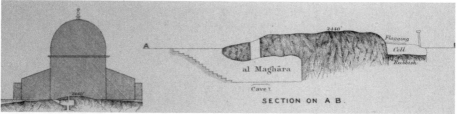

This cross-sectional diagram of the Dome of the Rock shows the vertical shaft of the Well of Souls and the horizontal floor of the first level. Below the floor is the word "cave?" Does this suggest additional levels below were documented by Charles Warren during his excavations in Jerusalem, from 1867-80, but were intentionally left off the sketches? (Warren, 1885)

Continuing with the narrative inside the chamber we learn it has, "...a trough and water within, a ritual bath perhaps." Zena Halpern interprets this trough as a Jewish Mikvah bath used for rituals of purification which require running water. This description is reminiscent of the ritual practices of the Cistercians (and Knights Templar) of washing their head, hands and feet before and after every meal. Every medieval Cistercian abbey had a structure located in the cloister, called a lavatorium, for this sacred daily cleansing ritual. As mentioned earlier, these structures were usually two stories in height, hexagonal or octagonal in design with fresh water constantly running through the central fountain.[134]

The author of the Cremona Document describes the group of knights finding four limestone boxes next to an altar stone. This fits the description of an ossuary which I have already discussed regarding the Talpiot Tomb in chapter 9. The author then refers to *loculi*, also called *kokhim*, which are tunnels cut into the bedrock connected to the central burial chamber. Arcosolium are shelves cut into bedrock, where bodies of the deceased, first wrapped in a shroud, were placed to decompose before their bones were placed inside an ossuary.[135] At his point, the ossuaries were then placed inside the tunnels/kokh-

---

134 Könemann, pages 64-65, 2006.

135 https://en.wikipedia.org/wiki/Arcosolium

im. However, human skeletons have also been found laid out inside first-century burial chamber tunnels so it is possible the author of the narrative could have been referring to either. It should be noted ossuaries were constructed to be sizable enough to accommodate the two largest bones in the body, the femurs, that were placed inside the bone box crossed into an *X* shape with the skull going in last. This is believed to be the origin of the skull-and-crossbones symbol featured prominently in the clock tower carvings in Tomar, Portugal.

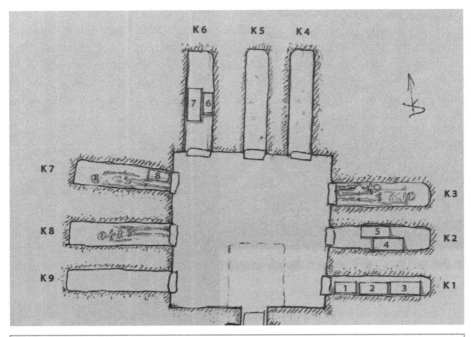

This first-century tomb in Jerusalem has nine burial tunnels called Kokhim and shows eight rectangular boxes called ossuaries. Additionally, Kokhim numbered K-3, K-7 and K-8 clearly show skeletons indicating bodies were placed in the tunnels, including K-3 which appears to have an adult along with a child. It is unclear whether the bodies were intended to remain permanently interred inside the tunnels or whether the bones were never collected and placed in ossuaries due to the destruction of Jerusalem in AD 70 that ended the ossuary culture at that time. (Drawing by Amos Kloner and Shimon Gibson in 1981)136

The passage that states, "…a rosette of six petals interlaced with small dots…" is describing a Flower of Life symbol carved on the ossuary that includes a name carved into the side. These same Flower of Life symbols are also carved into the "Mariamene Mara" and the "Judah, Son of Joseph" ossuaries in the Talpiot tomb. The narrative goes on to describe the condition of the bones that suggest the deceased was beheaded. These facts, together with the name Yon, or John, implies they were the mortal remains of John the Baptist. If so, this opens up a huge new avenue of research and possibilities that are profound to say the least.

---

136 Charlesworth, page 73, 2013.

Israeli archaeologist, Amos Kloner, took this photograph of one of two benches, or niches called Arcosolium, cut into the northern wall of the burial chamber of the Talpiot Tomb in 1980. These spaces are where the body of a deceased loved one, wrapped in a shroud, was placed to decompose before the bones were placed inside an ossuary. In the lower right and left sides are two of six tunnels where ossuaries were interred called loculi or kokhim. Both were partially filled with sediment that flowed into the burial chamber after it was entered and not properly re-sealed approximately 900 years ago. (Internet)

This artist drawing (left) illustrates how the Flower of Life symbol is simply a series of carefully placed interlacing circles that form seven interconnecting vesica pisces symbols in flower design (left). Two six-petaled flower of life symbols are beautifully carved on this first-century ossuary (right) in the museum inside the Lion's Gate in Jerusalem. Interestingly, there are also two spiral symbols and nine pillars carved in the middle, possibly alluding to the nine arches of the Enochian legend of the secret vault. (Courtesy of Vanessa Espinosa/2015)

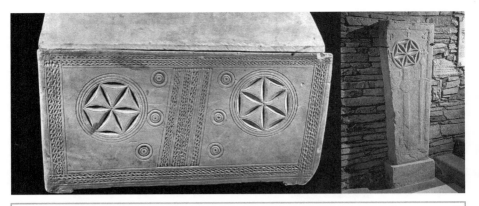

The ossuary (left) found in the Talpiot tomb in Jerusalem with the words "Mariamene Mara," carved on the opposite side, has two Flower of Life symbols carved onto the surface. The Cremona Document describes a "rosette of six petals interlaced with small dots" on one of the four ossuaries found under the Temple Mount that likely is the same symbol. This thirteenth-century Knights Templar tombstone (right) at Kirkwall Cathedral, Scotland, has the same Flower of Life symbol suggesting a likely ideological connection. (Internet/Internet)

This passage is incredible and lends a huge amount of credibility to the argument I have been making for years that part of the Templars' early twelfth-century mission in Jerusalem was to locate and collect the physical remains of important historical figures as leverage against the Roman Catholic Church. Keep in mind, the specific individuals who comprised the group of Templar knights mentioned in the narrative were also bloodline descendants of these historical figures. This could explain how they knew where places like the Talpiot tomb, and the secret underground chamber below the Temple Mount revealed in the Cremona Document, were located in the first place. There is evidence that suggests this happened in the Talpiot tomb where the remains of Jesus, Mary Magdalene, and members of their immediate family resided. At least some of their physical remains appear to have been collected and taken away; possibly by this same group of Templars who descended below the Temple Mount described in the Cremona Document. I fully understand this is pure speculation on my part, but it makes sense, and as you will see reading on, the facts logically fit the overall thesis.

The discovery of what are likely the physical remains of John the Baptist should be especially profound to my Masonic brethren who will read this book. All Master Masons know that our lodges are "…dedicated to the Holy St. John…," not Jesus, or any other important biblical figure. I was always confused by that, but now it suddenly makes perfect sense. Assuming the Cremona Document passages are true, for those six Templar knights to have discovered the mortal remains of the Baptist beneath the Temple in Jerusalem would have been a profound experience. Since these events are believed to have occurred at the time of the First Crusade sometime around 1110, this would have been before the order was officially founded at the Council of Troyes in January of 1129. To discover the actual remains of one the original teachers of the ancient mysteries and the person who initiated Jesus, along with whatever knowledge and teachings were in the scrolls they also discovered under the Temple, would have been arguably the most profound and important moment in the history of the order.

What we will see in the Cremona Document is evidence of the unmistakable evolution of medieval Templarism into modern Freemasonry. While undoubtedly many things within Templar/Masonic rituals and tenants have evolved and changed over the centuries, most notably the gradual veiling of the previously outward veneration of the Great Goddess, the utmost reverence for John the Baptist remains. In the "Cryptic Code" chapter, I expounded upon the idea that real historical truths are imbedded within the rituals of Freemasonry. The difficult part is mining that historical truth out.

Baphomet

It occurred to me the discovery of the mortal remains of Yon by Hugh de Payens and the other knights under the South Wall of the Temple Mount in Jerusalem described in the Cremona Document was likely what inspired the deep reverence of John the Baptist by the early twelfth-century Templars. That discovery could also be why Masonic lodges today are "…dedicated to the Holy Saint John…" The ossuary they discovered with remains, "…Hugh notes it is strange the head is separated not on the spine but cleanly severed. This man died when his head was cut off with a very sharp axe. The bones show little splintering where the axe slid over them." Clearly this person was beheaded and if there is any doubt who this person is, his name was inscribed on the side of the stone box, "Yon" [137](John).

What had been a mystery each time I recited the Masonic obligations, from Entered Apprentice thru the Master Mason degrees, began to make sense. In Minnesota, the language in our obligation refers to a singular John, whereas most of the northern United States are dedicated to the "Holy Saints John," referring to the Biblical figures of John the Baptist and John the Evangelist. Within Freemasonry today these two saints are associated with the summer (John the Baptist) and winter (John the Evangelist) solstices, but this wasn't always the case. Albert Mackey wrote the following about John the Baptist:

> One of the patron saints of Freemasonry, and at one time, indeed, the only one, the name of Saint John the Evangelist having been introduced subsequent to the sixteenth century. His festival (John the Baptist) occurs on the 24th of June, and is very generally celebrated by the Masonic Fraternity.[138]

This means the elevation of John the Baptist within Freemasonry happened sometime prior to the 1500s and could indeed be associated with one of the most enduring mysteries connected to the Templars: the Baphomet. The Baphomet was believed to be a mysterious idol representing Deity worshiped by the Knights Templar with unfounded depictions of a human body with the head of a goat and long horns. This image later became associated with dark-leaning occult and mystical orders. This cor-

---

137   As found in the cipher pamphlet authorized by the Minnesota Grand Lodge. Revised in October 2007.
138   Mackey, page 659, 1921.

rupted version of the Baphomet was likely the genesis of the blasphemous idea the Templars worshipped the head of an idol during the Inquisition. While definitely not the head of a goat, it appears the charge leveled against them may have been true.

Another clue to the identity of the Baphomet is found in the Inquisition charges the Roman Catholic Church leveled against imprisoned Templars after the put down of the order in 1307. A review of the list of charges shows an emphasis on their venerating the head of an idol, as seen published by Oddvar Olsen:[139]

1. The knights adored a certain cat that sometimes appears to them at their assemblies.
2. In each province they had idols, namely heads (some of which had three faces, and another only one) and human skulls.[140]
3. They adored these idols, especially at their assemblies.
4. They venerated these idols as representative of their God and Savior.
5. The Templar said that the head could save them and provide them with riches.
6. The idols had provided all of the Order's riches.
7. The idols made the land germinate and the trees flower.
8. They surrounded or touched each head of the aforementioned idols with small cords, which they wore around themselves next to the shirt or the flesh.
9. During one's reception, the aforementioned small cords (or some length of them) were given to each of the brothers.
10. They performed all of their activities in veneration of their idols.

The specific mention of human skulls is interesting and one could argue the accusation was possibly true if one of the skulls were presumably that of John the Baptist who, the Cremona Document tells us, the Templars discovered under the South Wall. We have already established the importance of the Baptist which I saw prominently displayed inside the charola in the altar of the church inside the Templar castle of the Convent of Christ in Tomar Portugal. I had assumed the carved head on the clock tower in Tomar, Portugal, was Jesus. However, upon reflection it may actually be John the Baptist. This is supported by the fact the clock, and the carvings, are attached to the church dedicated to John the Baptist.

In fact, we have already seen another very powerful piece of evidence that shows a clear connection of John the Baptist to the medieval Knights Templar order in the late twelfth century. Written in Old French on the Nova Scotia map in the Cremona Document are the words *Le Vingt Quatre de Juin* (The twenty-four June). All Freemasons know this date is the feast day of John the Baptist. Assuming the map was copied from the original created in 1179, we then have the earliest known occurrence of an apparent direct association of the Knights Templar with reverence for John the Baptist. This would explain and provide factual evidence to support one of the enduring mysteries

---

139   Olsen, page 163, 2006.
140   The mention of heads that "had three faces" is likely a misinterpretation of the Templar ritual and the carving of the "man with three faces," which I discussed in Chapter 1 of this book.

Inside the charola in the Templar castle of the Convent of Christ, in Tomar, Portugal, is a statue with the symbolic gesture of his index finger on his right hand pointing to a painting of an angel holding the head of John the Baptist on a cloth. There is no doubt about the reverence the medieval Knights Templar (and modern Freemasonry to this day) had for this important first-century historical figure. (2015/2015)

within Freemasonry as to why the Templars venerated John the Baptist above all other first-century biblical figures, even Jesus of Nazareth.

If the secret identity of the Baphomet was indeed the head of John the Baptist, then only those at the highest levels of the Templars, and traditions that evolved from them, would have known this. Thomas Jefferson, the third President of the United States, must have been one of those who knew the secret. During our tour of Monticello in the summer of 2015, Janet and I were especially taken with a particular painting he purchased in France in 1785. It was a copy of a painting of Herodias bearing the head of John the Baptist by Guido Reni. There could be many reasons why Jefferson purchased this painting. However, in light of the Nova Scotia map, the Johannite tradition, and the likelihood the Baphomet was the head of John the Baptist, this painting could be a memento of his knowledge of a very important Templar secret.[141] It could also explain the motivation behind his secret communications with Meriwether Lewis during the

141   https://www.johannite.org/

Thomas Jefferson acquired this copy of a painting of Herodias bearing the head of John the Baptist by Guido Reni, while in France in 1785 (left). The presence of this painting still on display in his home at Monticello, is compelling evidence he knew the secret of the Baphomet. If so, then he likely also knew where the Templars took those remains at some point prior to Lewis and Clark's now famous expedition. This stained-glass window (right) at the Cathedral of the Immaculate Conception in Kansas City, Missouri, shows John the Baptist, with his feet forming a square, initiating Jesus in the Osiris pose. All modern Masonic lodges are dedicated to the Holy St. John. Could this modern-day Masonic tradition of reverence for the Baptist have its origins in the discovery of the mortal remains of Yon the Baptist under the Temple in Jerusalem by the Templars at the time of the First Crusade? (Internet/2011)

Corps of Discovery Expedition of the Louisiana Purchase. I will explore this in more detail in chapter 12.

Also to be discussed in the coming chapter, are the artifacts found in the remaining three ossuaries that are surprisingly consistent with what we will learn about other Templar artifacts that fit with known facts related to this incredible story. Ancient scrolls, gold, and scientific devices must have been an amazing sight even back then. The unknown author who wrote this section of the narrative in Italian went on to describe the five devices in detail; four used for navigation and the fifth device to have been used in the decipherment of coded texts.

†HE FIVE DEVICES

It is believed the treasures and remains discovered by the Templars were taken back to Castrum Sepulchri, in Seborga, Italy. There the scrolls were deciphered by Cistercian monks under the direction of Bernard de Clairvaux. The ancient texts reportedly told the story of more first-century scrolls that had been taken to the land called Onteora including maps explaining the route of how to get there. One artifact which provides conclusive evidence that not only was a journey from the Mediterranean region to North America in the first century possible, but it must have taken place, is the Bat Creek Stone. This four-inch long by two-inch wide stone is inscribed with first-century Aramaic characters translated by Hebrew scholars to "for the Judeans," and was discovered in an ancient Cherokee burial mound in what is now Tennessee in 1889.[142]

Another very important point regarding the motives of the Templars is found within the following statement in the Cremona Document narrative, "This will help with the money moving plans." This implies the Templars' mission to Jerusalem to explore under the Temple Mount, along with many other important places they visited such as the Talpiot tomb, was part of a carefully crafted long-term plan by the extremely patient Venus Families. Alan Butler and my wife, Janet, wrote about the ideology and mission of this group of families in their 2015 book, *America: Nation of the Goddess; The Venus Families and the Founding of the United States.* Quoting Butler and Wolter:

> Probably the most significant fact about the Venus Families is that generation after generation they remain incredibly patient. They clearly recognized that creating the idealized version of the New Jerusalem that is described in the Book of Revelation was never going to be something that could be achieved in a short period of time. They have undoubtedly realized all along that their efforts would take centuries to mature.[143]

We will revisit this amazing early first-century story, and the items found by the Templar knights inside the four ossuaries in later chapters. For now, let us continue with the story of the Cremona Document that picks up several decades later with the voyage to Onteora led by a Templar Knight named Ralph de Sudeley beginning in 1178.

> **Device I**—It is a bronze cup about a hand wide lined with fired clay of a brown color. At the center bottom of the cup embedded in the clay rises a glass spike about two fingers high coming to a point. A small conical-shaped piece with a thin iron needle protruding from two sides of it balanced on the tip of the spike. No matter which way we face the needle still points the same but if we bring a sword by it, it spins around settling back to its original position when the sword is removed.

It is pretty clear the device is a directional compass with a magnetized metallic needle most likely comprised of magnetite. If indeed the artifacts found by Hugh de Payens and his colleagues under the South Wall date back to at least the first century, then it can be presumed knowledge of how to make a compass goes back even further. This was likely secret knowledge passed on within certain traditions through rituals

---

142 Wolter, pages 117-127, 2013.
143 Butler and Wolter, pages 112-113, 2015.

to individuals that earned the right to receive it. Those people would most likely have been trained as land surveyors, engineers, architects, cartographers, stone masons, and navigators.

> **Device II**—It is about a hand by a link and is made of brass. There is a basket of wire formed in a round shape upon its flat surface. The flat surface is cut so as to resemble the shape of an animal with four small feet a wide head at which is a hole and through it a metal brass rod about the size of a small finer about one link long and fitted at its top a square piece of metal like a shield boss slightly conical in shape with two flat handles. The handles have horizon way slots in them and across each is a fine thread of silver so fixed that it can be moved along the length of the slot. At the center of the boss is a hole square in shape and two silver threads are in this also sky way fixed the horizon way movable as the other two. A round piece of bronze weighted on its underside with two lead rests in the basket so as to be turn able in it and is inscribed with odd characters I recognize as those on scrolls. A five-pointed star surrounds them and the numbers I, III, V, VII, IX and some markings that look as the Arab script but I am not sure that is what it is.

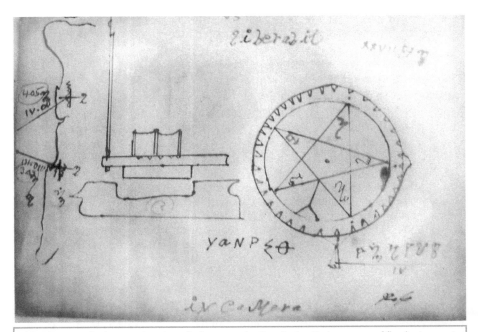

This photograph shows a drawing of a brass navigation device that was one of five instruments reportedly found by the Templars under the South Wall in Jerusalem as described in the deciphered first section of the Cremona Document. The device used the precise and predictable movements of Venus as evidenced by the five-pointed star symbol the planet makes when viewed from earth during its eight-year cycle. (Courtesy of Donald Ruh)

It is very difficult to visualize what Device #3 actually looked like as described in the Cremona document. However, I imagine an instrument similar to the "working cross" patented by researcher, Crichton Miller, that he believes was the genesis of the Celtic Cross originally used to measure angles for calculating depth, measuring the height of hills, mountains or structures, and for calculating latitude. (Courtesy of Crichton Miller)

Upon reading this description the brass device found inside the decorative ornament Donald Ruh found off the shores of Bannerman Island was the first thing to come to mind. After discussing the device Don found with the one described in the Cremona Document things became clearer. He said the brass seal he found inscribed with the five-pointed star and Theban symbols was a modern version of "Device II" made by Roche and McDonald, associates of Francis Bannerman, in 1916. Don said they used the device to locate the Temple of the Goddess on Hunter Mountain over a century ago. He then directed me to the photo of a page from the Cremona Document that was a detailed drawing of Device II. Like the brass seal found off Bannerman Island, there was a round plate with a five-pointed star. Don said, "The instrument is called an Abetor, and it was used to track the path of Venus over its eight-year cycle." As we learned earlier in this book, the movements of the planet Venus are extremely accurate and predictable and therefore was used to make accurate measurements for navigation. That is why the five-pointed star and the number eight are considered sacred symbols to so many cultures and traditions, both today and in the past. It also meant the device could only have been used for a few hours at daybreak and sunset when Vesus is visible to the naked eye.

> **Device III**—A tube of metal could be armor but thinner shaped square the length of two man's feet and smaller at one end but a hand square at the other. Again, silver threads are placed equal spaces apart both horizon way and sky way along the sides of the square at the large end. The small end has a little lip on it and makes a small hole. Above the large end on one side is a triangle of metal from whose point hangs a cord with a small

pointed weight. Along the bottom of the triangle forming the top of the tube are lines in equal spaces and markings that appear to be numbers as appear upon an astrolabe. It may be to measure inclines.

> It is very difficult to visualize what Device #3 actually looked like as described in the Cremona document. However, I imagine an instrument similar to the "working cross" patented by researcher, Crichton Miller, that he believes was the genesis of the Celtic Cross originally used to measure angles for calculating depth, measuring the height of hills, mountains or structures, and for calculating latitude. (Courtesy of Crichton Miller)

Device IV—This is best described as sailor's hooks. It consists of metal rods small and bendable in size formed into a square with one vertical side bent like a longbow. Above the center of the bow is a horizontal rod to the opposite side with one curved above and below forming a fowl wishbone. Towards the bottom end is another horizontal rod to the opposite side with one curved above and below forming a fowl wishbone. Towards the bottom end is another horizontal rod to the edge. Diagonally across these are four other rods not evenly spaced running from top to bottom. Across the top in the first and second squares formed by the rods are two small wire loops centered on each square. On the second horizontal rod is a third and fourth wire loop. On the lower wishbone line two more and on each near the bottom on the diagonal rods. There is a small flat plate fixed with wires to the bottom edge on which is an arrow depicted by hammered indents pointing to a star shape and the word "KOLCHABE." Below this are the following words, "LUPUS, CORNIA, ARA, AQUARIUS, ROM, GEMINI." Opposite each are the following, "MOON FULL, LYRA, SYGNUS, MOON FULL, MOON PERTH."

Device V—This is a large brass circle with small hole in the center and a triangle shape at the top and bottom. These triangles are not on the same radii. At the edges of these on the smaller radii are a square hole and an oblong. One closer than the other. There are two smaller holes equal distance either side of the central one. Through these are two pins that are fixed to a second disc below of the same size and of bronze. A pin passes from this second plate into the center hole of the upper one. The two smaller pins pass through this plate also and are joined by a piece of flat strip at the back. Between the two pins at the back is a cross piece much like a shield strap but rigid. When the flat piece is pulled the two pins retract from the top plate and it can be turned on the center pin its end flattened out. The flat strip between the pins at the back acts as a spring to push the pins back in when the next set of holes is reached. There are twenty-four sets of holes around the center of the top plate. Between the two plates is a piece of dried leather fixed to the back disk by four small tabs bent over the back disk. The twenty-four sets of holes are through this piece as it is the two small rods and the center pin. Burnt into the leather on three circles of various diameters are three series of letters. When the Arabic letter is in the upper triangle then the other letter is in the lower an Ivri letter in the right square and a series of dots in the oblong but an Arabic A does not repeat an Ivri A but of the other symbol and the dots I don't know. It is some sort of coding device. Purpose unknown. When we emerge from the caverns we in time for None."

It appears the "coding device" incorporated at least two alphabets, Arabic and Ivri (Old Hebrew), as well as an apparent dot code and possibly other symbols.

A Year We Remember

The third part of the Cremona Document was entitled in Latin, "La Voyage de MCLCXXVIII A Onteora A Moine de Dominicus Il Revevoit La Depsition Avec M Svedley;" when translated into English is, "The Voyage of 1178 to Onteora a Monk of Dominicans Received the Deposition of M Svedley." The deposition chronicles a three-year voyage by the Knights Templar that began in Gloucestershire, England, Sir Ralph de Sudeley's hometown.[144] The following is the story of the de Sudeley voyage, as translated into English by Dr. William Jackson in its entirety, that begins with the following commentary:

Dr. Jackson wrote:

> There are three pages of drawings of the devices. There is a space of missing paper here due to deterioration and on page 11 the narration begins in Old English. The names here are not the same and these are different persons writing at a later time I believe. In Camera.

We have followed the writing found to be in the Theban alphabet translated to Greek and Ivri from Adoniram's scrolls that were found below the stables of Solomon to Palmyra and have the devices with us. The ancient maps show a land of Onteora far to the west but the route is far from certain. With the round disks we can read some of the ancient scrolls that reveal how the unclean fled to Tigwa and set sail for the Kingdoms of Woton far to the North. To the place in the past where the Goddess commanded the outcasts of Solomon to erect a temple in her honor in the land of Onteora. There they hid the ancient writings, the secrets of the ages, the facts about our (L)ord."

Dr. Jackson interjects: "There is a hole in the paper where I believe the (L) should be."

The disk is the key to unlock these. The North Finder and Star Finder will help plot the way laid out in the sailor's loop but

144 https://en.wikipedia.org/wiki/Ralph_de_Sudeley

to read it we must seek the help of the King of the North. The Spaniard of Leon and Hubert Le Montier and Beaumont de Wurttemberg and Lionel de Walderne, The Celt: Eldric of Clan MacDonald, Ishma'il al-Mutamid and I Ralf de Sudeley shall undertake this quest by the Grace of God and the order of the Grand Master Amand.

It is clear from the entries the mission was based upon the contents of the scrolls, which included maps, found by the six Templar knights under the stables near the South Wall on the Temple Mount roughly fifty to sixty years earlier. This fact is especially interesting as the enduring legends had the Templars digging under the gold dome of the Temple built over the Dome of the Rock. While in the same vicinity, the area under the stables now called Al-Aqsa Mosque is quite a distance apart.[145] In 2015, I spent most of a day walking the area between these two historic structures and they are at least a couple hundred yards apart. While it is certainly possible underground tunnels could connect the two areas the narrative seems to suggest the entrance to the tunnel system that led to the secret chamber is likely closer to the South Wall than the Dome of the Rock. If so, the persistent Templar legend of their digging under the Dome of the Rock could have been intentional to put later treasure hunters on the wrong trail.[146] The party of seven Templar knights included one Muslim. This should not be a shock to those who understand how the medieval Templars really operated. De Sudeley also mentions the mission was per orders of then Grand Master, Odo of Saint-Amand, who served from 1171-1179.[147]

We sail in the spring from Luongo for Esbjerg. We make landfall at Dunwich Engeolnde to receive funds and the Bishop's blessing and stay in the Templar Hostelry near the church of St. Peters but the Celt and the Spaniard seek rooms in the local tavern because of the nearness of the Blackfriars [Dominican monks]. There is but one horse at the Hostelry and it has a bruised leg but the Spaniard make poultice of Fenugreek and by the morrow it is well enough for me to ride to my kinfolk. I stop at Shopshire for the hammersmith to make a copy of the discs. It is crude work but will be good for use. We will stay a fortnight [14 days] awaiting the storms to abate. The Celt has found an Anam Cara whom he shares with the Spaniard and are quite content. So much for the vow of celibacy.

Dr. Jackson interjects: *"There is again a missing area here due to a hole in the paper. The narrative begins again midsentence with:"*

"...at the Court of the King of the North and are well received. We are here introduced to a priestess of the Goddess named

Altomara and the Spaniard is besotted with her much to our shame but the King is not offended. She leads us to the quay and states, "Fater Kat Bot" Lion(e)l translates as he is a cousin of the queen and speaks some of their talk, "Father gives a boat." It is a long craft of the North with two decks one below the other, a high prow adorned with a symbol of the Goddess and one strong mast. Altomara states she has been to the Temple before and will guide us but she says we must leave soon as the North waters will ice up.

Readily apparent is the emphasis on the veneration of the Goddess that I have argued in my last two books was at the core of the true ideology of the leadership of the Templars. The Cremona Document certainly supports this.

We must also ask permission of the local people [Native Americans] to pass through their land and we stock up with some odd items for them. There is beads of colors, axes, kettles and wool blankets. There is an ongoing mistrust with some of the local people as the Temple is within a place sacred to them but so far no open hostility. The wind will take us most of the way and we will make landfall once at a place they have a settlement to take on fresh water and food. So our year begins with Beltane.[148] To follow the loops exactly requires that we start at a place unknown to us so we will make for Gwynedd (Wales) and await favorable winds and then head west by Altomara's course. To appease the priest, the Spaniard takes the priestess to wife. We are all in her hands and she revels in this but the Spaniard puts her in place. We have provisioned now with six ships and one hundred forty men and women. The women fight with the men and are held equal by them. A strange practice to us.

Dr. Jackson interjects: *"Page 14 is missing and the narrative begins at page 15 in the middle of the sentence with…"*

Aequinoctuim [Latin for Equinox] has passed long since. The Spaniard suffers greatly from the cold but she keeps him warm as we await one moon past Midsummer's Eve. We set sail north by northwest till below the North Star then west as the wind takes us we make landfall in a fortnight. There are a dozen mud huts here but the hospitality is warm and we are well cared for. Here we take on a man called Clyphus who is said to have knowledge of the waters ahead. Two ships remain here. Four now set sail again and we make landfall on an island of oak trees where on ship is to be laden with wood and will return. We have seen no natives of this place. Hubert will return with the copy of the discs and maps of the way thus far. It is insurance.

Halpern assumes the reference to "an island of oak trees" is the same Oak Island, in Nova Scotia, made famous by the legend of lost treasure and the popular cable tele-

---

148   https://en.wikipedia.org/wiki/Beltane

vision program on History Channel. Of the hundreds of islands along the coast of Nova Scotia, the odds this is the same Oak Island are next to impossible. I was impressed de Sudeley made sure that copies of the vital information on the discs and maps for navigation were replicated. This does not surprise me as the Cistercians were known for copying manuscripts in the scriptoriums of their abbeys. The tradition of making copies of important documents within Templar and Masonic orders is likely the reason the Cremona Document exists today.

> Again we set sail but now three days out the wind fails us and no prayers can set it to blow again. We must take to the oars and pulling the drogue [Funnel shaped device towed behind to slow a ship or pulled to move forward]. This is a slow and tedious process but we move after several hours with a northerly current. Fog very heavy settles around us and the Celt and Beaumont set to sending fire arrows aloft as the top of the mast one man sits to see by but it is in vain as strike solid on rock or ice and have torn a hole in the bottom and are sinking. Both Eldric and I see land and sing out. The other ship takes us in tow and then comes about and pushes us so that we land on a rocky hillside. We take off enough provisions to sustain us and part of the decking from which we will make smaller craft to row to the mainland.

Sailing to North America along the northern route of the Atlantic Ocean was extremely dangerous in medieval times and still is to this day. It was this ship Dr. Jackson and Donald Ruh would find while scuba diving in 1971, but more will be said about that.

> Night is coming and the other ships fearing a similar fate head out to sea and south. One makes landfall south and west and sets about a fire so that we may take heart from its sight. Altomara takes sky bearings and in the morning we begin to build rafts. Wood is scarce here. Four days have passed and three rafts have gone to the other place but one has not made it and all were lost Beaumont among them. Eldric the Celt, The Spaniard, Altomara and the one called Clyphus who so far has been of no good help to us and I set sail in a larger made boat with part of our masts top cut for a mast and sail and reach the other place where we set up to an anchor ashore. Rocks have been laid into the water without fear of her running to ground held fast to the shore by the great round anchor there.

The loss of Beaumont brought the number of Templar knights on the voyage to six. Already the trip has experienced tragedy and there is more to come. Dr. Jackson and Don believe they found the "great round anchor stone" on the shores of Prince Edward Island where it appears de Sudeley and his party used the stone to secure one of the ships.

These pictures were taken by Dr. William Jackson, in May of 1971, of what he and Donald Ruh believed was the same anchor stone on the shore of Prince Edward Island used by Sir Ralph de Sudeley and his party to secure a ship during their voyage to North America in 1178. (Courtesy of Donald Ruh)

We decide to proceed with the one ship as of the other we have seen nothing since we parted at the sinking of our vessel as it towed it out to deeper water. No sign of our passage must remain. These are not friendly waters. Many fish here and they do not respect strangers to their fishing grounds. We will take the smaller ship we have constructed with its sail and flat bottom behind the other and will reach the mainland in two days' sail with the new wind. First, we round the point and again set ashore on another isle so that Altomara can take sky bearings. There rests an anchor rock here not of our making and we leave below it a record of our passing. The tides are monster.

Dr. Jackson: *"There is a hole in the paper here."*

"...ch and are greeted well by the strange inhabitants of the main island. They are of a bronze color tinged reddish are dressed in furs and have various feathers of birds upon their heads. Those with many feathers have higher rank among their peoples. They refer to themselves as "The People" in a language unknown to us. It sounds as Pasa mac quaid ee. They live in houses some thirty feet long of sticks, bark and mud. There are no windows and a fire in the center makes it very smoke laden. The land is heavily wooded and is teeming with game and birds of many kinds unknown to us. The deer are much larger than at home and Eldric brings one down with his long bow. The head of these people is much impressed with Eldric's skill with his bow as theirs is shorter but they are excellent with them and with a weapon of three stones at the ends of three ropes hurled about their heads and thrown. With these they bring down birds of large size.

They are much afraid when we bring off the horses from the ship but it turns to amazement as no such animal resides here. They will provide us with one hundred dogs to pull our gear but the wheel is not known to them either and a drag of poles is all that the dogs will pull. We will spend a time with them and when Midsummer's Eve has come again Altomara will make her sky measurements for the location of the Temple of Goddess and it is decided that Hubert will return with the ship and twenty and six of us with Eldric, Ishma'il, Lionel, The Spaniard, Clyphus, and Altomara and I will travel first by water then by land over the mountains, beyond the mountains, over the mountains to other mountains, south by west three points less than half the lesser. This is a year we may surely not forget should by the Grace of God and the blessings of the Goddess we survive.

De Sudeley and his party of "twenty and six," was undoubtedly the number of individuals intentionally selected for symbolic reasons, most likely because it is two times the sacred number thirteen. As we have seen, thirteen is intimately associated with the Goddess and when acknowledged they believed She would provide protection on the journey. With Hubert Le Montier returning with the ship, this leaves only five remaining knights including de Sudeley to lead the party overland to the Temple of the Goddess. It is patently obvious how important Altomara was to this mission given her knowledge and skills in navigation using the stars, constellations, and planets. All indications show she had been to the Temple of the Goddess and makes one wonder if she was of Native American descent.

Hubert has taken the ship into a large river and set ashore upon an isle to the left. Upon the right bank, we encounter several hundred of the inhabitants dressed colorfully with bodies painted red and white and black. Altomara states that they are ready for war but when they see me in full armor sword unsheathed facing the rising sun so that it reflects from me they run away in fear. We cross over in the smaller boat and sound for depth to bring the ship to bear. Then we unload the dogs and the twelve horses, our supplies and we say god speed to our brethren. Hubert set off straight away with the tide and we are alone. Altomara has spoken with the head man of these peoples and they have word of us. It comes to pass that word travels fast among the different groups here. We are made welcome and learn that it is not us they were expecting to make war on but an enemy to the south. They call themselves the Mikee-Macks [Mi'kmaq] and the daughter of the head man finds Lionel most pleasing. Altomara has spoken to by her mother and some arrangement is come to that she spends time with him but not alone. He is able to provide some communication with her as some of the words of Gwynedd are most similar. I find this most amazing. Her name is Woe-a-tweez- Mita-mu we call her Wasa-bee.

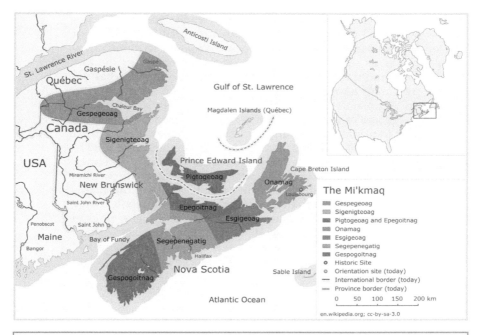

This map shows the geographic territory of the eight clans of the Mi'kmaq Indians. It is unclear which area Ralph de Sudeley and his party were dropped off. (Internet) See color section for detail.

We agree to aide these peoples in their fight against the enemy. Lionel and Eldric take charge of the battle plans. Eldric charges Wasabee's people to build a wall in a big circle nine chains round with an opening to the east. The wall is of stone three hands thick but at the east only one course on the ground some one hand high. A rod inside the circle he instructs them to dig three trenches a rod or two deep and one wide the length of the opening and several men's feet apart. The women weave from a water plant with wide flat leaves and long slender stalks with a brown seed atop which is good tinder long mats that will cover the trenches on sticks below and with dirt and leaves over them. Behind the west wall on the outside several less deep trenches are constructed but these are not covered with mats only branches and some hides and leaves. In the wood to the north Gertrude the spear maiden sets about some twenty men with spears. Eldric has some two dozen (spear) points he sets upon the poles. These are to lay upon the ground with the men. Clyphus, Adric Galen and I will take some twenty of Wasabee's people and form a phalanx inside the wall behind the trenches. The rest of them are to the south in the wood. The head man sends some of his best to wait in the water and to scout ahead to the south over the river to spy on the advancing army.

Some four hundred of them come over in boats made of bark and wood with a short oar having a thin flat blade on them some thirty men to a boat all painted up and screaming they charge us though the opening lightly jumping over the low rocks and thus pay no heed till they fall into the trenches the next wave jumps this to find themselves into another and so on. Altomara blows a horn of a goat. It makes a long low deep sound and at this Eldric's archers raise up from the outer covered trench to the west and fire volleys into the enemy within. They quickly see that it is a trap and attempt to come around to the west behind Eldric. Then does Gertrude send the spear men at them and our people mounted as cavalry charge them also. At the same time the head man's people set about the guards on the boats and burn them. Then the rest of the people charge as I command our group to move forward. The enemy takes to the water some swimming others in partly burnt boats or those they have put aright. Now a surprise. Eldric blows a horn and from the island comes twenty bark craft pushing a raft ablaze into the retreating boats. Those swimming are clubbed in the water. These people show no quarter. We are victorious.

Alantha Rolf's woman, Galan and Cedric of Londonary have been lost and some dozen of Wasabee's people. More than one hundred of the enemy are dead and many more wounded. They are dispatched but the women are taken as a prize. The circle of stones that was the battle ground rests upon a hill and the village behind it still higher up both overlook a fertile plain. This would be a good place to reside. I have mentioned this in my letters to the Temple and hope that Hubert will not mention it to the Holy Father.

Rolf, Adirc and Sven decide to remain with these people and are accepted into the group. Lionel has eaten the twelve cakes and thus Wasabee travels wither he goes. For his plans and valor in battle there in nothing else I can give him so I have him kneel and with my sword unsheathed he rises Sir Eldric. The King may not approve but he is far away and we all recognize him as such. It is the right thing to do."

The details of the preparation and execution of the battle between warring native tribes is impressive. Because so many intricate details are recorded by de Sudeley, it is obvious he kept a personal journal on the trip which is confirmed when he mentions, "…my letters to the Temple."

In a moon [Month or 28 days] we take our leave and with the boat head down the coast stopping each night so that the party ashore with the dogs and horses can regroup. The Al-no-bok's enemies of The People try to steal our horses but we strike a deal with their head man and Lionel leaves his Breast Plate, Shin Guards and Gauntlets with him. They also provide a man called Tamo who will guide us through the many passes as the forest is thick with growth. The wood are so close together in some places a man can not pass between. Tamo takes us over a mountainous route but we see few other of the inhabitants of this land. We come to another large river with a swamp at its mouth and pushing through this bring the horses and dogs over the south side. Here we will abandon the boat taking the sails and some tools with us.

As we will see in later chapters, having local natives as guides was common practice. In this case, Tamo was a man, but it appears most guides in the Native American tradition were women, like Altomara in the case of the Templars.

Then we arrive on the bank of a river with a tall mountain on our right. Altomara states we have come too far. We must go back ten leagues [League ranges in distance between 2.4 to 4.6 statute miles] north by nine east, but Tamo will go no farther with us. We give him the beast but it is the only one that remains. We have eaten the rest. The next day we realize that Malcom's crossbow and a quiver of twenty arrows with steel points is missing. We search for them but they cannot be found. We believe Tamo may have taken them. At the top of this tall mountain is water. This is unusual and Altomara states it is the mountain of a great God of the inhabitants of this land and is sacred to them. There is a large pile of stone here with a clear crystal one at the top with a point worked in its top. South from here we see a rock with a design of the Goddess on it and the name of the people that live here. The three spirals mark a passage of time Eostre. I marveled that they have writing. It is the first I have seen but Altomara and Wasabee tell us these people are not native to the land but live here as guardians of the mountain. We see none of them but feel we are being watched. They are called the Cone (Cohan?) or the Elohim.

There are multiple triple spirals carved into stone at the megalithic site of Newgrange in Ireland. This curbstone at the entrance to the chamber is one of many that line the outer perimeter of the ancient structure. (2012)

What jumped out in this passage is, "…we see a rock with a design of the Goddess on it… The three spirals mark a passage of time…" The triple spiral is indeed an ancient Goddess symbol that represents, among other things, the three trimesters of a woman's pregnancy.

> When we have gone north and east we begin to see large stone piles about a rod or two high and all topped with the clear or white shining stone. We follow these as they border a wide road free of brush and trees. We approach a wide river and Lionel goes to cut trees to bridge it but I cry "Nay" for upon the far bank stands some several hundred of the reddish people and they have many bows and they suddenly raise a cry of war. I stand forth in armor but several arrows hit me before they all become silent. Then as one they turn and face an opposing force of tall men in leather vests with a copper colored plates front and back with many spears with green tips of metal and they all stamp their feet and beat upon drums and cry out. Then a horn as Altomara has is sounded and the spears are lowered to breast height and they advance to the beat of a drum. These people are fair to look upon with many having blonde hair and blue eyes. The native group break and flee as the phalanx reaches the bank opposite us and one hails Altomara. We are taken aback the language is of that of Gwynedd [Welsh]. We are welcome. These are the people of the Temple of the Goddess. They are stately and tall. The shortest is two heads over me. They are fair of skin with large heads and dress much as we do but have a cloth type robe about their girth that extends over the shoulder.

The implication here is obvious, the people of this area are both the ideological and bloodline descendants of earlier visitors to this part of North America—presumably Wales or the British Isles.

> In the confrontation with the natives one was struck in the chest with an arrow but the metal plat(e)s caused it to not adhere as did they with my armor. He then used a short spear thrown from a straight stick with a hook at the back and flung much as a catapult. It pierced the throat of the warrior and he went down. We were taken to the mountain top and shown a structure with a sharp pointed roof made of stone and banked with mud. A wattle wall surrounded it…

Dr. Jackson interjects that this next part is out of chronological order in the story:

> The rest of this page is intentionally left blank due to computer restraints on the size of the file. There appears to be no sequence to this part of the narrative I believe it to be by de Sudeley as it is in Old English I also believe it is an account of his travels with the one called Tamo and before they reach the people of the Goddess. It is part of something I don't have as it begins in mid-sentence.

"...leaves are turned so we change course and at the sign of the bear we head east. We now enter the land of the Pan Cookie people (Penacook Tribe). Altomara, Tamo and Wasabee with the Spaniard who is learning their talk go to see their head man. These people are very hungry. The game has fled as there has been no rain for a while, two moons. Our provisions are no less thus I order twenty dogs and one horse slaughtered for them. They hold a great feast in our honor. This is a strange place. Altomara states she must prepare to give her offering of blood to the Moon Goddess. The moon is full. She enters a long structure of stone covered with earth some half a chain [33 feet] long and several rods [rod = 16.5 feet] wide. A channel brings water from a spring up hill to the rear. The Spaniard states he will stay with her but she kicks him out. There are many women here all for this purpose. They will stay seven suns. There are several more of these places and we take refuge in them.

The horses are restless. The storm is fast approaching. These people have a person of age who dances around with the necklace of bear teeth and claws around his neck and many feathers in bands about the legs and arms. He also has silver bracelets on and rings in his nose and ears and one through his lip. He has something about his person that rattles as he moves and he blows a whistle of willow wood. He also has a grotesque mask on a stick and much as a yester [Dr. Jackson: "There is no 'j' in Theban thus I believe this to be Jester."] puts it into faces of others. Tamo states he is chasing away bad spirits which is what the jester would do. The practices are not that different. He is called the Shay-Man or Shaw-Man and is considered a healer and religious leader among his people.

He tells the children a story. As I understand it once there were no people on the earth and the animals had to decide if they wanted light or dark all the time. The bear wanted dark. A small ground animal wanted light and so did the deer. Others wanted both. Those that wanted light did a dance and it stated to get light. At this the bear ran after the little animal, the leader of the group and it ran down a hole but not before the bear's claw raked its back. In the meantime, the animals that wanted both did a dance and the Great Spirit, this I suppose is God, chose half light and half dark but the little animal to this day has a dark stripe down its back. [Dr. Jackson: "I think this describes a chipmunk."] The children are pleased with this story. Lionel states it is just a story for children but Wasabee looks at him and states. "Is it?" He looks mollified. I am a second son but his place is a third son and is worse off than I. As I see him now I realize that Wasabee has tamed the animal within and am pleased for him. I ask Wasabee if she will go with Altomara but she states that she has no gift for the Moon Goddess. The storm rages without. Trees are uprooted. A horse is killed. It will be consumed as well. Nothing goes to waste here.

After the storm and the next morning, I have a chance to look around this place. There are about five hundred persons here some are with men and of the north who live here also and have families here. These people have a custom strange to us. All things have a separate Spirit to them and each must be kept in balance with all the rest. They tell this story to explain. Once the ground shook and a spring came up. The underworld Spirit gave freedom to the water Spirit. It ran from the north to west and then east till it dropped into another hole but soon emerged again from a split in the rocks at the base of the hill. The people went into this split in the rocks following the course of the water and found a silvery rock. The north people made of wood and hide a device to make fire hotter from below as does the Hammersmith. [Dr. Jackson: "Bellows"] There is a black rock here and it is hard to light but burns very hot when put on a stone pile with the device of the Hammersmith below. [Dr. Jackson: "Coal?"] A large caldron with this silvery rock broken up and water in it is cooked and what rises is removed. A place in hard clay is cut or in rock in a snake or round pattern and the residue of the caldron is run in it. When it is cold it is worked with stone and bone. The silver ornaments are made thus and these people would give us half a hundred weight for the Ass. We took it and divided it up among us. That Spaniard gave all his to Altomara and this they are held in higher regard by the people.

Where the spring came from the earth the people made a stone hut covered with earth as the Sun Spirit was angry with the Water Spirit for showing the people the silver metal and was out strong and held back the rain and the water dried up. To protect it the stone hut was built over it and the stream that ran a chain to the hole of the silver cave was covered in stone and a wall half my height built over it to protect the water from the wrath of the Sun Spirit. This wall serves no other purpose. This is not of good and sound mind. The children use sticks to annoy the ass and it bellows and kicks and this they find most amusing. We are glad to be rid of it.

When the seven days are over the women come out and with them they bring their blood and it is given in a ceremony to the Moon Goddess. There is on the hill top a small circle of three rods across and in it two uprights and a cross piece all of stone. This resembles the Greek letter pi. When the moon is not seen the blood is poured into the circle by the Priestess. This has to my knowledge no effect on anything except the area smells bad always. Not much grows here but one plant that it is stated the roots in a strong drink made of honey will win a woman for a man. This sounds to me as the tale concerning the Mandrake root back home but I am silent. It does no good to argue with our guest and it is much safer too. The Spaniard states he will try it on Altomara that causes Lionel to ask why. She is already yours he says and that ends that idea.

We have been a fortnight [two weeks] and are given a strip of hide with tortoise claws and shells long and shiny and said to come from far to the south in the waters of the great sea sewn onto it. [Dr. Jackson: "Dentalium Shells?"] It will be a mark of protection of these people on us and we will pass through the land of others called the Pea-coot. They will honor the passage and we again return on course."

Dr. Jackson interjects: "*This ends this portion of the account. The remainder of this page is blank on the original document. The text begins again I believe with a continuation of the sentence...*"

A wattle wall surrounds it and around this a high palisade of wood some half a chain in height and pointed at the top. A heavy gate laden with flat stones was barred from within and there were sentry posts upon raised mud and stone platforms within. There were windowed rooms with fireplaces some ten in all with a central chimney to all and a central hall with a banquet table of oak and wood benches about it. As we entered the smell of cooking meat assailed us. A woman called Gianna plays an instrument making a tinkling sound and a clapping sound alternatively. It is an elongated piece of wood tear shaped with two metal thin plates across the width on swivel rods. A drum and horn also accompany her. It is not unpleasing to the ear. I am told it is called a cistrum. To the back was a doorway and a way down to a large chamber but if constructed or natural I could not tell. Many candles provided light while only rustlits did so above. [Dr. Jackson: "Rushlights."] To the rear on the wall was an effigy of the Goddess with much flowers about her and pine sprigs over her and a well of water before her and lamps of oil about her. To the left was the sign of Blodeuwedd[149] and Cymidei Cymeinfoll[150] with her cauldron of Regeneration the three spirals circling the dot ever present. Also, was the sign of Gwyn ap Greidiawl Creiddlad Gwyn ap Nudd. about the sacred triangle and to the right the sign of Arianrhod.[151]

There are about forty soldiers here under the command of Darius but some one hundred and fifty are stationed in the valley below though we saw no signs of them upon our advance. In the Temple area the women rule but within the enclosure of the valley it is a mutual rule with Ishtar and Govenor and

Gwyn his partner. There is no king or ruling class and all agree on what should be done by equal votes both men and women. I find this strange. I am told this is a spiritual place and the body of the community resides to the west many days' journey upon a great lake where they dig and process the copper metal. Some is traded with the local people but most is traded with the north men. This has been the way of things for hundreds of years I am told."

These last few lines really hit home and confirmed how important the copper trade was to the indigenous people in the Lake Superior region. This goes back at least 1500 to 2000 years before present. There is every reason to believe the copper trade involved many cultures who traveled the globe to the richest and purest deposits in the world. This important precious metal fueled the Bronze age.

Dr. Jackson picks up with the following:

The remainder of this page is obscure and missing the Theban letter have been rendered unreadable. The ink has been smeared or other-wise distorted from water or some acidic liquid. The readable text begins again on a new page. The drawings included were most likely from the original find in Jerusalem and were at some time in the past backed on goat skins.[152] Being very brittle I photographed them and sketched them and that appears here. Due to the use of charcoal in the drawings some of it is very light, some has been retouched with ink at some time in the past and this has run. That could be due to dampness where this was kept. Those that did not reproduce well I have omitted. One of the small papers found with the medallion is pictured herein as is several of the items found in the Tomb and sold off. Elsewise my drawings have to suffice.

Upon the floor of the cavern of the Goddess was a circle of holes around the altar which from five of these holes' lines extend-ed to seven more holes in a semicircle before a square stone upon which sat a clay cauldron with the spirals on it. The seven holes formed a small semicircle much in the shape of a smile. A woman with a circle of entwined vines about her head and in a white garment of some kind of leather spoke to Altomara: "Are you a virgin of the Goddess?" Altomara went upon her knees and with outstretched arms spoke in language I could not fol-low ending with Ga-Sto [Dr. Jackson: "I am."] The woman then addressed me stating she was called Gywn Mother Goddess of the Temple. Lionel translates. She explained that the holes on the floor represented days of the year. Where the five were was a letter *N* for the Nones of the month and it was of this part of the year that as the five lines showed they came together at the

---

152 Here Dr. Jackson clarifies the document he purchased is a copy, or possibly a second or third generation copy, of the twelfth-century original. Even these later copies were in fair to very poor condition requiring him to reproduce them to the best of his ability.

third hole which was of the bright star of the Borialis symbol of Arianrhod. When a wooden peg with a carving of a phallus on it was in the the hole there would be a great festival.

The Spaniard did say unto Altomara that she lied for she was not a Virgin but she stated that she was for virginity is rather a state of mind than physical condition brought about by the lack of sexual contact. She was a free woman complete unto herself and without any ties to a man that she did not wish to have. This is in fact the basic form of the worship of the Goddess and though it is foreign to me as is the belief of the Prophet of Islam I can understand both from having now read one of the scrolls of Adoniram. I expressed a fervent desire to know more of them and stated this unto Gywn. Thus, I was told I must prepare."

This passage is very interesting as it demonstrates what many people with conservative views, even to this day, would consider to be very progressive thinking. This mentality would have been especially progressive in the fear-driven time of twelfth-century Europe that was Ralph de Sudeley's world. Essentially, Altomara is saying she is not beholden to a man, or "owned" by a man. As a woman who has been initiated with a particular philosophy and being able to think for herself, Altomara understands she has as much right to choose her mate, and her own destiny, as de Sudeley does. By sharing examples of when he took the time to learn and understand the philosophies of other traditions foreign to him, de Sudeley shows how open-minded and curious he was. More impressive still, he took the time to participate in the "Goddess" ritual.

"I was taken from the Temple structure and led by a winding path down the side of a mountain opposite that from which we arrived to an overhang of rock blocked up on all sides to its top with a small opening at one end. I was told to spend the night here after bathing in the stream to its left and to which a fall of water preceded from above. On the morrow she would come and get me. I was to eat nothing and to drink no wine. This I thought a yoke [Dr. Jackson: "I believe this to be "joke."] as we had no wine since we left Braich Y Pwill in Gwynedd.

Upon the rising of the moon however, she came to me and with a light of an oil lamp the oil of the rendered fat of the goose she stated as the lady of the Silver Wheel descends to earth to watch over the tides of the sea and the tides of human fertility so does her maiden come to me. I told her I had taken a vow of celibacy that I could not break as it was before my God and of this she seemed pleased. I have tested you and have not found you wanting. She speaks in the language of my land, of Engeolnde [England] much to my surprise. She states she knows many languages and is gone.

On the morrow she returns clothed again in garments and

shows me a winding path to the right that leads through a small opening in the rock as one would enter a vagina through a long passage that represents the womb into a large chamber and via a small opening at the back into the light of day in an alcove surrounded by rock. Following a narrow path to a small cave we enter here and she states I must leave within the sand here an offering. She leaves a likeness of the Goddess Blodeuwedd and I leave some trinkets I have carried with me from home.

Incredible as it may seem, the "likeness of the Goddess Blodeuwedd" might be the same artifact Don found in the Sand Cave in the 1970's during the search for the Temple of the Goddess. If so, this brass artifact is at least 850 years old and could be evidence to support the veracity of this incredible story. Other artifacts found by Don in the Sand Cave appear to further corroborate the de Sudeley narrative.

In the center of the photo, partially buried in a sand covered ledge, is a small brass bust of a goddess. This and other artifacts were found inside a small cave on Hunter Mountain, by Donald Ruh, in 2007. The bust, the clay lamps and other artifacts could be the same artifacts mentioned in Ralph de Sudeley's narrative in the Cremona Document. (Courtesy of Donald Ruh/2017)

She lights two lamps and by them I see that others have left things here also. At the very rear, she states I am to reach into a hole and remove what I feel. It is an uneasy feeling to place your hand into a hole that you cannot know what is inside but I do so and remove four long clay tubes as were seen by me at the Temple. Within are four rolled scrolls. I will return them to the Grand Master as I was so instructed and for which I was to be rewarded. It is the purpose of my venture here. We leave the way we have come. She states to me that as I have received knowledge from my parent at birth so have I received knowledge now. But as to the birth knowledge it must be learned how to unlock it and this is acquired knowledge. So now as I exit from the vaginal opening symbolic of rebirth so I must wash in a pool for a baby is washed at birth and then climb a set of stone steps to the top of a great rock set in the stream of the pool and sit at its top in a depression there with the carving of the goose at my feet to let the noon sun bath me with its warmth.

She also states that of the four tubes I may choose one as my own. Looking at them I see that each has cut into the clay a letter of the Greeks and I see Alpha, Beta, Eta, Onicron and being anew I choose Alpha. She states that I have chosen wisely. Now I must pass through a long dark corridor between two rocks that has been covered with stone and earth to signify my passage from birth into knowledge. She states I must now spend a night in a different cave opposite the one I spent last night in. On its roof are strange symbols and lines. She states they are rivers showing the way to their brethren far to the south. There are called the Man-Den, [Mandan Indians?] Cone, Navasak. She also states that Altomara shall not return with us. The Goddess has called her name. She has seen the owl. But of this I do not understand until later.

De Sudeley explains that "Seeing the owl" foreshadowed Altomara's death. This passage also sparked a realization I have missed for the past ten years. The carvings on the roof of the cave de Sudeley spent the second night triggered the idea the famous Spiral Petroglyph in Frost Valley likely is a map of nearby river systems. Could the carvings have been a map of the river systems for travelers to follow? Perhaps the spiral represented the Temple of the Goddess described in the Cremona Document located at the top of Hunter Mountain?

The author poses with the Spiral Petroglyph in Frost Valley, New York. The carvings are likely a symbolic representation of a map of river systems that lead to the Temple of the Goddess on Hunter Mountain. (2009)

When I was alone in the small cave I set about making a light and by it examined the tube I had chosen. The others were held by Gwyn. In it were four documents. A map on parchment and signed Tantin d Mandrakis. [Dr. Jackson: "At the *d* there is a hole in the paper and I believe the missing letter may be an *a* but am uncertain."] The second document was in Theban and said nothing till I used the discs and then it told of a vast treasure in gold and gems and precious relics including parts of the tablets given by Moses from God and held in a golden chest feared taken by the Romans when they overran Jerusalem and it was hidden below in the tunnels cut for water in the ruined city of Petra in the Valley of Edom and in a cavern with the mark of the crescent moon upon the mountain of Jebel Madhbah. The third document also encoded was of a journey of the Spirit and told of the True teachings of our Lord who came to reveal rather than redeem. Also of a Seal of Herod to an agreement of union between one Hasmonian princess, Myrian of Migdal and Yeshua ben Yosef ["Jesus, son of Joseph"] of the Royal House of David at Cana.[153]

This passage has not one, but two bombshell historical revelations that, if true, serve as twelfth-century evidence to support two of the greatest legends in biblical history. The first supports the central point of the discovery I present in Chapter 6 concerning the Enochian legend of the nine arches and the secret vault. The second revelation is the long-rumored marriage of Jesus and Mary Magdalene is indeed fact. I will have more to say about the Jesus and Mary Magdalene subject in the next section.

When I emerged from the cave the next morning Cedric who had taken Benedictine cowl[154] at Shewsbury[155] admonished me for my actions reminding me of my vows to Our Lady and the Holy Father. I in turn felt the need to respond in kind and did thus remind him of the vow he took with us at the Temple so stating that what I do now is by the order of the Temple and for the Glory of God. If he came upon this quest with other intentions, then his venture has been in vain and he was silent. However, I know that should by the Grace of God he returns from whence he came that his tongue will be well oiled.

Gwyn has stated that on the morrow is a meeting with the local group at a great rock set on the banks of a river at the base of the mountain by a bald. Both she and Altomara want to meet a man called the Sac Man or Quicksa-Piet. A great healer among the local people called Le Nee Lan-ap-pee which I am told means First People. This mountain we are on is sacred to them as they believe their Great God lives on it but upon the opposite moun-

---

153   Yeshua *ben* Yosef is somewhat surprising. *Ben* is the Hebrew for *son of*. However, Jesus was assumed to be an Aramaic speaker so one might expect to see the Aramaic word for *son of* which is *bar*, thus yielding *Yeshua bar Yosef*. Importantly, the Talpiot Tomb ossuary gives his name as "Yeshua bar Yosef."

154   http://www.osb.org/gen/habit.html

155   http://www.shrewsburyabbey.com/

tain lives the Pan-si-kee a trick player and I think a form of dev-
ilish demon. This may prove to be informative.

Clyphus, The Spaniard, Altomara, Lionel, Sir Eldric and I went
with Gwyn down the steep slope of the mountain on the side
where the caves were the next morning. As we approached the
bottom of the ravine through which a river ran we could see to
our right a bald and a large rock set beside the stream. It had a
particular shape and reminded me of a grave stone.

Ralph de Sudeley's description of the large rock that reminded him of a "grave
stone" has to be the large tabular-shaped sandstone boulder standing upright in the
bald, or treeless area, in the valley at the base of Hunter Mountain. This massive block
of stone is now called the Devil's Tombstone.

Grant Wolter examines the large stone in the valley at the base of Hunter Mountain called The
Devil's Tombstone on June 30, 2009. This stone with a plaque commemorating the centennial
of the state of New York's forest preservation and is likely the same one Ralph de Sudeley described in the Cremona Document, "It had a particular shape and reminded me of a grave stone."
(2009)

To its left was a spire of rock, gray in color spersed with white
and the top rounded by man to resemble a phallus. To the right
was a rounded large rock that was split through its center. Gwyn
stated that on the first day of the third month the sun's rays cast
a shadow at midday upon the phallus which then entered the
split in the rock to the right towards eventide symbolizing im-
pregnation and marking the next day of festival of the Goddess.
[Dr. Jackson: "*The months of the year I believe are counted from*

spring to the equinox. Thus, this event described are counted was about June 21st or close enough to be the mark of Mid Summer's Eve which also coincides with John the Baptist's birth date as set by the Roman Catholic Church."]

Within the left side of the great stone and about the Phallus stone at the edge of the bald were several striking persons one of which was dressed in the hide of a bear with the head and skull of it over his own. He carried a short stick with two shells of a tortoise joined together at the top which he periodically shook making a rattle noise. He had a metal ring through his nose and one through his right ear which looked like silver. He appeared very old and Gwyn identified him as the Quicksa-Piet we were there to meet. The others were dressed in skins and furs with the feathers in their heads and painted up in red and white one in red and black. They were the escort. We approached over a tree set across the stream which had the top flattened to make walking easier. Thunder rolled in the distance and it was a cool morning.

Clyphus was looking to his left and staring into the forest beyond when I, taking up the rear and in full armor came to him asking what he was looking at. Something is a stir in the forest me thinks he replied. An animal no doubt I stated but he said, "Nay" and just at that point Altomara was seen making hand signs to the Quicks-Piet with her back to the wood. She pitched forward and the Spaniard cried in a loud voice. Lionel, Gwyn, and Sir Eldric covered the Quicksa-Piet and his people with their shields and drew weapons. I saw that there were feathers sticking out of Altomara's back. Instantly, the Spaniard dove into the woods screaming and flailing his great axe. I was hit with several arrows but only one penetrated the armor and struck flesh in my left shoulder. It was a bolt of a crossbow and I felt the steel point hit bone. Still I stood but going to one knee rested a moment before charging after Clyphus and the Spaniard. He had no armor but his mail over a gambeson[156] and some furs yet all of the arrows hitting him in the chest didn't strike home.

At this juncture, the story is tailor made for an action scene in a movie, almost to the point of seeming a bit contrived. On the other hand, conflict among Native American tribes and factions was commonplace as it has been among human cultures around the world throughout time. It is very plausible to imagine an ambush by a tribe fearful of strange visitors dressed in metal armor carrying swords and spending many months at such a sacred place. While the motivation for the attack is unclear in the narrative, the outcome of the conflict is not.

He was among the attackers in a short time rushing up hill and

156   https://en.wikipedia.org/wiki/Gambeson

the first three went down, one his head rolling down hill and the other an arm missing, the third was cleaved from skull to waist and the axe stuck. Then drawing blade and dagger he charged on. Clyphus dropped two as a third jumped from a rock upon his back but Gianna of Gwyn's people hit him with his dagger. Sir Eldric now entered the scene and he too was struck with an arrow in the side between his breastplate and the waist guard but it was a stone point and turned on his mail. The attacker was sliced both bow and man across the middle and left with his guts spilling out over the earth. Another attacker jumped on Lionel's back but Wasabee defended her man and cut him across the throat burying her dagger of flint in it. The Spaniard had reached a man pulling something and bending over to do so and was relieved of his head. Thus, Ponce recovered the missing crossbow. The head of this one was presented to Quicksa-Piet by the Spaniard on his knees. I had dispatched several and taken one as a prisoner. The attack was over.

The Spaniard having presented the head which was taken and thrown to the warriors and they began to kick it around among themselves, then went to Altomara.[157] She spoke to him in a whisper and kissing him she passed to the Goddess. He turned to me and said, "She stated she had seen the owl. The Goddess had called her home. I will honor her as she wished." The attackers were enemies of the Quicksa-Piet and his people and of the people of the Goddess. They are known as the Cat-skins [Catskills?] and the Sac-Man stated that because of their actions in making war in a sacred place all other groups will not befriend them. Only the five groups of the many fingered rivers to the west (Fingers Lakes of upstate New York?) would be friends to them. For our actions on his people's behalf there would be peace between his people and those on the mountain for as long as the trees grow, the four winds blow and the sun shines.

Altomara was taken and wrapped in a mat and placed upon the top of the stone tunnel upon a great pile of oak wood of the pine tree and a fire set below her and she was consumed. The bones were gathered and placed in a special box of oak wood and Ponce took her ash and placed it in the jar he carried Myrrh that he had used to wash her body with.[158] Gwyn had her placed in the cave with the carving atop its roof both ash and bone box and each of us left a grave good. Gwyn left the three scrolls and I the disks but the scroll of Alpha I took with me and later secreted the Eta one also.

---

157   This scene with the heads of the enemy being kicked around brought to mind a little-known fact about the Talpiot Tomb described on page 4 of *The Jesus Family Tomb*. The day after the archaeologists ceased their excavations, on the morning of the Sabbath, a mother saw children "playing soccer" with skulls they had found inside the unguarded tomb. It is unknown if the skulls were taken from the ossuaries or from the floor of the tomb.

158   https://en.wikipedia.org/wiki/Myrrh

This last paragraph is especially interesting as it appears Altomara's body was processed using a tradition very similar to the first-century ossuary culture in Jerusalem. In this case, likely out of convenience, her bones were placed inside "a special box of oak wood." I find it interesting they choose oak to make the bone box. This wood species suggests a sacredness for it to be chosen to contain the mortal remains of a person who was so highly revered. The box with important offerings was then placed inside a cave which again is reminiscent of the first-century practice of the Essene.

De Sudeley admits he essentially stole the Eta scroll, the ethics of the action can be debated, but it must be remembered the purpose of his mission was to recover as many of these precious first-century scrolls as possible.

> Talismans[159] [objects thought to have power to bring good luck] were set upon the cave and Clyphus and Sir Eldric pushed a great rock from above to block the entrance and then we made upon the hide of a deer a chart with the sky tool to mark the place where she was and to mark the place of the [navigation] disks for I knew that Hubert held the others. If the Goddess Priestess thought we could not read the scrolls she may let us have more. It was a good thought as Gwyn had Sir Eldric and Lionel also choose scrolls. We laid out marks on the rocks so that the chart would be better followed in the future. Clyphus had a chart of the stars for Beltane at Cypress and he felt he could track a course home by making one of the stars here. A large natural stone formation on the side of the mountain of the Goddess suggests a human face in its shape and at the right of this is a ledge that allows one to stand with a complete view of the south, east and north. So, did Clyphus prove of some worth after all. Clyphus did however choose to check his measurements upon the morrow at eventide and as he was at work did a rain begin and he cried, "Oh Astroth" and upon this utterance did a lightning bolt strike his metal and he was killed as the rain turned to snow. Gwyn claims it is an omen but I believe it to be an accident of timely proportions. Now only those of the Templars know the disks are within with Altomara's ash. He is also laid to rest in a cave upon the top of the mountain near the living structure of the Goddess.

When I first read this passage of the lightning strike it sounded a bit like fiction. However, it seemed more plausible than I originally thought since I have been on the mountain three times and witnessed how quickly the weather can change in the summertime. Don, who has been on the mountain many times, also shared stories of the often-violent weather.

> I have been laid out in a hut of sticks bent over round and covered with hides. A fire is within and some evil smelling dried plant is placed in it. The smoke is overpowering and I become dizzy as though drunk with too much wine. Then I remember nothing. When I awake the arrow is removed and a poultice of

159 An object thought to have power to bring good luck.

the sap of a wide leaf plant covered with the inside bark of a tree and then a leather cuff strapped with lacing about my arm and shoulder has been applied. It is changed four times a day and heals well. The Quicksa-Piet tends my wound himself with a woman called Gerillius of the Temple who is learning this method of healing from him.

With a course set we prepared to depart. Gwyn gave us the blessing of the Goddess and of Arianrhod, Mother of Dylan and Lleu Llaw Gyffes, sister of Gwydion, Niece of Math ap Mathonwy daughter of Beli wife of Nwyvre ruler of Caer SIdi and Caer Arianrhod. More substantial she provided us with a guide as did the Quicksa-Piet of the Len-ap-pee who would guide us to the valley of the Cone for it was in the mind of Lionel that he and Wasabee should reside with them if they would grant them succor [to give assistance or aid] as it was now evident that Wasabee was with child. Lionel did put in my care the scrolls given him and stated that he now had all he ever wanted and with the birth if all went well he would seek the People of the Goddess to the south that Gwyn called the Man-Den so that Wasabee could be with people she could speak with in her native tongue. It would be his gift to her for the child. I have agreed to release him from his vow and we set out on thus.

As de Sudeley prepared for the journey home, the experiences he and the others had on Hunter Mountain reads like a movie script. I was on Hunter Mountain in 2009, 2010, and again in 2018. For me, this adds authenticity to the story as the terrain, petroglyphs, and the Devil's Tombstone are all consistent with de Sudeley's descriptions. There is a lot described on the mountain I haven't seen, but I suspect if I spent more time looking around, especially near the top, I would find more that relates to the story that has survived the elements over the centuries.

It is very cold and snow has fallen but the guides Sif and Dane of the Goddess know the way well. From a mountain top we can see far to the west the land of the many rivers as the disconnected fingers of a hand lives the enemies of the Len-ap-pee. We arrive in two days at a sheltered cave near a waterfall on the bank of a large river to the west of the Tall Mountain with water at the top and for the first time meet one of the Co-Han. They look to me as the Ivri. They wear a small hat of woven grasses upon the top of their heads [Yamulka?] and unlike the natives of this place all have much facial hair and long beards. They are of a darker color than those of the Goddess but lighter than those of the native peoples. They have heard of our exploits with Len-ap-pee and the death of Altomara. We are made welcome. Lionel is to be made a member of their group and will be given a place of honor in the Circle. I am happy for him.

Sif tells us we must leave when the snow melts a little and before the river ices up. We will go by water most of the way but must take the boats around a great cataract four days' travel south and then we will reach a greater river. We will wait there till it freezes over and walk to the other side. Then we will travel overland half north to east following the ridges descending all the while till we make a sharp change and go south. We reach a high bluff overlooking another greater river with a small island upon its far shore. Here the river narrows and it is here we will cross. We begin to fell trees for rafts and are soon upon the far shore. This river is of salt. We pass in three days several stone and earth covered structures but don't stay in them. They are for the women. We cross another river with the help of the local people and to this to an island of great size and travel in a sheltered water way by great bark boats along this to where we can await the thaw to build a boat and sail east to our homeland across the great ocean.

This passage about building a boat during winter and sailing back to Europe first struck me as far-fetched. What seemed incredible beyond belief, to think about with our twenty-first-century mindset, apparently wasn't that big of a deal at that time. In fact, the more I thought about it, the more it made sense building a seaworthy boat over several months' was not only doable, but likely standard practice in their time.

It is strange these people set great importance upon such little things as beads of color which we give them many. As Sif has said it has been accomplished and our year is completed upon the banks of the Great Salt River at the Island of the Man-ap-ti-en peoples. Our escort has left us two days ago at a stone shelter covered with earth and have returned with Dane but Sif has found it good to stay with us. Ship building will commence soon. I have asked the Spaniard about when he charged up the hill the day Altomara died. He wore no armor but mail yet the arrows did not stick into his flesh. He cannot explain this except to say that Altomara had given him a copper disk some hand and half round with the symbol of the Goddess on it and wore it on a cord under his coat. It was swinging back and forth so it may have stopped the arrows but he is not sure. He shows it to me and it has several dents where points may have struck. I think however it occurred it was a miracle and a result of the Grace of God and he agrees.

The mention of "…a stone shelter covered with earth…" rang a bell as there are literally hundreds of stone shelters in the northeast part of North America. Since the area where Sir Ralph de Sudeley and his party wintered was most likely the easternmost end of Long Island, it is quite possible the shelter was connected to the people who built the multiple earth-covered stone shelters at Gungywamp in Groton, Connecticut. The structures at Gungywamp date back prior to contact and are likely a thousand or more years old. It has been speculated by many researchers these structures were built by Pre-Columbian Europeans. I have personally inspected many of these structures and am convinced most predate a colonial origin. The most impressive site with several stone structures and numerous astronomical alignments is America's Stonehenge in Salem, New Hampshire.

This pre-colonial earth-covered stone structure ,with David Brody inside for scale, is one of many at the Gungywamp site in Groton, Connecticut. It was likely a similar structure Sir Ralph de Sudeley described wintering inside of in the Cremona Document. (2008/2007)

> The ship is in the style of the North men [Norwegian Vikings?] but with the sail lateen as has been constructed by Ism'il al-Mutamid who has accepted the Cross of Christ and taken the vows of the Order and is related to Hugh de Payens by the union of his ancestors Abdullah al-Kamal and Zohra. It is of one mast and spar and of only one deck with a portion for some shelter of the stores. We take on skins of water a plant called mace [Dr. Jackson: "Maize?"] dried and ground. It is filling food with a little water. Some dried meats and fruits also are provided and when Sif tells us the winds are favorable we will set her to sail and will make land in two moons and half another by the Grace of God and the Goddess Arianrhod of whom Sif is a Priestess. She will go to the King of the North to tell him of the passing of Altomara and so will the Spaniard go with her as does Ishma'il and Gretchen.

It is worth noting that Ism'il al-Mutamid had taken the Christian vows to become a Templar knight, but was obviously Muslim beforehand. This lends credence to the point I have argued in the past that Christian Templars interacted with Muslims in the Holy Land during the Crusades. They would periodically meet in lodge with their enemy while on the battlefield.[160] It is reasonable to assume that diplomacy included sharing knowledge if for no other reason than as a bargaining chip. Higher mathematics, geometry and astronomy were extremely valuable. The use of Pentadic numbers which are Arabic in origin, such as used on the Kensington and Spirit Pond Rune Stones and believed by scholars to have originated in the Far East, supports medieval Templars creating these artifacts.

> We have finished the oars and they are in place. The ship rides high in the water and we add ballast of stone. We take it into the sheltered bay with six small islands but stay in the deep channel as there are shoals here. We must practice much with a small crew till we are satisfied that it handles well for us. This island forms two fingers with a bay between and upon the leftmost point we land and Sif marks a stone by the stars as to where the Temple lies. Eldric makes a chart and calls this place aligning place as it points both west to the Temple and east towards home. Now we set sail and go with the scrolls to the Temple at Castrum Sepulchri.

Dr. Jackson: "*There appears to be a missing page here and the narrative begins again mid-sentence after this title. "Conamur Tenues Grandia", the first line has been obscured.*"

> ..orm [Dr. Jackson: "*I believe this to be storm*"] and the mast is damaged and lower spar cracked but the sail is not damaged. We are all wet and except for Cedric who was aloft all are safe. He has gone to God. May he be received well. God has certainly protected the location of the Temple of the Goddess and the disks as now the Holy Father can hear of it only from one of the Order of the Knights Templar. We are now XII (12 people) without the Spaniard and Sif. He may return with her to the Temple as his love for Altomara warrants it. I have released him from his vow. Sir Eldric sights land and we are soon upon a rocky shore but the hull is undamaged. It is an island on the XL (40 degrees' latitude?) course.

> We make landfall at Eris Head in two days and three days hence we are at Gwynedd and make for Merthry Tydfil. I have thus returned to the Cistercian Abbey at Castrum Sepulchri in three moons. My shoulder has healed well but pains me a bit when the damp sets in. Father Abslem has sent us brother Antoninus to take down my story so that it can be added to the record by order of the Grand Master, Odon de St. Amand.[161] He has informed me that the map and instructions to the treasure of the Alpha scroll shall be my reward for the valuable service I have provided and having received the Sacraments and been given Absolution I shall be given a command of the Garrison at Petra. This is more than I could hope for.

160   Bernard, page 76, 2012.

161   https://www.geni.com/people/Odo-Eudes-de-Saint-Amand-8th-Templar-Grand-Master/6000000009440523704

We have returned with the nine tubes many having several scrolls within, but the marriage document master Odon state is valued beyond measure. Unfortunately, Hubert and his ship was lost at sea thus no discs (used for deciphering scrolls) remain. A quest is to be assembled to recover the ones with Altomara de Leon but I shall not be a party to it nor shall Ponce, he hated that name and always wanted to be called the Spaniard. However, the new Grand Master, Arnould de Torogo decides to delay it. I state that all of the above is as I remember it and to so place my sign and name below to so attest this by the Grace of God in the Year of our Lord 1180. (MCLXXX) Ralph de Sedley

This concluded the report by Sir Ralph de Sudeley and the recounting of his incredible journey to North America. He was partially successful in his mission having recovered many, but not all, of the first-century scrolls hidden within the Temple of the Goddess on what is now Hunter Mountain in the Catskill Mountains of upstate New York. We have to remember, the only reason there is knowledge of this story today is primarily because of two men, Donald Ruh and Dr. William "Bill" Jackson. As previously mentioned, it was Dr. Jackson who purchased the document in 1971 and spent two years getting it translated from Theban into multiple languages, Latin, Italian, Old English, and then eventually into modern English. Keep in mind this was done before the advent of the internet which made the task much more difficult and required Dr. Jackson to travel to Europe to find people with the right expertise. Realizing his failing health in 1996, he wrote a lengthy narrative about the document and his experiences vetting it, which included a scuba diving expedition in Newfoundland and multiple hikes up Hunter Mountain with his friend Donald Ruh and others. To put this entire story into proper perspective it is important to understand it from both of their perspectives and Dr. Jackson's narrative is a good place to start.

Dr. William D. Jackson

Donald Ruh kindly gave me permission to publish Dr. William Jackson's commentary on the Cremona Document. I consider Dr. Jackson's commentary to be almost as important as Sir Ralph de Sudeley's narrative itself. Dr. Jackson also provides important context about the challenges he faced obtaining and translating the document along with clarifying important aspects behind its discovery and the people who were involved. Dr. Jackson's narrative also provides additional facts and breathes a convincing air of authenticity into the Cremona Document and the incredible history it contains. In addition to offering comments based on my own experience with the story, I will also provide input from Donald Ruh to help bring additional clarity to the events described in Dr. Jackson's narrative.

This is an immensely complicated and confusing story with multiple events that took place over the course of two-and-a-half decades. For all intents and purposes, Donald Ruh is the last man standing with reliable first-hand knowledge of these events. In May of 2017, I asked Don to write about his experiences with Dr. Jackson and the Cremona Document material. Within a few months, Don completed the initial draft of his yet to be published book that I will frequently refer to in my comments about Dr. Jackson's narrative.

Commentary on Un Anno Che Noi Ricorda

A Year We Remember—By William Jackson M.D.

When I first went on a diving trip in the Hudson River near Cold Springs, NY U.S.A. I never dreamed that events would unfold that has encompassed almost twenty years of my life. Juan Nefitelri, Jake Stevens, Don Ruh, George Porter and I went for two weekends diving in the Hudson River in May and June of 1968. I had just been certified as a Scuba Diver and wanted to try it out. The Hudson River was a poor choice. It has up to a 3-knot current in some places, and the water is very murky reducing visibility to about 3 to 6 feet in most places yet it proved to be a fun experience. Between Pollepel Island and the mainland there are very shallow areas and we anchored the boat upstream and used a line connected to a winch aboard for safety, two divers down and one up always. We set on the island and looked around. We walked through the ruins of the Bannerman castle and took a few pictures with a 135 insta-matic camera in black and white so I could develop them myself. Two things of interest I noticed there which were important later on. First was the Bannerman's Coat of Arms, something he designed himself I believe. It shows an arm holding a flag with an X on it in the upper right quadrant. In the upper left is a sailing ship in the lower left a sea anchor and in the lower right an exploding bomb. The second was that above each fireplace was a carved scroll with Biblical passages on them. The one pictured here is, "Surely goodness and mercy shall follow me all the days of my life.", and another was, "She looketh well to the ways of her household, and eateth not in the bread of idleness.

We then went to the mainland and tied up to the shore using a skiff to reconnoiter the banks and do a little fishing. There were several pieces of cement we located, two of which were shaped as ornaments on the island and very similar to the one in the photo I took, reproduced here, of the superintendent's house but with the ball on the top orange-size rather than bocce-ball-size. Two of these I felt would look good on the stone pillars of the gate posts from my wife's flower garden and Don Ruh gave them to me since he had gotten very muddy pulling them from the bank. A year later I was mortified when my son had damaged one by removing the ball atop it. It was then that I noticed that the ball was in fact a sort of key fitting a keyway in the base and locking a cover in place. This all was not stone but iron, very rusted, and covered with plaster. Within was nothing but dried seaweed. In the other however was a layer of hard earth either clay or dried mud under which was some dried seaweed and a small clay tube about 4 inches long by ½ inch wide sealed with a zinc or lead seal, and having a coat of arms on it of which a ship and an anchor and a hand holding a flag with an *X* on it was barely visible. Below this was a layer of beeswax and a cork stopper. Inside was a piece of oiled cloth holding what I originally believed to be a single sheet of paper with strange markings on it and a red wax seal with a Fleur-de-Lies on it. Later I was able to separate this into two separate fragments about 4 inches long by 2 wide. Also in the cavity of the iron box was a green metal round object about one inch thick.

Bannerman Castle is now in ruins on the island near where Donald Ruh, along with his friends Dr. William Jackson, Juan Neftileri, and George Porter were in the Hudson River where he discovered two gate post stone pillars, in 1968 (left). The three images (right) show a reproduction made by Donald Ruh of one of the gate post pillars he discovered that was hollow and could be opened by turning the ball on top which unlocked a secret compartment. Inside the compartment was a brass seal and a sealed clay tube that contained two small scrolls. (Internet/ Courtesy of Donald Ruh)

Inside the secret compartment of the gate pillar was a brass seal with Theban text symbols on the side that opened, a five-pointed star on the bottom, and inside were metal plates and a small brass inscribed nail. (2008/2017)

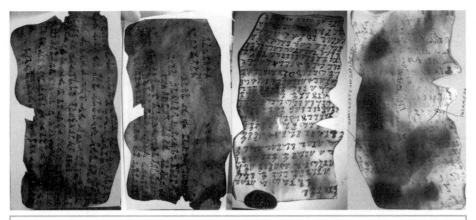

These two, 4" long by 2" wide fragments of paper (both sides of each shown) with Theban script, one with a wax seal stamped with a Fleur-de-lis symbol was found inside a clay tube sealed with a cork stopper and beeswax, inside the gate post stone pillars found by Donald Ruh, along the Hudson River off Bannerman Island, in 1968. (Courtesy of Donald Ruh)

Page 2

This cleaned up to be a brass seal or medallion mentioned in the de Leon Report by Mr. Denton Maier.[162] I was not familiar with the markings either on the papers or the seal but after some time my friend Don Ruh found a book with this alphabet in it. He said that he chose to look in books that dealt with witchcraft as the Medallion had a pentagram cut on one side with strange markings on it that reminded him of something he had seen in a book about Necromancy. When I knew that the language was Theban I tried to translate the papers but got nothing intelligible. I now tried to locate any information on this strange language and this led to a lengthy search culminating in three books. One was the Socoturn [spelled Socotra] translation of parts of the Constitution of Honorious that I intended to see the original of which was said to be in the Vatican Library in Rome Italy.[163] The second was by a Danish author named Lundquist, entitled *A Method of Ancient Measure.* This was published in 1956 by Lomb and was a first edition given to me by my friend Ms. Arkinson. The third was a rare pamphlet written in 1715 by Galvao Benvenuto and Gauden Roache entitled, *La Applicazione de le Francese, Gallese et Scozzese a la Lingua di Indiano Americano.* This I purchased from Mr. Spartan's friend Mr. DeValzac in Paris, France. It was in this one that I found mention of the American Indian word ONTEORA, meaning Land in the Sky, being reference to another document written in Italian and located in Cremona, Italy. It was in the possession of the great-grandson of one of the authors, Gustaveste Benvenuto.

---

162   In a telephone interview on November 5, 2017, Donald Ruh said Mr. Denton Maier was a computer programmer and a member of the same archaeology club as Dr. Jackson. Maier kept a journal on behalf of the archaeology club during the search for Altomara's Cave on Hunter Mountain in the 1970s. Excerpts from his writings dubbed "The de Leon Report" will be mentioned further on.

163   According to Donald Jackson he met Benvenuto at the Vatican, but reviewed and purchased the Cremona Document at Benvenuto's hotel in Rome.

He was going to donate it, with other letters and documents to the Vatican. I was able to view it in the Vatican Library and after translating the first page from the Theban I knew it was something of value. I bought it. I then set about trying to locate the family of the other author. They have an ancestral home in France and from a woman there I was able to locate a member of the family that had emigrated to America. Although the spelling is slightly different it is the same base family. This person, John Paul Roche, was active in the movement that President Theodore Roosevelt championed setting aside an area in Yellowstone as a national park. A relative of this man, Mr. Henry Roche, I was able to interview in Wyoming.[164] He had a picture on his wall of a photograph taken by his father. It showed a rock in the forest with a flat top and an eroded clay portion between a hard quartz base. Below this was Theban writing. Mr. Roche didn't know what it was of or said but his dad had and valued it so he kept it hanging in the home.

The picture mentioned of a flat rock in Henry Roche's home, taken by his father while searching on Hunter Mountain, instantly resonated with me. This had to be the same Table Rock we climbed during our hike on Hunter Mountain in 2009 and again in 2018. After studying the Roche picture with the ones I took, there was no doubt in my mind they were the same.

STONE TABLE (#1)   JUNE 1976
NORTH UPHILL VIEW

Brother Lou Emery stands at the base of the roughly fifteen-foot natural column of bedrock called Table Rock. At the base of the cliff face is a small cave filled with ice during our hike up Hunter Mountain on April 21, 2018 (left). The entrance can be seen in this picture (right) of Table Rock taken by Dr. William Jackson in June of 1976 and confirms it is the same feature Donald Ruh showed us on July 1, 2009. Table Rock was one of the landmarks mentioned in Sir Ralph de Sudeley's narrative that helped Dr. Jackson and his colleagues find Altomara's tomb in 1977. (2018/Courtesy of Donald Ruh)

164   Henry Roche was Philip Roche's uncle. It is unclear, but it appears from Jackson's writings that he met with both Henry and Philip Roche in 1973.

At the base of Table Rock is a tall narrow space that leads to a small cave that is roughly ten feet deep. Inside the cave on the left side is a small ledge covered with sand. The bedrock on this part of the mountain is comprised of strongly bedded sandstone that weathers relatively easily producing the tall cliffs, large blocks of stone, crevasses and small caves all over the mountain. Based on de Sudeley's deposition, this could be the very cave where the scrolls brought to the land of Onteora in the first century to the Temple of the Goddess were hidden:

> Following a narrow path to a small cave we enter here and she states I must leave within the sand here an offering. She leaves a likeness of the Goddess Blodeuwedd and I leave some trinkets I have carried with me from home. She lights two lamps and by them I see that others have left things here also. At the very rear she states I am to reach into a hole and remove what I feel. It is an uneasy feeling to place your hand into a hole that you cannot know what is inside but I do so and remove four long clay tubes as were seen by me at the Temple. Within are four rolled scrolls. I will return them to the Grand Master as I was so instructed and for which I was to be rewarded. It is the purpose of my venture here.

I took this photo (left) of David Brody with the stream flowing down the steep rock face standing on Table Rock. My son, Grant Wolter, can be seen inside the small cave (right) located at the base of Table Rock. This cave is likely where Sir Ralph de Sudeley discovered the first-century scrolls during his expedition in 1178-80. (2009/2009)

If this is the small cave Sir Ralph de Sudeley discovered the first-century scrolls, then it must be the large rectangular boulder with the Goose carving only tens of yards away across the small stream that he sat upon to warm in the sun:

> So now as I exit from the vaginal opening symbolic of rebirth so I must wash in a pool for a baby is washed at birth and then climb a set of stone steps to the top of a great rock set in the stream of the pool and sit at its top in a depression there with the carving of the goose at my feet to let the noon sun bath me with its warmth.

Donald Ruh points to the Goose carving on the large rectangular shaped block of sandstone not far from the stream and Table Rock. (2009)

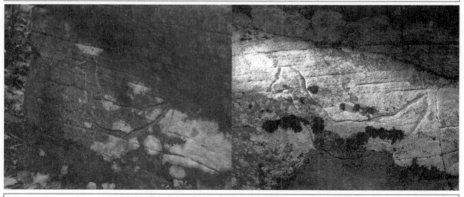

Closer view of the Goose carving taken by Dr. William Jackson on September 25, 1977, (left) and my picture showing multiple generations of lichen growth covering the carved lines taken on July 1, 2009. (right) (Courtesy of Donald Ruh)

Dr. Jackson then wrote about how he contacted Dr. Barry Fell at Harvard University:

> I translated it into a poem called Clyphus Sojurn. Once I had translated the Benvento document, it took two years, I had all I needed to try and find the Tomb. I wanted to trace the original voyage but the device referred to as "Sailors Hooks" I had no recourse as the drawings had no scale to them. Then I found that the words mentioned in its description were star clusters and I could trace this voyage using a computer clock in the University of Harvard. This was before the use of digital computers. Most computers of the analog type were huge. The university put me in touch with a Dr. Fell. When he wanted to know why I wished to do this research I showed him the Benvenuto (Cremona) document. He instantly wanted it and I had difficulty in getting it back from him. He offered to buy it and I refused. He intended to put mention of it in his book, *America B.C.* but a friend of Dr. Carruso, Juan Mateo, a friend of mine and fellow researcher in our Amateur Archaeology Club, who worked for Fell's publisher and was acquainted with our work alerted us and we demanded recompense. Dr. Fell removed the reference. He did however circumvent the University Court Order by taking a group of students with his protégé Mr. Williams to the area in a ploy to look at Ogam writing they also took core samples in an exercise designed to look like student practice. I accidentally met him there with my friend Don Ruh and that ended it. Denton left him a gift in the cave which he didn't appreciate but we all got the last laugh.[165]

This is a fascinating and important story Dr. Jackson wrote about in regards to his interaction with Harvard Professor Barry Fell. From Dr. Jackson's perspective, Professor Barry Fell was behaving unethically. Thankfully, we get another perspective about this incident with Professor Fell in the form of a journal written by the now deceased, Denton Maier. A friend of both Don Ruh and Dr. William Jackson, Maier was part of several trips into the Catskill Mountains between 1971 and 1977 in search of the cave where the Priestess Altomara's ashes were buried. Denton Maier, a computer programmer and member of the archaeology club Jackson also belonged to, wrote extensive notes about their years-long search. It is clear from Dr. Jackson's narrative, and from my conversations with Donald Ruh, that Maier didn't always get his facts correct such as the historical dates for the age of certain artifacts cited in his journal. However, his recollections of the events he witnessed were portrayed accurately. Maier also wrote extensively about the problem with Barry Fell that resulted in a race to find the tomb in the fall of 1977. I believe it will be helpful to include some of the typewritten passages written by Maier about the discovery of the tomb that read like an *Indiana Jones* movie beginning on October 10, 1977:

---

165   According to Don Ruh, an unflattering message was carved on a stone using Ogham script for Dr. Fell to find. Dr. Fell was renowned as a world expert in Ogham, and Dr. Jackson and his colleagues knew he could easily decipher the message.

It is no longer necessary to prove my theory. As Dr. Fell draws nearer to the conclusion of his calculations Dr. Jackson has located a goldish color rock ledge about 12' up the wall and about 15' west of last dig site that has been cut out of the original wall with a crude chisel that could have been done about the time of the entombment of Altomara de Leon. The cutout lies over what appears to be a shallow cave that is blocked by a large rock that has fallen since. We feel we have located the tomb entrance. Mr. Vincentio suggests that we manually dug out the base of the rock and he will attempt to place a charge of explosive at the base of the excavated rock to blast it free and cause it to tumble downhill. I have suggested and accomplished the rigging of a lever behind the rock to aid in its removal, with the aid of the above-mentioned charge. It is now dark and for the sake of safety we retire to our hut to await morning and either the jubilant end of a long search or the disappointment of failure as we feel that this is our last chance to beat Dr. Fell to the tomb. A light snow has started to fall at this altitude while it is still raining below. We are optimistic.

```
Oct. 10, 1977
        It is no longer nesseesary to prove my theory.  As Dr. Fell draws nearer
to the conclusion of his calculations Dr. Jackson has located a gold-ish
color rock ledge about 12' up the wall and about 15' west of our last dig site
that has been cut out of the original wall with a crude chisel that could
have been done about the time of the entombment of Altomra de Leon.  The
cutout lies over what appears to be a shallow cave that is blocked by a large r
rock that has fallen since..  We feel we have located the tomb enterence.
Mr Vincentio suggests that we manually dig out the base of the rock and he
will attempt to place a charge of explosive at the base of the excavated
rock to blast it free and cause it to tumble down hill.  I have suggested and
accomplished the rigging of a lever behinD the rock to aid in its removal
with the aid of the above mentioned charge.  It is now dark and for the sake
of safety we retire to our hut to await morning and either the jubilant end
of a long search or the dissapointment of failure as we feel that this is our
last chance to beat Dr. Fell to the tomb.  A light snow has started to fall at
this altitude while it is still raining below.  We are Optomistic.
```

Denton Maier's entry in the original typed draft of The de Leon Report he made on October 10, 1977. (Courtesy of Donald Ruh)

October 11, 1977 6 a.m:

We ate no breakfast this morning but made straight for the excavation site. The snow had not lain on the ground but there was a dew making it necessary to recheck and readjust all our work of the night before. With binoculars, we observed as best we could the camp of the competitors on the opposite mountain. All was quiet. They had taken refuge in the cave and no one could be seen at the entrance. I positioned myself downhill of the charge while associates positioned themselves under the cover to the left of the charge. The condition of the rock can be clearly seen from the diagram below.

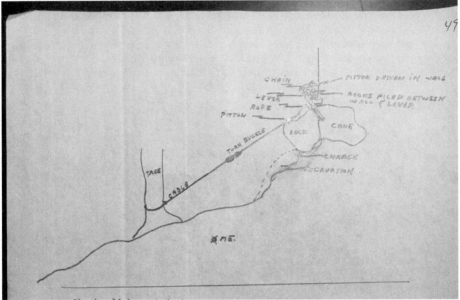

October 11, 1977 6:A.M.
We ate no breckfast this morning but made straight for the excavation
The snow had not lain on the ground but there was a dew making it nessesary
to recheck and readjust all our work of the night before. With binoculors
we observed as best we could the camp of the competitors on the opposite
mountain. All was quiet. They had taken refuge in the cave and no one cou
be seen at the enterance . I positioned myself down hill of the charge
while my aseociates positioned themselves under cover th the left of the
charge. The condition of the rock can be clearly seen from the diagram bel

These sketches drawn by Denton Maier in his journal detail the configuration of the large boulder that blocked the entrance to Altomara's tomb. The boulder was blasted and then winched until it rolled down the hill exposing the cave entrance. (Courtesy of Donald Ruh)

It should be noted that the weight of the rock being thirteen tons approximately estimated should be sufficient to snap the rope at the turnbuckle as the rock passed the tree.

8:58 A.M. Mr. Vincentio set off the charge. The explosion was deafening and the rock and earth it spewed up were tremendous but the rock didn't move. I realized at once that a rope on the turnbuckle to a pulley and over a limb of the tree would give the added leverage needed. We woke up Dr. Fell. His party was looking back at us with binoculars from the cave entrance but due to the morning fog it was difficult to make any clear observations. They were yelling and waving their arms but we soon realized that they were laboring under the impression that someone had a rifle and was shooting at them. No one had seen the flash from the cave so they did not know where it had originated and the echo of the sound through the valley only confused them more. Their main concern was not to be shot at.

We continued working and by 9:45 A.M. we had rigged up the pulley. I pulled. The rock instantly and almost easily came loose and began tumbling down hill towards me. I ran to the right and the rock followed me so I jumped to the left and the rock passed within three feet of me. I grabbed my camera and took a shot of it as it tumbled down the hill a total of 168' from its original resting place. Jackson and Vincentio were already at the entrance of the cave when I joined them. To the left side of the cave was a pile of rocks that looked as though they had been laid there one on top of the other. In front of this was a slab of sandstone about three inches thick and one foot by six inches with the cutting of OCTONOUS on it.[166] We had found the purpose of the little devil after all. We had also found the TOMB. Dr. Jackson threw his hard hat in the air and was jumping up and down."

These journal entries by Denton Maier are compelling for many reasons. First, they corroborate Dr. Jackson's narrative about these events. Second, they add additional context to the story about Professor Barry Fell's interactions with Dr. Jackson after he had seen the Cremona Document that led to the drama in the mountains that brisk

This photograph was taken by Dr. William Jackson just after the rock blocking Altomara's tomb was loosened and went rolling downhill, reportedly almost hitting Denton Maier, who apparently wrote the caption beneath the photograph. (Courtesy of Donald Ruh)

ROCK TRAVELING DOWN HILL AFTER LEVERING AND BLASTING. NOTE PIECES AT LEFT FORGROUND AS IT BOUNCED OFF OF FLAT ROCK NEARLY KILLING ME.

---

166 The Octonous symbol is likely the wilted rose symbol found on the In Camera Stone we discovered on Hunter Mountain in 2010.

OCTONOUS STONE AFTER REMOVAL
FROM BASE OF STONE PILE.

AT CAVE AND NICHE ENTERANCE
LEFT SIDE: CONTAINER #2, PESTLE,
SCRAPER, QUARTZ, TIGER EYE, LOADSTONE,
DRILL POINTS? TO RIGHT ABOTOR, URN
AND CONTAINER #1 - EDGE OF CONTAINER
#3 LOWER LEFT --

These photos of the Octopus Stone Dr. Jackson called *Octonous* (left) and some of the artifacts (right) were taken in the field at the time of the discovery of Altomara's tomb on October 11, 1977. (Courtesy of Donald Ruh)

fall day in 1977. The Maier journal also details the financial settlement which appears to confirm there was a significant ethical breach by Dr. Fell.[167]

It would be unfair to judge either man too harshly since they are both deceased and we have not heard Fell's side of the story. However, the important points we can draw from this story is Dr. Fell was apparently persuaded enough with the veracity of the Cremona Document to want to include it in his groundbreaking 1976 book about pre-Columbian contact, *America BC: Europeans Living in America at Least 4,500 years Before Columbus*. He was also moved enough to cross ethical lines at the risk of damaging his personal credibility when he assembled a party of students and others under false pretenses to search for the location of Altomara's tomb. I must admit to being impressed by these accounts that in my view provide additional support to the veracity of the Cremona Document. Of course, the detailed description of the discovery of the tomb and its contents provides conclusive evidence to accept the account as true and accurate.

The next section of Dr. Jackson's narrative deals with the trip to Newfoundland in 1971 to search for one of Ralph de Sudeley's ships that was scuttled after hitting rocks near the shore. Incredibly, not only did they find and recover artifacts from a ship, but they also discovered another artifact buried under an anchor stone along the shoreline

---

167   In a telephone conversation with Donald Ruh on November 12, 2017, he said he thought there was a non-disclosure agreement signed between the parties in the settlement which would explain why we have been unable to find any record of a lawsuit.

near where the ship went down. Whether the ship was actually de Sudeley's has not been definitively proven, but the apparent artifacts discovered and photographed are very compelling.

> Prior to that however I was able to trace a portion of the Benvenu-
> to bar with the Ogam on it below the anchor stone as mentioned
> in the work. I knew this was real and not a hoax.[168] The brass mast
> strap and stone with the octopus and Goddess symbols on it was
> an even greater plus.

This part of the Jackson story was very confusing until Donald Ruh shed addi-
tional light in chapter 4 of his book titled, *The Scrolls of Onteora*. Don retells the story of how he, Dr. Jackson, and their friends Dominic Pellora and Al Heard flew, drove, and finally took a ferry to Newfoundland in August of 1971. Their goal was to scuba dive in 30 to 60 feet of water to find the wreck of one of the ships in Ralph de Sudeley's fleet that sank off the coast of Newfoundland in 1178. After three days of dives they eventually pulled up a, "...piece of rounded mast about four feet long." Don wrote the following:

> The wood was squishy in nature. Between the strap and the wood
> partially embedded in the rotted and waterlogged wood was a flat
> stone shaped in a figure eight pattern much like an hourglass. On
> it were two carvings, one at each end, about two inches long and
> a half [inch] wide. One was of what looked like a five-legged oc-
> topus with one eye and little antenna on its head. The other was
> formed like a stick figure with a triangle with a round circle at its
> apex through which a balance arm passed with the ends turned
> up like raised arms. This I later learned was a depiction of the God-
> dess TANIT.[169]

That Dr. Jackson, Don and the others were successful in finding debris from the twelfth-century shipwreck from Ralph de Sudeley's expedition, if true, is nothing short of incredible. The most impressive artifact was the stone with the carvings strapped to the mast that will take on obvious significance toward the end of this chapter. My lingering thought after reading these accounts is whether anything remains of the ship beneath the waves. If so, similar to the words of Dr. Jackson, I would also be convinced the Cremona Document was "...real and not a hoax." Continuing with Dr. Jackson's narrative:

> I should mention here in all fairness that Denton did a fabulous
> job with the amount of information I supplied him with for you
> see that I never showed him or anyone the above actual docu-
> ment.[170] Mr. Denton Maier developed his own ideas about the

---

168   What the author calls the Cremona Document was referred to as the "Benvenuto Document" by Dr. Jackson because he purchased it from Gustavo Benvenuto in Italy in 1971.

169   Ruh, page 20, 2018.

170   Don confirmed that he never saw the actual Cremona Document during all the years of research-ing it with Dr. Jackson.

project including some mistaken ones such as the association with Quetzalquatl and South America, though a Mayan woven silver necklace in the cave points to some possible contact, trade is another explanation, and the use of some fictional works to support our research.

This passage alludes to the contributions made during the search and discovery of Altomara's tomb, as well as the subsequent research and testing of the artifacts discovered in the tomb, by his friend Denton Maier. This might be a good time to share Maier's journal entries about what was discovered in the cave in his own words:

"June 10, 1978

As of this writing all identification, testing and analysis of the containers and their contents have been completed.

Container #1 This container is made of two pieces of bronze each folded into box shape and fitted together to form a cube. It held 5 rough polished semi-precious stones. Two more such stone were found near the urn. All these stones measure approximately 5/8" long by .960 to .569 inches wide and the thinnest is .230" while the thickest is ¼." All stone have since been polished and waxed. They are all made of silicon dioxide (Crystalline Qtz). Contained in the box were:

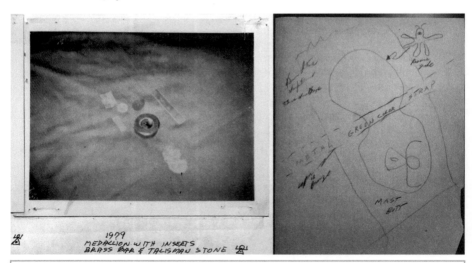

This Polaroid photo (left) taken circa 1971 includes the brass seal with the inserts discovered inside the decorative gate post while Don Ruh was scuba diving in the Hudson River off Bannerman's Island in 1968 (center and upper left). The brass strap (upper right) and the hourglass shaped stone (lower right) used to tighten it around the mast of one of Ralph de Sudeley's ship that sank off the coast of Newfoundland in 1178, was discovered by Dr. William Jackson, Dominic Pellora, Al Heard and Donald Ruh in August of 1971. Dr. William Jackson drew this sketch (right) of the brass strap and the stone used to tighten it with the carvings of the five-legged octopus and the Phoenician Goddess symbol of Tanit/Tanith. (Courtesy of Donald Ruh)

- **Amethyst**—Pale bluish Violet/South African/prevents intoxication.

- **Lace Agate**—Opaque multi-colored/ South America, Mexico

- **Carnelian**—Translucent Orange red/ South West Africa/ protects against we(a)pons.

- **Jasper**—opaque mottled red rust/ South West Africa/ draws poison from snake bite.

- **Turquoise**—opaque green blue/Orient, South America, U.S./ Wards off illness and misfortune.

Found near the Urn (One stone on either side, gave the appearance of being deliberately placed there.):

- **Tiger Eye**—translucent striped brown and gold/ South Africa/ wards off evil spirits.

- **Pumice**—greyish brown and porous/ South Africa/ produces tranquility and heals rough skin.

Also found in Container #3:

- **Iron Pyrite**—(Fools Gold) gold-rust, opaque/ South America, Africa, U.S.

- **Meteorite**—magnesium iron content/ greenish black/ space.

Also found near the containers:

- **Slate**—charcoal grey/ U.S./ tooled and could have been used as a scraper or knife.

- **White crystal quartz**—silica/ silvery translucent white/ U.S.

- **Sandstone and granite**—this piece was definitely tooled into a pestle. Several smaller pieces were also tooled and appear to have been either drill points or arrows points.

Container #2

This piece was made from several pieces of brass cut roughly and smooth or hammered and held together by brass and copper straps threaded through holes punched or drilled into the metal. It took quite some time to figure how to open it but finally it was found that the top pulled off. Inside was much to our surprise a silver necklace about 3 feet long made of .850 pure silver with a nickel lead base and woven into strands to form a box stich style common only to the ancient M(a)yan weavers whose ancestors still make this type of woven silver necklaces today. It dates about 2000 years old and although tarnished is in excellent condition.[171] This the second most valuable piece found.

---

171 Dr. Jackson wrote that he never told his friends Denton Maier, or Don Ruh, the full story about what he called the Benvenuto (Cremona) Document. This is likely why Maier erroneously believed the artifacts they discovered on Hunter Mountain were a millennium older than they actually were.

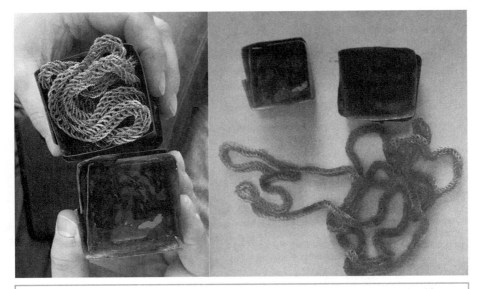

I took this picture (left) of the silver necklace with the box it was inside during my visit with Donald Ruh in May of 2017. It was discovered in a small cave where Priestess Altomara's ashes were interred on Hunter Mountain. Don explained that Dr. Jackson sold the necklace to a man named Charlie Muttunburg, who then gave it to Don seventeen years later. The photo on the right is the same necklace that was taken shortly after it was discovered on October 11, 1977. (2017/Courtesy of Donald Ruh)

Container #3

This is the best made of the containers and the most ingenious. It appears to have been fashioned using well-made but ancient tools. It is also the largest container. Its age is about 2000 years old. I took several months to clean this container as it was the worst of them as far as tarnish and corrosion. Like the others, it also is made of brass. To open it the two small protruding boxes must both be pulled up. This enables a drawer in the side that has only a portion of it hollowed out to be pulled out. The solid portion of the drawer is made of pored lead. The contents consisted of the two stones already mentioned and the residue of what appeared to a parchment. The document however, was not contained within. Either it was removed befor(e) being entombed or it was removed since which seems unlikely due to the condition of the container. It also may have been just a small piece of parchment and due to the fact that the container was not air tight it may have decomposed except for the tiny residual fibers that remained to give us the clue to its one time presence.

Container #4

The URN. Both the urn itself and the entrapping's are fine work of apparent craftsman. The urn appears to have been tooled on some form of jig enabling the lines to match exactly. If they had met perfectly then it would be apparent that the piece had been turned on a motor driven lathe. The entrapping's are not quite of the same workmanship but are well made, better than the containers except for #3. The Urn is about 2000-year-old but its entrapping's including the tear shaped glass dome and machined or cut glass base are only three hundred years old. The entire assembly was found through spectro scopic analysis to be slightly radioactive. For this reason, it was opened in an environmental chamber in a Long Island Hospital by Dr. Jackson. The contents were most astounding. The urn contained the following elements whole total equals one gram:

Element	Percent	Color	Breakup Of Elements
potash	76	white	58% incarnate
lime	18	white	18% pure
potassium (nitrates)	2.3	silvery white	6% lime
magnesium	1.2	reddish white	12% cal. carbonate
iron	0.38	black	
phopherous	0.72	yellowish	
sulphur (incarnate)	0.64	yellow	0.57% pitchblende
uranium (raw)	0.76	mineral-black flecks-white	0.19% uranium
Total	100%		

Except for the uranium, the contents in the portions listed above could be that of human remains of some organ tissue. The quantity is insufficient to be that of a whole human body. The presence of the uranium throws off any attempt to date the remains by conventional means. The dating process shows that the remains are about 1200 years old. If we consider the amount of radiation the quantity contained produces and add the C-14 factor for this amount to the age we arrive at a figure of about 2500 years.

Also in the container was a roughly cut stone about .375" by .2600". This stone is commonly called diamond.

This Polaroid photo of the artifacts from Altomara's Cave was taken in 1977. The X arrow (left) is pointing to the piece of uranium and the black arrow points to the large rough cut diamond found inside the urn with ashes which along with the two-section box (Container #3) is not pictured. The silver chain encircles all the artifacts. (Courtesy of Donald Ruh)

Maier then listed the specifics surrounding the items from the cave that were sold, including pricing. The urn was one noted exception about which he wrote the following:

> The urn itself has been offered 300 dollars but I intend to keep it and its entrapping's as a souvenir of the adventure. The ashes have been placed in a newer receptacle and reburied at the site of the tomb, a gesture by Dr. Jackson that while a bit silly does show a certain amount of humanity for what may be the last remains of Altomara de Leon. It may also aid in the lessening of the Curse providing you believe in such things, Dr. Jackson, a man of intellect and science does. Including the sale of all other artifacts and less all our expenses to date we are realizing a net profit of 1400 dollars each.

Maier's final entries dealt with the little joke Dr. Jackson mentioned in his narrative, along with his closing remarks:

> Two weeks after we had found the tomb Dr. Fell's staff notified Dr. Jackson that they had found the tomb site. We acted very surprised. We were notified that they had uncovered besides the

238

stone with the Octonous on it a tablet written in Og[h]am and a brass vessel called a drip.[172] It was located to the back of the cave and about 28" into the floor of the cave. This is one of the artifacts we missed. The tablet I knew would prove to be worthless as we had arranged to have it made up and left it for the good doctor to locate which he obligingly did. It said:

I do not like thee I can tell,
I do not like the way thee smell.
I do not wish thee well,

thou goest thou to Hell Dr. Fell. de Leon

A short note some two weeks later from the scholar himself revealed that the effort was not wasted. It read, 'Very funny, ha ha. I can tell your efforts have not been wasted, your theory intact, I shall see it remains just that for as long as I can. In your future endeavors I wish you well, but please do not come again to Dr. Fell.'

There was no signature nor was one needed.

There have been some follow-up investigations to certain aspects of this search that when they are complete shall be included herein. They center mostly around the mention of a Kabalistic circle in the Rituals of Honorius Constitution, The Roche incident and his purposes towards the tomb, the purpose of Mepnorius in returning to the tomb, and the significance of our find on the archaeological society today. With these exceptions, we can say that after

nine years of searching the de Leon File is closed.

Picking up again with Dr. Jackson's narrative, he confirms Denton Maier played a little fast and loose with other people's research. Dr. Jackson's speculation about how to find Altomara's tomb in the early pages of his journal called, "The de Leon File."

He also had the habit of writing up other people's work as his own. My friends Juan Matao, Don Ruh, Dan Spartan and George Porter were not pleased with this but let it slide for my sake. When I finally presented the de Leon File to my friend Dan Spartan the truth dawned on us both that most of its first twenty-five pages was a combination of fact and fantasy that we decided not to correct or publish. In point of fact, the Benvenuto document, the Clyphus poem by Roache, the pamphlet mentioning Onteora, the Socoturn work and the Lindquist book with the Medallion were all that was actually needed to find the Tomb. The Constitution of Honorious was just icing on the cake and Denton mistook most of it to mention specifically the de Leon voyage which it didn't and with the exception of the Red Birds of Death mentions nothing about North America specifically or cryptically. Also, my wife did most of Denton's typing and mine too for Spartan Enterprise's work so unlike this work there were a lot of errors.

---

172   The likely reason Ogham script was chosen by Maier to write on the stone left in the tomb for Professor Fell to find was he knew Fell was one of the few world's experts at reading it in the 1970s.

```
Two weeks after we had found the tomb Dr. Fells staff notifed Dr.
Jackson that they had found what they felt was the tomb site.  We acted
very surprised.  We were notified that they had uncovered besides the
stone with the Octonqus on it a tablet written in Ogum and a brass vessle
called a drip.  It was located to the back of the cave and about 28" into
the floor of the cave.  This is one artifact we missed.  The tablet I knew
would prove to be worthless as we had arranged to have it made up and
left it for the good doctor to locate which he obligingly did.  It said
I do not like thee I can tell
Ido not like the way thee smell
I do not wish thee well
Thus goest thou to hell
Dr. Fell-De Leon.

     A short note some two weeks later from the scblor himself revealed that
the effort was not wasted.  It read.  Very Funny, Ha Ha.  I can tell yor effons
have not been wasted, your theory intact,I shall see it remains just that
for as long as I can.  In your future endevors I wish you well but please
do not come again to Dr. Fell.
     There was no signature nor was one needed.

   •  There have been some followup investigations to certain aspects of
this search that when they are complete shall be included herein.  They
center mostly around the mention of a Kabalistic circle in the Rituals
of Honorius Constitution, The Roche incident and his purposes towards the
tomb, The purpose of Mepnorius in returning to the tomb, And the significance
of our find on the archeological society today.
     With these exceptions we can say that after nine years of searching
the De Leon File is CLOSED.
```

Denton Maier's entry in the original typed draft of The de Leon Report, made on June 10, 1978, relates messages received from Dr. Barry Fell and his staff concerning their reported discovery of artifacts found two weeks after the initial discovery of the cave on October 11, 1977. Written in what appears to be Dr. William Jackson's hand are the words, "Disbeliever Assholes," that leaves little doubt concerning Dr. Jackson's opinion of the academic archaeological community. (Courtesy of Donald Ruh)

I have taken some liberties with this translation. The original document was not in pristine shape. Also, it was written in a continuous manner that produced no sentence or word structure. There were no periods and little punctuation except on occasional hyphen. There were names in both Latin and Welch that I have left as I translated them. Further, I have left some of the working in the Old English portion as I found it. This was done to provide a "Flavor" to the text and often because I didn't see the error till later and then just left it. There are some words that I could not fathom and those I left as I found them written. An example would be de Sudeley's translations that are obviously written from a phonetic standpoint resulting in the Welch form of using "ap" in a context, Len-ap-pee and Man-ap-ten. There [are] also words such as CONE and SHAW-MAN or Quicksa-Piet that could be sachem but I left as translated it hyphen and all. My friend Jake Stevens of the Onadaga tribe states to me that Quicksa-Piet could be a phonetic rendition of an Algonkin word for Medicine man, Quecksa' piet and Wasabee's name could also be Algonkin for Flower Woman, Woa'twes [the e is long] Mita'mu. Also, the Pan-si could be an Athabaskan word for Coyote but that is not certain. Later in the text de Sudeley came to hear CONE first hand from the people called that by others and here he wrote COHAN. I have not altered this. All of the numbers were written as letters and correspond to Latin form. Portions are missing and I have tried to fill in some letters as I thought they should be to make sense of the text. If my choice is wrong I'm sorry. Also, there is a mention of sky way and horizon way in the document. I realized this meant horizontal and vertical but didn't change the original form to that of the modern wording. There are three writers to this document. They all didn't write at the same time. This was some kind of record meant to be longer than what I bought but the rest is nonexistent. If I could not find an English word for the foreign language portions I left it in the original language. I often used modern words to replace the arcane ones used in the original text. There appear to be two persons with similar names one spelled Lional and the other Lionel. I left the spellings as I found them. I believe the first part to have been written between 1118 and 1139, the years Hugh de Payens was Grand Master of the Templars as he appears to have been the first writer I think that this incident occurred early on and when he remained in Jerusalem and most of his fellow knights left.[173] Originally, I chose 1130 for the date based on a test of the paper but it could be anywhere between 1100 and 1200 A.D. This is based on the oak gall content of the ink. Also, there is mention of "money moving "PLANS" and this could only refer to the Templars institution of the world's first international banking system set up early on in their existence. The second portion was written later by some Knight that was Italian. One of the original nine knights was Italian I believe. It is a continuation of the events that de Payens details but I think it was written down at a later time as a recollection. The third portion is attributed to one Ralph de Sudeley who signed it Ralp but the *h* may have not remained. This is true of a number of letters throughout the document. I believe also that this was written after the events occurred but that either de Sudeley or another member of the party possibly the Arab took notes. This is why some portions translate in the present and some in the past such as, "we must ask permission" and, "There is beads of colors. There is a Latin phrase that heads several sections of the text. It is the phrase required to decode that portion. Although each portion is written in a different language they all use Latin phrase as the coding medium. The document was meant to be a chronology of events for the initiated of the Temple but at the end of it de Sudeley mentions that a brother is sent for to record his events presumably for the R.C. Church and the Pope. That document I believe was signed not only by de Sudeley but by Eldric, perhaps the Spaniard and others as a statement to what they held in their possession and how it came to be so. That was the object of mentioning in this document the monk being brought in to record the testimony. I believe de Sudeley carefully worded it so as not to offend the Rule of the Church. His mention in this document of the administration of the sacraments and of absolution is proof.

173   http://www.encyclopedia.com/history/encyclopedias-almanacs-transcripts-and-maps/hugh-de-payens

There are some questions with the document also especially with regards to some of the place names. Where are or were they? Gwynedd I believe is Wales. Dunwich I can not locate. Why did de Sudeley head for a place in Wales upon his return? It was close by? They were familiar with the waters through Eldric, or was there some not mentioned reason such as dropping off items of value prying eyes and wagging tongues didn't need to know about. De Sudeley mentions at the end of the document two Grand Masters. Odon de St. Amand[174] and Arnould de Torogo.[175] The first was Grand Master from 1171 to 1180. The other from 1180 to 1185. Since de Sudeley calls the second the New Master I believe that the voyage took place during the tenure of Odon de St. Amand and since his narrative is about a period of time encompassing three Mid Summers Eve's I would guess 1177 or 78 to 1180. The document entitled, "A Year We Remember" but it encompasses several years. The first part of the document was titled in Latin but due to a misrepresentation by my researchers of this I chose the Italian to title this translation but the meaning remains the same. Is the "we" mentioned referring to each of the writers separately or collectively. I believe it is separately. I also believe that there had to be copies of the disks made and that is why de Torogo delayed the return mission. What was on the map signed by Mandrakis? De Sudeley does not say. Why? I think it told of treasure hidden somewhere and it was acquired by de Sudeley.

There are many questions about this document in regards to the people that they went to meet in America. From the eventual translation of the two scraps of paper with the Medallion I surmise that one group was in some way connected with the removal of Jesus Christ from the tomb. From *Joseph of Arimathea at Glastonbury* by Lionel S. Lewis, London: James Clarke & Co., 1955, comes the supposition that he was in fact James the brother of Jesus and the Roman Catholic Church purposely misinterpreted his Essene title. If this is in fact true, then the persons involved in the removal of Christ were part of a conspiracy and that they fled Jerusalem either without or with him or his body. They then went to the Nordic tribes and according to the document settled in America. Their descendants intermarrying with either the Nordic group or the natives were the people Lionel stayed with called the Cohan. I place this group in either Woodland Valley or Frost Valley in the Catskill Mountains of New York State U.S.A. The Nordic group is another matter entirely. It should also be noted that persons in the time frame when the fragments were comprised didn't have the education we have now. Only those of the wealthy classes could read and write.[176] Most persons could not speak several languages and could not read or write. The language structure was

---

174   https://translate.google.com/translate?hl=en&sl=fr&u=https://fr.wikipedia.org/wiki/Eudes_de_Saint-Amand&prev=search

175   https://en.wikipedia.org/wiki/Arnold_of_Torroja

176   I made a similar argument about the author of the Kensington Rune Stone inscription having been a highly-educated member of the clergy in the fourteenth century because the common people weren't educated.

based mostly on phoneticism. That is to say as people spoke local-
ly. The two fragments appear not to have been written by natives
of Portugal and France but that may be only our misinterpretation
of the language of the time it was written or they were purposely
depicted as non-grammatically correct to further hide the context
from the uninitiated.

There are two forms of thought in regards to early Jewish beliefs.
This is one of them. In older forms of the English Orthodox Bible translated from the Greek it states. "In the beginning was the
Word and the word was GOD." This implies that GOD is a concept
rather than an entity. What make Homo Sapiens what they are is
their ability to perceive consciousness in themselves and to convey it to others. Millions of years ago some animals must have developed a nervous system capable of carrying out perceptual cate-
gorization and memory. At that point, this animal could construct
and set discriminations. It could create a scene in its mind and
make connections with past scenes. At that point, primary consciousness sets in. But that animal cannot narrate. Some time later in hominid evolution [neural] circuits connected in the brain
that resulted in language. We were then freed of the remembered
present, of primary consciousness, and could invent all kinds of
images, fantasies and narrative systems. We could talk. This then
set us apart from all other forms of animal life including other
strains of Hominid existence, Neanderthal, Cro Magnon etc. The
WORD is what set us apart and that the WORD was the highest
creative THING in the universe of man. It was GOD. If GOD then
man must have visualized from his environment that there must
also be a GODDESS. It requires a male and female of all visual
species to procreate. She is symbolized in many forms throughout human history but in the Jewish faith she is ostracized during
the reign of Solomon. Those however that refused to accept this
monotheism were either killed or they fled to where they could
practice their TRUE religion, to the NORTH. As a footnote here I
would add that the early Greek Scriptures refer to the Holy Spirit
as She. In Latin there is no word for Spirit and it is translated as
Holy Wind and Wind is a masculine word. Jesus mentions to his
disciples that they will be visited by the Holy Spirit and she will
descend upon you it is written in the Aramaic and this I got from
a Bible in the Vatican Library. Now I must delve into the realm of
supposition and say that if de Payens and his fellow knights found
scrolls below the ruins of the temple in Jerusalem and below the
Location of the stables of the Temple of Solomon could it not be
that those scrolls told of the plight of the followers of the GOD-
DESS. Jesus never referred to himself as Divine. He refers to himself as the Son of Man as did all high-born Jews of their time. He
refers to the ONE that sent me and to his FATHER in heaven but
not to a specific individual referred to as GOD. Therefore, both the
Templars and the followers of Islam had it in common that they
didn't accept the divinity of Jesus as set forth by the Holy Roman
Church. If de Sudeley brought back evidence to prove their case

then they would have held it over the Pope which would explain the Papal reluctance to sanction, excommunicate or threaten the Knights Templars.[177] Further those persons involved in the finding could testify to the authenticity of the documents. For in that time frame copies had to be done by hand and a forgery was easy to make. By 1307 none of the original witnesses were still alive and the Papacy could act against the Templars without fear of reprisals. Did he find the Ark of the Covenant? No. But he may have found parts of the tablets of Stone given to Moses. How does a Concept write? Ideas upon the mind of man in a Protoplasmic experience would do just as well. The mountain of GOD was an active volcano and it erupted at just the right time. Petra was known for its protoplasmic disturbances and de Sudeley built his Templar training center in England in an area of similar occurrences. Coincidence? I doubt it.

Christ is reported to have said, "In my Father's house there are many mansions. I go to prepare a place for you. If I were not so I would not have told you." He meant that he would go in the spirit. As Abraham was to sacrifice his son to make a new Covenant with God based on Love, Unity for all and Self-esteem. He did nothing to save himself from death after he instigated his arrest. He would only be saved by the will of God not by his hand. If he were saved from death then God would have rejected his sacrifice and his Covenant. To say that he was raised from the dead was to say that his Covenant with God was rejected. This was the Cathar belief and it was embraced by the Templars who befriended them. Even when the Pope declared that de Payens should rebuke them he did so half-heartedly and feigned illness thereafter to keep from further abuse. With de Sudeley's findings the Templars intended to set themselves where he went in order to worship and live as they believed without interference from the Pope. Thus, the secret of the Temple of the Goddess etc. was of paramount importance to be kept. Jacques de Moley gave his life rather than reveal it. Too bad it didn't work out.

Could it be that Hugh de Payens' Islamic ancestry gave him some idea of what could be below the Temple in Jerusalem.

From the Charles Morrison collection in the Grand Lodge of Scotland comes a book, item #432, by James Burness titled, *Knights Templar* published in 1837 in which I find the following information:

Jacques de Moley when summoned by Pope Clement V put together ten ships and an astronomical sum of gold bullion to mount a new Crusade. He sailed from Cypress to La Rochelle a Templar port. These ships should have sailed to Marseilles rather than make their way through the Pillars of Hercules both sides

---

177 Not only would first-century documents be powerful leverage for the Templars to use against the Roman Catholic Church, but as I proposed earlier, having at least some of the mortal remains to go along with the documents would be even more devastating to the myth of Jesus if need be.

of which were still in Moors hands. He even left Jerusalem and traveled through Palestine to the port of Tyre, crosses to Cypress, where he is elected Master of the Order of Templars and makes his way back to Jerusalem without being molested by either Moors, Turkish, Saracen, or Arab followers. That is because there was very cordial relations between the Templars and Muslim groups and there was a non-aggression treaty with the Moors and the Templars excluding the Papacy at that time. Some of the charges brought against the Templars by Phillipe of France and the Papacy included the worship of a head called Baphomet.

From *Essens Odysey* by Dr. Hugh Schoenfeld, published in 1984, I found this interesting bit of knowledge that sheds light on de Sudeley's story:

The Essenic and NAZOREAN Church used a cryptographic system to disguise theological concepts or names of individuals. The word Baphomet when decoded is Sophia which is the Greek equivalent for the Judiac name for "WISDOM" this has always religiously been related to the female aspect of the Godhead. This head was therefore a reminder that though the Order came under the male dominated Papacy it acknowledged that Wisdom came from the female aspect of the deity that had been worshiped long before male form of worship raised its ugly head. Wisdom is referred to in Genesis as, "she who flies over the waves of the waters."

Continuing on with Dr. Jackson's narrative:

When I mention that pages are incomplete it is that they have been torn out. This I surmise was the work of Roache and the Mc-Donald group in their search for the hidden disks. I also believe that they found them. From the document I purchased anonymously but thanks to my friend Mr. Spartan I now know that it came from a MacDonald [sic] I think the vandalism theory not to be too far-fetched. Some pages are missing. This could also be due to the same source or just been mislaid. The binding was not in good condition when I purchased the document. At one time these pages may have been scrolled as the scrolls of the Bannerman Castle depicts and the unrolling left holes and deterioration. Later they were bound in book form as they are now. This resulted in missing parts of the text in both lines, pages and letters.

Recent archaeology discoveries in Europe and Asia have uncovered corpses that have evidence of Syphilis. This disease has been originally thought to have originated in North America and Columbus brought back to Europe but these findings produce the Archaeology community to revise that and state that it developed earlier in Europe. I believe they are all idiots. It developed in America and was transported to Europe and Asia because there was a regular trade route several thousand years prior to Columbus. The de Sudeley document proves this. I believe the chronology goes like this. About 950 or so BC a group of Jews not wanting to convert to monotheism and give up Ashura, Goddess and consort of YHWH left Solomon's Temple for parts unknown and ended up in America perhaps with the Nordic peoples and at some point began to mine copper. They traded it for supplies with the Nordic groups who eventually traded it to the inhabitants of England to be mixed with tin and made Bronze. This continued throughout the Roman occupation and I think a two-way trade route was at some point established for there to be scrolls under the Jerusalem Temple in AD 1100 At some point around AD 30 or 40 , a second group of Jews following Essenic and Gnostic teachings and connected to Jesus's family, remember Jesus father had shipping contracts for bronze with the Celts, chose or had to flee Jerusalem and went to Wales and the Brits. From there they went to the Nordic peoples all of whom were connected to those that worshiped the Goddess. They transported them to America and introduced them to the people of the Temple. They became the Cohan. The Temple descendants became the Mandan Indians. The Templars wanted to create a separate place so they could live free of Roman Catholic rule and they may have set up a group in Canada and worked with the Mi'kmaq Indians. They all probably perished around 1337 when the Plague broke out in Europe and trade brought it to them. Of course, this is all conjecture on my part.

This is where I disagree with Dr. Jackson. I have no doubt the plague was brought over to North America and likely decimated native populations as well as many of the Templars who stayed behind. However, I do not believe they, "all probably perished around 1337." All the Templars who stayed behind quickly assimilated with the various tribes they were accepted into. After one or two generations they had become completely native. Their impact on Native American culture, especially their rituals such as with the Mandan Okipa ritual, as documented by painter and writer George Catlin, is evidence of profound European influence.[178]

With regard to the sale of the document I have asked my friend Mr. Peter Carson to investigate Alexandros Andreadis. Based upon his findings I doubt that he wishes as he stated to buy the document for the Onassis Foundation. Stelios Papadimitriou, president of said Foundation, was unaware of such a purchase on its behalf. Thus, I can conclude that Andreadis is acting as an agent for either the Russian Orthodox or the Greek Orthodox Church and if I sell this document to him they will destroy it because it does not support THEIR Christian concepts. Rhinhardt has not offered as much money yet I am certain based on Mr. Carson's investigation that he represents an order of Masons and probably the one to which my father was a member but exactly which one precisely he won't say. I however think he will get this document. I believe they will preserve it. In any event, I think that whether it is a conceptual idea in the mind of man or a Spiritual Entity, GOD will approve of what I have done.

178   https://www.smithsonianmag.com/arts-culture/george-catlins-obsession-72840046/

A final word about the symbolism at the Temple of the Goddess. De Sudeley does a good job at this but leaves out one important item and that is the Triskele. This is a representation of the Three Worlds of the Celtic Myth. For this I am indebted to Ms. Roberta Arkinson, Iudaea, both for her paintings and for introducing me to Jerry Fox and Simon Rhinhardt without whose help much of my historical research could not have been accomplished successfully. Thank you all. The number three was revered by the Celts. It symbolizes three worlds the Other World of Spirits, the Mortal World, and the Celestial Sphere from which comes sunshine, rain to nourish the land, the moon to mark time in months and the stars to guide the traveler. The Mother Goddess was a triple Goddess; her three forms separate but still blending into one form creating a powerful whole. The three whorls represent stability, wholeness and completeness of the body, mind and spirit, earth, sea and sky. The interconnections of life and the nature of all things are enshrined in the whorls, spiraling, outward looking yet connecting veins, blood and arteries to the body as a whole. The three spirals also represent three times three months of pregnancy this connecting to the Great Mother, the Earth.

One final notation and that is that among the artifacts in the cave was a small brass container containing a diamond uncut, and a piece of uranium. Where they came from I don't know but must have been left as grave goods by some member of the group when Altomara was buried there. I have located the small cave where I believe Clyphus was interred. The text does not say he was cremated. I found it through Ms. Dede Phelps the forester at the Devil's Tombstone Campsite run by the State of New York and she learned of it from her father who preceded her in that position. It was not blocked up and was vacant. If anything remained the animals would have eaten it and the first people in it would have removed the grave goods. This area saw many persons in the 1800's with the building of a railroad at the base of the mountain. That is all but gone now. The other smaller cave where the scrolls were originally housed with the sand I may have located above and behind the natural stone formation of a human head but it is a dangerous place with much loose rock and is struck by lightning often so I have not investigated it thoroughly. There were some carvings on stone within and it was blocked up when I saw it first. Now that I have been diagnosed with Arteriosclerosis I don't think I ever will get to investigate it. I'll leave that for the next daring person to take up the torch of discovery from my failing hands. Thus, do I pass it.

Because my dear wife Murial believes that digging in the mud and dirt is beneath the stature of a man of the medical profession I am compelled to hide any artifacts and information I discover from her or she will simply throw it out. In this vein, I have disguised most of my finds and this document so that I believe they will be preserved for if man learns where he has been then he may learn not to repeat the mistakes of the past and so preserve his future. This is in effect the essence of both Medicine and Archaeology, only the medium is different.

Also, I may add good friend and former patient Ms. Arkinson chose the title Iudaea from the Book of Kells, Gospel of Matthew, as it represents the Monogram of the Greek form of Christ's name [CHI-RO-XP]."

Lastly, I would be remiss if I didn't comment upon the symbolism depicted upon the roof of the cave where Altomara's ashes were interred. De Sudeley records that he is told that the lines represent rivers and the way to "Brethren far to the South called the Man-Den, Cone and Navasak." When I saw this depiction upon the roof of the cave I could not discern what some of it was to the southern end as it had been worn down too much. I had the surface scraped and had Professor Ronald Cowee test it. He discovered it was not rock in the natural sense but a mixture of sandstone, pulverized with shells probably of snails, mud and cattail stalks. The cattail stalks were woven into a mat form and stretched over the natural rock surface that had a layer of this mixture added to it. Then more of the mixture was added to cover the mat. This then was partially dried and then the surface was scored to depict the characters and lines. When this dried firm it was like rock as long as moisture did not permeate the cavern. Over time moisture from above not only deteriorated the work it also caused the top rock surface to separate from the rest of the roof. This we supported with available wood logs but it will not remain for much longer. I surmise that the lines depict the East and West branch of the Neversink River and either the East and West branch of the Delaware or just the West branch of the Delaware and the Ohio River. At the very edge of the mural is the shape I have drawn below and I believe this is the representation of the Man-Den Group. Of course, the symbol that Denton thought was an octopus is actually the wilted rose of the house of Migdal and is a Teutonic Templar sign. The Menorah like design is of course the Cohan, the broken branch of the Jewish faith, thus the six candles instead of the seven. The vulva symbol is for the Goddess group and the notched feather is for the Katskyn natives to the West."

This part of the narrative especially perked my interest. In 1994, Dr. Jackson depicted the carvings in plaster-like material within a drawing. Coincidentally, all four symbols carved into it including the horizontally aligned vulva, the wilted rose, the six-candle Menorah and the notched feather have been discovered on inscribed stones in the area of Hunter Mountain.

When I first met Donald Ruh, he had already discovered what I call the Vulva Stone. Don said he found it near the YMCA camp in Frost Valley, in 2001. On July 1, 2009, while traveling with Don, Steve St. Clair, David Brody, and my son, Grant Wolter, I discovered a carved stone within a small pile of stones. The carving on the stone I found is nearly identical to the notched feather symbol on the tomb roof drawing. Since this area was a known fertility site to the local indigenous people, I suspect it was left as an offering. How long ago is impossible to say.

Donald Ruh discovered this stone inscribed on both sides with Phoenician characters in Frost Valley, New York, in 2001. The age and origin of the inscribed stone is unknown. (2007/2007)

Donald Ruh also discovered this six-armed symbol (left) with a triangular shaped base near the YMCA camp in Frost Valley, New York. Some have interpreted it as a Hebrew menorah, while others associate it with a deer refuge known to be in the area in the early 1900s as reported by Ruh. The author found this stone within a small pile of stones near a small stream in the woods of Frost Valley, New York, on July 1, 2009 (right). (Courtesy of Donald Ruh/2009)

On July 1, 2009, on Hunter Mountain David Brody and Donald Ruh unearthed the In Camera Stone that had Roman numerals XLV XXX (45 degrees 30 minutes) for latitude and LXXV LIII (75 degrees 53 minutes) longitude (left), and the Tanith and Wilted Rose symbols carved on the back side (right). (2009/2009)

On the original document following the word *Navasak* there are 12 characters badly smudged or deteriorated. I make them out to read *mmbe dadoniram* and I believe that this could be *tomb d'Adoniram* or the tomb of Adoniram. I put this from the cross on the mural at the source of Deer Shanty Brook but when Don Ruh, Jake Stevens and I went there there was nothing evident to suggest a tomb on the surface nor did Jake feel the presence of the dead. It is also possible that the area showing the way to the Man-Den was obliterated on purpose to hide the route from others.

Yours Truly,

Bill Jackson 1994

P.S. The mural tested out based on the shell content at a little over two thousand years old give or take 200."

Turning now to the actual contents of the document, I was impressed with the insightful comments Dr. Jackson wrote about concerning various aspects. He obviously put in a lot of time researching the history of the Templars and quoted his sources. I was especially moved with Dr. Jackson's thoughtful theory about how the Templars had leverage against the Church in the form of first-century scrolls recovered on Hunter Mountain that contained, among other things, the truth about Jesus:

Now I must delve into the realm of supposition and say that if de Payens and his fellow knights found scrolls below the ruins of the temple in Jerusalem and below the Location of the stables of the Temple of Solomon could it not be that those scrolls told of the plight of the followers of the GODDESS. Jesus never referred to himself as Divine. He refers to himself as the Son of Man as did all high-born Jews of their time. He refers to the ONE that sent me and his FATHER in heaven but not to a specific individual re-

ferred to as GOD. Therefore, both the Templars and the followers of Islam had it in common that they didn't accept the divinity of Jesus as set forth by the Holy Roman Church. If de Sudeley
brought back evidence to prove their case then they would have
held it over the Pope which would explain the Papal reluctance
to sanction, excommunicate or threaten the Knights Templars.
Further those persons involved in the finding could testify to the
authenticity of the documents. For in that time frame copies had
to be done by hand and a forgery was easy to make. By 1307 none
of the original witnesses were still alive and the Papacy could act
against the Templars without fear of reprisals. Did he find the Ark
of the Covenant? No. But he may have found parts of the tablets of
Stone given to Moses. How does a Concept write? Ideas upon the
mind of man in a Protoplasmic experience would do just as well.
The mountain of GOD was an active volcano and it erupted at just
the right time. Petra was known of its protoplasmic disturbances
and de Sudeley built his Templar training center in England in an
area of similar occurrences. Coincidence? I doubt it.

Christ is reported to have said, "In my Father's house there are
many mansions. I go to prepare a place for you. If it were not so I
would not have told you." He [Jesus] meant that he would go in
the spirit. As Abraham was to sacrifice his son to make a new covenant with God based on Love, Unity for all and Self-esteem. He
[Jesus] did nothing to save himself from death after he instigated
his arrest. He would only be saved by the will of God not by his
hand. If he were saved from death then God would have rejected his sacrifice and his Covenant. To say that he was raised from
the dead was to say that his Covenant with God was rejected. This
was the Cathar belief and it was embraced by the Templars who
befriended them. Even when the Pope declared that de Payens
should rebuke them he did so half-heartedly and feigned illness
thereafter to keep from further abuse. With de Sudeley's findings
the Templars intended to set themselves where he went in order
to worship and live as they believed without interference from
the Pope. Thus, the secret of the Temple of the Goddess etc. was of
paramount importance to be kept. Jacques de Moley gave his life
rather than reveal it. Too bad it didn't work out.

Dr. Jackson did not seem to have much respect for the conventional thinking of
archaeologists which, I have to confess, I agree with in far too many cases. His specific
complaint was geared to the debate about when syphilis was brought to Europe:

Recent archaeology discoveries in Europe and Asia have uncovered corpses that have evidence of Syphilis. This disease has been
originally thought to have originated in North America and Columbus brought it back to Europe but these findings produce the
Archaeology community to revise that and state that it developed earlier in Europe. I believe they are all idiots. It developed
in America and transported to Europe and Asia because there was

a regular trade route several thousand years prior to Columbus. The de Sudeley document proves this. I believe the chronology goes like this. About 950 or so BC a group of Jews not wanting to convert to monotheism and give up Ashera, Goddess and consort or YHWH left Solomon's Temple for parts unknown and ended up in America perhaps with the Nordic peoples and at some point began to mine copper. They traded it for supplies with the Nordic groups who eventually traded it to the inhabitants of England to be mixed with tin and made Bronze. This continued throughout the Roman occupation and I think a two-way trade route was at some point established for there to be scrolls under the Jerusalem Temple in AD 1100. At some point around AD 30 or 40 a second group of Jews following Essenic and Gnostic teachings and connected to Jesus's family, remember Jesus's father had shipping contracts for bronze with the Celts, chose or had to flee Jerusalem and went to Wales and the Brits. From there they went to the Nordic peoples all of whom were connected to those that worshiped the Goddess. They transported them to America and introduced them to the people of the Temple. They became the Cohan. The Temple descendants became the Mandan Indians. The Templars wanted to create a separate place so they could live free of Roman Catholic rule and they may have set up a group in Canada and worked with the Mi'kmaq Indians. They all probably perished around 1337 when the Plague broke out in Europe and trade brought it to them. Of course, this is all conjecture on my part.

While the term, "Triple Goddess," had come to my attention earlier in my research, Dr. Jackson provided a pleasant surprise in one of his final thoughts about the concept of Goddess veneration. It was something I had never heard before.

Dr. Jackson's summary of the Triple Goddess is fitting, as it is the most important aspect as to why the medieval Templars, and the first-century Goddess worshippers who came before them, had so much success with the indigenous people. When the Templars first encountered Native Americans they had compatible ideologies. This served as the foundation for the relationship that allowed the Templars to assimilate over the millennia. It was gratifying to read Dr. Jackson's eloquently stated conclusion in 1994, which was the same conclusion I reached a decade later. This also explains the origin of many of the mysterious artifacts and sites found on this continent. Just like how we were taught to believe about pre-Columbian history in North America, the discoveries and research, has changed the historical paradigm.

For the purposes of my research there are several interesting facts that emerge from de Sudeley's narrative that, assuming the document is authentic, adds a critical piece to the already massive body of evidence proving pre-Columbian contact by medieval Templars in North America occurred. Here is a list of the relevant points to keep in mind:

1. Templar knights from multiple countries made the voyage to North America, including Scotland, Denmark, what is now Germany, France and Spain.

2. The Templars discovered human remains under the Temple in Jerusalem. In this case, they appear to be those of John the Baptist.

3. The Templars discovered gold bars under the Temple in Jerusalem referring to, "…money moving plans."

4. The Templars discovered ancient scrolls and maps under the Temple in Jerusalem which told of first-century voyages to North America, where other scrolls from the first century were hidden.

5. Repeated references to the veneration of the Goddess which includes the knights' search for a reported "Temple to the Goddess" on Hunter Mountain.

6. Mention of "…precious relics including parts of tablets given to Moses from God and held in a golden chest feared taken by the Romans when they overran Jerusalem and it was hidden below in the tunnels cut for water in the ruined city of Petra…"

7. First-century documents that include, "The third document also encoded was of a journey of the Spirit and told of the True Teachings of our Lord. Also of a Seal of Herod (Agrippa) to an agreement of union between an Hasmonian Princess, Myriam of Migdal and Yeshua ben Yosef of the Royal House of David at Cana."

8. Priestess Altomara's body is processed in a manner similar to the ossuary culture in Jerusalem in the first century. The only difference is her body was burned, as they did not have the time necessary for desiccation of the flesh:

Altomara was taken and wrapped in a mat and placed upon the top of the stone tunnel upon a great pile of wode [wood] of the pine tree and a fire was set below and she was consumed. The bones were gathered and placed in a special box of oak wood and Ponce took her ash and placed It in the jar he had carried Myrrh that he had used to wash her body. Gwyn had her placed in the cave with the carving atop its roof both ash and bone box and each of us left a grave good.

9. That de Sudeley traveled overland to Hunter Mountain in a party of "twenty and six" people may seem like a minor point, but we have already seen the number 26, which is 2 x 13, is a sacred number that was likely not chosen by accident.

10. De Sudeley and his men built a boat over the winter to sail back to Europe, "…to where we can await the thaw to build a boat and sail East to our homeland across the great ocean."

11. Several Hooked X symbols are presented in the table of contents, on the signature page, and three times on the Nova Scotia map, all within the Cremona Document.

Perhaps the most interesting revelation in de Sudeley's deposition is one of the scrolls recovered from the cave at the Temple of the Goddess on Hunter Mountain. It was essentially a marriage document, most likely a copy of the original, between "Myriam of Migdal" (Mary Magdalene) and "Yeshua ben Yosef" (Jesus, son of Joseph). This was not shocking news to me. When I first read it, I had already reached the conclusion that Jesus and Mary Magdalene were married after researching the ossuaries from the Talpiot tomb. However, in the early 1970s when Dr. Jackson first read this it must have come as a real shock. It was a different time and thirty years before Dan Brown's *The Da Vinci Code* first awakened the world to this heretical idea in 2003. In Dr. Jackson's time, this would have been an explosive thing to make public to the point of being dangerous in certain circles. This explains why Dr. Jackson kept knowledge of the marriage document, and the explosively controversial information it contained, so quiet. Assuming the Cremona Document is authentic, the Jesus/Mary Magdalene marriage scroll was likely the primary thing that prompted the first-century party, possibly the Essenes, to travel across Europe, and then the Atlantic, to protect this long-suppressed truth.

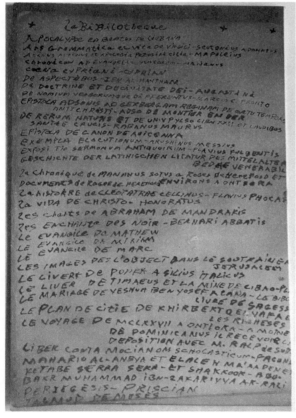

This page from the Cremona Document contains the list of scrolls Ralph de Sudeley recovered from the Temple of the Goddess on Hunter Mountain. The most notable scroll title is just over two-thirds of the way down, "Le Mariage de Yeshua Ben Yosef a Cana" (Yeshua Ben Yosef's Wedding in Cana). The presumption is he married Mary Magdalene. (Courtesy of Donald Ruh)

To add more fuel to the fire concerning the marriage of Jesus/Yeshua and Mary Magdalene, on February 7, 2015, I received an email from a friendly fan named "Dave" who said he was a retired Navy Commander and shared the following information:

Dear Mr. Wolter:

I saw your season finale (Season 3). While I am not a geologist, I am a professor of Jewish history. Especially back in the days of Yeshua (Jesus) there would have been tremendous pressure on Him to make his mother, Mary... a grandmother. Under the Jewish tradition of that time, for His child to be recognized as legitimate, Yeshua would have to be married BEFORE the child was born. To make his mother a grandmother would be a societal honor bestowed upon her. It would be in modern parlance, a feather in her cap.

Now, the RC (Roman Catholic) church has been anti Mary of Magdala since the earliest days of the church. Modern research and inquiry has indicated that 1) Yeshua and Mary of Magdala were indeed married and 2) Mary, about 7 months after the crucifixion gave birth to the daughter of Yeshua.

As a Freemason, I cannot give you exact knowledge, but let's just say that your assumption that the Templars became part of Freemasonry and your assumption that they brought the truth of Yeshua's daughter and skeletal remains to North America are not unfounded.

There was a parchment delivered to the RC church in 1927 by an antiquities collector. It was dated by experts in 1945 to around AD 120 and it details the marriage of Yeshua and Mary and her birth of his daughter... and the fact that Mary of Magdala was in fact the head of the Christian church for several years.

The document was called the Catholicos Mysticus. It was apparently penned by the bishop of the church of Galatia and many requests to view it over the decades have been denied... and as of 2012 the RC Church officially denies its existence.

I cannot and will not offer any more info on this subject... it's just not prudent for me.

Cordially

This prompted an exchange between us where Dave shared additional information:

Between you and me... YOU and ME, you should know that the Templars hid MANY valuable religious artifacts in North America, places like Oak Island, Vermont, Philadelphia (as recently as 1870 one of the items was relocated to some location near the original Pennsylvania Statehouse in Philadelphia) and these items include the remains of the daughter of Yeshua, the Ark of the Covenant and the chalice Yeshua drank from at the Last Supper. I don't know where each individual item is, but I do know that there is definitely something of tremendous religious significance buried on Oak Island... but you have not heard this from me... I'm risking complete expulsion from the Order for divulging even this scant information.

The Catholic church has certainly infiltrated the Craft. I am not asking you to stop. Of all the people I've seen on TV, you are getting the closest to the truth... I'm sure of that. The Catholic church is MOST worried about the truth of Yeshua and Mary of Magdala coming out.

As for Yeshua and Mary, I believe it was true... I mean, a Vatican Monsignor admitted it was true. So why would there be any reason to doubt the great relics of the old and New Testaments exist somewhere in North America?

In light of the Cremona Document and mention of a marriage scroll hidden on Hunter Mountain that was recovered by the Templars in the twelfth century, this mysterious information passed along to me by a Freemason is more than a little interesting. The weight of evidence has shown this is real historical truth.

An anonymous Freemason sent me a copy of an email correspondence dated May 12, 2009, a colleague shared with him where a Vatican Monsignor named Francis Marchetti, confirmed the existence of a document recording the secret marriage between "Mary of Magdala" and "our Lord and Savior." (Anonymously submitted, 2015)

Because I first published the connection between the Hooked X with modern Freemasonry and the medieval Knights Templar in 2009, it is not possible a forger could have created this lengthy and extremely detailed document using several Hooked X's properly before that time. In my eyes, this strongly supports the Cremona Document's authenticity, but for something of this historical magnitude it has to be carefully and thoroughly vetted before being fully accepted. This must be kept in mind while considering the points about to be presented that pertain to the contents of the document.

If true, this incredible story is amazing on the one hand, and confusing on the other. It has long been rumored the Templars found gold under the Temple, but the human remains, the ancient scrolls, and the scientific instruments were somewhat of a surprise. My first thought was the person in the ossuary whose head was severed by an axe was likely John the Baptist. If so, it would lend credence to the Templars', and Freemasonry's, reverence for the Grand Master who initiated/baptized Jesus. According to tradition, he was another bloodline ancestor of certain Venus family lines that later included the Templar knights, along with Hugh de Payens, who recovered the contents of ossuaries in the de Sudeley narrative.

CREMONA DOCUMENT MAPS

Arguably, the most captivating aspects of the Cremona Document are the four maps of easily recognizable locations on the northeastern seaboard of North America. One in particular, dated to 1179 (MCLXXIX), includes southern Newfoundland and Nova Scotia cut into two pieces, with the eastern half stacked on top of the western half in an apparent space saving exercise. There were several interesting symbols and Roman numerals marking specific latitudes as well as *longitude*. Conventional wisdom says the ability to accurately calculate longitude was not discovered until the latter part of the seventeenth century. Many researchers, myself included, believe ancient navigators understood how to calculate longitude with reasonable accuracy. The four metal devices used for navigation provide evidence that ancient mariners understood this vitally important knowledge. Keep in mind the drip cup found by Barry Fell in Altomara's cave was used as a clock. To accurately determine longitude requires a device that records time, like a sundial. The drip cup, left as an offering to the fallen princess, was designed to do the same thing. Further, if the information in this document dates to the twelfth entury, then these maps definitively prove the Templars understood how to determine longitude at that time.

What are now called the Nova Scotia and southern Connecticut maps haves words and phrases in Old French peppered throughout them. On the Nova Scotia map, some of the French words are numbers, one is the name of an indigenous tribe, the "Inuhit" (Inuit). Another correctly documents where the largest tides in the world are found in the Bay of Fundy, *La Courant de Monstre* (The Monster Current). Others are interesting short phrases. After translating the phrases using Google Translate, several immediately caught my attention, *La Mere de Deus* (The Mother of God), *La Deesse* (The Goddess), and *Le Vingt Quatre de Juin* (The Twenty-Four of June). The twenty-four of June is now known within Freemasonry as John the Baptist day. In addition to John the Baptist, the Templars also revered Mary Magdalene. It occurred to me this might be evidence to support the rumored Cathar legend that Mary Magdalene married and had sons with both John the Baptist and Jesus. This would be a bombshell that went far beyond the heretical claim of *The Da Vinci Code* that Mary Magdalene married and had children only with Jesus. It is also possible the phrase refers to something else entirely. However, if the history of the Cremona Document is true, it was a highly dangerous document and was held in utmost secrecy for almost nine-hundred years.

For the reported date of 1179, the Connecticut map is amazingly accurate. Like the Nova Scotia map, it also contains interesting words including: *Nord d'apres treize* (North after thirteen), *Onze* (Eleven), *Douze* (Twelve), *Treize* (Thirteen), *Point de Étranger* (Point of Stranger), and *Neuf* (New). It is presumed the words *Peacoot* and *Penecookie* are referring to local indigenous tribes. The phrase *North after thirteen* seems to suggest movement of what we presume was the de Sudeley party. When considered with another previously unpublished map in the Cremona Document, this suggestion appears to be accurate as it represents a stretch of the Hudson River.

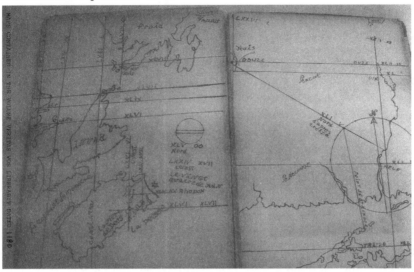

The Cremona Document includes these two maps that shows Nova Scotia (left) drawn as two sections, with the northeastern half stacked on top of the southwestern half, and the apparent connection point designated with a Seal of Solomon symbol. Both latitude and longitude are depicted using Roman numbers on horizontal and vertical lines. The text used is Old French and includes interesting phrases like *La Deesse* (The Goddess), *La Mere de Deus* (The Mother of Two), and *Le Vingt quatre de juin* (The twenty four of June) that are featured prominently in medieval Templarism and modern Freemasonry. What I find most interesting are the three Hooked Xs, one found in the word "six," the second as the last *X* in the date 1179 (MCLXXIX) and the most obvious found directly adjacent to the circle with two horizontal lines in the *X* in latitude forty-five (XLV), zero (00) minutes. (Courtesy of Donald Ruh)

Moving on to the next map, there is one very interesting feature on the Narragansett Bay map that appears to have a tie with a site still extant to this day. The line angling from southwest to northeast has the French words *La Place* (The Place) and *Le Tresor* (The Treasure) with a small dot marked where the line meets the edge of a semicircle in the top right side of the page. Curiously, the location of the dot is eerily close to the present-day Cistercian Monastery in Cumberland, Rhode Island.[179] Construction of Our Lady of the Valley monastery in Rhode Island began in 1902 on a 530-acre parcel of land. Home to roughly 140 monks, in 1950 a devastating fire broke out that destroyed the guest house and most of the church. Deciding not to rebuild, the monastic

179   http://www.cumberlandlibrary.org/monastery-history

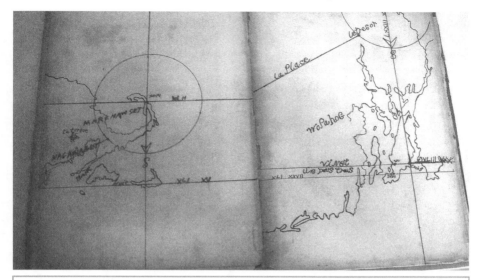

The Cape Cod and Narragansett Bay maps are pictured here in the Cremona Document purchased by Dr. William Jackson in 1971. The map on the right clearly shows Narragansett Bay, with what has to be the local Native American tribe of the Wampanoag, spelled "Wopahog," in the center. Interestingly, *"Un," "Deus,"* and *"Trois"* appears between the latitudes 41 degrees, 27 minutes (XLI XXVII) and 43 degrees, 30 minutes (XVIII XXX) with a single longitude line marked at 73 degrees, 35 minutes. The *Un* dot is at the approximate location of the Newport Tower, and the *Deus* dot is very close to where Fort Adams was built in 1812. (Courtesy of Donald Ruh)

community decided to relocate to a larger parcel of land in Spencer, Massachusetts, where they remain to this day. However, what is most interesting is the history of the order that began in Nova Scotia.

The Cumberland monastery was founded in 1892 after the monks relocated from Nova Scotia, Canada after a fire destroyed the Abbey of Petit Clairvaux.[180] The Trappist order of strict observance was originally founded by Father Vincent de Paul Merle (1768-1853). Of the original twenty monks who were sent from the hostile environment of post-French Revolution Europe to Halifax, Nova Scotia, Father Vincent de Paul Merle, was the only one who stayed behind. His efforts resulted in the foundation for the abbey being constructed in 1819. Despite the harsh conditions the order grew to as many as forty-five members only to have their refuge, records and sanctuary, destroyed by fire sapping the energy and will of the monks. Besides sending a contingent to Cumberland to relocate and begin anew, another group of monks related to the Cistercian order in Nova Scotia found their way west. They eventually settled at the incredible ancient Native American city called Cahokia.

Monks Mound was named after the Cistercian Trappist monks who sailed from France in 1802 and eventually settled, albeit briefly, at Cahokia, in St. Clair County, Illinois, from 1809-1813.[181] Not only is there an ironic connection with St. Clair County

---

180 https://www.spencerabbey.org/our-history/the-foundation-of-petit-clairvaux-1825-1857/

181 http://penelope.uchicago.edu/Thayer/E/Gazetteer/Places/America/United_States/Illinois/_Texts/journals/IllCHR/8/2/The_Trappists_of_Monks_Mound*.html

that brings to mind Earl Henry Sinclair, the Cistercian Templar knight who landed in Nova Scotia with seven ships in 1398, but the name of the monastery at Cahokia, *Notre Dame du Bon Secours,* will enter our story again very soon. What I find to be the most interesting event related to the Trappist monks at Cahokia was the connection to the famous Shoshone Native American, Sacagawea (circa 1788-1812). She guided and essentially saved the lives of Lewis and Clark during the Corps of Discovery expedition. In 1809, Sacagawea traveled to Cahokia with her husband, Toussaint Charbonneau (1758-1843), to have their four-and-a-half-year-old son, Jean Baptiste "Pompey" Charbonneau (1805-1866), baptized. The resident priest of the Trappist monks at Cahokia, Father Urbain Guillet, performed the service in St. Louis, Missouri, on December 28, 1809.[182]

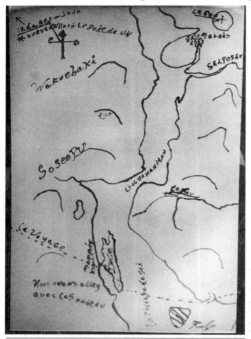

What this tangled web of historical figures, Cistercian monks, and important Native American sites has to do with our investigation is somewhat murky. However, the thick, dark smoke of coincidental connections of time, places and people has to be connected to a fire burning somewhere. As if this boiling cauldron of related facts weren't enough, it should be remembered Sacajawea was living with the Mandan and Hidatsa in North Dakota, not far from where the Kensington Rune Stone was discovered in 1898.[183] Some researchers believe the Mandan, known for a high percentage of people having blonde hair and blue eyes, and whose Okipa ritual contained numerous identical elements to the Hebrew Exodus story, were direct descendants of the Kensington party who assimilated with the local indigenous people in the fourteenth century. I believe the theory has a lot of merit and although Sacajawea was originally part of the Shoshone, she could have

This map appears to be of the Hudson River which shows the route Ralph de Sudeley and his party took on their way back to Europe. The dashed line at the bottom of the map traces their route and is labeled *Le Voyage* (The Trip), and at the west edge of the river says, *Nous avens allez avec les radeau* (We go with the rafts). In the upper left corner are the words, *IX dager* (9 Days), which appears to suggest how long it took to travel overland from the Temple of the Goddess on Hunter Mountain. (Courtesy of Donald Ruh)

182 https://books.google.com/books?id=tdMX9lJf5u0C&pg=PA62&lpg=PA62&dq=Sacagawea%27s+son+baptism+by+trappist+monks+at+Cahokia&source=bl&ots=MnRFquIVzn&sig=h_KlwE6qjoGfZW0QEljxCH5YgOE&hl=en&sa=X&ved=0ahUKEwj5iuOQpeXbAhWlwVkKHZJ0DxY-Q6AEILDAA#v=onepage&q=Sacagawea's%20son%20baptism%20by%20trappist%20monks%20at%20Cahokia&f=false

183   https://www.nps.gov/lecl/learn/historyculture/sacagawea.htm

obtained knowledge of her people's interactions with the Templars and understood aiding Lewis and Clark was her destiny and obligation. I suspect Sacajawea may even have been a direct bloodline descendant of one of the Templar knights who assimilated with, and whose descendants were, Mandan and/or Shoshone.

Along with the Corps of Discovery expedition, there appears to be more going on with these seemingly obscure historical individuals and events than our history books tell us.

The Hudson River map shows what appears to be a river with an Isle (island) in the southern end, mountains, a dashed line marking *Le Voyage* (The Trip), and a coat of arms next to the name *Ralp*, of Ralph de Sudeley. A quick Google search finds the coat of arms for the de Sudeley family at Weddington Castle, in Warwickshire, England. It is a yellow shield with two diagonal red bands running across from the top left to lower right. This is a match to the coat of arms roughly drawn on the Hudson River map. Between the island in the river and the French words *Le Voyage*, is the word *Marias* (swamp). Below that are the words *Nous avens allez avec les radeau* (We go with the rafts). This dashed line that crosses the river, via the swamp and island, corresponds with the de Sudeley deposition describing when he and his party are making their way home: "We reach a high bluff overlooking another greater river with a small island upon it's far shore. Here the river narrows and it is here we will cross. We begin to fell trees for rafts and are soon upon the far shore. This river is of salt."

While this passage seems to correspond with the Hudson River map, under examination there is some confusion as to which river they crossed. From Hunter Mountain, the quickest route would be a relatively short trek east to the Hudson River which runs due south to the sea. The areas depicted on the map appear to fit most closely with the section of the Hudson River between the *Isle* of Iona and the round protruding landmass to the north with the swamp, in what is now called Constitution Island. At this point, after crossing the Hudson, de Sudeley continues:

> We pass in three days several stone and earth covered structures but don't stay in them. They are for the women. We cross another river with the help of the local people and to this to an island of great size and travel in a sheltered water way by great bark boats along this to where we can await the thaw to build a boat and sail east to our homeland across the great ocean.

The island of great size appears to be Long Island and the "sheltered waterway" is Long Island Sound. Where the de Sudeley party wintered before they sailed home appears to be answered on yet another, and perhaps the most mysterious, map in Dr. William Jackson's collection of documents.

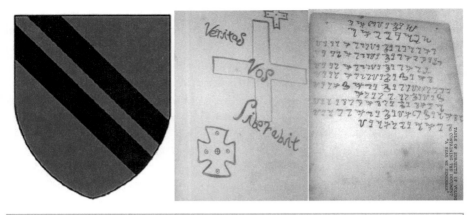

The de Sudeley coat of arms (left) matches the one drawn at the bottom of the Hudson River map with the name *Ralp* next to it.[184] The cover page of the Cremona Document (center) includes the phrase, *Verita Vos Liberabit* ("he Truth Will Set You Free). See color section for detail. The title page (right) contains a list of subjects using Theban symbols and translates into French. When translated into English it is as follows: "Lines 1 and 2: Table of Subjects; Line 3: The Gospel of Miriam (Mary); Line 4: The Gospel of Matthew; Line 5: Gospel of Mark; Line 6: Gospel of John; Lines 7 and 8: The Voyage of 1178 with M[aster?] of Sudeley; Lines 9 thru 11: How to Get Water Out of the Tunnels." On line 7, the two Roman numeral *X*s are Hooked *X*s. (Internet/Courtesy of Donald Ruh/Courtesy of Donald Ruh)

The Ark Page

Arguably, the most surprising page of the Cremona Document is filled with Theban text—wavy lines that look like a river or stream—a drawing of a box with a lid and two compartments, and what looks like two puppets facing each other with a sun symbol between them. Don Ruh shared a picture of the page during my visit in May of 2017.[185] I carefully studied the drawing and it quickly dawned on me this had to be the Ark of the Covenant! The open lid,

with lines pointing to specific things attached to the lid, led me to believe this page had to be instructions about how the Ark operated, or more likely, how to build one. When Don shared the English translation of the words it made all the sense in the world. This revelation put an entirely different spin on the pervasive legend of the Ark of the Covenant that the world has been led to believe.

Without going too in-depth, there are connections in these instructions that directly connect to specific degrees in both the Scottish Rite and York Rite Freemasonry. In fact, the Select Master degree, where I discovered the Cryptic Code on the Kensington Rune Stone, also reveals specific details about what is on the outside, and inside, of the Ark of the Covenant. To learn more about those details one must become a York

---

184   http://www.weddingtoncastle.co.uk/sudeley-castle.html

185   Donald Ruh will share a photo of the entire page along with his translation of the Theban text in his forthcoming book titled, *The Scrolls of Onteora*.

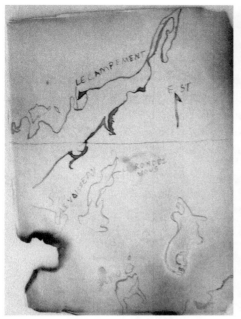

The origin of this partially burned map is unclear, but it is believed to depict the extreme northeastern end of Long Island where it is thought the Ralph de Sudeley party wintered prior to sailing back to Europe in 1180. The drawings thought to have been made using lemon juice were brought out by heat that eventually caused the paper to ignite and completely burn to ashes. (Courtesy of Donald Ruh)

These drawings are from a page in the Cremona Document that deals specifically with the Ark of the Covenant. The left drawing appears to show a diagram of the opened box that is divided into two compartments. To the right of the box are what appear to be two crudely drawn angels with a sun (energy?) symbol in the middle. The image on the right in the upper right part of the page shows Theban text and Roman numerals with a Hooked X in the second numeral ten. (Courtesy of Donald Ruh)

Rite Freemason and go through the Cryptic Council degrees, or carefully read the Ark page section of Don's forthcoming book. Of course, for the most thorough examination, one would do both.

As fantastic as the Ark page is in revealing secret information related to what is arguably the most mysterious artifact in history, the page also revealed something else that is secret and sacred. In the upper right edge of the page is a series of four Roman numerals (XVIX). As if confirming the importance of this page, the second *X* was a Hooked X.

Ramses ii Obelisk Page

Another remarkable page in the Cremona Document, like that of the Ark Page, has Theban text and interesting drawings. The Theban text has been translated by Donald Ruh and is presented in *The Scrolls of Onteora*. The message claims the pyramidion at the top of the obelisk erected by Ramses II, that once stood outside the entrance to the Temple of Luxor, in Thebes, was reportedly stolen in the sixth century BC.[186] The motive for the theft of the pyramidion is depicted in drawings that show three holes cut into the bottom of the stone that once contained scrolls with maps of the world's continents and oceans drawn by ancient cartographers. Curiously, there are detailed maps surrounding the drawing of the obelisk that include the eastern Mediterranean region—including the Red Sea and the Nile River in the upper left—the Americas in the lower middle, and the west coast of Africa in the lower left.

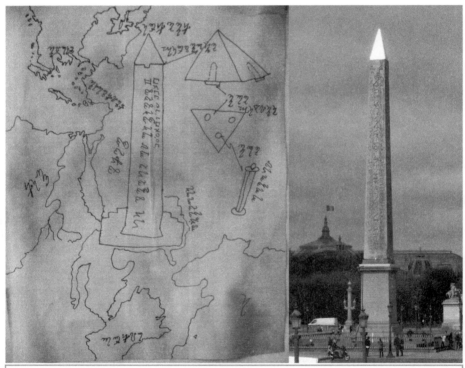

Another page with Theban text from the Cremona Document (left) appears to definitively answer the question about pre-Columbian exploration of the world by cultures that had the sailing technology and the secrets of global navigation. The obelisk drawn here, erected to Ramses II, depicts the pyramidion on top being detachable with three holes drilled into the bottom where scrolls of ancient maps of the world were reportedly hidden. The drawings around the obelisk represent the eastern Mediterranean region in the upper left, North and South America on the bottom, and the east coast of Africa on the bottom right (Courtesy of Donald Ruh). In 2010, I visited Paris and took this photo (right) of the Ramses II obelisk that was one of two that once stood in front of the Temple of Luxor in Thebes. The gold top replaced the now missing original stone and is consistent with the story of the original top being stolen, likely for the hidden maps it reportedly once contained.

---

186   https://en.wikipedia.org/wiki/Luxor_Obelisk

This illustration is from a fictional book published in 1858. One of the twelfth-century Templar maps with parts of the northeast coast of North America is copied on the back side and may have secretly been copied and removed from the Vatican archives in the latter part of the nineteenth century. (Courtesy of Donald Ruh)

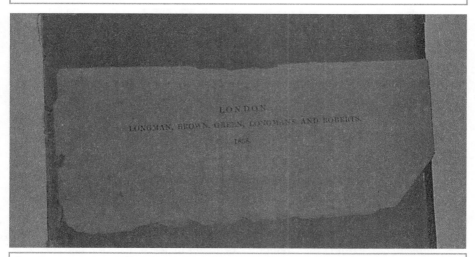

On May 28, 2018, Donald Ruh sent this picture of part of a page listing the year of publication of a book in London, lying on the back cover of the Cremona Document. Ruh recalled this was the title page of the fictional book that contained the illustrations with the maps drawn on the blank back sides. This confirms the book the maps were drawn in, their origin likely being in the Vatican library in Rome. (Courtesy of Donald Ruh)

This obelisk was one of the original two at the entrance to the Temple of Luxor that was moved to Paris, in 1832-1833.[187] In March of 2010, I traveled to Paris and photographed the obelisk, unaware of the history of why it is now topped with a gold leafed cap. The Cremona Document appears to explain the mystery, but also begs the question: where are those ancient maps now?

There is an overriding question about the Cremona Document. Is it an authentic record of the origins of the Knights Templar and their activities in Jerusalem and North America prior to European settlement beginning in the late sixteenth century? Based on my collective research to date, it appears the answer is yes. If so, it puts emphasis on understanding the origin of the Cremona Document purchased in 1971 by Dr. William Jackson. What is the age of the document we still have original pages of, and where did it originally come from? At this point it boils down to speculation based on the known facts at hand. The best explanation of the origin of the document that contains the maps published here, and several additional pages to be published in Donald Ruh's forthcoming book, was put forth by fellow researcher and friend, Jovan Hutton Pulitzer in early 2018.

In private conversations with Pulitzer, he speculated the detailed maps were likely copied from older versions, or possibly the originals, he believes were stored in the Vatican archives. When I asked how the maps could be copied and then taken from a facility with such high security, he presented his theory. Don has two of the original maps in his possession that were drawn on the blank side of the illustration pages. Pulitzer speculated the pages were from a book published in the mid-nine

teenth century. Future C-14 testing of the pages will reveal the actual age of the paper, but it appears Pulitzer is probably right. But how could someone have made copies of vitally important Templar-era maps at the Vatican and simply walked out with them? Pulitzer was able to track down the book the illustrations were published in. The book is a fictional work and may have been easily brought into the archives. The maps could have then been quietly drawn on the blank back side of the illustration pages and brought out again without raising suspicion. Security was likely more lax at that time, and a mission of espionage to steal these early twelfth-century Knights Templar maps was successful.[188]

ODD LIПE OП UPPER RiGHT QUAD OF X

Shortly after Zena Halpern's book was published in March of 2017, I learned that Donald Ruh was very unhappy that Zena had not followed through on the terms of their agreement regarding the Cremona Document material that Don had the exclusive rights to. We made plans to meet at his home to discuss working together. During my visit on May 19, 2017, Don shared a handwritten note by Dr. William Jackson that included the year 1973, presumably when he wrote the note. The single sheet of paper

187   https://en.wikipedia.org/wiki/Luxor_Obelisk
188   The two hand drawn maps on the back side of the illustration pages will be published in Donald Ruh's forthcoming book, *The Scrolls of Onteora*.

included tidbits of information apparently shared with him in conversations with a man named Philip Roache. Dr. Jackson commented in his own narrative that Roache was the descendant of Gauden Roache, who co-authored a pamphlet published in 1715. Dr. Jackson bought this pamphlet in 1971. Surprisingly, one of the topics of discussion included the apparent meaning of the Hooked X symbol:

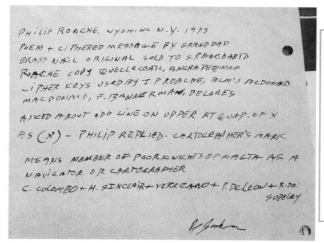

On May 19, 2017, Donald Ruh shared this letter written by Dr. William Jackson recalling comments made about the Hooked X symbol he noticed within the Cremona Document. A man named Philip Roache said it was a "cartographer's mark" made by "...members of the Knights of Malta as a navigator or cartographer." (Courtesy of Donald Ruh)

Philip Roache, Wyoming, N.Y. 1973

Poem + Ciphered message by granddad

Brass nail original sold to S. Rhinehartd

Roache copy Quezlecoatl, Angra Pequena

Cipher keys used by J. Roache, BLM's McDonald

MacDonald, F. Bannerman, Delores.

Asked about odd line on upper rt quad, of X

As (X)—Philip replied—Cartographer's Mark

Means member of Poor Knight of Malta as a

Navigator or cartographer.

C. Colombo + H. Sinclair + Verrazano + P. Deleon + R. de Sudeley

B. Jackson

What first struck me was that Dr. Jackson noticed the Hooked X and, further, thought it important enough to want to understand it better. The opinion he received was the Hooked X was a navigator or cartographer's mark which makes a lot of sense. Further, the opinion expressed in this note is consistent with the conclusion I drew several years ago that the Hooked X symbol was connected to the Knights Templar, or as written here as the Poor Knights of Malta, which was the same order in the twelfth century. What I find very interesting is the list of names of famous historical navigators who, in the opinion of Philip Roache, were connected to the Knights of Malta/Templars. I have already pointed out in *The Hooked X* that Columbus (C. Columbo) used the symbol in his sigla after returning from the New World on his first voyage in 1492.

I also find it interesting Dr. Jackson's inquiry into the Hooked X was done more than three decades before I published my research. Therefore, this document represents independent corroboration by another researcher of the symbol's association with the medieval Knights Templar order. It is also worth mentioning this conversation between Philip Roache and Dr. Jackson took place in 1973. This was long before the internet, which made Dr. Jackson's research much more difficult and time-consuming, yet he was still able to make good progress and eventually reached the same conclusion as I did. This note is a very important new discovery in the Hooked X research and further supports not only the authenticity of the Cremona Document, but by association, the Kensington, Spirit Pond and Narragansett Rune Stones.

As I have pondered the unexpected appearance of this important note, along with other new documents Don shared with me, it prompted me to ask a few questions. Why did Dr. Jackson go to such lengths to secretly hide pages, pictures and notes related to the Cremona Document inside books and behind pictures, but in the end, make sure his twenty-three years of research ended up with Don? Don said there were two reasons. The first reason was Dr. Jackson's wife Murial. In fact, at the end of his 1994 narrative Dr. Jackson explained that his wife would likely throw away all of his research she believed was a waste of his time.

> Because my dear wife Murial believes that digging in the mud and dirt is beneath the stature of a man of the medical profession I am compelled to hide any artifacts and information I discover from her or she will simply throw it out. In this vein, I have disguised most of my finds and this document so that I believe they will be preserved for if man learns where he has been then he may learn not to repeat the mistakes of the past and so preserve his future. This is in effect the essence of both Medicine and Archaeology, only the medium is different.

After reading this I realized how fortunate I have been to have a spouse like Janet, who has not only embraced the excesses of my hobbies and passions, but encouraged them. It must have been difficult for Dr. Jackson to have a wife who was not supportive of this research that was obviously very important to him. I then asked Don about Murial and, choosing his words carefully, he added additional context to his late friend's words, "Murial came from a wealthy family in Ireland and thought this research, and frankly, some of his friends, were beneath the time of a physician of his intellect and status." I completely understood where both Don, and Dr. Jackson, were coming from, and now had a better understanding of why this convoluted and complicated story has unfolded the way it has.

I then asked Don my other questions, "Why you? Why did Dr. Jackson want Donald Ruh to end up with all if his research and artifacts? Why not one of his other friends?"

Don sat his tall, lumbering, six-foot eight-inch frame in a chair and paused a moment before answering, "I was the only one who took an interest in his archaeological research. Every time he wanted to go up on Hunter Mountain he dragged me along. When he went to Newfoundland to dive on the shipwreck, I went with him. Bill and I grew up together and have been friends since I was seven years old. What else can I tell you?"

Don paused for another moment and then continued, "Bill Jackson saved my life one day. I was scuba diving in the Hudson River and it was muddy with poor visibility. When I came to the surface I was under the boat motor propeller, hit my head, was knocked unconscious and then started sinking. My friends jumped in the water and pulled me out, but my heart had stopped. Bill quickly rigged up wires connected to the battery on the boat and shocked my heart into beating again. He saved my life; we were good friends..."

Before leaving, I encouraged Don to write a book about his experiences with Dr. Jackson and the Cremona Document. I said to him, "You're the last man standing in this chapter of this incredible story and you need to write down everything you can about what you have experienced. It's really important that you do that." Don demurred for only a moment and then said he'd do it. Don completed his book, *The Scrolls of Onteora: The Cremona Document*, in 2018.[189]

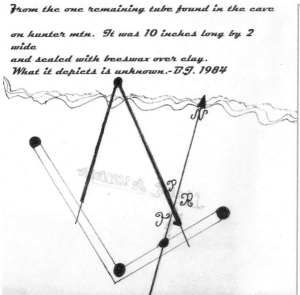

From the one remaining tube found in the cave on hunter mtn. It was 10 inches long by 2 wide and sealed with beeswax over clay. What it depicts is unknown.- BJ. 1984

This page was drawn by Dr. William Jackson in 1984 and depicts a stream with an asymmetrical compass and square symbol. Written above it states, "From the one remaining tube found in the cave on Hunter Mountain. It was 10 inches long by 2 [inches] wide and sealed with beeswax over clay. What it depicts is unknown. BJ. 1984" On July 1, 2009, Don Ruh and David Brody discovered the In Camera Stone after digging down roughly two feet. The location on Hunter Mountain where they dug was marked by Steve St. Clair and me where the right arm of the compass meets the right side of the square (tongue which is typically 16 inches long). (Courtesy of Donald Ruh)

After reading the narratives in the Cremona Document for the first time in 2009, I remember thinking this story was too good to be true which raised immediate skepticism and doubts. I also knew it had to be thoroughly investigated. In *Akhenaten* I relayed the exciting discoveries my son Grant, David Brody, Steve St. Clair, Donald Ruh and I made on Hunter Mountain in the Catskill Mountains of New York, on July 1, 2009.[190] Without question, the most important discovery of the day was the In Camera Stone, dug up by David Brody and Don Ruh. They dug down roughly two feet on the exact spot where Steve St. Clair and I had placed a flag in the ground after measuring out the coordinates we obtained from the Lionel de Walderne map Don provided.

The de Walderne map closely resembles the Compass and Square symbol of Freemasonry, and where the point of the right arm of the compass touches the right arm of the square is where I put a flag in the ground to mark that spot. Steve St. Clair and I used a tape measure to determine the distance between rock outcrops with Theban *A* and *B* symbols carved roughly two feet above the ground, representing the ninety-degree corner of the oblong square. Don explained the carving had been destroyed when a large tree, whose roots had grown around the part of the outcrop, had fallen in a storm.

Within minutes of placing the flag in the ground, Steve, Grant and I decided to climb up the mountain to look for a small cave Don found years earlier he called the Sand Cave, which contained artifacts. Don had shared pictures and video of the cave,

PER SEAL MEASURMENTS
ROCK "B"

David Brody stands next to the sandstone outcrop where the Theban *B* symbol was carved, representing the bottom corner of the square symbol on the Lionel de Walderne map (left). Dr. William Jackson's picture of the same outcrop, from 1975, confirms it is the correct location (right). (2009/Courtesy of Donald Ruh)

---

190   Wolter, pages 215-221, 2013.

THE BAN "B" (9) LOWER CENTER
INSCRIBED ON ROCK AUG 14, 1975

This is a closer view of the Theban *B* symbol carved on the sandstone outcrop in 2009 (left). Dr. William Jackson's picture from 1975 (right) of the same symbol, marked by a red arrow in the center of the photo, confirms it is the same carving. (2009/Courtesy of Donald Ruh)

While visiting Don Ruh on May 18, 2017, I took a photograph of a picture Don had taken of the flag I had put into the ground where the In Camera Stone was discovered on July 1, 2009.

so we felt confident in what to look for. He then pointed in the direction where it was located and off we went. We searched the side of the mountain, often scaling dangerous cliffs, for roughly two hours but were unsuccessful in finding the Sand Cave.

Meanwhile, Don and David excavated the spot where we had placed the flag into the ground. Upon our return, Don and David relayed how they pulled the In Camera Stone out of the ground at a depth of roughly two feet. Later, we hiked down Hunter Mountain and drove several miles southwest to a site along the Neversink River that Don wanted to show us. After walking a short distance into the woods, Don pointed to a small mound comprised of flat stones. We decided to remove the stones to see what might be inside the pile. As Grant and Steve removed the stones they handed them to me. I then brushed off the dirt and examined each one for possible carvings. As they got near the bottom of the pile, Grant handed me another stone. After rubbing the dirt off the surface, I realized there was a carving that resembled a feather with a notch at one end. It looked reminiscent of a dove. It was clearly man made and was yet another inscribed stone to add to the collection of mysterious artifacts discovered in this area.[191]

Although many questions remain, the collected artifacts and documents related to Dr. William Jackson's research are of great historical value. I am especially intrigued by the Cremona Document deposition of Ralph de Sudeley and the important historical context breathed into it by the thoughtful Dr. William Jackson narrative.

Alpha-Omega Tradition

I would like to circle back to the moment Steve St. Clair, Grant and I came down from the mountain and David Brody first handed me the In Camera Stone. After the initial excitement of the discovery, we looked more closely at the Roman numerals carved into the stone. We quickly determined they were Roman numbers for 45 degrees, 30 minutes (XLV XXX) of latitude and 75 degrees, 53 minutes (LXXV LIII) of longitude which eventually led to exciting discoveries in Montreal. I wrote about these findings in *Akhenaten*. While rotating the stone at a low angle toward the sunlight to highlight the carved lines, I noticed an extra line angling down and to the left of the lower right leg of the first *X*, or Roman numeral ten, in the number 45. It still had dirt in the groove and did not seem to belong where it was, but a line was clearly there. After examining all the carved numbers, I found another line out of place on the last number on the second line, a Roman numeral *I*, that looked like the letter *L*. It later dawned on me what these short carved lines added to the first and last numbers were meant to represent. They were added as something akin to a watermark meant to add legitimacy to a message typically written on parchment or paper. In this case, the two added carved lines served as a coded message of legitimacy, apparently using the concept of alpha-omega (beginning and end).

---

191   For additional insight into our discoveries that day on Hunter Mountain please refer to pages 219-221 of my book, *Akhenaten to the Founding Fathers: The Mysteries of the Hooked X*.

The In Camera Stone has a carved line added to the bottom right leg of the first Roman numeral ten (*X*) on the top line (white arrow from left and inset image) and to the last Roman numeral one (I) on line two (white arrow from right). Could these lines have been added by the carver to the apparent latitude and longitude numbers to invoke the esoteric tradition of alpha-omega, and/or as a watermark of authenticity? (2017)

I believe we also see the same esoteric concept of alpha-omega on the Kensington Rune Stone. The first two symbols carved in the inscription are the pentadic number *8* and the unusual runic symbol for the letter *G*. The last symbol carved on the face side of the inscription is a never-before-seen runic symbol for the letter *U*. The *U* symbol has a horizontal line carved across the lowest part of the vertical line, or stave. Dick Nielsen and I determined in 2004 that this was part of the Dating Code. The carver of the Kensington Rune Stone appears to have employed this alpha-omega tradition, while at the same time incorporating the Dating Code. Two of the three things needed to create a date using the medieval Easter Table, the column number 8 in this case, and the Sunday Letter crossed *U* on line nine, are the first (alpha) and last (omega) symbols carved on the face side of the inscription. Since the Templars were Christians, they believed in the teachings of Jesus (and Mary Magdalene). Therefore they understood and revered the significance of the concept of the beginning and the end, as evidenced by these two symbols singled out by the carver.

Janet and I found an example of the alpha-omega tradition during the Christmas holidays of 2016. We decided to see the *Martin Luther: Art and the Reformation* exhibition at the Minneapolis Institute of Art. After purchasing our tickets, we entered the very crowded exhibition hall to take in the artifacts on display. While looking for symbolism in the various works of art we found Luther's will written the year before his death in 1542. While scanning the letter, I noticed a familiar symbol Luther had written in the extreme upper left and lower right areas of the paper: the triple-barred, patriarchal Cross of Lorraine. I recognized instantly this symbol was a coded reference to the secret esoteric teachings in the Tree of Life of the Kabbalah. The vertical line of the cross represents the central pillar of the Tree of Life with the three horizontal bars, or Three Mothers, represented by the Hebrew letters, *shin* (top), *alef* (middle) and *mem* (bottom). The presence of this symbol suggests Martin Luther was initiated in the teachings of the Kabbalah.

The carver of the Kensington Rune Stone singled out the first and last symbols on the face side. On line one at the far end of the second horizontal bar of the pentadic number 8, a punch mark was added. Additionally, a short horizontal bar was added to the strange *U* rune at the end of line nine. By modifying these two symbols the carver appears to have employed the esoteric tradition of alpha-omega as yet another code, or watermark of authenticity to the initiated. (2017)

The beautiful triple-barred Cross of Lorraine on this jewel (left), presented to a Grand Master of the Masonic Knights Templar in Canada, represents the esoteric teachings of the Tree of Life in the Kabbalah the Templars have been initiates of for over 900 years. The two triple-barred Cross of Lorraine symbols (circled) in opposite corners of this letter (right), written by Martin Luther in 1542, suggests he was also initiated into an order that taught the ancient Hebrew mysteries of the Tree of Life. (2014/2016)

Let us also not forget what is arguably one of the most important discoveries to date that relates to the concept of alpha-omega reported earlier in this book: the Hooked X/Tau Cross on the Jesus Ossuary from the Talpiot tomb in Jerusalem. As I have argued repeatedly regarding this entire corpus of research, each piece of evidence must be consistent with the overall thesis. The ever-growing body of evidence remained consistent to the point of reaching critical mass and these three examples of the alpha-omega concept clearly maintained that overall thread.

DE WALDERNE XXI LETTER

As has become the norm with this incredible, constantly unfolding story, the ghost of Dr. William Jackson provided yet another surprising and vitally important document that he had squirreled away before his death in 2000. On August 30, 2017, I received an email from Donald Ruh while Janet and I were in Phippsburg, Maine, for a lecture. Don explained he received a message from Dr. Jackson's daughter, Melissa, who said through a third-party intermediary she had discovered a very old unopened letter with a wax seal adorned with a fleur-de-lis symbol. Attached to the email was a photograph of the letter addressed to, "Maître Robert Cavelier de la Salle, a la Parsiesse de Saint Harbland, Rouen, France."

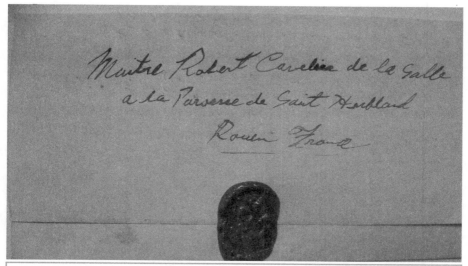

On August 30, 2017, Don Ruh forwarded a photo of an old unopened letter sent to him by Melissa Jackson who had recently moved to the British Isles. (Courtesy of Donald Ruh)

Don and I were puzzled about the letter, but we realized if Jackson had left it to his daughter it must be important. We just didn't understand why as of yet. It would be another month before we would learn the contents of the letter and realize how several important pieces of this giant puzzle suddenly fell into place. Don relayed that Melissa's husband wanted to keep the letter, as it was very valuable, but they did agree to open it and share photographs of its contents.

While waiting for the letter to be opened, I did a little research on the individual it was addressed to. Robert Cavalier de La Salle (1643-1687) was an early French explorer who was born in Rouen, France, and became a Jesuit priest at the age of fifteen.[192] Reportedly having a hopeless case of a wandering spirit, La Salle left the priesthood due to "moral weaknesses" and traveled to Ville Marie (Montreal) in New France, in 1667. In 1669, La Salle began a series of exploratory journeys that made him famous. He discovered the routes along the Ohio and Mississippi Rivers to the Gulf of Mexico. His explorations were riddled with difficulties, many brought on by his own stubbornness, lack of preparation, and questionable judgment that would ultimately lead to an early death, but he is credited with the discovery of a large tract of the Mississippi River.

It was amazing to see an unopened letter written to the famous seventeenth-century explorer, especially a name so familiar to Minnesotans, where buildings and streets are named after him, like de LaSalle High School in Minneapolis. This promoted a lot of speculation as to what was written inside the letter, and who had written it. I also wondered why the letter was never opened in the past three-and-a-half centuries, and how did it end up with Dr. Jackson, and eventually his daughter. After all that time, the letter was finally going to be opened and both Don and I were riddled with anticipation.

On October 1, 2017, Don called and said he had received pictures of the opened letter that also contained a small piece of paper with strange drawings he correctly thought were Masonic symbols. He asked if I would look at it to tell what the symbols might be. Shortly thereafter, Don's email arrived and I opened the pictures. The letter was written in French and dated "Eighth Day May 1656." The second and third attachments were the letter written by Melissa to Don that included her translation:

> This day is our last in the Temple of the Goddess on the mountain of Manitou. Flat Landers and Hollanders encroach daily and the people are much afraid. I have set a message in stone and one in the cave of Priestess Altomara to tell of our passing. I go be with the people of my mother to the south by water. Have gotten a missive from Father Oiler to go to his place of the Sulpicians to the north, beyond the great north river. Twenty-six soldiers and Imogene and all the faithful go also north. I send four bound boxes with thirteen scrolls of Adoniram, twenty-six of Pharos Scrolls, one hundred and twenty-nine of Euripides, nine of the Cohan, sixteen of ours, eight of Yeshua and the history with the Celts. I have also sent the book of the wars of the Lord. All go north.
>
> —M. Lionel de Walderne XXI

---

192   http://www.biographi.ca/en/bio/cavelier_de_la_salle_rene_robert_1E.html

Melissa added, "I hope this is of some interest to you. I have no idea where dad got it from or what it refers to but I am sure you will have a better understanding of that." I understood instantly what it meant and called Don back to discuss it. He agreed the words, "I have set a message in stone..." had to be referring to the In Camera Stone we found on Hunter Mountain in 2009. Don then clarified the passage, "...and one in the cave of Priestess Altomara to tell of our passing," referred to the clay tube Dr. Jackson found in 1977 inside the cave where the urn with Altomara's ashes had been interred.

Suddenly, the answers to all the questions I had pondered relating to the In Camera Stone the past eight years came roaring into my brain like a flash flood. I never understood where the Compass and Square map originated, which we used to find the In Camera Stone. Incredibly, it appeared the map was made by the direct descendant of Lionel de Walderne, one of six Templar knights who traveled to Hunter Mountain with Sir Ralph de Sudeley nearly five hundred years earlier. Lionel de Walderne XXI had carved the In Camera Stone and left a note sealed inside a clay tube in Altomara's

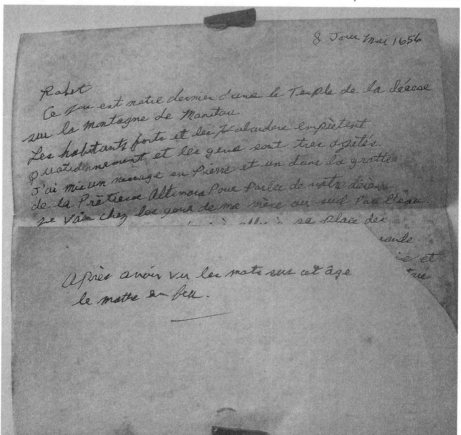

Melissa Jackson sent this photo of the letter written to Robert Cavalier de La Salle after breaking the wax seal and opening the first flap. Written in French were the words, "After reading, set this message to flame." (Courtesy of Donald Ruh)

Jean Jacques Olier was the founder of the Sulpician Order in France and was responsible for establishing the first parish in Ville-Marie (Montreal) in 1654. (Internet/2014)

cave of how to find it. It was the latitude and longitude carved on the stone, corrected to the Paris Prime Meridian of the Templars, that led us to Montreal where the French Sulpicians had established themselves as early as 1642.

Over the next several days, more answers to the questions I had pondered for nearly a decade would come. Father Jean Jacques Oilers (1608-1657) was one of the leaders of the Société Notre-Dame de Montreal who started the Sulpician missionary project at Ville Marie (Montreal). Later, Olier was the driving force behind the establishment of St. Sulpice Church, in Paris, when the cornerstone was set in 1646.[193]

In February of 2014, we filmed an episode of *America Unearthed* at St. Sulpice Church with Alan Butler. We were amazed at the astronomical aspects that had been intentionally incorporated into the structure. This included a brass line embedded into the floor where a small spot of sunlight was created by a small hole engineered into one of the south windows. At noon every day of the year, the spot of sunlight moves along the brass line and marches vertically up the line on a white marble obelisk until it illuminates a gold orb at the top on the winter solstice. In many ways, this church is a monument to astronomy that is further evidenced by a giant symbol that spoke loud and clear to me even before I was made a Freemason. The bold green and white marble solstice symbol stood proud and tall, hidden in plain sight from those who could not "see."

This symbol of two parallel vertical lines on opposite sides of a perfect circle, often with a dot in the center representing the sun, is familiar to most Freemasons. The circle represents the orbit of the earth with the opposing vertical lines representing the

---

193   http://www.sulpc.org/sulpc_fondateur_en.php

On the north wall in St. Sulpice Church in Paris stands a roughly twenty-feet-tall white marble obelisk with a gold-colored metal line that runs across the floor of the church and up the middle of the obelisk, which is topped with a gold orb (left). On the south side of the church, on pillars on either side of the pulpit, are two white marble Masonic symbols commonly associated with the summer and winter solstices (right). (2014/2014)

summer and winter solstices, commonly associated with John the Baptist and John the Evangelist, respectively. If St. Sulpice Church is anything, it is in large part a monument to astronomy.

The missive received by Lionel de Walderne XXI proves Father Olier was aware of the scrolls de Sudeley was not able to get and still remained in the Temple of the Goddess by the mid-seventeenth century. This begs the question: how did he know about them? Did the information come through the Vatican or through Templar/Masonic channels? A small piece of paper found tucked inside the letter when it was opened appeared to provide some answers.

Upon opening Don's email, I instantly recognized the Masonic symbols of the ink drawing in the photograph. The twin pillars with the globes on top of the earth and the twelve primary constellations of the Zodiac are known within Freemasonry as Jachin and Boaz. It is between these two pillars, allegorically representing the gate between heaven and earth, initiates must walk through during the beginning of the Fellowcraft, or Second degree. The six-pointed Star of David, also called the Seal of Solomon when the six lines alternate and overlap, is familiar to most people as the symbol of Jerusalem. It was drawn within a circle resting against the twin pillars that could represent the earth's orbit and the vertical solstice lines as seen in St. Sulpice Church. Drawn on the pillars were two Cross of Lorraine symbols, commonly associated with the medieval Templars, along with two Tau Crosses. The circle inside the Seal of Solomon, along with the equilateral triangle, are symbols of Deity making the entire arrangement of symbols deeply significant to Masons as well as the Knights Templar. Despite the Latin phrase at the top of the paper having smeared, making a few of the letters harder to read, the English translation was clear: *Sit Luxet Lux Fuit* or "Let There be Light and There was Light."

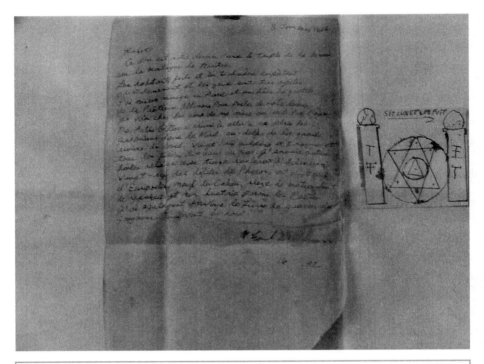

On October 1, 2017, Don Ruh emailed four photographs of the mysterious letter and its contents from Dr. William Jackson's daughter, Melissa. The first two images were of the typed letter Melissa had written to Don that included her English translation of the de Walderne letter written in French. The third image was a picture of the opened letter dated "Eighth Day May 1656," signed by M. Lionel de Walderne XXI, with the small piece of paper found inside the letter covered with Masonic symbols. The fourth image was a closeup of the back of the piece of paper. (Courtesy of Donald Ruh)

As interesting as the drawings were on the front side of the slip of paper, the writing on the back side was even more fascinating. It contained a second Latin phrase, *Vincit Omni Veritas* (All Truth Prevail), angled across the page. Both Latin phrases had the same general Masonic/Templar meaning of the importance of truth, reminiscent of the cover page of the Cremona Document, copied circa 1856, *Veritas Vos Liberabit* (The Truth Will Set You Free).

Below the Latin phrase were four cursive letters and three Roman numerals, "L de W" which I deduced was likely shorthand for Lionel de Walderne. It was the three Roman numbers (XXI) that confirmed the identity of the individual who made the drawing. That person was the same Lionel de Walderne XXI who wrote the letter to La Salle that contained this unexpected note.

The note had one more surprise that was the most exciting of all. The second X in the Roman numeral twenty-one had an extra line in the upper right arm making an undeniable Hooked X symbol! While the Hooked X jumped out immediately, not long after two other symbols became apparent that, in my opinion, were no accident. A ver-

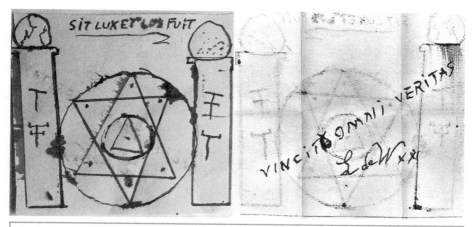

The front and back sides of the piece of paper found inside the recently opened letter that had the Latin phrases *Sit Luxet Lux Fuit* (Let There be Light and There was Light) written across the top of the front of the page (left). Angling to the upper right of the back side is *Vincit Omni Vertas* (All Truth Prevail) (right). Below the Latin phrase on the back side, in cursive writing, were the letters "L de W XXI." Surprisingly, the second *X* was a Hooked X! (Courtesy of Donald Ruh)

tically-aligned fish symbol, with the tail up, was drawn after the Latin word *Vincit*. Just below that fish symbol was an opposing fish symbol with the tail down, in the upper part of the cursive *L*. These opposing fish symbols appeared to be a Pisces code drawn by de Walderne XXI. As will become obvious in a later chapter, the fish symbol weaves throughout the last two millennia as an apparent code, or watermark of authenticity, similar to the alpha-omega used by initiated members of a secret Templar tradition.

As incredible as the letter and note were in helping to answer many of the nagging questions since our hike up Hunter Mountain and our discovery of the In Camera Stone, there were still a few questions that may never be answered. The first is, why did Lionel de Walderne XXI write this letter that reads like a report to a then-thirteen-year-old Robert Cavalier de La Salle? It seems the letter never reached the future explorer, or maybe it was intended to be opened later in his life? The second big question is, where are the cache of scrolls today which Lionel de Walderne XXI recovered? We likely will never know the answers, but the connections of the known historical facts about de La Salle's explorations, and his ties to the Sulpicians in Montreal, are consistent with this incredible still-unfolding story.

CHAPTER 12:

MERIWETHER LEWIS IN MONTANA

With so many new doors of research opened, with the revelations of the Hooked X/Tau Cross on the Jesus Ossuary, the Cryptic Code on the Kensington Rune Stone, and the Cremona Document, it is hard to wrap one's head around it all. Hopefully, I have made it clear how important the implications of these important discoveries are to understanding North American history. However, there is still one burning puzzle that needs to be addressed after considering all we have learned and where things stand today. Arguably, the most shocking and important new revelation of the Cryptic Code is the discovery that the Kensington inscription could contain directions to the secret Templar vault in Montana. If our interpretation of the Kensington inscription is correct then the first Templar party to reach what is now Montana to hide treasures collected in Europe and the Middle East was one of those earlier trips, or even the Kensington party itself may have deposited treasure. Knowing the Templars were in the Catskill Mountains of New York in the late 1170s leaves open the possibility that many Templar expeditions over the next two centuries could have made their way to Montana with treasure, and maybe even the Baphomet.

New speculation has been spurred about known historical events that have transpired, due to the shocking description of the treasures discovered under Jerusalem's South Wall in the Cremona Document. The most notable discovery appears to have included the head of John the Baptist (the Baphomet) that was brought to North America on or before 1362. Based on William Mann's research published in his 2016 book, *Templar Sanctuaries of North America*, he makes a convincing case that there was a "crown jewel" in the land to the west. I now add my own research that supports Bill's conclusion there was a secret vault filled with Templar treasures in what is now Montana. At least some of Bill's information came from Native American story-keepers in Canada who have retained this knowledge and felt compelled to pass it along to him because of his heritage: Bill is half Algonquin on his mother's side, who is full blood.

If we look back at how early American history played out, there appears to be a connection to the legend of a Templar secret vault in Montana with the Louisiana Purchase in 1803.[194] Famous explorers, Meriwether Lewis and William Clark, set out on their expedition to explore the territory, newly acquired from the French in a deal with Napoleon who, at the time, was desperate for money to continue fighting his wars.

If we assume one of the top secret goals of the Corps of Discovery Expedition was to confirm the existence and security of the secret vault, only those at the highest levels of the then very young United States government would have any knowledge of it. The ones most likely to have had that knowledge were Benjamin Franklin, Thomas Jefferson and Meriwether Lewis. Both Franklin and Jefferson were in France during the time when the eventual third president was the American ambassador from 1785-89, and both are listed on the rolls of a secret society known as the Lodge of Nine Sisters.[195] It is all but certain Jefferson and Franklin heard whispers about the secret Templar vault in the foothills of the Rocky Mountains of western North America through contacts within the brotherhood while attending the French lodge. If so, this could explain some of the events associated with the Louisiana Purchase just over a decade later. It is well documented that Jefferson gave specific instructions to Meriwether Lewis on what to look for while on the expedition.[196] If Lewis was told by Jefferson to check on the secret vault, this could explain one of the reasons why Lewis, who was a Freemason at the time, separated from William Clark (who wasn't made a Freemason until after the historic expedition) in what is now central Montana in July of 1804.[197]

This is a good time to return to the mysterious events related to Sacagawea and her time with Lewis and Clark. Born into the Shoshone tribe, whose territory was mainly in present-day Idaho, her brother, Cameahwait, would become chief. She was only twelve years old when she was kidnapped by the Hidatsa, enemies of the Shoshone.[198] Sacajawea was sold and married off to a French-Canadian fur trader, Charbonneau, who, along with his wives, lived at times with the Mandan and Hidatsa. In November of 1804, Lewis and Clark wintered with the Mandan where they met Charbonneau and convinced him to join their expedition as an interpreter. Sacajawea was also chosen by Lewis and Clark, for they knew, being Shoshone, she could help them get the horses needed to succeed in their mission. The other benefit was, shortly after they set off Sacagawea's son was born. Having a woman with her newborn child sent a message to potentially hostile tribes that their intent was not to make war.

194 https://en.wikipedia.org/wiki/Louisiana_Purchase
195 Weinberger, McLeod, and Morris, page 295-6, 2002.
196 https://www.monticello.org/site/jefferson/jeffersons-instructions-to-meriwether-lewis
197 Ambrose, pages 379-405, 1996.
198 https://www.biography.com/people/sacagawea-9468731

It was a Charles Russell painting that sparked the idea of possible intrigue between Meriwether Lewis, a Freemason, and Cameahwait, an initiate who would have been versed in the Native American mystery schools as a tribal chief. The artist captured what appears to be the Masonic greeting called the Five Points of Friendship. In maritime tradition dating back many centuries, an approaching ship would fly the proper signs and colors on flags to communicate their intentions. This practice was also true when parties met that did not speak the same language. In Russell's portrayal of this historic meeting the familiar colors of red, white, and blue are presented.[199]

In Charlie Russell's painting (left)of the meeting between Cameahwait, Chief of the Shoshone and brother of Sacajawea, and Meriwether Lewis, their embrace is reminiscent of the Masonic greeting known as the Five Points of Friendship (right). (Internet/Secret Society Illustrated, page 26, 1900)

One of the central tenets of my research into pre-Columbian activities of the Templar order in North America is they shared a similar Monotheistic Dualism ideology with Native Americans, which included similar rituals. Like Freemasonry today, the medieval Templars and Native Americans initiated into their own secret societies, signs, symbols and tokens that were, and still are, part of standard operating procedure. This was especially true for a meeting between strangers of two warring cultures in the open west of the very early eighteenth century. Greeting what could be an enemy with familiar signs, seals, tokens, colors, and an embrace would set the proper tone of friendship and trust.

I firmly believe, after hearing an Ojibwe shaman tell me personally about oral tradition that speaks of their Templar blood brothers who stayed, assimilated, shared rituals and ancient knowledge, that chiefs like Cameahwait knew all about the medieval Templars. Not only did he speak of the interactions with his people in the past, but also knew men like them would return. He and other Native chiefs, elders, and shaman would know them by certain signs of recognition. Whether Cameahwait knew about the secret vault himself, or knew the person or tribe that did, is unknown. William

---

199   https://franceshunter.wordpress.com/2009/12/09/charlie-russells-lewis-clark-art/

Mann maintains it was the Blackfoot who were charged with guarding the secret vault as it is now within their territory. For those who doubt, remember the Blackfoot shaman Smohalla sitting with his brethren within the sacred lodge flashing the *M* sign (See page 151). For a brief moment when the image was captured, Smohalla revealed to the initiated he held secrets that stretch back to the time of the medieval Templars. At this point it is only speculation, but it would be foolhardy to dismiss the notion of secret communication between Lewis and the Shoshone, and possibly the Blackfoot as well. This appears very plausible considering Meriwether Lewis' actions on the return trip at the mouth of the Blackfoot River.

On July 3, 1806, on the return trip, the explorers split into two groups, with Lewis taking nine men (perhaps a symbolic number related to the nine arches of the secret vault?) and leading them up the Big Blackfoot River, and Clark leading another group up the Bitterroot River. They would not reunite for another six weeks until August 12th. During their first week apart, the Lewis group made their way up the Big Blackfoot River, traveling essentially due east. This put the Lewis group within a day's ride of the location where William Mann was told the secret vault is. Due to the highly sensitive nature of a matter of such importance it is not at all unexpected there is no mention of a vault, or caves, in Lewis' journals during this time. Lewis may have had a private second journal and was likely told only to confirm the vault's existence and whether treasures brought over from Europe by the Templars were still there.

William Mann has known about the legend of the secret vault in Montana for several years, and in the spring of 2011 he shared where it is believed to be located. Upon receiving the coordinates from Bill, we zoomed in on Google Earth and quickly noticed the cluster of trees near the top of the mountains that looked like the giant snapping turtle Bill had described. Staring at the several-acre-sized, turtle-shaped cluster of trees brought to mind what many Native American tribes, like the Ojibwe, call the continent of North America: the Great Turtle. Sure enough, when zooming out on Google Earth the continent does vaguely resemble the shape of a turtle. We asked Bill if he was interested in making a trip to Montana to check out the site and see if we could find any clues to the secret vault. He was not able to get away, but encouraged Janet and me to go. We were planning a family trip anyway and decided that visiting Glacier National Park and then taking a day to try and find the turtle would be fun.

It was a perfect sunny day on August 20, 2011, when we turned off highway 287 south of Helena, Montana, and started making our way up gravel roads into the mountains. Before long the gravel tuned to twin ruts littered with ever larger gravel and rocks as we inched higher in elevation. After a couple of hours we emerged from the forest into beautiful, rolling treeless prairie terrain as we neared the top of the pass. On the last couple of miles we passed two abandoned decaying wooden cabins that had not been occupied in decades, and criss-crossed a small creek multiple times as we made our way to the top. I parked the car just short of the edge of the cluster of trees next to the right front leg of the turtle. We compared the map with satellite photos and concluded this was definitely the spot Bill pinpointed as the location of the secret vault. I looked at my family who were ready for a hike and said, "Let's go find it!"

Janet, our children Grant and Amanda, along with our friend David Brody, who flew in from Boston to join us, exited the vehicle and took in the amazing view. We decided to first hike around the perimeter of the turtle and then traverse across it through the trees looking for anything that could be a man made entrance or markings. I reminded everyone this was bear country and to be extremely careful not to surprise any wild animals. Not long into the hike we noticed the ground was wet and the grass was bright green. We quickly realized we had crossed water flowing from one of the numerous springs that dotted open areas around the turtle. Bill told us there would be springs associated with the correct location, but there were springs coming out of the mountains throughout the Rockies. The question was were these the correct springs?

Bright green grass marks natural springs flowing out of the ground surrounding the turtle of trees at the headwaters location where we searched for the secret vault. This location was less than a day's ride from where Meriwether Lewis separated from William Clark on July 3, 1804. (2011)

The exposed bedrock we did see was peppered amongst the trees and grassy areas dotted with small springs flowing out of the ground. At one point near the center of the turtle the terrain suddenly steepened as we walked out onto a small ledge. This lone projection of bedrock formed a twenty-foot tall vertical face that we slowly walked around to the base. Looking back up at the rock face we noticed it was different than the rest of the area. I had the feeling if something was hidden below the surface in this area, this was most likely where the entrance would be located. We carefully scanned the rock face looking for anything that might indicate the workings of man. There was plenty of loose rock laying on the downside slope, but it was difficult to determine if it was the handiwork of man or simply the result of natural weathering. After a half hour of searching we did not find an entrance and were unable to make a determination if the small cliff face had anything to do with the influence of man.

Pic 12-4

After roughly four hours of searching with no luck, we decided to call it a day and head back down the mountain. The discussion in the car was filled with speculation and possibilities but surprisingly little disappointment. I think we all understood it was

Janet Wolter paused next to a curious outcrop of rock within the turtle of trees at the top of the foothills of the Rocky Mountains near Helena, Montana, where Templar historian, William Mann, says the secret vault is located. (2011)

a long shot to find the secret vault constructed centuries ago on our first attempt. Even though everything Bill had told us was here, the entrance to the vault, if it indeed exists, it was not going to reveal itself that day.

At this point we are left wondering where the vault is exactly located. It seems we now need to reach out to the indigenous people, who say they know the location, and see if they are willing help. If so, they will likely insist the location remain hidden, and if they would only bring us there blindfolded that is fine with me. Because Benjamin Franklin was also a member of the Lodge of Nine Sisters and one of the foremost Founding Fathers of the burgeoning nation, he certainly would have known about the treasures hidden "far to the west." If so, he likely also knew about the Kensington Rune Stone land claim shallowly buried along the east-west continental divide that made up the northern boundary line of the Louisiana Purchase.

We can also surmise that whatever information about these treasures that Franklin knew, Thomas Jefferson would have had that same knowledge. In light of what we now know, it seems a near certainty that Jefferson secretly assigned Meriwether Lewis to locate the repository of treasures we now know were brought over from Europe by the Kensington party in 1362 and/or by a different Templar party centuries earlier. Let us assume Meriwether Lewis confirmed the treasure was there and reported back to Jefferson it was still secure, we are left with the lingering question of what happened to it after the Corps of Discovery concluded? Were the treasures left by the Templars, along with the Baphomet, inside the vault in Montana or has some, or all of it, since been recovered? If so, then surely it would have been brought to Washington, D.C. The burning question is where are those treasures and the remains of John the Baptist now?

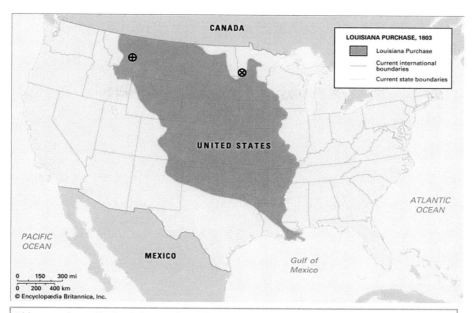

This map shows the land that made up the Louisiana Purchase that includes the secret vault in Montana (circle cross) and the location along the north-south continental divide where the Kensington Rune Stone was discovered in Minnesota (circle X), in 1898. (Internet)

CHAPTER 13:

THE FINAL REPOSITORY

If Meriwether Lewis did confirm the location of the crown jewel of the Louisiana Purchase in 1804, or the secret vault holding at least some of the Templar treasures, where is the treasure today? Surely, it was eventually recovered by the United States government, which I suspect did not happen for several decades after the Corps of Discovery expedition. My hunch is the treasure, and the Baphomet, were moved to Washington D.C. sometime after the Civil War ended in 1865. To determine the location of the final repository in the nation's capital, we first have to think like an enlightened Freemason, one who understands esoteric symbolism. Keep in mind these treasures likely included many sacred objects beyond silver and gold currency. Things most likely included are ancient religious relics, documents, ossuaries with human remains and who knows what else that are likely still in Washington, D.C. somewhere, but where?

Working closely with me and her co-author Alan Butler, my wife Janet was the first to find the clue that might lead to the correct answer. Being well-versed in the signs, symbols, and tokens of Freemasonry, and the principles behind the ancient phrase, *hidden in plain sight*, she had an idea that led to a watershed of discoveries and resulted in Janet and Alan's book, *America: Nation of the Goddess*.

Her discovery started as an outgrowth of a satellite image search of the National Mall in the late spring of 2014. Janet noticed the prominent shadow being cast by the Washington Monument and wondered, "Could that shadow be pointing to things in the nation's capital?" What followed was an avalanche of discoveries Janet and Alan made of certain monuments and locations throughout the National Mall where the tip of the shadow of the Washington Monument points to sites at specific times on specific days of the year. Arguably, the most important shadow play occurs on the winter solstice on December 21ˢᵗ, which also happens to be my birthday. In my most recent books, *The Hooked X*, and *Akhenaten to the Founding Fathers*, I shared two amazing illumination events that occur on the summer and winter solstices. The first was the illumination of the egg-shaped keystone in the Newport Tower in Newport, Rhode Island. This event, which happens at 9:00 a.m. EST, was intentionally engineered by the builders to document the rebirth of the sun on the Earth's annual journey around it.

In the mysterious underground stone chamber in Pennsylvania, featured on an episode of *America Unearthed*, the original builders captured the setting sun on the summer solstice as its final rays reached the farthest point deep within the manmade structure where springwater continuously flows from a natural fracture in the bedrock. Who built it and when is unknown, but whoever it was certainly designed this ritualistic solar event into the chamber to mark the beginning of the annual shortening of the days in the eternal six-month march toward the winter solstice. Obviously, the designers and builders of the nation's capital had similar thoughts in mind.

Realizing how important the solstices were and how the Washington Monument shadow play must be tied to them, Janet and Alan researched the shadow's movement throughout the National Mall on various days and made an important discovery. In the back of our minds we knew part of the Templar treasure included some or all of the mortal remains of important historical figures, most likely John the Baptist and possibly Jesus and Mary Magdalene. To solve the mystery of their whereabouts it seemed plausible, if not likely, the location would be related to the biblical Resurrection story. That time is December 20ᵗʰ-22ⁿᵈ, which is the annual rebirth of the sun when it stands stil" for three days at its southernmost point in the sky. Many believe these three days symbolically represent the three days Jesus was inside the tomb hewn into rock prior to his Resurrection. They believe the biblical story was not about the resurrection of the Son of God, but the allegorical resurrection of the Sun God. It is on December 21ˢᵗ that the tip of the shadow of the Washington Monument points to what could be the final resting place of at least some of the remains of Mary Magdalene and her two husbands, John the Baptist and Jesus.

What Janet and Alan discovered is the shadow of the Washington Monument makes a west to east traverse as it moves toward the Ellipse, one of the least understood and most innocuous landmarks in Washington, D.C., which lies just south of the White House, hidden in plain sight. The official latitude of Washington, D.C. is 38.8951 degrees north, and the monument shadow reaches the southernmost tip of the Ellipse at 11:00 a.m. EST on December 21ˢᵗ. This was an amazing discovery, and as the 2014 holiday season approached, Janet and I decided we needed to verify this brilliantly engineered alignment with our own eyes. While we trusted Alan's computer models which predicted the alignments actually happened, we still needed to confirm them in the field.

As the days before our flight to Washington approached, Janet and I laughed each morning as Alan's growing insecurity about his calculations became ever more humorous. He knew the computer models were right, but worried they might not line up.

After landing at Reagan National Airport on December 17th, we jumped into our rental car and headed straight to the National Mall. The partly cloudy skies opened as we drove past the Washington Monument casting a long afternoon shadow over the Smithsonian African American Museum building, then under construction. We were very excited to see the massive shadow being cast by the monument we had taken for granted during past visits. It was too late in the day to check the shadow on the Ellipse, so we made our way to the other important site we wanted to revisit situated on the north side of the Capitol grounds.

Janet had stumbled onto this site while searching the mall on Google Earth a year-and-a-half earlier in May of 2013. She noticed a curious, hexagonal-shaped, terracotta red-brick structure and learned it was officially called the Summerhouse. The unofficial name for the structure was the Grotto. Intrigued, we vowed to investigate this mysterious structure during our upcoming trip to D.C. while filming the *America Unearthed* episode based on Alan's megalithic yard research titled, "Secrets of D.C."[200]

During a break in filming, the three of us made our way to the Capitol grounds and quickly found the structure nestled into the gently sloping landscape facing the southwest. We recognized the familiar architecture as we entered the structure with the circular fountain in the center. The Summerhouse has three prominent sides with built-in chairs and three entrances with rounded arches between making it hexagonal in shape. The east-northeast side has a large oval-shaped opening with ornately designed wrought iron. Behind the window an artificial cave was constructed with water flowing into it resembling a spring. We all smiled at the not-so subtle reference to the legendary stories of Mary Magdalene and the grotto. Legends about Mary Magdalene are pervasive, most notably those of the Black Madonna.

There are over 500 known statues of Black Madonna throughout Europe and the Mediterranean region, but the highest concentration of these statues are found in churches and cathedrals in France. To the Gnostics, the Black Madonna represented knowledge of the Merovingian bloodline that traced back to the secret marital union of Jesus and Mary Magdalene. According to author Ean Begg,

> Historically, the Black Virgin cult seems to point in the direction of two alternatives in particular. One, the alternative Church of Mary Magdalene, James, Zacchaeus, Gnosticism, Cathars, Templars and alchemists, we have circumambulated many times, peering at it from different angles. It contains much of the wisdom of the old religions as well as certain new phenomena that reached consciousness in the twelfth century, such as the Holy Grail and the courtly love.

---

200   Janet Wolter and Alan Butler have a new book coming to present their discovery of a late-nine-teenth-century structure in Washington, D.C. that early architects and land surveyors used to accurately calculate the megalithic yard using the planet Venus.

As my research continued, it became increasingly obvious that the cult of the Black Virgin and the history of the Merovingian blood-line were inextricably linked. [201]

In Washington, D.C. (38.8951 degrees north latitude), the sun rises 30 degrees north of east on the summer solstice, casting a shadow to a point at 240 degrees on a circle around the Washington Monument. At sunset of the same day, a shadow will be cast to a point at 120 degrees, thus dividing the circle into three equal parts, when connected they create an equilateral triangle. On the winter solstice, the shadow touches the 60 and 300 degree points on the circle, creating an opposing equilateral triangle. When joined together the opposing triangles theoretically create a Seal of Solomon symbol over the city. (2015)

Landscape architect, Frederick Law Olmsted, designed the Summerhouse and one can assume he was likely versed in the legend of the Black Madonna and its connections to the Merovingian/Venus families.[202]

After peering through the wrought-iron railing covering the grotto opening, we turned one hundred eighty degrees and looked out the entrance opening to the southwest. Realizing the mall was aligned east-west, I noticed the direction the entrance was pointing toward was close to where the sun sets on the winter solstice. It was one of those things you get a feeling for after researching this subject matter for a long period of time. Both Janet and Alan agreed the angle of the opening looked close and we all knew there was something special about this structure, but did not fully understand it just yet.

Since our priority was to confirm Janet and Alan's Washington Monument shad-

201   Begg, page 145, 1996.
202   https://www.aoc.gov/capitol-grounds/summerhouse

ow play they were about to publish in their book, Alan had written to Janet who read his comments aloud to me. She relayed how there was no need to be concerned about shadow play ever occurring in the area to the south of the Washington Monument since the sun is never in the northern sky. Because the sun rises thirty degrees north of east on the summer solstice, the shadow can never reach the area between azimuths of 120 and 240 degrees on a circle around the Washington Monument. Upon hearing Janet read this, my mind put these points on a circle and I realized they divided the circle into three equal points, at azimuths of 0, 120, and 240 degrees, creating an equilateral triangle. It didn't take long to realize an equilateral triangle in the opposite direction was created on the winter solstice with azimuth points at 60, 180 and 300 degrees. Superimposed one upon the other, it dawned on me the two equilateral triangles created a theoretical and highly significant symbol over the capital city that can only happen at this exact latitude: the Seal of Solomon.

This realization prompted a flurry of new thoughts and ideas. Most importantly, it underscored the value of collaboration of like-minded people. One of the thoughts we agreed on was this theoretical Seal of Solomon that only occurs at this exact latitude, and is directly over the nation's capital, was not a coincidence. It likely explains why the final location of the city was largely built upon a swamp. They would have needed to choose a location along that latitude that was on a river to provide access to the Atlantic Ocean for shipping, which was vital for commerce and the economy at that time.

The next thought that came to our minds was if there was any tangible evidence on the ground that connected this Seal of Solomon symbolism over the city. It did not take long for us to focus our attention on the Summerhouse. Alan went to work and the next morning Janet read his latest email. It contained another interesting bombshell that once again could not possibly be a coincidence. Starting with the location of the Summerhouse and extending the solstice line thirty degrees southwest of due west, the line went directly through the center of the Pentagon—within inches. Could this possibly be another coincidence?

The bronze statue of the sitting Franklin Delano Roosevelt has his hands crossed with his right hand making a subtle *M* sign (left). FDR's memorial is a simple rectangular block of white marble on the lawn of the National Archives Building (right). (2013/2013)

Later in the day, Alan started digging and discovered there was supposed to be a matching Summerhouse built on the south lawn of the Capitol, but apparently lawmakers failed to approve funding. It appears certain the intended twin Summerhouses were designed and placed to symbolically create the Seal of Solomon over the capital city by marking the rays of the sun at sunrise and sunset on the solstices. Add in the connection to the Pentagon and suddenly a conspiracy of secret knowledge within an exclusive unknown group, most likely an exclusive Masonic side order, becomes apparent. This group likely had members that included President Franklin Delano Roosevelt, for it was he who insisted the Pentagon be placed where it is only days before groundbreaking began on September 11, 1941. Both the Pentagon and the FDR memorial stone that sits on the lawn of the Archives Building along Pennsylvania Avenue, conform to the ancient megalithic yard system of measurement (which based on a 366 degree circle, calculated using the planet Venus, and is 2.72 feet), as does the distance between the Capitol and the White House.

Since the Pentagon evidence points to President Roosevelt being a member of this very exclusive secret society, and since he was also a 33rd degree Scottish Rite Freemason, it is highly likely this group was then, and still is, connected to Freemasonry. So why would the president insist on having the Summerhouse and Pentagon line up to create a symbolic Seal of Solomon with two important points on the ground? My guess is it was for the same reason the Templar Knights encircled the charola with their horses inside the altar of their church prior to going into battle. Just as the Templars raised their swords to call down the power of the Deity to give them courage and strength in battle, I would bet President Roosevelt, who was about to declare the United States' entry into World War II, was secretly doing the same. I am certain he said to himself, what harm could it do?

President Franklin Delano Roosevelt certainly was not the only person who understood the symbolic importance of the Seal of Solomon over the capital city of the most powerful nation on earth. It might also explain why much of our nation's capital was built on a swamp! To create this important symbolic Seal of Solomon the early city planners had to build the city along a major river for it to be a port city, important for development and commerce, but it also had to be at the exact latitude to create the symbol. Much of the west end of the National Mall near the Potomac River is constructed on fill to provide structural support for massive stone monuments, like the Abraham Lincoln, Martin Luther King Jr,. and Franklin Delano Roosevelt Memorials to name a few.

While searching for more clues that might provide support for the symbolic Seal of Solomon over Washington D.C., I found arguably the most compelling evidence of all. This evidence convinced me it was all planned by a high-powered, very exclusive and secretive group of people. The most meaningful symbolism is hidden in plain sight. This holds true in the intentional placement of where the Founding Fathers chose to build Washington D.C. The clue to the sacred latitude that creates the Seal of Solomon is hidden in plain sight in virtually every person's wallet in the United States. On the back side of our currency, in the great seal of the highest government institutions of America, we find the Seal of Solomon. It is created by the intentional placement of thirteen stars, symbolically hovering like Deity in the heavens, over the iconic symbol of the United States: the bald eagle. Add to this the Goddess/Venus symbolism of the number thirteen on the back of the dollar bill, where we have the number of leaves and berries in the left claw of the eagle, arrows in the right claw, Latin letters in *E Pluribus Unum* (Out of many, one), and finally the thirteen vertically aligned red and white stripes on the banner which are horizontally aligned on the United States flag.

These three examples of the symbol of the United States' bald eagle contains interesting symbolism. The number thirteen is symbolic of the Goddess and can be seen in the number of arrows, berries and leaves in the olive branch, red and white vertical stripes, letters in *E Pluribus Unum*, and in the number of five-pointed stars, another symbol of Venus/Goddess, above the eagle's head. The arrows in the right claw are symbolic of America's willingness to fight, the olive branch on the left is a symbol of peace. The eagle is looking left which indicates America prefers peace, but is willing to fight for freedom if necessary. (Internet)

There is one more interesting number in the Great Seal of the United States that brings our minds back to the 'nine arches' of the Royal Arch and the secret vault in Montana. Could the nine tail feathers of the eagle, pointing downward, be a symbolic reminder of the nine arches below the Temple of Solomon? And could those tail feathers also be a reminder of the Royal Arch resurrection story woven throughout the history of humanity, the Kensington Rune Stone, and this research?

The bald eagle on the one-dollar bill also has nine tail feathers pointing downward. Could this be a secret symbolic reference to the nine levels of the secret vault? As if to confirm the United States is indeed the New Jerusalem, twelve of the thirteen five-pointed stars above the eagle's head form the fourteenth star in the cluster, the Seal of Solomon, which symbolically flies over the capital city of Washington, D.C. (2015)

So what about those treasures the Templars brought to the secret vault in Montana? Is the treasure and the Baphomet still in Montana, being guarded by the Blackfoot tribe, or were they moved to Washington D.C. with the responsibility of guardianship transferred from the Blackfoot to the Founding Fathers? This would have been the logical thing to do as the treasures had for centuries been constantly on the move, always one step ahead of the Roman Catholic Church and its agents. The Holy See would do anything to recover the sacred religious items and historical documents listed in the Cremona Document, and they would have been frantic to recover the human remains of historical figures like John the Baptist, Jesus, and Mary Magdalene that could potentially bring down the entire religious institution. If so, where would those treasures and sacred remains of the Venus families' bloodline ancestors be? They have now been on the move for a thousand years, where could they finally be safe in a repository in perpetuity? Where else but in the capital city of the New Jerusalem, almost certainly hidden in plain sight.

On a trip to D.C. in February of 2017, Janet and I walked the Capitol grounds checking out new astronomical alignments when we noticed something interesting. Sitting atop the ornately carved sandstone pillars at the entrances to the grounds directly in front of the Capitol building were familiar-looking ornamental light fixtures. There were three different styles and sizes that brought to mind items featured in multiple pages of the Cremona Document.

"Janet, doesn't that light fixture look like the Ark of the Covenant?" I said.

"Sure does," she responded.

I then looked down the wall next to the street and noticed another light fixture that was even bigger and also looked like an Ark with a slightly different style. The top part of the light fixtures were brass, and the copper within it had oxidized to the familiar green color of copper carbonate or malachite. The bottom sides were made of panes of white frosted glass. A few minutes later we found a third light fixture adorning another entrance to the grounds, but this one was much smaller.

On ornately carved sandstone pillars at multiple entrances to the Capitol grounds are bronze and frosted white glass lanterns that look similar to depictions of the Ark of the Covenant. Could certain knowledgeable people within the United States government in the late 1800s have provided a clue to what must be in a hidden archive somewhere? (2017/2017)

After photographing the three different light fixtures we walked back to our rental car and studied the images. It was then the Baphomet from the Cremona Document popped into my head, "It is Yon. Bernrd bags the bones." Sure enough, the smallest ark-shaped gas light looked just like an ossuary. We let ourselves entertain the possibility that this could be the ultimate example of hiding something unquestionably important and sacred in plain sight for all the world to see. The more we thought about it, the more it made sense. Those in the know in the late nineteenth century could very well have decided to quietly share some of the most important treasures that Earl Henry Sinclair and the Templars had brought to the New Jerusalem.

As Janet and Alan so eloquently revealed in *America: Nation of the Goddess*, after following the clues the most logical final repository would be under the Ellipse, on the Jefferson Meridian, directly in front of the White House. It seems to me the resurrection story of the rebirth of the sun on the winter solstice, which has played a key role in the mysteries woven throughout this investigation, must play a pivotal part in the final chapter. It was Janet who first wondered if the shadow of the Washington Monument could be a clue to the secrets hidden in D.C. Our story throughout this book has also been inextricably linked to the Enoch legend, and it is yet again with the tallest obelisk in the world. The answer to why it is 555 feet tall is found once again in the Hebrew science of Gematria. In the ancient Enoch legend, he reportedly built two giant hollow pillars containing the world's sacred knowledge. When adding the numeric values of Enoch spelled in Hebrew (He [H] = 5, Nun [N] = 50, and Kaph [K] Final = 500), it adds up to 555.[203]

Of the three different designs of the late 1800's era brass light fixtures at the entrances to the Capitol grounds the smallest ones reminded me of first-century ossuaries that contain human remains. (2017)

203   Hogan, page 69, 2009.

I will always remember those late fall days in 2014, when Janet would read Alan's emails first thing in the morning regarding his astronomical program findings of the movement of the Washington Monument's shadow toward the Ellipse on the winter solstice. Amazingly, his program predicted the tip of the shadow would barely penetrates the outer edge of the Ellipse on the southernmost end, representing an allegorical fertilization just like the illumination of the egg-shaped keystone in the Newport Tower. This happens exactly on the day of the resurrection of the sun on December 21st.[204]

We were all excited about the discovery, but I then chimed in with the words we knew needed to be said, "Now it's time to test your theory in the field." They both agreed we had to see it with our own eyes to ensure the computer program calculations were correct. From the observation window on the north side at the top of the monument, Janet and I watched for the sun to come out on a cloudy day, and it did right as the tip of the shadow of the giant hollow pillar just barely passed through the outer edge of the Ellipse at 11:00 a.m. For Janet, Alan, and me, it was one of those epiphany moments, like seeing the illumination of the egg-shaped keystone in 2007, when you get confirmation you have been on the right path all along.

I took this picture of the shadow of the Washington Monument just after the tip had entered the edge of the ellipse on December 21st, 2014. (2014)

Later that day, Janet and I took a walk around the Ellipse and enjoyed the holiday displays and National Christmas Tree on the north end closest to the White House. We pondered where the most likely final resting place of at least some of the Templar trea-

---

204   Butler/Wolter, pages 192-209, 2015.

sures and mortal remains of the first-century royal family members were located. We imagined their millennia-long journey from Jerusalem to sacred temporary sanctuaries across medieval Europe until their perilous journey across the Atlantic. Not long after arriving in North America, they made their way to the secret vault in the Rockies. In the late 1800s these Templar treasures and sacred remains were most likely moved to their final resting place, a secret chamber at the center of our nation's capital. As Janet and Alan wrote about so eloquently in their book, the beautiful, oval-shaped sanctuary is emblematic of the ancient threshing floors which have always been a place of utmost importance, where sacred rituals were performed by so many cultures across time. Near the center of the Ellipse we stopped and smiled at another prominent symbol of the December holidays, a giant nine-candle menorah. At this point, we laughed at the irony and at how we were not surprised by anything anymore. Was this yet another incredible coincidence? Or, was this another piece of evidence that somebody still knows about the treasures and where they now reside? It turned out this was a foreshadow of things to come in the near future.

While Janet and I walked around the White House in Washington D.C. on December 20, 2014, we could not help noticing how appropriate it was to see a giant nine-candled Jewish menorah near the center of the Ellipse, just past the Christmas tree. (2014)

On our trip to Washington in 2017, Janet and I did a little sleuthing around the Ellipse after our discovery of the mysterious light fixtures on the Capitol grounds and found something else that was very interesting. Knowing how speculative the theory was of the Templar treasures being beneath the oval-shaped barren ground in front of the White House, we hoped to find more evidence that might support it. As we walked around the area near the center of the giant oval we noticed two metal grates covering concrete shafts that descended below the surface. As I knelt down to look through the openings in the grate, I heard a low humming sound and felt a slight breeze on my face. Peering down I saw a whirling fan about a foot below the grate providing ventilation. Janet and I both realized ventilation was not necessary for a simple storm drain system.

The second metal grate was about 30 feet from the first, and before investigating I remembered the story of the helicopter Alan Butler said appeared overhead when he was snooping around this same area of the Ellipse a few years ago. While Janet stood guard several yards away, I scanned the grounds and sky for law enforcement that might be watching us. Peering through the holes again, I saw a metal ladder that descended roughly ten feet to a concrete chamber. It looked like an emergency escape ladder but I could not tell if it was an isolated space or connected to the other chamber with the fan, but it sure looked suspicious and served to fuel our imaginations even more. I quickly snapped photos with my cell phone and then Janet said, "Let's get out of here." Will we ever know the truth about what is under the Ellipse? Not likely, but we will continue to look for clues that support the Templar treasures being hidden some-where in Washington D.C., most likely in plain sight.

At the center of the Ellipse in Washington D.C. there are two steel grates covering concrete shafts that descend roughly ten feet. On February 12, 2017, I took several cell phone photos of the two chambers through holes in the grates. One has a steel ladder and the other a high speed fan providing ventilation for a space below. (2017/2017)

As I finished writing this book, I reflected on how I was able to find so many an-swers to the questions I have researched for the better part of two decades. I was also reminded of the huge surprise that happened when I finished my previous book. It was 2012, and Jorge Mario Bergoglio, who took the papal name of Francis for Saint Francis of Assisi, had just been elected Pope. After being elected, the world wondered what kind of man he would be.[205] Would he follow the same stringent Catholic dogma the Roman Catholic Church has preached for so many centuries, or would he be different? It did not take long to get the answer. The first time he stepped out onto the balcony

---

205   https://en.wikipedia.org/wiki/Pope_Francis

and raised his hand to wave at the massive crowd welcoming their new Pontiff, I was shocked at first, and then very pleased to see a clear and obvious *M* sign. I knew right then he would be different and, in fact, he has been a huge breath of fresh air with his progressive and common sense proclamations and policy changes ever since.

Many changes in the world have been prophesied to occur at the end of the twenty-six thousand year-long cycle of the Precession of the Equinoxes, also called the Great Year. The Age of Pisces (the fish) marks the end of the reign of the Fisher King, also known as the biblical Jesus. Pisces is now giving way to the new Age of Aquarius, which marks the beginning of a new Great Year when one of the mystical prophecies, the decline of the Roman Catholic Church, is set to occur. All indications of this seem to be happening. Young people are not attending church services as they once did, and churches of many denominations are closing at an accelerated rate. In 2016, the Catholic Church in the state of Minnesota filed for bankruptcy after ringing up a mountain of debt due to the settlement of lawsuits for covering up the sexual abuse of priests. Clergy abuse has long been an epidemic, due largely to an antiquated institution that has been terribly out of balance for far too long. The young people today still ask the same big questions about life every other generation has, the difference is they are searching for the answers in places other than organized religion. I believe Freemasonry, and related orders for women and men, offers a wonderful alternative for people, young and old, to explore with like-minded people the ancient mysteries. Perhaps the most important spiritual pursuit of all people is to discover the meaning of Deity, or what Freemasonry calls the Great Architect of the Universe.

8/22, the Megalithic Yard, and the Golden Ratio

Having learned long ago the concept of *hidden in plain sight,* you would think I knew better. While working with Janet and Alan Butler on the eight numbers in the Cryptic Code that appear on the Kensington Rune Stone, and in the Select Master degree of the Cryptic Council of York Rite Freemasonry, something dawned on us as we chatted on a Skype call about the numbers eight and twenty-two. It was so simple we all chided each other for not having seen it years ago. In Alan's book, *City of the Goddess: Washington, D.C.,* he presented his discovery that the Founding Fathers of the United States secretly used the megalithic yard measuring system in the layout and placement of roads, buildings, and monuments in the capital city. The megalithic yard is a sacred, ancient measurement calculated using the movement of the planet Venus, a pendulum, and a 366 degree circle to consistently and accurately determine its length of 2.72 feet. While discussing the relevance of the megalithic yard relative to the Kensington Rune Stone Cryptic Code numbers, it dawned on us to do a simple calculation of dividing 22 by 8. The answer shook us to our core; the answer was 2.75 feet which is, symbolically, close enough. The implications of this simple calculation didn't take long to sink in.

The ultimate mission of the fugitive order of the medieval Knights Templar was to establish the Free Templar State which was certainly considered to be a sacred act, or covenant, made with Deity. That mission was of utmost importance which demanded extreme secrecy and devout loyalty. Even though 2.75 feet is not exactly the same as 2.72 feet, it was close enough using whole numbers to make a reasonable connection to the sacred measurement. So what does all this mean with regard to the Kensington Rune Stone Templar land claim document? To make more sense of the intentions of the medieval monk who crafted the inscription we need to understand the context of that time. In fourteenth-century Europe, Deity was forefront in the minds of the general population, far more than people today, and more especially in the minds of clergy. In light of this, it is self-evident the coded numbers within the inscription, most notably eight and twenty-two, besides having astronomical and navigational significance, were intended to first acknowledge and then ask Deity to bless and protect the land claim document the Templars saw as critical to the eventual establishment of their sanctuary. As if for emphasis, not only did the carver split the larger slab of stone down to the sacred symbolic 2:1 dimensions of an oblong square, but he also made the overall length, diagonally across the face side of the artifact, exactly one megalithic yard (2.72 feet = 32.65 inches).

As if the Kensington Rune Stone megalithic yard length wasn't amazing enough, there was one more incredible surprise that had been staring us in the face for the past eighteen years. Of course, it would be the eyes of a sacred feminine to see it first—Janet

When measured diagonally across the face side of the Kensington Rune Stone, the distance the carver intentionally split the once larger slab of graywacke down to is exactly one megalithic yard (2.72 feet or 32.64 inches). Janet Wolter discovered the Hooked X symbol holds the magical proportions of the Fibonacci sequence, also called the Golden Ratio, found throughout the universe. (2018/2018) See color section for detail.

Wolter. In April of 2018, she was studying the magical aspects of the Golden Ratio found in nature and used throughout history by the Venus families she and Alan were researching. I was sitting right next to her, working on this manuscript with a pile of books in front of us. Suddenly, Janet turned to me in wide-eyed amazement. I looked at her and said, "What?"

She then pointed to the cover of my Hooked X book and said, "Oh my God, there it is. The Hooked X has the Golden Ratio too."

Confused at first, I looked at the cover and then it hit me too. The Fibonacci sequence was definitely there. After absorbing the initial shock of the discovery I came to a realization as to why the Hooked X symbol was so important. It was not just the symbolic representation of the Templars, and Monotheistic Dualism, it was the magical appeal of the Golden Ratio that fits so perfectly into the human brain. No wonder I picked the first Hooked X symbol on line six of the Kensington Rune Stone inscription. Of the twenty-two examples carved on the stone, this is the one that best fits the magical proportions of Phi.

As hopeful as Pope Francis has made the world feel with his common sense ideas, progressive spiritual guidance, and perpetual optimism, the world might finally be figuring things out. Current world events suggest we still have much work to do to find the balance needed for the long term survival and prosperity we are all hopeful for. As we begin this uncertain journey we can only hope for the best.

Coincidentally, as I was finishing this manuscript another unexpected and pleasant surprise came along. One of my Twitter followers posted a photo taken on Inauguration Day for Donald Trump on January 20, 2017. It was Barack and Michelle Obama standing together, hands over their hearts listening to the National Anthem. There it was again, Michelle Obama was clearly making the *M* sign! I took it as a hopeful sign that all is not lost, and along with the discovery of the Cryptic Code, the Hooked X/Tau Cross on the Jesus Ossuary, the Cremona Document, and the wonderful secrets and truths they all reveal, I am confident there is hope for humanity. Time will tell.

This picture of an apparently forlorn Michelle Obama making the *M* sign while listening to the national anthem with her husband Barack, on Inauguration Day for Donald Trump, was posted on my Twitter account on January 21, 2017.

REFERENCES

Ambrose, Stephen E., *Undaunted Courage: Meriwether Lewis, Thomas Jefferson and the Opening of the American West,* Touchstone, New York, NY, 1996.

Begg, Ean, *The Cult of the Black Virgin,* Penguin Books, London, England, 1985/1996.

Belán, Kyra, *The Virgin in Art: From Medieval to Modern,* Barnes & Noble Books by arrangement with Parkstone Press Ltd, New York, USA, 2005.

Bernard, Raymond, *A Secret Meeting In Rome,* CIRCES International, Aurora, Colorado, 1965/ 2012.

Burnes, James, *Sketch History of the Knights Templar,* WM. Blackwood & Sons, Edinburgh, Payne & Foss, London/John Cumming, Dublin, Edinburgh, 1840.

Butler, Alan, and Janet Wolter, *America, Nation of the Goddess: The Venus Families and the Founding of the United States,* Destiny Books, Rochester, Vermont, 2015.

Callahan, Charles H., *Washington: The Man and the Mason 6th Edition,* Memorial Temple Committee of the George Washington Masonic National Memorial Association, Alexandria, Virginia, 1907/1913.

Capps, Benjamin, *The Great Chiefs: The Old West Series,* Editors of Time-Life Books, Time-Life Books, New York, NY, 1975.

Charlesworth, James H., *The Tomb of Jesus and His Family?: Exploring Ancient*

References

Jewish Tombs Near Jerusalem's Walls, The Forth Princeton Symposium on Judaism and Christian Origins, Sponsored by the Foundation on Judaism and Christian Origins, William B. Eerdman's Publishing Company, Grand Rapids, Michigan/ Cambridge, U.K., 2013.

Cook, Ezra A., *Secret Societies Illustrated: Comprising the So-called SECRETS of Freemasonry, , Adoptive Masonry, Oddfellowship, Good Templarism, Temple of Honor, united Sons of Industry, Knights of Pythias, and the Grange,* Ezra A. Cook, Chicago, I.L., 1900.

Emerys, Chevalier, *Revelations of the Holy Grail: Bringing to Light the Secrets of the Knights Templar, Rosicrucians, Freemasons, The Ark of the Covenant, Rennes-le-Château, Atlantis and Alchemy,* Emerys, 2007.

Finegan, Jack, *The Archeology of the New Testament: The Life of Jesus and the Beginning of the Early Church,* Princeton University Press, Princeton, N.J., 1969/1978.

Godwin, David, *Godwin's Cabalistic Encyclopedia: A Complete Guide to Cabalistic Magick,* Elewellyn, 1979.

Hall, Manley P., *The Secret Teachings of All Ages: An Encyclopedic Outline of Masonic, Hermetic, Quabbalistic and Rosicrucian Symbolic Philosophy, Golden Anniversary Edition,* The Philosophical Research Society, Inc., Los Angeles, California, 90027, 1975.

Halpern, Zena, *The Templar Mission to Oak Island and Beyond/Search for Ancient Secrets: The Shocking Revelations of a 12th Century Manuscript,* Zena Halpern, 2017.

Hogan, Timothy, *The 32 Secret Paths of Solomon: A New Examination of the Qabbalah in Freemasonry,* Timothy Hogan, 2009.

Hogan, Timothy, *The Way of the Templar: A Manual for the Modern Knight Templar,* Timothy Hogan, 2015.

Hutchens, Rex R., *Bridge to Light: A Study in Masonic Ritual & Philosophy,* The Supreme Council (Mother Council of the World) of the Inspectors General Knights Commander of the House of the Temple of Solomon of the Thirty-third and last degree of the Ancient and Accepted Scottish Rite of Freemasonry of the Southern Jurisdiction of the United States of America, Washington, D.C., 2010.

Hutchens, Rex R., *Thinking Outside the Box, The Geometry of the Oblong Square,*

Philalethes: The Journal of Masonic Research & Letters, Volume 70, No. 2, 2017.

Jacobovici, Simcha, and Charles Pellegrino, *The Jesus Family Tomb: The Discovery, the Investigation, and the Evidence That Could Change History*, Harper Collins Publishers, New York, N.Y., 2007.

Jacobovici, Simcha, and James D. Tabor, *The Jesus Discovery*, Simon & Schuster, New York, NY, 2012.

Jefferson, Thomas, *The Jefferson Bible: The Life and Morals of Jesus of Nazareth Extracted Texturally from the Gospels in Greek, Latin, French & English, Smithsonian Edition*, Smithsonian Books,Washington, D.C., 2011.

Jones, Bernard, *Freemasons' Book of the Royal Arch*, AERRP Books Limited, Kent, Britain, 1957/1991.

Kaplan, Aryeh, *Sefer Yetzirah:The Book of Creation in Theory and Practice,* Weiser Books, San Francisco, California, 1997.

Knight, Christopher, and Robert Lomas, *The Hiram Key: Pharaohs, Freemason and the Discovery of the Secret Scrolls of Jesus,* Fair Winds Press, Glouchester, Massachusetts, 1996/2001.

Könemann, *Cistercian Abbeys: History and Architecture*, Tandem Verlag GmbH, Paris, France, 2006.

Mackey, Albert G. M.D., *Encyclopedia of Freemasonry and its Kindred Sciences Comprising the Whole Range of Arts, Sciences and Literature as Connected with the Institution*, The Masonic History Company, New York, N.Y., and London, England, 1921.

Mann, William F., *The Templar Meridians: The Secret Mapping of the New World*, Destiny Books, Rochester, Vermont, 2006.

Miller, Crichton E.M., *The Golden Thread of Time: A Voyage of Discovery into the Lost Knowledge of the Ancients*, Pendulum Publishing, Rugby, Warwickshire, United Kingdom, 1998.

Olsen, Oddvar (Editor), *The Templar Papers: Ancient Mysteries, Secret Societies, and the Holy Grail*, The Career Press Inc., Franklin Lakes, New Jersey, 2006.

Page, R. I., *Runes: Reading the Past,* University of California Press, Volume 4 in the Reading of the Past series, Berkeley and Los Angeles, California, 1987.

References

Ralls, Karen, Ph.D., *Knights Templar Encyclopedia: The Essential Guide to the People, Places, Events, & Symbols of the Order of the Temple,* The Career Press Inc., Franklin Lakes, New Jersey, 2007.

Richardson, Jabez, *Monitor of Freemasonry: Being a Practical Guide to the Ceremonies in All the Degrees conferred in Masonic Lodges, Chapters, Encampments, and Explaining the signs, Tokens, Grips, and Giving all the Words, Pass-Words, Sacred Words, Oaths, and Hieroglyphics used by Masons,* David McKay, Publisher, South Washington Square, Page 82.

Sinclair, Gerald, and Me, Rondo B. B., *The Enigmatic Sinclairs: A Definitive Guide to the Sinclairs in Scotland,* St. Clair Publications, McMinnville, Tennessee, 2015-2018.

Stein, Susan R., *The Worlds of Thomas Jefferson at Monticello,* Harry N. Abrams, Inc., New York, 1993.

Weisberger, William R. (Editor), Wallace McLeod and S. Brent Morris, *Freemasonry on both Sides of the Atlantic: Essays Concerning the Craft in the British Isles, Europe, the United States and Mexico,* Columbia University Press, New York, 2002.

Wolter, Scott F., *The Kensington Rune Stone: Compelling New Evidence,* Lake Superior Agate Inc., Chanhassen, Minnesota, 2006.

Wolter, Scott F., *The Hooked X: Key to the Secret History of North America,* North Star Press of St. Cloud, Inc., St. Cloud, Minnesota, 2009.